CONTEMPORARY SPANISH PHILOSOPHY

CONTEMPORARY

José Luis Aranguren

Luis Díez del Corral

José Ferrater Mora

José Gaos

Pedro Laín Entralgo

Luis Legaz y Lacambra

Juan José López Ibor

Julián Marías

Eduardo Nicol

Juan Zaragüeta y Bengoechea

Xavier Zubiri

SPANISH PHILOSOPHY

AN ANTHOLOGY

Translated and with an Introduction
by
A. ROBERT CAPONIGRI

NOTRE DAME & LONDON
UNIVERSITY OF NOTRE DAME PRESS

Copyright © 1967 by
University of Notre Dame Press
Notre Dame, Indiana
Library of Congress Catalog Card Number 67-22141
Manufactured in the United States of America

To
Adolfo Munoz-Alonso
in grateful appreciation

INTRODUCTION

The presentation of an anthology of contemporary Spanish philosophy to the English language reading public requires justification for a singular reason: such a presentation should need no justification. Knowledge of Spanish speculative thought, as indeed of Spanish culture in all its forms and dimensions, should in the normal course of things constitute an integral part of the cultural formation of every Western mind. In fact, the very concept of Western culture, with its American and other overseas extensions and developments, is historically impossible without the Spanish presence. The Spanish spirit (one is tempted to say the Spanish *style* of the spiritual life) is at once so distinctive and yet so representative a development and expression of all the basic values of Western culture that its absence or alienation must figure as the absence of the base note of a chord. The truth of this proposition draws irrefutable evidence from cultural history in all its dimensions. Both the study of Western European culture, consequently, and the formation of every cultured mind in the English-speaking world as elsewhere in the West should include an acquaintance with Spanish thought and expression as a matter of course, and to speak of justifying the presentation of an anthology such as the present, in that case, would be absurd.

Such, however, is manifestly not the case. What has, as a matter of history, developed is a situation of absence, of alienation, between Spanish culture and that Western European culture of which historically and spiritually it forms so integral an element. It has existed and does exist extensively as an element of the consciousness of the other elements or components of Western culture; critics, historians of ideas, and other writers of other tongues have addressed Spanish matters as something exotic and apart, withdrawn from the main stream of Western cultural life, drawing inspiration from other sources and finding expression in only obliquely apparentated forms. Even more arrestingly, this sense of absence from the rest of Western European culture—of alienation, of a dissociating distinctiveness—has entered into the consciousness of Spain itself. It has found expression, for example, in the somewhat exacerbated "Spanishness" of an Unamuno (an essentially universal European spirit who forced himself to think and feel himself—and in his person, Spain—as something apart); or again, in the strange effort of so eminent a historian as Americo Castro to find the Spanish identity in its African affiliations.

To trace the process by which this situation of absence, of spiritual distance, came into being is clearly not the task of the present introduction; it is a task which demands the efforts of the most gifted historians. It is enough to note here that it is a process whose origins may be traced, without doubt, to the Counter-Reformation in its cultural, religious, and political aspects alike, a process which by slow and corrosive stages advanced through the centuries. It seemed to reach its ultimate point in the final loss of the Spanish overseas empire and the defeat in the Spanish American War; deep as this crisis was, however, the nadir of that process had not yet been reached. That nadir was to be reached only as the aftermath of the conflict of 1936–1939; it was then that the isolation of Spain and its alienation seemed complete.

As a consequence, Spain entered the world which emerged from World War II almost completely isolated, surrounded, as it were, by a wall of silence and incommunication, physically contiguous, historically apparentated, yet spiritually remote from the world of the West. One is reminded of Garcia Dorca's plaint over Cordoba "distant and solitary."

Yet it was at this very point, this nadir of isolation, that the modern resurgence of Spain began. The notion of "generation" had been very influential in Spanish cultural history, and the notion serves very well for the understanding of this process of resurgence. For the decades since World War II have seen the emergence of a generation of thinkers and writers whose spiritual center may be said to reside precisely in this sense of the basic unity and integrity of Spanish culture and the Spanish spirit with the whole of Western European culture and with the European spirit in its historical depth and its geographical breadth. The isolation in which that generation found itself did not blunt this sense. On the contrary, it sharpened it, gave it an edge. Even more, it gave the spiritual resources of that generation impulse and direction. It pointed its efforts toward a purpose.

This purpose has been complex. It has consisted in giving an expression to the Spanish spirit which would vindicate its unity with the culture of Western Europe and, at the same time, exhibit the positive contribution which Spain, in a wholly distinctive and induplicative way, could give to the values of that culture. This purpose involved, on the one hand, the reweaving of all those multitudinous strands which unite the elements and components of a culture and which bind Spain historically and spiritually to the culture of the West; and, on the other, the constant quest for the true center of the Spanish spirit, from the creative force of which Spain's contribution to the values of Western culture must spring.

The pursuit of this purpose has engaged that generation in interests as wide as the theme of Western culture itself. Among these interests, however, philosophy must be recognized as occupying a very special place. This is not a matter of surprise in a country which produced Vitoria and Suárez and, at another date and in a different spiritual climate, Unamuno and Ortega. The speculative strain in the Spanish spirit is powerful and fruitful even when transplanted to another clime, as in the case of Santayana. As a consequence, the evidences of this effort at reintegration of Spanish culture with the culture of the West are especially strong in philosophy. Accepting the model of Unamuno, in respect, for example, of Kierkegaard, and of Ortega and Zubiri with German philosophy, the men of this generation made contact with all of the strongest currents of Western thought. In every case they have sought to reach the living center of those movements interpretatively and to give them a fresh expression in which the particular insights of the Spanish mind itself would be reflected.

It is with the men of this generation that the present anthology is concerned, and it is in their effort to reintegrate Spanish and European culture that it finds its justification. It seeks in a small way to complement this effort, as it were, from the other end, so far as the English speaking world is concerned, by making representative examples of their work available in English idiom, and in this way helping to re-establish that lifegiving flow of ideas by which every culture lives. It is a modest task, undertaken in the present work in a modest way, but one whose value, we feel sure, will recommend itself immediately.

When with this purpose in mind the compiler addressed himself to contemporary Spanish philosophical literature, he found himself involved in an *embarras de choix*. Within the limited means of publication open to him, his task was to choose and select from among a wide range of writers representing a great diversity of points of view, thematic and problematic. Even more importantly, he had to choose a principle of selection; and this principle of selection, no matter how prudently determined, must inevitably result in certain exclusions which must bear the appearances of injustice. He solved the problem as seemed best to him and fixed on a pattern which would exhibit both a line of continuity in time—establishing contact with the Spanish past in philosophy, short of Unamuno and Ortega—and the complexity of themes and problems which preoccupy contemporary Spanish thinkers. The authors presented were selected within this pattern. Their presence does not argue lack of acquaintance or underestimation of others who do not appear. Such names as Millan Puelles, Cruz Hernandez, Munoz Alonso, Gonsalez Alvarez, and many others are both known and immensely esteemed. On another occasion, when more ample means may be available, it is the present compiler's hope to make their ideas, too, more readily available to the American scene; and it is also his hope that such an occasion will not be too long in presenting itself.

A. Robert Caponigri

Notre Dame, Indiana
July 6, 1967

ACKNOWLEDGMENTS

The expression of one's gratitude to those who have assisted in the accomplishment of any work is the greatest satisfaction attending its completion. In the present case, the very Spanish and profoundly Christian courtesy extended me on every hand during my sojourn in Spain intensifies this satisfaction a hundredfold. I regret only that their very number makes it impossible to name individually all those who extended me courtesy and counsel; space makes it necessary to limit myself to official agencies. Chief among these are the director of the Fulbright Program in Spain, Dr. Ramon Bela; his executive director, Senorita Matilda Medina; and their staff; the staff of the office of the Cultural Attaché of the American Embassy in Madrid, and, in a very special measure, Miss Joy Dickens; and, finally, the Spanish Ministry of Information, especially in the persons of His Excellency Sr. D. Manuel Fraga Iribarne, Sr. D. Carlos Robles Piquer, and Sr. D. Luis Artigas. The Ministry made possible the translation of a substantial portion of the material included in this anthology. The generosity and courtesy of the individuals whom space makes it impossible to list is neither forgotten nor unappreciated; occasion must eventually present itself to acknowledge publicly what privately is cherished so warmly.

A. Robert Caponigri

CONTENTS

        Juan José López Ibor

VII.   THE MORALIZATION OF POWER
        THROUGH ITS SELF-LIMITATION   220
        José Luis Aranguren

VIII.   THE DOCTOR-PATIENT RELATIONSHIP IN THE
        GENERAL FRAMEWORK OF INTERHUMAN
        RELATIONSHIPS   250
        Pedro Laín Entralgo

IX.   ON THE SINGULAR CHARACTER OF THE
        HISTORICAL DESTINY OF EUROPE   278
        Luis Díez del Corral

X.   ON TAKING THINGS FOR GRANTED   304
        José Ferrater Mora

XI.   THE IDEA OF METAPHYSICS   324
        Julián Marías

        NOTES   371

        INDEX   379

CONTEMPORARY SPANISH PHILOSOPHY

Juan Zaragüeta y Bengoechea

Don Juan Zaragüeta (b.1883), the dean of living Spanish philosophers, a teacher of Xavier Zubiri and teacher and colleague of Ortega y Gasset, has touched directly or indirectly every philosophical writer in Spain. Professor Zaragüeta represents basically the scholastic tradition of the Louvain school, broadened considerably, however, under the influence of German philosophy. He has made contributions to value theory and pioneered the introduction to Spain of the problem of language and philosophy. Among his major works are El languaje y la filosofia *(1945),* Filosofia y vida *(1950–1954), and* Vocabulario filosófico *(1955).*

"Being and Value" appeared in *Estudios filosóficos* (Madrid: Instituto de Filosofia "Lius Vives," 1963) 205–237. © 1963 by Juan Zaragüeta. Grateful acknowledgment is made to the author for permission to reprint.

I. BEING AND VALUE

Under the above title I would call attention to a theme that is playing a cardinal role in contemporary philosophical thought. Indeed, modern thought, finding itself largely impregnated with "positivism," has been trying by various means to overcome its positivism, especially in the very area where positivism has proven to be inadequate, namely, that of knowledge. However, since Lotze, who seems to have been the first to introduce the term "value" into our philosophical vocabulary and to have recognized it as a problem (as until his time only the economists had done), a new philosophical attitude has been establishing itself. It is an attitude which seeks not so much to know the "being" of the world and life as to "estimate" their authentic "value." Indeed, these four verbs—to know and to be, to evaluate and to have value—mark a complete revolution in the thought of the present period, a revolution that touches past thought as well. For we find no special place in traditional thought for value in contradistinction to being or for valuation as opposed to knowledge. The only sense in which the scholastics used the word "estimative"

3

amounted to the sense in which modern thought uses the term "instinct" in animals. At times very different meanings are contained in a single expression, and widely contrasting expressions are at times identical in meaning. Thus we must not accentuate counterpositions that may conceal more than a single point of agreement, nor vice versa. But all these considerations only invite us to clarify this entire problem, and this is what I propose to do as briefly as possible.

I
BEING AND VALUE

1. The most common sense of the word "value" is its economic meaning. "What is this worth?" is a question we are constantly putting to ourselves. Indeed, we often put it in another form: "What does this cost?" The two questions formulate the two aspects of value which economists call "value in use" and "value in exchange." A hunter thinks that his hunting exercise "has value" in that it can lead him to get a "good bag," and such a "bag" will be good inasmuch as it is tasty or nutritious. Thus we have the "value in use" of hunting. It also happens, however, that the hunter thinks, not of tasting and enjoying the game he has shot, but of selling it and thus of acquiring thereby money which, in its turn, will permit him to obtain other things more attractive for him. Here, on the other hand, we have the "value in exchange" of the hunt in question. In both cases a "cost" is involved. In the first, the bagging of the game requires of us the expenditure of some shells, the endurance of certain discomforts, and even certain risks. In the second, the collection of the money means giving up the game we have bagged. In the final analysis, both types of hunter—the consumer and the seller—take their hunting "seriously," and both differ essentially from the "sporting hunter" who dedicates himself to hunting as a kind of play, who converts the means into ends and the ends into means and gives himself to the hunt for the pleasure of physical exercise and of enjoying

the unexpected things it often entails. In all these cases there are beings and things which we know and deal with regularly, but beings and things which we also appreciate and value and without which the hunt would be utterly senseless.

Now the philosophical problem of being and value is nothing other than the generalization or extension of the above to the entire range of human life and the world around us. In what does this world and that life consist? At least three answers to that question are possible:

First. According to the so-called phenomenists, the world is a series of physical appearances and life is a series of mental processes, both of which are purely immanent in the subject, hence relative to the subject, variable with the subject, and differing from subject to subject. The subject is wholly reducible to a number of "states of consciousness" either simultaneous or successive, cognitive or affective, which (in this last case) constitute our "estimation" or "evaluation" of the cognitive impressions. In this radical psychologism there is no occasion to speak of beings or values in the strict sense; beings are simple sensations or images, and values are the feelings of pleasure or sadness and the tendencies of attraction or aversion they elicit.

Second. Others, by contrast, recognize being as something lying beneath its phenomenal appearances, an authentic objective or subjective reality. But as far as value is concerned, they continue to understand it as purely sentimental appreciation. They regard being as something transcending our consciousness of it, but value only as immanent. They are "ontologists" with respect to being, but "psychologists" with regard to value.

Third. Finally, with a fully "metaphysical" sense of the world and life, the classical philosophers regard them as transcendent to our consciousness of them and hence, to a certain extent, independent of our consciousness which is called upon to recognize and even to create them, never arbitrarily, however, but according to the norms that command the respect of consciousness itself. Within this group we note two subgroupings.

a) In classical philosophy no distinction was ever made either between being and value or between knowledge and valuation. Among the transcendental properties of being are mentioned truth, goodness, and even beauty, but purely as "ontological" properties which, for this reason, can be known. The pure knowledge of the good, for example, is followed by the appetite for it, but no distinction is made between knowledge and valuation.

b) By contrast, in the modern "philosophy of values" or "axiology" it is supposed that there is, alongside the world of beings or even within it, the world of values; and while the world of being is the object of knowledge, the world of values is the object of valuation, which is a specific function of our mind and therefore irreducible to pure knowledge. At this point our problem emerges in all its clarity. Is there or is there not in our consciousness a valuative function, distinct from the cognitive function, the first dealing with values and the second with beings, so that being and value are not to be identified?

2. Value thus appears as something relatively distinct from being, as valuation is distinct from knowledge, but never separable from being except by abstraction. In relation to being, value stands much as an adjective stands in relation to a substantive. They appear separately in dictionaries but never in real discourse. Every value adds something to pure being, but it also supposes its presence. Thus, for example, the ancients used to define the value of glory as "clara cum laude notitia." To the simple knowledge of something or someone glory adds praise, which is no longer knowledge but a valuation. In this fusion of being and value, this union of the cognitive with the estimative, differences appear between them which fully justify (as long as it is not exaggerated) the modern distinction between "ontology," or the science of being, and "axiology," or the science of values. To begin with, we note "quantitative" differences. Thus we may encounter, for example, a person having vast knowledge of a thing with little estimation of it—hence the exaggerated indifference of some men

of science toward what they know. Or we encounter, on the other hand, high estimation together with little knowledge. Thus a man who is ignorant of medicine but who is preoccupied with his health may have an intense esteem for a medicine the efficacy of which is unknown to him, or for a physician whose knowledge he cannot really measure. A child does not know what it is to be a father or a mother, but he loves his own parents dearly. On the other hand, all men are equally convinced that they are going to die, but all do not show the same sensibility to the high moral lesson for one's life that can be taken from death. Then there are "qualitative" differences where, with reference to a reality that is equally known by different persons, the different individuals (or even the same individual) will develop an estimative scale in different directions: one esteeming the reality as good or as beautiful, and with this or that type of goodness or beauty; or even in contrary directions, one esteeming the reality in question as good and the other as bad, or as beautiful or ugly, as just or unjust, or perhaps as valuable or worthless. The so-called polarity of values about a point of indifference rests on this phenomenon. I know that it is difficult to present two examples of absolutely equal knowledge, but the purely cognitive difference existing between them does not always justify the difference of appreciation to which they lend themselves, such as occurs, for example, in courts of justice when, with the proofs in fact exhausted and the judges likewise convinced of what has transpired, the judges differ concerning the juridical qualifications or value that should be ascribed to the facts.

All these differences between being and value, or between knowledge and valuation, are found in the three essential functions of our thought: "conceiving," "judging," and "reasoning." In concepts, as well as in judgments and in reasoning, we are presented with "mixed" forms of the one and of the other and with forms which we shall call "interferential" forms of the one and of the other. The rest of my essay shall be dedicated to an elucidation of these various forms.

II
PURE FORMS

3. In the area of pure "conceptualization" signified by terms, it would be of great importance to establish a demarcation between a vocabulary that is strictly "cognitive," to be used in referring to concepts that represent real or ideal beings, and a vocabulary that is purely "valuative" or that refers to value.[1] A classification, not so much of words—since in every word there are ordinarily to be found meanings in each of these orders—but of the purely ontological or axiological senses of the words, would contribute enormously to clarifying the subject that we are examining. However, there are "ontological" concepts such as those which in our sciences refer to material, mental, or mixed beings and, again, in each of these refer to their quantitative, qualitative, or mixed aspects, distinct from purely ontological concepts abstracted from all those mentioned above. But there are also "axiological" concepts which reflect the values of such beings, and they also—and this should be underlined because this distinction is not often encountered even in the axiology of our day—are divided along the lines of the quantitative and the qualitative.

4. Let us first of all consider the "quantitative." As an example which points up the confusion prevailing in this whole area, we frequently read in books on mathematics that that science is concerned with "magnitudes." Nothing could be further from the truth. "Magnitude" comes from the term "magnus," which means "large," and there is no mathematician in the world whose science authorizes him to attach such an epithet to numbers or to any reality. Its measure, which is the only thing proper to mathematics, yields a certain number of units or fractions of a unit. But that such a number deserves to be called "large" or "small" is a problem of valuation, not of knowledge. This simple distinction, which is of capital importance in the material, extends to all forms of quantity whether continuous or discrete, spatial or temporal, static or dynamic, simple or complex, actual or vir-

tual. All of them, in addition to their *dimension*, which lends itself to mathematical knowledge, also lend themselves to being estimated or valuated, and this means being not merely counted but appreciated. Thus a distance will be regarded as short or long; a duration as brief or prolonged; a movement as rapid or slow; a plurality of beings as numerous or few; a plurality of events as frequent or rare, and so on.

5. Passing from the quantitative to the qualitative, we should note before all else the twofold sense of both being and value in the very word "quality." A double sense of being when, for example, we say of a piece of cloth that its quality is silk and, similarly, a double sense of value if we say that it is "quality silk" or even silk of "high quality." It is a very common error to reduce values of quality to values of "goodness" and disvalues to values of "badness." Since good and bad are so outstanding in the order of values, they are also extended to cover "beauty" and "ugliness," while many types or forms of these values are to be distinguished. In the order of the good, the distinction between the "useful," the "pleasing," and the "noble" is classical—a distinction which may very well be considered exhaustive. The useful is the good that belongs to the means leading to ends which are, as ends, either pleasant or noble, or both. With this broad division all pleasures enter into the order of values and with them the entire psychologistic (i.e., subjectivist, relativist, and therefore variable) area of valuation to which many modern axiologists seem to refuse to apply the term value at all. The scholastics, on the other hand, did not hesitate to include them among values—nor did they limit themselves to calling a condition of pleasure good. They went on to inquire into the why and wherefore of pleasure in life, and they subordinated it to "nobility," which corresponds to what we today would call the "dignity" of being. Now dignity or worth is the ontological value par excellence, for a being is the more worthy or dignified as it is more elevated in the hierarchy of beings.

Let us also indicate here the inadequacy of the point of view

of the ancients when they defined good as "id quod omnia appe-
tunt": "that which all beings desire." First of all, a being is not
good because it is desired or desirable; rather, it is desired or
desirable because it is good. More especially, a definition like
this regards as good only the objects of desire or appetite, and
not the act itself of desiring or the subject that desires. Each one
of these capital aspects of being—the object or quasi object as
being, the act as being, and the subject as being—possesses its
own goodness and is susceptible to peculiar valuations, a matter
which in some of my works on this theme I have tried to define
as constituting the proper perspectives of a complete system of
ethics.[2] Similarly, from its own point of view, the same could be
said of the value of beauty in the esthetic order.

6. If such is the condition of concepts of value viewed with
respect to those of being, something analogous occurs with judgments, whose division into "judgments of reality" and "judgments of value" has found universal acceptance. Personally,
however, I have found it useful to distinguish "value judgments"
from the "value of judgments." "Value judgments" refer to values
as objects, whereas the "value of judgments" refers to judgments
as acts whose value consists in being true and whose disvalue
consists in being false. For the rest, it is a matter of judgments
referring to realities or to values as objects. In this way a mathematical theorem and the affirmation of a historical fact, which
by their very nature are totally foreign to the realm of values as
objects, also possess their proper value, which is their conformity
with reality peculiar to each case. The same can be said of value
judgments, for example, in the ethical or esthetic area—that they
possess, besides the value to which reference is being made, the
value of being true or false.

7. Ontological judgments are divided into "theoretical judgments," which are limited to knowing things as they are,
and "practical judgments," which are concerned with making
things. The first constitute science; the second constitute tech-

nology or art. Similarly, axiological judgments can be clearly "appreciative" of the value of a given reality or "appetitive" of the value of that which is about to be done or made, and this by reason of the value which makes it attractive. To say "it is raining" ("I believe that" is understood here) is to formulate a theoretical judgment, just as it is a practical judgment to say "I am going to open my umbrella." The first enunciates knowledge; the second enunciates what is to be done, an act toward which I feel myself neither forced nor impeded but of which I am simply capable. If I go on to say that "this rain is troublesome or harmful," my judgment will be appreciative of a value. If I add "How I wish the rain would stop!" my judgment will be appetitive. It will be observed that both the theoretical and the appreciative judgments are "apprehensive": the first of a being and the second of a value, while the practical judgment and the appetite are, rather, "expansions" of the subject toward its respective objects, being and value, which are nonetheless still discontinuous, since I can do nothing about the rain.

In any case, the judgment is composed of concepts—the subject and the predicate—and that judgment will be purely ontological whose subject and predicate are pure beings (e.g., "John is writing a letter") and will be purely axiological if both terms represent pure values (e.g., "moral evil is more serious than physical evil"). The distinction between these two classes of judgments is of maximum importance in the analysis of our thought, whether it be cognitive or estimative. These are modalities of one same thought which nevertheless do not appear in their pure form, separated from each other. The estimative form of thought, moreover, can be found without cognitive thought only by abstraction, since value is something adjectival with respect to the being it affects.

8. This brings us to the problem of the justification of our judgments, a justification obtained by a process of immediate or mediate evidence, called in the latter case ratiocinative. But the monstrative or demonstrative methods of arriving at the truth

of a judgment of reality are very different from those used with judgments of value, in spite of the omission of these latter methods in ordinary criteriologies which are set up almost exclusively with a view to judgments of reality and ideality. Intuition or perception as a means for laying hold of the real; induction as a way of passing from the real to the ideal; deduction within the ideal order and in order to return to the real order (all of which is also conditioned by the intrication of reasons with objections): such is the cycle of the methodology which our books recognize, the method of "intrinsic evidence" or "self-evidence." To this is added the method of "extrinsic evidence" employing an extrinsic criterion, whether immediate or mediate, subsequent to a critique of the authenticity and inerrancy of an affirmation on the grounds of whether the affirmer knows what he is saying and says what he knows. The movement from "theoretical" judgments reached in this way to "practical" judgments or the transition from science to technology or to art is made by means of a change from a contemplative to an active attitude, from knowing to doing, a doing based on knowledge and preceded by "know-how." Thus, for example, the technique of swimming is based upon the laws of balance and movement of solid bodies in a liquid mass, and the consequent disposition of the members of the body to such a purpose. This whole criteriology is irreproachable, but it is insufficient for the solution of life-problems which involve, for the most part, judgments of value.

9. These latter also begin with an "intuition"—not an intuition of a pure reality, however, but of a value dependent upon it, such as a concert's esthetic value relative to acoustics, the moral value of a human act, or even the value of a person's state of health. There follows thereupon the "induction" of some values from others, an induction which is at times positive—as when we infer the goodness of something from its large size, or beauty from goodness, and vice versa; and at other times negative—as, for example, when we eliminate a real value by subjecting it to ridicule or by approaching it for purely scientific curiosity. There

is also the deduction or concatenation of some values with others, again either positively or negatively. All of this can occur not only with values but also with defects provoked as reactions to those values, and vice versa. Thus we say, and with good reason, that the ridiculous is only one step removed from the sublime.

10. The difference between ontological criteriology and axiological criteriology is underlined by the fact that in the order of values that principle which is universally admitted in the order of being holds no longer, namely, "magis et minus non mutant speciem," or "more and less does not alter the specific nature of beings." For example, a hundred yards of silk are neither more nor less silky than one yard. Such is not the case with values, ruled as they are by a law of the "average" of the realities they modify or affect and in virtue of which we find that, to the extent these realities are pushed to the extremes of excess or deficiency, their value is transformed into a defect or the opposite of value: virtue is changed into vice, beauty into ugliness. The relative weight, the harmony, the balance of the ingredients of a value are an indispensable condition for its continuation; therefore it is not the measure, as in judgments of reality which are dominated by mathematics, but the "sense of measure"—that which Pascal called "ésprit de finesse," as opposed to the geometrical spirit—which constitutes its supreme criterion. This is evident even in morals, whose principles and prohibitions suffer from the effects of the ever-present exceptions (dispensations and privileges), and even in jurisprudence, where justice appears modified by equity, without which one ends up in the paradox of the "highest justice being the greatest of injustices": "Summum jus, summa injuria."

11. There also belongs to the methodology of values the "comparison" of some values with others that are either simultaneous with or follow upon the first, which places in relief their historical relativity; in this perspective we can speak not so much of "goods" and "evils" as of "benefits" and "sacrifices." A "benefit"

is, more than anything else, the acquisition of a heretofore non-existing good or, once obtained, its conservation. But this word also designates, in respect to evil, the preservation or the restoration of the good. On the other hand, the word "sacrifice" is not only applied primarily to falling into a previously nonexistent evil or to persistence in it but also to the loss of a good previously possessed (damage) or the deprivation of its possession (injury). Likewise, a part of this methodology leads to the formation of value judgments which we might call "related" or which are expressed with homogeneous qualification with respect to beings that imply values and disvalues, but with one predominating. Hence one proceeds to initiate the valuation with an analysis of the constituent elements of such a complex of values in order then to qualify it synthetically, bearing in mind the relative weight of its single elements. All of this is common practice with our philosophers in their work in ethics, jurisprudence, or esthetics, but it has not yet found its proper expression in their criteriological systems.

12. Finally, all of our valuations depend also upon the principle that we could call the "hierarchy of values," which has the double sense of intensity and elevation. As regards intensity, it is logical that our concern with one value easily dislodges another from our consciousness, unless the latter value is accentuated as a reaction against the former. But this happens especially with respect to "elevation" in that indifference to superior values (ideal or altruistic values) is felt, while inferior (material and self-centered), though vitally more urgent, values receive no satisfaction whatever. This is what lends some legitimacy to the so-called materialistic interpretation of history. It is erroneous insofar as it supposes ideal values to be simple disguises or at best a sublimation of material values (though such artifices are indeed possible in certain cases); but it is true and realistic when it limits itself to recognizing that inferior values constitute an ordinary condition for the generation of higher values.

III
Mixed Forms

Let us consider now the mixed forms of being and value and of knowledge and valuation as they present themselves to us in life and as they affect life's three logical functions: the concept, the judgment, and the ratiocination, which are implicated in both ontology and axiology.

13. To be sure, concepts of "pure value" are rare since value, as we have said, is not substantival but adjectival to the being it affects, and hence can be considered in separation from that being only by way of abstraction. Such is the case of the values of goodness, beauty, and greatness. Those of wisdom, richness, or virtue, on the other hand, already suggest a relation to a determinate order of beings by reason of which they are already mixed concepts of being and value—or, to put it more exactly, concepts of a valuated reality or of a realized value. Such concepts are sometimes expressed by different words that are significative of pure realities. Thus, with the word "house" we signify a reality, and with the word "monument" we bespeak a value; the word "palace" means a house outstanding for its size, beauty, or quality. By contrast, sometimes several significations are linked to the same word: thus "accident" refers to a reality or property of a substance, or to something lacking value and, hence, without importance ("accidental"), or to some misfortune fallen upon someone ("victim of an accident"). It can even happen that the condition of possessing value is not indicated save as implied in the definition of a concept which apparently refers to a pure reality. Thus, the concept of "island" (land surrounded by water) or of "lake" (water surrounded by land) ceases to be applied to such realities when they are too large (they are then called continents, like the American continent, or seas, like the Caspian Sea), or when they are too small (in which case the island will become a reef and the lake a pool). A certain qualitative value is

also at times required for the definition of a being. Thus, when referring to an automobile which is broken down, even though it still runs, we are not content with saying that "it is a bad car"; we may go to the extreme of saying that "it is not an automobile." In such an example, the fusion of the real with the valuative in a single concept can be made under the rubric of "quantity" or "quality."[3]

14. Thus we have concepts which, being "qualitative" or "quantitative" with respect to the knowable reality, are likewise so with respect to a determinable value. Thus we have (a) concepts "qualified" as realities and as values, e.g., that of "calumny" which consists in attributing to someone a specific character, one which is esteemed to be at the same time blameworthy and false; (b) concepts "quantified" analogously as realities or as values, e.g., the results registered numerically as real by a statistical process which are then valuated according to the frequency or rarity of their occurrence; (c) concepts which are "qualitative" in regard to their reality and "quantitative" as to the value they imply, such as is inferred in using the expression "it is warm" to mean "it is hot" and in the series of words "breeze," "wind," "gale," "hurricane," etc., with which we refer to the graduations of the air in motion; (d) concepts which are "quantitative" as to reality and "qualitative" as to value, e.g., the lack of a part belonging to a whole is esteemed a "defect," just as perfection is the condition of a thing already brought to completion within its proper being; analogously, beauty supposes a plurality or variety of elements according to a law of harmony, and in social and political life numerical votes are translated into indications of valuative approval or disapproval. In the order of discrete quantity, its values generally tend to stand in inverse proportion to the qualifying adjectives applied, whence one comes to the point of qualifying something as "middling" simply by saying that it is "vulgar, ordinary, trivial," while to exalt its quality one is satisfied to say that it is "unique" in its kind.

15. In the mixed concepts given above the reality is the substantive, and the value appears as something adjectival to that reality. But there is also an inverse way of conceiving the matter, namely, that of "values" which come to be translated into "realities." Thus, (a) the "qualitative" value of justice comes also to be realized "qualitatively" in the person responsible for it and in the act of applying it. Generally, the inspiration of great men of thought, sensitivity, or action and the so-called spirit of good or bad will with which one conducts oneself in all the actions of life signify nothing else than a certain pre-eminence of the consciousness of value over that of being; (b) the "quantitative" values of "little" and "much" are then "quantified" or determined in concrete numbers, e.g., when we fix a salary or calculate in pounds the impression we have of the weight of an object; (c) a "qualitative" value is cifered "quantitatively," as a teacher does when he corrects the work or examinations of his students and assigns them a grade which gives or deprives them of a passing mark or a better mark; a "quantitative" valuation gives rise to entitative "qualifications," e.g., many physical properties and psychical functions, various mineral and biological species and their temperaments and characters, political regimes, languages, doctrines, geographical territories, and historical periods are frequently defined as qualitative entities when they are such only in degree, although with a "considerable" difference in degree.

16. It is interesting to observe, in the light of these distinctions, how the hierarchical scale of beings (Porphyry's Tree) lends itself to being interpreted ontologically by some as comprising "qualitatively" discontinuous categories and by others as "quantitatively" continuous levels; though the first do not cease, for this reason, to evaluate it "quantitatively" (considering some categories as "superior" to others: man to animals, animals to plants, plants to minerals) or the second to evaluate it "qualitatively." An evolutionist will take offense at being called an animal, in spite of the fact that his doctrine regards the difference between man and animal as one only of degree.

17. What occurs in the case of mixed concepts of being and value also proves to be true with "judgments" when they are composed of a real subject affected by a predicate of pure value (as when I say "that man is just"), or of an evaluated reality ("John is ill"), or, conversely, of a subject of value or of evaluated reality ("justice makes a nation great" or "the illness took his life"). Such judgments are mixtures of reality and value by reason of the "concepts" which constitute them.

The judgment, however, contains, in addition to concepts, a "verb" which relates the concepts and which is, as it were, the soul of the affirmation or negation. This verb can be the impersonal verb "to be" or any verb reducible to the verb "to be." It can state a simple reality or the adjectival reality of a value: when one says "it is good weather," that "good" may be sunny or rainy according to whether it is evaluated by a city-dweller or by a farmer who depends upon rain for his harvest. But if this man of the country says, "I am going to have a rich harvest," he is enunciating not a simple fact but the prospect of an event which is valued and hence desirable for him and, in addition, realizable through his voluntary effort. If he adds, "I ought to sell it for the set price," he signifies a precept; and he signifies a prohibition when he affirms, "I can't hide it from the market authorities." In each of these judgments, he recognizes a moral or juridical "obligation" from which he declares himself exempt when he says, "I can sell my harvest or use it for making bread." Note the contrast between the verbs "must" and "can" when they signify moral values or pure necessities, possibilities, or impossibilities of reality, as occurs in the following judgments: "If this ladder should break, I must fall"; "I can't get up with this broken leg"; "It may be that I will never recover from this fracture." As a rule, moral "obligation" (must) is not only not incompatible with the physical power of violating it but is, in fact, linked with it. As far as the verb "can" is concerned, the differences are clear in its three meanings: that of simple possibility or doubtful reality theoretically known ("it's possible that it may rain"); that of the practical capacity for action ("I can take refuge in that entrance");

or that of moral or legal permission which is thought to be effective ("I can buy an umbrella"). Analogously, the negation "I
can't" sometimes has a physical or psychological meaning, and at
other times a moral or juridical meaning. It is of capital importance to distinguish between all these meanings if we are to come
to grips with the double physiognomy of being and value that
our judgments can assume.

18. The mixed forms of reality and value in our ratiocinations merit very careful attention. Judgments of this type appear
in demonstration as conclusions of two premises, one of which
affirms the aspect of its reality and the other that of its value.
Thus, the judgment "that man is generous" will be the conclusion of a syllogism which might say, "That man has contributed
a thousand dollars to this cause; but such a donation indicates
generosity; therefore, that man is generous." To arrive at such
conclusions, we ordinarily content ourselves with formulating
the first or second of its two premises, assuming the other as
understood, and with that the argument takes the form of enthy-
meme. Now let us take a look at the various types of reasoning
of this character which we encounter in life.

19. The most patent meeting-point of ontological and axiological factors in ratiocination is to be found in those inquiries which
attempt to fix the value called "utility." A being is useful, above
all, to the extent that it is "efficacious" (i.e., that it is a cause
capable of producing an effect) but also on the supposition that
that cause is a means and that effect is an end: not a simple term
of the action, but a valuative and hence attractive term (when it
is not disvaluative and, as such, repulsive, in which case one will
speak, not of usefulness but of harmfulness). Thus utility can be
the conclusion of a reasoning process whose premises are the
affirmation of the above mentioned causality, on the one hand,
and of that finality, on the other. Accompanying this twofold
"ontological" and "axiological" aspect of reasoning, of being and
value, indissolubly united in the usefulness of any means, we find,

also inseparable from it, the "logical" aspect of the greater or lesser certainty or security which one has of attaining an objective as end. Thus in life we regard as useful natural and artificial things, the acts which we perform on these things, and even subjects, all equal to each other to the extent that they are applicable or are in fact applied to the realization of a determinate end. It is also interesting to note, apropos subjects, the activity dedicated to modifying usefully their proper structure and their consequent function by means of education and instruction. All pedagogical values serve this purpose.

We find a special kind of usefulness in the "economic" order. Here, the problem of linking the means of production with the ends desired or desirable for consumption is complicated by the contrast between the limited character of these means and the unlimited character of the ends and even between the quality and the quantity of the one and the other, which causes those of inferior condition to abound and vice versa. From this arises the distinction between articles of basic necessity, those of convenience, and those of luxury, in decreasing degrees of quantity. All of this is translated into the introduction of disjunctive evaluation —the attainment of an end by this or that means among those considered available—in which the value of each item will be in inverse proportion to the number of items as far as "value in use" is concerned. As to the "value in exchange" in social life, the price of an article will be in inverse proportion to the number of sellers that represent the market of the means and in direct proportion to that of the buyers which reflects the market of the ends to be satisfied. All of this is translated into money as the common denominator of all values, and monetary units will also have value for their possessor in inverse proportion to his fortune. In the face of such a condition of human life of which all who share it are creditors, there arises the value of the "common good," the good common to all, which is the ideal of justice (just as "partiality" is the token of "injustice"). This last is value with respect to the alien person—the stranger—and is excelled only by love.

20. But it is not only in the order of the value of usefulness of means for an end that the above mentioned fusion of the cognitive and the valuative is manifested but also in that of the ends or beings in themselves. This holds true with respect both to "quantitative" judgments and to "qualitative" judgments.

To begin with, let us consider "quantitative" judgments. If I say, "The Eiffel Tower is very high," it will not suffice—to justify my affirmation—to show that that tower is nearly one thousand feet high, for I shall have to show at the same time that such an elevation constitutes a great height. Thus, I will say, "The Eiffel Tower is nearly one thousand feet high; now a tower one thousand feet high is very high; therefore, the Eiffel Tower is very high." This spreading out of the ratiocinative process leading to such judgments brings out what there is in them of cognitive and valuative content, what there is in them of reality and of value. What occurs in this example of continuous quantity also occurs in others of discrete quantity (e.g., "Barcelona is a heavily populated city"), of complex quantity ("the airplane is a very complicated apparatus"), and of quantity of efficiency ("the atomic bomb is an extraordinarily destructive weapon"). In all of them it becomes necessary to distinguish the measurable reality, which is the basis of valuation, from the evaluation of its value in the strict sense. Let it be noted, in this connection, that the meaning which the word "value" has in mathematics, where it signifies a knowable fixed quantity, is different from that which it has in axiology, where it designates a determinable quantitative value. The same distinction is observed in statistics when one passes, for example, from the number of times it rained in a given country during a year, and from the quantity of precipitation entailed, to the affirmation that that country "is very rainy."

21. The same occurs with "qualitative" judgments (also comprising known reality and evaluated value) as the necessary premises of a ratiocinative conclusion. Thus, in moral matters, if we say that "Guzman the Good performed a heroic deed," our demonstration first will have to register that fact of his having

refused to surrender the Tarifa Square before the threat of the execution of his son, so as then to qualify such an act as heroic. Likewise, in order to find someone guilty of dishonesty, it will first have to be demonstrated that all insincerity is reprehensible and that the subject in question has conducted himself insincerely. The same occurs in esthetic matters. If I say, "The picture by Las Lanzas is a model of historic composition and artistic execution," my affirmation involves the twofold judgment of a pictorial reality and of its exemplary worth, with regard to both its content and its form. The same composition is observed in a ratiocination such as the following: "Snow is a very pretty spectacle; it snowed last night; therefore, we are going to enjoy a pretty sight." Thus every reasoning process in "moral" and "esthetic" casuistics will consist of a primary premise of valuation of an abstract or hypothetical fact which a second premise will give as realized, so as to affirm its value in the conclusion. In "historical" disciplines, not limited to the mere statement and explanation of facts, one will proceed in the opposite direction, registering in the first premise a fact as realized, valuating it abstractly and hypothetically in the second, so as to valuate it absolutely in the conclusion. When one takes up problems of facts not yet realized, but to be realized without the intervention of the human will, one will proceed analogously.

22. The distinction we are referring to can be more clearly noted in the juridical order where it is always necessary to justify a primary "veritas facti," which refers to a situation of an act performed or to be performed, or another "veritas juris," the right in the strict sense affecting such a situation or issuing from it. Consider, for example, the structure of a judgment in "civil" law ("property is a natural right") or in "penal" law ("this man is guilty of theft"). Regarding the first, property is primarily a possession, i.e., the physical possibility of disposing of something, and, as such, it is the object of a judgment of reality which becomes a judgment of value with the recognition of the morally inviolable condition of said disposability or disposition. Similarly,

in the second case, to demonstrate the culpability of someone in a question of theft, it will not suffice to prove the fact that he took possession of what did not belong to him, not even if it were against the owner's will, but it will be necessary to evaluate the owner's will as to its reasonableness and the supposed thief's will as to its freedom. The distinction between juridical reality and juridical value is clear and manifest in the "laws," whose preamble frequently contains the motives and values that justify them, just as their text regularly contains the acts to which they bind those subject to them. Indeed, these acts at times also include a value, such as that of requiring a physician to attend to his patients "diligently" or a teacher to teach nothing but "truth" to his students, to educate them "morally," and to give them "good example." Judicial "rulings" are also preceded by "establishments" of fact and by "considerations" of evaluation. And the same ruling obligates to acts which may be defined as simple acts (e.g., restitution of property), as acts involving value (e.g., satisfaction), or as pure values (injury). "Crimes" are defined in terms of pure acts (e.g., falsity), of acts involving value (e.g., calumny), or of pure values (e.g., injury). Penalties are likewise meted out as treatment of fact (so many years of prison) or of evaluated fact (so many years in a correctional institution). Generally, all "right" is defined in relation to things or powers of which one may "make use" at one's own discretion (liberty) but without abusing them indiscreetly (license). In the exercise of public power, one distinguishes between its "legality" or proportion to the norms prescribed in fact by the constitution and its "legitimacy" or spirit of justice in the laws and rulings. It often happens that rulings within the legal norms are treated as unjust and that illegal attitudes of rebelliousness presume justice which, by chance, is recognized as theirs when rebellion triumphs.

23. To conclude, the realm of values, freighted with realities, constitutes the "moral order" when it is organized hierarchically by subjecting inferior values to values superior in dignity, and hence pleasure to virtue or dignity, whatever the intensity with

which they are made to prevail in life. The proclamation of this
order by the twofold avenue of the knowledge of the realities
which constitute it and the establishment of the values which
give it life is the essence of moral reasoning. To this is joined the
"juridical order" from the moment that the moral order is shared
by a plurality of persons equally bound to it who, consequently,
must respect and assist one another in order to fulfill it and who
regard the "good" which constitutes it as a "common good," as
far as is possible within human limitations, and thus recognize,
"altruistically," the value of the other person (whether individual
or collective) as an end in himself in the same terms with which
"egoism" proclaims the value of one's own person.

24. Mixed forms of reasoning are not limited to recognizing
values linked to determinate beings in "theoretical" judgments
of value but tend toward realizing values as they are proposed by
so-called practical judgments. The fundamental axiom of ethics
is "Bonum est faciendum, malum autem vitandum," or "Do good
and avoid evil." This axiom presupposes a definite good and a
definite evil, and it imposes as an absolute norm (and in this it
differs from technique, which is hypothetical) the seeking of the
first and the rejection of the second. This passage from the theory
of the good to its practice is a conclusion "sui generis," for in it
there is something more than in the premises ("This is a good,
and I can do it; therefore I must do it")—all the more to the
extent that, while all evil is forbidden (as far as possible), not
all good is commanded (for there are good actions which are
"optional," of pure counsel or permission). "Obligation," then,
presupposes "capability," and "value," consequently, constitutes
a new problem: the problem of ethics and law in their practical
application, which adds something to the problem of the simple
appreciation of the good in its theoretical character, especially
to pure psychological knowledge of human acts and even to
their psychotechnology. "Moral" obligation is spelled out in the
counsel "live honestly." Besides this moral obligation, which can
take on juridical character, "juridical" obligation can be reduced

to the negative maxim of "do not harm others" and to the positive maxim to "give to each his due."

All of these norms are designated by the word "law." We use the term "natural" law for the most abstract and universal norms and the term "positive" law for those norms incarnated in customs and in the will of lawmakers for collectivities, though limited in time and space. In positive law there are individual "intentions" and interindividual "contracts" that set bounds to the range of the liberty of political organization and thus oppose the state authority which tends to absorb that liberty in so-called socialist or communist regimes. All of these are "moral facts" or "political facts," i.e., realities that give rise to maxims of action inspired by a value to be realized. Such is the condition of the "moral and juridical order" confined to the imperfect and transitory goods of this world. Different from this is the "religious order" that crowns it with the reference of man to God, the supreme Being and the highest and most excellent Good, in whom all other beings and goods participate and to whom they all aspire and from whose will, also called the "eternal" law, all other laws receive their force and authority.

25. The realization of values under the dominion of law by means of human activity is achieved, up to a certain point, in the form of mental and locomotive "spontaneity." This spontaneity also has its values: acuteness of the senses, fidelity to the memory, the ingeniousness of the inventive imagination, discretion in judgment, muscular ability, and so forth. But the efficacy of such activity, which is attentive only to the present or to the past and which is incapable of disposing the destiny of the human person, is very limited and accordingly deprived of all subjectively moral value. Only the will, with its affective and effective prevision and intention—where it overcomes, while continuing to use, the automatism of pure spontaneity—distinguishes itself for its sovereign fecundity in facing the real and mental future, to order it in conformity with the moral law.

It is easy to show how every problem of the will is a problem of mixed reality and value, of mixed knowledge and valuation. Thus, for example, before the reality of atmospheric weather, I cannot "love it"; I can at best "desire it" as long as I consider it independent of myself and not do anything with respect to it, such as to go out for a walk or to take an umbrella. But neither will I do any of these things if I am indifferent or uninterested in the weather as good or bad and if, consequently, I do not make it the object of an "intention." Thus, the will in general is the intention of an end through the proper means. But the end in question is not a simple termination of our activity, but a valuative or disvaluative object, one recognized as good or as evil, and consequently the object of pursuit or rejection. In the case of pursuit (and we would have to say the contrary in the case of rejection) it is a question of an object known as imperfect or as imperfectly known and an object whose perfection is sought because of its value. Concretizing this dynamism before the ordinary reality of life, the will has to face problems of choice between imcompatible goods, unavoidable evils, and combinations of inseparable goods and evils which put to the test the essential values of the human person in its highest prerogative: freedom.

26. The first task of the will before the complex situations of life is "deliberation" or weighing of available motives so as to adopt a line of conduct with respect to the greater or lesser goodness or badness of ends; with respect to the greater and lesser efficacy of the means of attaining or avoiding them; and, furthermore, with respect to the greater or lesser certainty or security of the judgment of that goodness or efficacy. This is translated—in order to conclude deliberation with "decision"—into the possible division of goods, compatible in themselves, from separable but inescapable evils: choice of good and evil which are inseparable but avoidable; among these solutions, choice intervenes. This choice, which is the second task of the will, is called "resolution,"

and the criterion necessary for it varies according to whether moral or juridical obligation has to intervene in it. When it is a question of choosing between alternatives that are found to be within the range of what is morally and juridically "permitted," either such alternatives appear as "equivalent" and the will arbitrarily elects any one of them, or one of them offers itself as the "prevalent" one and the will forthwith "prefers" it (unless it rejects it merely for the sake of demonstrating its autonomy) by reason of its greater goodness as an end (the axiological factor), its greater efficacy as a means (the ontological factor), and the greater certainty of the one or the other (the logical factor). These factors can be found to be in inverse proportion to one another, and they compensate one another mutually—a lesser, but more secure, good is preferred to a greater good which is less certain or vice versa. When the factor of "moral obligation" (which is not foreign to the criteria set forth before, though distinguished especially for the accentuated worth of the final object and the honesty of the means to attain it, and when the "juridical obligation" factor inspired by the universality of the subjects it benefits prevail, the will finds itself face to face with "temptation" if such a value does not coincide with the purely affective values leading to the pursuit of the pleasurable good and to avoidance of the painful evil, and this more for oneself (egoism) than for others (altruism). The solution will lie in overcoming the temptation with "moral effort," in preferring duty to pleasure and universalism to egoism, or in surrendering oneself to it, in opting for the side of greater vital intensity but of lower moral or juridical quality (Ovid's "videa meliora, proboque, deteriora sequor"). In this connection, it should be noted that temptation is subject to degrees which can rise even to the point of conflict between two obligations that must be resolved according to their importance in the hierarchy of values. Finally, the third task of the will consists in the "execution" of the adopted resolution, in carrying it to completion with firmness and perseverance but without refusing to subject the whole resolution to a possible revision with a

view to ratifying or rectifying it as may prove advisable in the
course of things.

In these three tasks, we catch sight, in the first place, of the
so-called human freedom, conceived, not as an actual condition
of the will that is equal in all men and in all human acts, but as
a possibility of "liberation" from the yoke of inferior values to the
reflective consideration of superior values; and witness is likewise
borne to values that are typical of the will: the quantitative value
of what goes under the name of "will power" and the more specifically qualitative value of "virtue" (incorporated with spontaneity by habit) which, with those that have come to be called
cardinal virtues—"prudence, temperance, fortitude, justice"—
places that power in the service of the moral good. It is, of course,
just the contrary with "fault" and "vice," which make it serve evil.
As far as the good is *possible,* man is responsible for its realization through his free will, and it is with that free will that he contracts the "merit" or "demerit" of his conduct as well as the obligation of consequent "reward" or "punishment" (which can also
be valuated as means or as ends) as a sanction of that conduct.
The "force" necessary for the imposition of a "punishment" by the
public authorities upon the guilty person has a moral value only
when it is placed in the service of the Law or when, in the form
of "war," it tries to settle an otherwise insoluble dispute between
two nations and two public authorities. Lacking these conditions,
it is a "brute force" possessing merely quantitative value. The
perspective of the present life, moving as it does toward corporeal
death, is broadened by the perspective of a happy immortality
of the soul in the bosom of God, the supreme Being and highest
Value. But he is such only in consonance with fidelity to the voice
of duty in the conduct of the present life and only as the recom-
pense of that conduct as well as in contrast with the castigation
deserved for unrepented immorality and injustice. Such is, then,
the scheme of the so-called logic of the will which is, as it were,
the culminating chapter of the "philosophy of values" and which
is treated so haphazardly in our books on logic, limited as they
are to what serves as an introduction to the "philosophy of beings."

IV
INTERFERENTIAL FORMS

Up to this point we have considered being and value, along with the mental functions that correspond to them, as distinct or as juxtaposed and combined but still independent of each other. We are now going to broach, however briefly, a third and final aspect of our theme which involves the most subtle problems of philosophy. It is a question of what I call the "interferential" forms of being and of value, the forms of the knowledge "of" valuation or vice versa and of a knowledge "by" valuation or vice versa. In the first sense, that of knowledge "of" valuation and vice versa, such interference is found in the domain of the concepts, the judgments, and the reasoning processes; in the second sense, that of knowledge "by" valuation and vice versa, it affects only the reasoning processes.

27. Human knowledge extends, in the first instance, to material objects, which alone may be properly called objects, and it manages to trace a knowledge of them that, in its scientific state, constitutes physical-mathematical science, made up of concepts, judgments, and ratiocinations touching upon the material world. Besides knowing, the human spirit "savors" the physical world, i.e., it enjoys its values, and thus makes it the object of its valuation. It is not only the physical world that is known and enjoyed by man but also the social world and even the very life of man's own spirit when it is objectified by reflection. So then, in the knowledge of the spirit by the spirit—which we designate with the name of psychology—we come upon the fact that among the functions of the spirit is found the valuative function, or the function of valuation, whose object is value and not being as such (for being is, rather, the object of the cognitive function). Here arises the first form of interference between the two functions, namely, the pure knowledge "of" valuation and of valuated values or, if one wishes, the pure knowledge of values and their valua-

tion. Let us take a look at the characteristics of such interference in the order of concepts and of judgments.

28. In the order of concepts, in the first place, we have an idea of beings which, strictly speaking, we call their concept or percept according to whether we are dealing with abstract or concrete beings, but here we shall refer to them as "concepts," covering both. However, we also have an idea of values and of the process by which we evaluate them. Here the question arises: "Is the idea of a value the same as the value itself?" The word "idea" has a purely cognitive meaning, and the word "value" has a purely "valuative" meaning. Does the idea I have, for example, of the value of humility manifest this value perfectly, or is it only a pallid and cold reflection of its true value, as the light reflected in a mirror has no heat? Is a cognitive concept of a value the same as a valuative concept of that value? The question becomes still more compelling when asked concerning valuation, i.e., concerning the act of valuating a value. I can imagine a man who makes a cult of modesty and humility, one who feels them in himself even though he is unable to define them (much as Thomas à Kempis says of compunction, that he would rather feel it than define it), since the most perfect definition of either of them is not incompatible with a limited or even a total lack of valuation of them. What shall we say of the "lived" consciousness the modest man has of his modesty, or the humble man of his humility— let us take the case of the publican in the Gospel—before the purely "representative" expression that a theologian, who may be proud of his knowledge, can give of those virtues? Everything insists upon our maintaining the distinction between the two in spite of the interference we have pointed out. I can have, to use a subtle verbal expression, an idea of the "value of justice" without having the idea of the "value of the idea of justice." The first is a purely cognitive idea, the second purely valuative. Or, to put it in other terms, the "idea of a value" is not the same as the "value of an idea," even though the idea is an idea of value. The first is a simple representation of an object, while the second is something felt and lived by a subject.

29. All of this can be seen still more clearly in the realm of "judgments." The psychologist has to take into consideration all the "facts of consciousness" and, among these, those called "judgments of valuation" of one's own or another's consciousness, but he must limit himself to their simple representation or statement. It may be that he does not share such valuations personally because either he does not agree with them or he once had them but has abandoned them. But even if he shares them, he must, as a psychologist, prescind from such valuation; he must forget that it is his valuation and consider it as a simple fact, but a fact "sui generis," consisting in the affirmation of a value. A man who becomes vitally involved in the emotional content of a concert is not practicing psychology nor is the critic who, even though in a state of greater serenity, observes its esthetic values. He alone is a psychologist who limits himself to describing, so as later to be able to explain the valuative process that such a concert evoked in him. If we say this of esthetic values, we must also say it of ethical values, of juridical values, and of religious values. But, let it be kept clear, this leaves intact the theme of esthetics, ethics, jurisprudence, or religion, which are eminently valuative disciplines and which cannot, therefore, be confused—in spite of all the attempts being made today in this direction—with purely cognitive sciences that are designated by the names of the psychology and the sociology of art, of customs, of law, or of religion. Beyond the pure and simple reality of such "facts of valuation," the frequency of which is registered by statistics (valuating them quantitatively in turn as "normal" or "abnormal," or as common or exceptional but without qualifying such exceptions, for example, the idiot and the genius, the criminal and the saint), we find the qualitative or "normative" valuation of the "valuation of such facts" which is incumbent upon the above mentioned disciplines and which consists in defining whether or not the facts in question are produced as they should be produced: the eternal contrast between "reality" and "the ideal," between "being" and "what ought to be," which because of "valuing" is imposed upon human acts.

30. And this relates the theme of such judgments to that of their "justification" which is found, for those who profess them, in the object to which they refer and which they suppose is manifested to them in its authentic valuative reality—sometimes directly and sometimes through a ratiocination. The psychologist, by contrast, cannot in that role subscribe to such a justification; nor can he, however, forego explaining such judgments; and in this explanation either he coincides with the reasons which objectively justify them or—as often occurs—appeals to subjective causes to explain them (though ipso facto, in the latter case, weakening his justification). This happens especially in what is called "psychologism," which is very much given to reducing the why and wherefore of everything that man thinks, feels, and desires to purely subjective factors; forgetting that this procedure, to be valid, must also be applied to the person who advocates such opinions and that such criteria, solvent of all the normative sciences, must also prove solvent of psychology.

31. The interferences which we are describing are reciprocal: they proceed not only from knowledge toward valuation but also from valuation to knowledge, and this in two senses.

First of all, the pure knowledge of being does not cease to retain its value, a threefold value: the value of "exactness" for concepts, of "truth" for judgments, and of "evidence" for ratiocinations. The spirit, in turning back reflectively upon its own act of knowledge, cannot fail to recognize and to evaluate these values. The value of "exactness" in a "concept" is reflected in its precise definition, reduced to registering the whole, but nothing else, of what pertains to the concept in question. The proper value of a judgment is, in its turn, "truth"—not the value of ontological truth which coincides fundamentally with the good, but the value of "logical" and even "psychological" truth which consists in the conformity of the affirmation of a reality with the reality itself, and the value of "veracity" or conformity of what one thinks or wishes with what one does or says, under the double rubric of the competency and sincerity of conduct and language. Finally, "ratiocination" also has a value peculiar to itself, which is that of "evidence," a value distinct from truth (since all truth is not evident, nor does all pseudo evidence constitute a false argument) and patent in that form of evidence, either immediate or mediate, and properly ratiocinative, called "consequence." Now that these values of pure knowledge have been made clear and distinct, we can apply to them what we established in connection with the psychological recognition of the strictly valuative values of greatness, goodness, or beauty.

32. But there is another very interesting sense in which a penetration of the valuative function into the cognitive function can occur. I am referring to the esteem we pay to the pure knowledge of being, the cultivation of "science for the sake of science," which inspires so many members of the scientific profession in their painstaking research and which, on a lower level perhaps, stimulates even the common man when, moved by pure "curiosity," he sets about verifying something. This "feeling of curiosity" is so different from other feelings that it may even conflict with and outweigh all other feelings, dominating the mind and leaving behind values or valuations of any other character. This also manifests itself in the threefold order of concepts, judgments, and ratiocinations.

With respect to concepts, there is an obvious difference between a chemist and a perfumist; the latter is dedicated to procuring the most gratifying fragrances and to eliminating fetidness, while the former will tolerate unpleasant odors provided they reflect the authentic odors of this or that body. The chemist is more interested in the representation than in the quality of the odor, while precisely the contrary occurs with the perfumist. In the order of judgments, the difference is observed between the historian and the patriot in registering and relating the events of their country's history. While the patriot selects the events that most exalt the country's glories and dissimulates the rest, the historian reflects them all, whether favorable or unfavorable: he is more concerned with the truth than with the content of his affirmations, concerned with the truth more than with the certainty of truth, and faithful to that double-edged axiom of the good historian for whom "there must be no truth that he does not dare to proclaim, nor error that he would not dare to admit." Finally, with respect to "ratiocinations," a difference is also to be observed between the apologist, the panegyrist of a doctrinal matter, or the lawyer who is the "accuser" or "defender" in the trial of a person (always inclined to be convinced by the proofs which tend to support his conclusions and to weaken opposite conclusions) and one who approaches the matter impartially, in a critical spirit, more interested in the value of the proof than in the nature of the conclusion, and seeking in the proof the evidence of the demonstration rather than the demonstration of the evidence.

In all of this, we are dealing with the parallel between the "intellectual" and the "sentimentalist," not meaning that the former is lacking in sentiment and that the latter turns his back on the expense of intelligence, but in the sense that while the sentimentalist subordinates knowing to feeling, the intellectual inverts this order, reducing sentiment to the satisfaction he receives from the knowledge of the truth, which, from other points of view, may be pleasing or unpleasing, good or bad, just or unjust, beautiful or ugly. In a word, the sentimentalist seeks "good news" in life; the intellectual seeks "news" pure and simple. The condition of the intellectual is rare despite all that we expect from it in human controversies which tend less to be discussions than disputes and in polemics where the disinterested love of truth is conspicuous by its absence and is supplanted by the more or less unconscious love for an object whether attractive or repulsive, or at least that of a subject bent upon "having his way."

33. The intersection of being and value in our mental life is to be noted not only in the sense of giving rise to a knowledge "of" valuation and, vice versa, a valuation "of" knowledge but also in the sense of producing at times the valuation of a value "in virtue" of a pure knowledge of reality and, at other times, a knowledge

of reality "in virtue" of a pure valuation of a value. Let us consider separately each of these interferences which directly affect
the order of proofs and ratiocinations and, through them, the
judgments derived from them.

It frequently happens, as a matter of fact, that for the affirmation of a value, including the value of pure truth inherent in
cognitive judgments, one accepts as proof the fact that such
a value is held in a determinate area of society, regarding as
good, as just, beautiful, or true what is recognized as such and
assuming that it should have been so recognized. This often happens in the case of a preference for the new (modernism), the old
(traditionalism), what is native (nationalism), or what is foreign (internationalism). Such is the criterion which inspires so-
called moral or juridical positivism—and we could say the same
of esthetic or religious, and even of scientific, positivism—which
either disavows the transcendence of all valuation or accepts it
as valid merely because it is produced in a determined sector of
geography or history, a fact which constitutes a presumption of
its value and which removes it—unjustifiably, to be sure—from the
scrutiny of criticism. Analogous to this acceptance of human
valuations is the acceptance of the values realized in nature
when they are taken as unimprovable, thus closing the door to
all progress.

34. In comparison to this interference, in which a reality is
given as possessing value, there is a greater range in the inverse
interference in which a value is taken as realized because it is a
value or in which a knowledge is founded upon the estimability
of its object. The value and the valuation in question can be
"quantitative" or "qualitative."

It is always a "quantitative" valuation that decides the process
of "empirical induction," which is the basis of all the natural sciences. It is known that the so-called experience on which these
rest is nothing but the repetition, in conformity with a precon-
ceived hypothesis, of a series of instances of results which are in
concord with the hypothesis in question. These results are always

limited in number. Induction, however, consists precisely in giving them the unlimited and universal range of laws, in virtue of
the "mathematical calculation of probabilities," which makes that
concordance inexplicable on the basis of pure chance and induces
one to recognize them as the effect of some cause. However, to
be exact, there is no fixed mathematical criterion for the transition
from one to the other, and it is ultimately entrusted to the valuative reasoning of the experimenter, who regards a certain number of registered concordances as sufficient to eliminate the
hypothesis of chance and to erect as a thesis that of causality.
Such is the meaning of Bernouilli's so-called law of large numbers
which betrays its valuative derivation even in its name. And it is
not only in the task of pure science, which extracts from reality
the laws it obeys, that one observes the importance of the valuative factor but also in that of the "applied sciences," the sciences
applied to reality under conditions which, to a large extent, pre-
clude a rigorous calculation and in which they must trust an
approximative valuation. Nor does this fail to occur even in simple
sense perceptions of real objects whose conditions of normalcy,
the guarantee of their truth, is as little susceptible to strict test.
Finally, in the extremely vast realm of so-called extrinsic evidence,
in which an appeal is made to an outside criterion to resolve problems inaccessible to an internal one (subsequently, to a critical
discussion of that criterion's authenticity, capacity, and veracity),
it is obviously not possible to eliminate all possibility of error
touching these extremes; obviously it becomes necessary to reduce
this process ultimately to a valuative judgment of its value,
founded on a greater or lesser sum of probabilities in favor of its
truth. Such is the first ingredient—that of "quantitative" valuation—of the value of "trust" or of "authority" that a person merits
from us.

35. Over and above this quantitative valuation—reduced, after
all, to an accumulation of probabilities which is estimated to be
sufficient to determine a certain conviction—we encounter the
"qualitative" valuation of the reality to be judged, with decisive

influence upon such a judgment, when its cognitive conditions do not impose it beyond question. It is an error to suppose, as is so often done in our criteriologies, that our cognitive faculty stands before its objects "tanquam tabula rasa" if by that we are to understand that it is indifferent to the valuative condition of the objects in question. On the contrary, such objects frequently contain great vital interest, to the cognitive acts and to the knowing subject: interest which is based upon their condition as possessing or lacking value, the values of delightfulness, goodness, beauty, or utility, or the disvalues of harshness, badness, ugliness, or harmfulness.

Then it happens that, by a sort of vital reaction of the valuative function—that which Balmes called the "influence of the heart over the head"—we easily regard as true, or perhaps as realized or to be realized, that which is good, beautiful, or useful, i.e., whatever has value (whence we have the "optimist" tendency) unless by a contrary reaction we are inclined to suppose as true precisely that which is bad, ugly, and harmful, or whatever is without value (which is the "pessimist" tendency). This occurs not only with values but also with the feelings in which they are reflected, the "motives" of which are at times recognized as real in advance of feeling but at other times under its influence. Thus the lover firmly believes whatever his love can conjure up (when it is something that does not endanger that love, as occurs with the jealous lover), and the animosity proper to hatred is translated into the facility with which one welcomes all that is unfavorable to its object. The only spirits that escape either the optimist or the pessimist tendency are those "dispassionate" spirits which, without ceasing to be sensitive to the attractive suggestion of the ideal, are no less sensitive to the "impurities of the truth" that cause them, on many occasions, to exclaim: "What a pity that such beauty is not true!" In this way, love and hatred exercise their seductive influence upon our convictions, making us see things and persons not as they are but as we would wish them to be according to our vital interests.

Personal interest is not the only thing that inspires our convic-

tions; equally effective is the tendency to regard as true that
which is convenient, the tendency to idealize, improve, and beau-
tify reality, a tendency that is evident in the arguments which the
ancient scholastics called "de congruentia," or the impersonal
and objective convenience of the realization of some value or the
frustration of some disvalue in the course of history. This occurs
not only in the order of human moral history—so frequently beau-
tified, but also disfigured, by legends—but also in the order of
natural history in which one sometimes reasons on the basis of
presumed axioms such as: "Nature does nothing in vain; it does
not proceed violently but obtains its effects in the most simple
ways," etc. Analogous to this is the tendency to believe in the
miraculous, i.e., in what is released from the yoke of the laws of
nature. The most synthetic formula of such arguments of congruency is given to us by the sword-work of Duns Scotus in defense
of the Immaculate Conception: "Potuit, decuit, ergo fecit"—"He
could, it was fitting, so He did it." Once the possibility of a fact
is supposed, its realization is inferred from its simple worth. Was
it worthwhile? Then it took place. This order could be inverted,
so as to say: "Did it take place? Then it was worthwhile," thus
inferring its worth from the fact that it took place. In neither sense
is the argument conclusive except in connection with higher
values—and then out of strict necessity rather than out of convenience—but in any case it offers us one of the typical forms of
interference of being and value, of knowledge and valuation in
the ratiocinative function.

36. All of these factors of qualitative valuation which shape
our convictions are present not only in valuations elaborated with
"one's own" criterion but also in those based on an "outside"
criterion which is offered by an equal to an equal or by a superior
to an inferior (in which case it is accepted, thanks to the "confidence" we enjoy) or by an inferior to a superior, to constitute
then the criterion of "authority." The authority of a person who
imposes himself upon others is not precisely a proof of his capacity
or veracity, nor even a quantitative valuation of the high proba-

bility of such capacity or veracity (which would give them as practically certain), but the valuation of a series of qualities—from physical excellence (especially that of age, of course) to the spiritual prestige reflected by that excellence, which may be intellectual, potential, moral, sympathetic, even that of eloquence with its countless resources of conviction—which very often subjugate spirits rather more effectively than do better constructed arguments. Let us not think that each one of the above mentioned qualities is a source of authority only for the problems peculiar to it, for they form among them a united front which often imposes itself indifferently upon the subject's consent. To the "objective" values, which of themselves suggest the proposed doctrine as very likely true, are thus added those that affirm it because of the admiration and love professed for the "subject" who proposes it and who happens to have lived it and realized it in his life. The "credit" granted to authority is then corroborated by the "success" or happy results which it predicted and in which, with some lack of logic, the person favored sees the best proof of its value, just as, for the person not favored, its failure is the principal motive of discredit with respect to the authority in question. One should also note the frequent process of "communication" or "chain" of authority through which a person derives his authority from another who guarantees it, and this other from still another, and so on until one comes to a person who has it in himself, in his own being. The process of "tradition" in history is nothing other than this. Likewise, there is the correlation of so-called authorities in carrying out some charge of social or political responsibility with those who, outside of any function of this type, enjoy a personal authority in their social ambient. The functional authority leads one to assume personal authority, just as the latter leads to the former, but such correlation is in no way rigorous. Finally, there is the interference, in our mind, of the authoritarian criterion with what is our own criterion—whether our own is indifferent, favorable, or adverse toward that authority—and even with the conflict of authorities among themselves which produces consequent doubt, from which we may or may not succeed in freeing ourselves, depending on whether one of the criteria in question prevails or all remain equal.

And with this I think I have terminated my presentation of a panoramic view of the problematic which, in my judgment, the being-value dualism presents in our day. This problematic, in its totality, has a physiognomy that is somewhat unknown to many who regard themselves as cultivators of traditional philosophy. Indeed, the word "value" does not even come up in that philosophy, and its counterposition relative to being, with the consequent counterposition of valuation relative to knowledge, does not appear in classical thought. This is not to say that it is not found hidden in that thought, or that the progress of philosophy does not consist precisely in bringing it out from that hidden position. The essential thing in the cultivation of the rich treasure of traditional philosophy is that we do not limit ourselves to repeating it under the guise of fidelity but that we understand this fidelity as the task of constantly enriching it with new additions in its own spirit of "Vetera novis augere et perficere." We are convinced that philosophy, although it is not a history, as some of our contemporaries claim, has its history, and indeed a history achieved in the past and to be achieved in the future, following paths that become constantly broader, though all originate in the secure and firm course of the "perennis philosophia."

Xavier Zubiri

Don Xavier Zubiri (b.1898), Spain's most eminent and representative philosopher, well versed in science (especially anthropology and allied fields), combines an impressive synthesis of Aristotelian thought with contemporary European philosophical movements. Representing a strictly disciplined concept of philosophy, Professor Zubiri forms a strong polar influence to that of Ortega y Gasset. Among his principal works are Naturaleza, historia, dios *(1944, revised 1964),* Sobre la esencia *(1962), and* Cinco lecciones de filosofia *(1963).*

"The Origin of Man" appeared in *Revista de Occidente* Ano. II 2a er. No. 17 (August, 1964) 146–173. © 1964 by Xavier Zubiri. Grateful acknowledgment is made to the author for permission to reprint.

II. THE ORIGIN OF MAN

The problem of the origin of man was almost exclusively a theological one until the end of the nineteenth century. Since then, surprisingly, the problem has entered a new phase, the phase of positive science. Human paleontology and prehistory have discovered a series of impressive facts whose volume and quality must be considered transcendental, since these scientific facts lead to the idea that the origin of man is evolutional: the human phylum has its evolutionary origin in other animal phyla; and within the human phylum, humanity has adopted genetically and evolutionally distinct forms until it has arrived at present-day man, the only one until now with which philosophy and theology have concerned themselves. Human evolution is certainly a subject which belongs to positive science. Though a question raised by facts, it is nevertheless one which affects philosophy and theology. Leaving aside, for the moment, the theological aspect of the question, the idea of the evolutionary origin of our humanity, though it is a scientific idea, is still an idea, which, like many others, is on the borderline of both science and philosophy. These ideas constitute borderline problems, two-sided problems. And inasmuch as they are two-sided, they should be considered philosophically. Speaking philosophically, what does the evolutionary origin of our humanity mean?

I

In the somatic, morphological order there is a strict evolution from animal to man. The mechanisms, scope, and character of this evolution might be argued, and are argued. But there undeniably exists a morphological evolution which places man in the line of the anthropomorphous primates, concretely speaking, at the division between the Pongidae and Hominidae. The anthropomorphous Pongidae lead to the great apes: the chimpanzee, gorilla, orangutan, and gibbon. Starting from the same point of reference, the anthropomorphos Hominidae follow a different line of evolution. Paleontologists use the term "hominids" for all the anthropoids which form a part of the phylum to which man belongs. They do so because there have been anthropomorphous members of this phylum which were not yet human but infrahuman (though not apes, as the Pongidae are). These not-yet-hominized hominids are the direct somatic ancestors of man. Since paleontology does not yet possess enough fossil remains, it cannot describe with satisfactory precision either the ways in which the hominids proliferated or the precise point of hominization.

However, this undeniable somatic evolution leaves untouched another fact that must be kept in mind and integrated with evolution if we are to explain the phenomenon of humanity completely: the essential irreducibility of the intellective dimension of man to all his sensory animal dimensions. An animal, being merely sentient, always and only reacts to stimuli. There can be, and there are, complexes of stimuli structured as units, often endowed with the character of a sign, and an animal selects from them according to their attunement with the tonic states it feels. Still, it is always a case of mere stimuli. In contrast to this, man with his intelligence, responds to realities. I have always maintained that intelligence is, not the capacity for abstract thought, but the capacity that man has to perceive things and deal with them as realities. Between mere stimulus and reality there is not a difference in degree but in essence. What we are accustomed to call, improperly, "animal intelligence" is the refinement of the animal's capacity to move among stimuli in a very diversified and fruitful way, but always on the level of giving an adequate response to the situation with which the stimuli present it; and this is why it is not, properly speaking, intelligence. In contrast, man does not always respond to things as stimuli; he also responds to them as realities. The richness of man's response is of an order essentially distinct from that of an animal's. This is why his life transcends animal life, and the evolutional lines of man and animal are radically distinct ones which follow divergent directions.

An animal, for example, may be completely classified; man cannot. For psycho-biological reasons, man is the only animal that is adaptable to all the climates of the universe, that tolerates the most diverse diets. But this is not all. Man is the only animal that is not imprisoned in a specifically determined medium but is constitutively open to the undefined horizon of the real world. While the animal only resolves situations and makes small predispositions, man transcends his actual situation and produces artifacts that are not only made ad hoc for a determined situation but are also situated in the reality of things, in what these things are "of themselves." Thus, he constructs artifacts he has no need of in the present situation against the time when he might have need of them. He handles things as realities. In a word, while the animal only "settles" his life, man "projects" his life. This is why man's industry is not found to be fixed or to be mere repetition; rather it denotes an innovation, the product of an invention, of a forward-moving, progressive creation. Precisely where the remains of tools allow the discovery of traces of innovation and creation, prehistory interprets them as rudimentary human characteristics. Such is the case with the pebble culture of Australopithecus, which we will speak of later.

This irreducibility does not imply a break, a discontinuity, between animal and human life. Completely the contrary. If the distinction between mere sensation and intelligence which I have just proposed is accepted, it is true that the animal reacts to mere stimuli and that man responds to realities. But in his individual life as well as in his development as a species, the first form of reality which man apprehends is that of his own stimuli. He perceives them not as mere stimuli but as real stimuli, as stimulating realities, so much so that the first function of intelligence is purely biological. It consists in finding an adequate response to real stimuli. This fact alone proves that the further we descend toward the beginnings of life in both individual and species, the more subtle the distinction between mere stimulus and real stimulus becomes until it seems to disappear—and that is exactly what proves there is no break between animal life and life which is properly human. It is abundantly clear that there is no such break in individual life any more than there is in the zoological scale. The life of the first beings with somatic, and perhaps psychic, traces of humanity, the Australopithecids, approaches very closely the life of other anthropoids. This is why it is so difficult, and at times impossible, to know if a hominid fossil does or does not represent a hominized hominid.

II

Since the human phylum is constituted by an intelligence, we find in it a true and strict genetic evolution due above all to the evolution of the somatic structures but also to the evolution of a type of intelligence expressed in industries characterized by an almost perfect evolutionary unity. This means that what we have been accustomed until now to call "man" in the singular, in reality includes types of humanity that are different somatically and industrially, that is, somatically and intellectively, produced by a true, genetic, intrahuman evolution. It is a question, not of men who are different only in their type of life, but of structurally distinct types, in regard to both their morphology and their mental structures. From among the most outstanding and well-known facts, let us note only some so as to add concreteness to our ideas.

1. From the beginnings of the early Quaternary (the Villafranchian) almost two million years ago, the Australopithecine hominids appeared. They seem to be the first beings who by then possessed traces of rudimentary human characteristics. The oldest relic known is the Chad skull. Later there is, on the one hand, the African group of Australopithecus, with its different varieties, and, on the other hand, Australopithecus of Java. These groups spread until well into the Middle Quaternary (Australopithecus Telanthropus and Australopithecus of Palestine). These, with the ones from Java, are the closest transition to the following type. Together they constitute a quite homogeneous group.

Except for later variations, they have short stature and an appearance similar to that of the Pongidae: a receding forehead and concave face. But their premolars are exactly of the human type and completely distinct from those of the Pongidae. They are almost perfectly biped and erect; their pelvis is already of the human type. This has left the arms and hands free to grasp and shape tools. On the other hand, they have an elongated and shallow brain: a cranial volume of 500 to 700 cc., notably inferior to that of later men but high in relation to the Pongidae and relative to their stature. Some of the skulls, as the Chad skull, present noticeable differences.

Let us take, under the heading of "information," the very recent discovery by Leakey in East Africa (1963–1964) of a fossil dating from the beginning of the Quaternary which he has named "Homo habilis." Some of its structures are intermediary between those of Australopithecus and those of the man who followed; others are more closely related to those of "Homo sapiens." According to this idea, "Homo habilis" would be a direct ancestor of later man, while Australopithecus would constitute a collateral branch of unhominized hominids. To "Homo habilis" would belong the Chad skull, Australopithecus of Palestine, as well as Telanthropus (who, then, should not be called Australopithecine), and perhaps the "enigmatic" Kanam jaw. All of this needs more careful and minute study before it can be admitted.

Australopithecus made rudimentary axes, if you could so call his sharpened pebbles (pebble culture). Considered within an extended temporal perspective, Australopithecus seems to present, according to some (and to this opinion the majority of researchers today incline), traces of a creative innovation differing from the fixity and repetition characteristic of instinct and animal imitation. As such they would exhibit a certain intelligence. In this case, the transmission of these characteristics from some beings to others of the same group would be a first trace of authentic society and tradition, that is, a first outline of rudimentary culture. He would be, then, rudimentarily hominized because he would have begun to have perceived things as realities, as things which are "of themselves." On the other hand, if one does not admit that there is creative innovation in the industry of Australopithecus, then it would be a case of unhominized hominids who would be, perhaps, either the immediate ancestors of man or a collateral branch of hominids that has gradually been extinguished. In Leakey's opinion, there is a pebble culture that is creative, but its producer is "Homo habilis" and not Australopithecus (who, he believes, also made tools from pebbles, but without creativeness).

2. At the beginning of the Middle Quaternary half a million years ago, the hominized hominids (whether Australopithecus or Homo habilis) produced by evolution a clearly human type: Arcanthropus, as Weidenreich calls him. The oldest type is represented by the Modjokerto skull. In order of age, Arcanthropus is followed by Pithecanthropus and Sinanthropus. The Mauer jaw dates very close to Sinanthropus, perhaps before, and the Montmaurin jaw comes later, preceding the next man. There are more recent relics from East Africa related to certain varieties of Australopithecus. After that appear Atlanthropus of Ternifine (Algeria) and, lastly, the Casablanca, Rabat, Temara, and Saldanha men. Arcanthropus, then, stems from Australopithecus or from very closely related forms (Homo habilis?), while the

Mauer and Montmaurin men, together with the Morocco and Saldanha men, represent the transition to men of a later type.

Arcanthropus has a dentition of the same type as that of Australopithecus. He has a very rudimentary trace of chin, very strong jaws, very large supraorbital ridges, a very thick skull with a strong crest at the occipital foramen, and a less pronounced occipital curvature than that of earlier types. The brain develops upward, from an elongated to a rounded form, its convolutions are still slight but more pronounced than those of Australopithecus; the frontal lobes are larger but still very inferior; there is probably a predominance of the left hemisphere; its average volume is 1,000 cc. Arcanthropus already produced very distinctive, two-faced stone implements. He did not know how to light fire, but it seems he knew how to use it or conserve it. He did not bury his dead. But the occipital foramen is artificially enlarged, which seems to indicate that he extracted the brain to empty the skull. Was this an anthropophagic rite or simply, perhaps, for the conservation of the skull as a relic of the dead? It is difficult to decide.

3. In the remaining part of the Middle Quaternary, about two hundred thousand years ago, there appeared another somatically and mentally different human type: Paleanthropus (Keith). This human type evolved in different phases. The oldest type is that represented by the pre-Neanderthal men (Steinheim, Ehringsdorf, Saccopastore) and the pre-sapiens (Swanscombe and, much later, the Fontchévade man). Then come the classical Neanderthal men, distributed throughout Europe, Asia, and Africa. Those from Palestine are, perhaps, pre-sapiens. Lastly come those which mark the transition to a later type: the Rhodesian man and the Solo man (a descendent of Pithecanthropus).

Their dentition is largely intermediate between that of Arcanthropus and the subsequent man. The older representatives have a less prominent chin (at times almost nonexistent) than that of the more recent ones, a weaker lower jaw than that of Arcanthropus, and concave maxillaries. The skull takes on a new shape but has a regressively lower vault, a receding and flattened fore-

head, and very large supraorbital ridges with a greater curvature
which at times approaches that of later man. The pre-sapiens
has a vertical forehead, almost without brow ridges. The bones
are not nearly so thick. The volume of the brain is about 1,425 to
1,700 cc., and remains so in later man. The convolutions are more
accentuated, with a greater development upward; the frontal
lobes are more accentuated but in general still poorly developed,
far below those of later man. His culture is typical: a lower
paleolithic culture. Some of these men begin to cut typical hand
axes that are much more perfect than the previous bifaced ones.
Others begin a chipped-stone industry. They live in the open
and in caverns. They are nomads; they store goods and hunt.
They use fire. They probably painted their bodies somewhat, and
some objects might be interpreted as amulets. It seems they wore
trophies during the hunt, which perhaps belonged to the ritual
of the hunt and which might indicate a certain idea of superior
powers. They buried their dead, surrounding them at times with
offerings, which denotes a certain idea of survival after death.

4. Only afterwards, in the Late Quaternary, about fifty thousand years ago, did a somatically and mentally different type
appear: Neanthropus, often simply called Cro-Magnon man. He
is the one who represents, strictly speaking, Homo sapiens. The
oldest examples known, until now, are the Kanjera man and,
a little later, the Florisbad man, both from East Africa. This is
the human type to which we belong. It has typically modern dentition. The chin is well formed; the face short and wide, with a
high forehead, elongated nose, and almost no brow ridges. The
bones of the skull are less and less thick as we proceed from the
Upper Paleolithic to the Neolithic period. The brain has definitely
acquired its rounded form, is very rich in its convolutions, which
are now permanent, and has fully developed frontal lobes.

In his first cultural phase (Upper Paleolithic), this man now no
longer carves axes; he polishes the stone (a flaked-stone industry).
He makes awls and bone needles for sewing. He begins to farm
and domesticate animals. He produces admirable rock paintings
and small relief work, sunken and raised; statuettes that could

be fertility idols (the earth mother) and protector idols; all of which indicates that he clearly shows magico-religious practices denoting a belief in spirits to which he makes offerings. He buries his dead, sometimes constructing small burial monuments.

After the last glaciation this man enters into the Neolithic cultural phase. He polishes stone more finely, works in ceramic, and develops textile arts. He constructs huts and sheds and begins shepherding animals. He possesses a clear cult of the dead in that he builds megalithic monuments (domens, menhirs, etc.). He has domestic gods (lares and the like), a god of fertility, and a cult of the bull and of the sun. He begins to use ideographic signs. And he develops an art, very rich in all aspects, at times of a very stylized character. Finally, he enters into a new phase, the metal age—not taking into account copper which could have belonged to the Neolithic phase.

These four types of men (the first hominized ones, that is, Australopithecus or Homo habilis; Arcanthropus; Paleanthropus; and Neanthropus) are not found stratified, but overlapped, sometimes for long periods. For example, we have already said that certain types of Australopithecus are so close to Arcanthropus in time that it is difficult to classify them in one or the other group, since the former extend into the Middle Quaternary when Arcanthropus is already fully developed. The same is true of Arcanthropus and Paleanthropus. And these latter lived at the same time as Neanthropus. As each type begins, it is contemporary with the previous type. We do not know, naturally, the social character of the diverse human types, especially of the more ancient ones, and know even less the social adjustment made between men of a previous type and those of a later type. The ethnology of certain present-day "primitive" peoples, utilized with the *utmost* prudence, may throw some light on certain aspects of the problem.

The succession of human types is not only a succession but a true genetic evolution. The comparison of the morphology of their fossil remains and the character of the fauna surrounding their resting places clearly suggest this. The evolutional continuity of their industries confirms it. It is not a case of absolute certainty—

science never obtains that—but there is the sufficient force of reasonable conviction. Opinions may differ, and do differ at times, about very important details. This is because it is not a case of the totality of one type being the genetic origin of another type.

Within each type there are forms that are surely collateral branches in the evolution of humanity. This is what occurs in general with Pithecanthropus, but even in this case let us not forget that the Solo man is probably a direct descendent of Pithecanthropus of Java. This is even clearer with Paleanthropus. The classic Neanderthal men, in general, are only collateral branches, but the pre-Neanderthal men and the pre-sapiens are in the direct genetic line of Neanthropus. The examples could be multiplied. New facts are constantly coming to light that demand a revision of the description of human types and of the precise genetic expression of their evolution. In fact, as we have already noted, paleontology does not yet know precisely how the hominids spread; nor, therefore, does it know the exact point of hominization. For a time it was thought that some form such as Oreopithecus was an example of what the hominids might have been before their hominization. Today, it seems, the investigators are not so firmly convinced.

We have also indicated the recent ideas in regard to Homo habilis. In addition, interpretation of the pebble culture is in need of more documentation—not only paleontological but also archeological—concerning the character of the culture and consequently the possible hominization of its producers. Finally, the constant discovery of new fossils which are clearly human ones will modify the morphological, geographical, and historical scheme of fossil man and his evolution. All this falls under the responsibility of science. What remains established is the great fact of the existence of very distinct human types linked by a true genetic evolution. And this is the one decisive fact in our problem: man as such is not a reality; only his distinct evolutional types are.

III

This granted, what does evolution mean? What are all these distinct types of humanity? Let us say first of all that, scientifically and philosophically speaking, these types are all strictly human; they are true men. Speaking philosophically, I think man is the intelligent animal, the reality-conscious animal, something essentially distinct from the nonhuman animal which is endowed only with mere sensation, that is, with a way of perceiving things and dealing with them as mere stimuli. This intellective dimension is found essentially united, in a primary coherential unity, with definite, structural, somatic intrinsic factors, that is, a certain type of dentition, of locomotive apparatus, of hands free for the seizure and fabrication of tools; a certain type of cranial configuration and volume; a certain type of shape and functional organization of the brain; and apparatus for articulate phonation; capable of being used at certain stages in the form of language. Language, in fact, is a question not only of macroscopic anatomical structures for phonation but of functional organization, which is perhaps achieved only in the more advanced stages of hominization.

The specific unity, then, of man is assured: it is the essential unity of intelligence and of a determined type of basic somatic structures. Therefore, in all the men of whom we have been speaking there is what I have called a constitutive scheme, transmitted by generation, that is, there is a true genetic phylum. In virtue of this, the structure is, scientifically and philosophically, a strictly specific structure. Reciprocally, the inclusion of an anthropoid in the human phylum constitutes its strict specific unity with man. (I have elaborated upon this concept of species in another publication, *Sobre la Esencia* [Madrid, 1962]).

The representatives of all these human types are, then, true men. Upon confirming the innovating and creative character of the industry of Australopithecus, we see that he possesses an intelligence, a true intelligence, no matter how rudimentary, because he apprehends things as realities. He is a true rudimentary man, as we shall see presently.

However, this phyletic, specific unit contains within it great diversity. This diversity refers first of all, not to different types of life, but to psychosomatic structural differences. Types of life are different because the psychosomatic structures that make them possible, and so define them, are different. Arcanthropus and Paleanthropus have different types of life because their structures are different. What we call diverse "modes" of life are differences within an already structurally defined type of life. Among the different arcanthropes and the different paleanthropes, as well as the neanthropes, some individuals may have had, and surely did have, distinct modes of life. But the different modes of life of Arcanthropus are lives of the same type, a type distinct from that of Paleanthropus. The primary difference, then, is a difference of "type" of life which depends on a difference in psychosomatic structure.

This structural difference is not merely individual. It is something much deeper: a pithecanthrope and a Neanderthaler differ much more profoundly than two Neanderthalers. That is perfectly clear. But we are not speaking of the quasi-structural difference we indicate by names for varieties and races. These differences, including the racial ones, fall always and only within a definite and already constituted primary unit. There are diverse races of Arcanthropus (for example, today it is considered that Pithecanthropus and Sinanthropus are different races), of Paleanthropus (the different Neanderthal men), of Neanthropus (the Cro-Magnon, Grimaldi, and other races in the Upper Paleolithic period). But the difference we are speaking of is a difference between the primary units themselves, the difference that allows us to separate Australopithecus (if hominized), Arcanthropus, Paleanthropus, or Neanthropus. Only within each one of these units can one speak of races or varieties.

That this difference between primary units exists is a fact that leaps to one's eyes when one merely reviews the characteristics which, taken together, distinguish them. However, in spite of being structural, this difference is not specific because we are dealing, not with a difference *in* species, but with a difference *within* a species. I will return to this point very shortly. It is in this precise sense that I have called each primary structural unit a "type." In each type the unit of the species has a distinct quality. A pithecanthrope and a Neanderthaler or a Cro-Magnon man are not only different men but are men of different human quality, if I may so put it. The *quale** of their humanity is different. And it is different as much in regard to the somatic as to the psychic in their structures.

In the first place, each of the types is qualitatively distinct from the others on the level of its somatic structures. The differences of appearance, of cranial volume, and brain development between Australopithecus and Homo sapiens are markedly qualitative. The brain of Arcanthropus is not of the same qualitative type as that of Neanderthal man. There is not the least doubt about this. Human morphology, like that of any living thing, is not constituted by the mere presence of characteristics each one of which is independent from the others. A morphology is the expression of a *correlative unity* between these characteristics and prior to them. In virtue of it these characteristic differences are not accidental. They are systematic and phyletic differences.

This is why for the paleontologist there is not the least doubt that Homo is a genus which contains various species of men: habilis, erectus, sapiens, etc. They are systematic and phyletic lines within a unique (generic) phylum from which they proceed, at times in branches and not straight lines. Since the taxonomic concept of species is purely systematic and, as such (as is recognized), somewhat indefinite and conventional, it is necessary to complement it with a phyletic consideration. Now, since this phyletic (at least generic) unity undoubtedly exists in humanity (polyphyleticists are an outstanding minority), I prefer not to prejudge here whether the units or systematic branches are or are not rigorously species but, for this reason, to limit myself

---

* Translator's note: "Quale" is Latin for "what kind."

to calling them qualitatively distinct "types," reserving the word "species" for what the paleontologists call genus. In this sense, I say there are types of men who are qualitatively distinct in their somatic morphology.

Moreover, the differences in the psychic constitution of the human types are also qualitative. As little as we know of them, the remains of their culture oblige us to form this conclusion. It is not by chance that some human types do or think things that did not occur to other types, for example, burying their dead or being farmers instead of mere hunters. The range of possibilities is prescribed by a primary and radical quality of the psychic constitution of each type. There are things which could not have occurred to certain human types, given that these types were of a determined quality. It is not, then, a question of what comes to mind but a question of quality of mental type. And this is above all true of intelligence itself. It is not only that some types of men, for example, the Neanderthal men, are more intelligent than others, for instance, the arcanthropes. It is not a question of "more and less" but of some types which have a class, shall we say, of intelligence distinct from that of the others. The intelligence of the Neanderthal man is qualitatively "other" than that of Pithecanthropus. Only within each type can one say that some individuals are more or less intelligent than others. There were certainly some Neanderthalers who were more intelligent than others. But the radical difference is the qualitative one.

These qualitative differences in psychic constitution could be interpreted in the sense that the psyche of the different human types was "substantially" distinct in each case. But it is not necessary to enter into this dimension of the problem because the undeniable fact that somatic structures determine the qualitative form of the psyche, the *forma animae,* is more than sufficient. And since the somatic structures are of distinct quality, so, inevitably, are the psychic structures. The unity of the psychic and the somatic is, in fact, in my opinion, an essential structural unity and, is, moreover, bilateral. It is an idea which I have repeatedly put forward. The psyche and the soma are mutually co-determined, not as potency and act, but as two actual realities. The unity of man is an essential unity but not a substantial one. In virtue of this, the relations in this co-determination vary through-out the course of the life of each man. In the germinal plasm it is the somatic structures, the germinal structures (that is, the progenitors), that determine completely the "first" mental state and continue determining for some time the other mental states. This occurs in any human individual at whatever level you consider him. It is in this way that the *forma animae* takes on its shape. When the moment arrives at which the psychosomatic development brings into play its properly intellective dimen-sion, it is certain that this dimension determines in good measure the development and the functionality of the somatic structures. But since these structures initially and radically shaped the qual-ity or form of the psyche, it turns out that even in this dimension the intellective function is already at its roots qualitatively dis-tinct between some human types and others. The somatic struc-tures not only *permit* the use of intelligence but also qualitatively *shape* this use in all the human types, including our own.

In this manner, each human type has a unitary psychosomatic structure qualitatively distinct from that of the other types. Be-tween these qualitatively distinct human types there is a true and strict genetic evolution, a psychosomatic evolution. The genetic evolution of the structures, in fact, completely determines the quality of the psyche, of the *forma animae*. In virtue of this, the genetic transmission of the structures determines an evolution in the form or quality of the psychic constitution. Therefore, there is, as I say, a strictly psychosomatic, genetic evolution of the human types. The typification of the species is the product of a strict psy-chosomatic evolution. Once evolution had begun, it was possible, as I have just indicated, that the functional organization—for example, that of the brain—might be determined in some sense by the use of intelligence within each type. Thus it has been said more than once that the tool precedes the brain and forms it, that it is not the brain that shapes the tool. This being the case, if these organizations were transmitted, the psychic constitution

itself would have been one of the factors in evolution. But in order for this to happen, the functional organization acquired by the
use of intelligence would have had to affect the structures of
the germinal plasm, if it were to be transmissible. Whatever was
the case, this psychosomatic structural unity had its beginnings
rudimentarily in Australopithecus and Arcanthropus and gradually perfected itself qualitatively and typically throughout the
process of evolution. Human evolution is above all an evolution
of the typical qualities of the psychosomatic unity.

What is the meaning, the orientation of this evolution? Is it the
passage from pre-men to men? I do not believe so. It is undeniable
that all of us sense a certain resistance toward calling all these
types of "humanity" men. We are accustomed, by a very old tradition, to defining man as a "rational animal," that is, an animal
fully endowed with the capacity for abstract thought and for
reflection. Such being the case, we resist, with more than enough
reason, calling such types as Pithecanthropus, and even more so
Australopithecus, men, even though their industry denotes intelligence. But if we force ourselves to call these beings men, we
incline toward considering them "rational." Both tendencies
spring from the same conception, that of man as a rational animal.

I think that this conception cannot be defended. Man is not a
rational animal, but an intelligent animal, that is, a reality-conscious animal. These are two completely distinct things because
reason is no more than a special and specialized type of intelligence, and intelligence formally consists, not in the capacity for
abstract thought and full conscious reflection, but simply in the
capacity to perceive things as realities. Intelligent animal and
rational animal are, then, distinct things. The latter is only one
type of the former. And this is just as true if we consider the
human individual of our epoch as if we consider his paleontological evolution. In both aspects and dimensions, the intelligent
animal is not necessarily a rational animal. The child, only a few
weeks after birth, undeniably makes use of his intelligence, but
he does not have, until years later, that special use of intelligence

which we call "the use of reason." From the beginning the child is an intelligent animal, but not a rational animal.

Now within the interior evolutionary line of the human species, man has been, from his origins in the Quaternary, an intelligent animal and has made use of his intelligence. Even the Villafranchian Australopithecus, if he had had a creative culture, would be a rudimentary but true man. The false identification of the intelligent animal with the rational animal is the origin of many of the doubts about the hominization of Australopithecus, as well as the reason why many speak timidly about whether he had intelligence and was only potentially or virtually what would later be man. I think, on the contrary, that if he possessed a creative culture he would have intelligence, in the sense I have stated it, and then we would have to decide to call him man, not virtually but formally. What *is* true is that he would be virtually rational. There is no reason why we should reserve the word and the concept of man only for the rational animal. All these types of men have slowly and during many millennia been progressively evolving from their level of intelligent animal to the level of rational animal, whose fullness is *Homo sapiens.*

When did he achieve this? At bottom, this question is absurd. It would be absurd to try to fix precisely with a calendar or watch in hand the precise moment at which a child acquires the use of reason. This acquisition is not a question of "moments" but is a "process" of human maturation, which, moreover, varies with individuals. As such, it is subject to variations, hesitations, and even regressions, even though for only a short time. Maturation is not and cannot be a rectilinear process. It is equally outlandish to try to fix precisely, chronologically, the evolutionary stage in which "for the first time" humanity became rational, *sapiens.* It is an evolutionary process of nonrectilinear rationalization which is not completed once and for all in only one human type. Furthermore, it is not even achieved uniformly. Forms appear at times, such as those "pre-sapiens" among the Neanderthal men, which testify to the truth of what we are saying. Within the same period there are points discernible even geographically which possess greater evolutionary potentiality in the line of ascending evolution than others at which, on the contrary, men disappear. Since it is a process, we can only say that there are evolutionary stages such as that of Arcanthropus which with certainty are not rational, and there are stages such as Cro-Magnon man which are fully rational, Homo sapiens. In the meantime, there are men who are becoming rational.

Consequently, man is an intelligent animal and not a rational animal. In virtue of this, it is not necessary to think, even remotely, that the first rational animal on earth was the first man in the evolutional scale nor that the first intelligent animal had to be a rational animal. All the human types prior to Homo sapiens are not "pre-men" but true men; however, not rational, only "pre-rational." Only the "pre-intelligent" hominids would be the authentic pre-men. The hominized types prior to *Homo sapiens* would be progressive sketches oriented evolutionally to the constitution of *Homo sapiens,* the rational animal. It is not an evolution of the infrahuman to the human, but the human evolution of intelligence to reason. *Homo sapiens* is not an exception in the evolutionary history of humanity; it is toward him that the evolution is directed.

This is true no matter what concrete detail of data science might possess at any determined moment. These data are necessarily modified and enriched constantly. But the knowledge that we have today is enough to support our affirmation. In fact, throughout the four great evolutionary stages, each of which fills almost all the continents with forms and varieties of great richness, one can discern on a large scale (with all the inexactitude it implies) something like a coordinate or vector of propagation of the human wave that flows from mere intelligent animal to rational animal—a vector oriented by forms which have characters progressively convergent upon *Homo sapiens*. It starts at the beginning of the Quaternary with the Chad skull (or *Homo habilis*). It continues, more or less, with Australopithecus of Java, Telanthropus, Australopithecus of Palestine, the Mauer man, the

Morocco man, the Swanscombe, Steinheim, Montmaurin, Font-chévade, Kanjera, and Florisbad men. Each one of them, according to the calculations of the majority of the investigators, follows the previous one chronologically and marks one step more in the direction of "sapiensiation." It is the axis of progressive rationalization from the mere intelligent animal to *Homo sapiens*.

In conclusion, once the specifically human phylum is constituted, all humanity procedes to constitute itself evolutionally through typically qualified, diverse stages, somatically as well as psychically; throughout these stages it ascends from the level of intelligent animal to the level of rational animal.

IV

What we have said does not exhaust all the problems. It all refers to the evolutional structure of an already constituted human phylum; it is what could be called the "typification problem" of the human species. But this phylum is inserted in an animal phylum that is not human, in the phylum of the anthropomorphus primates. It is in this phylum that the zoological line divides into two phyla: the phylum of Pongidae and the phylum of Hominidae. I have indicated several times that the manner in which the Hominidae spread and the exact point of hominization are not sufficiently known. But this is the affair of positive science and does not directly affect our problem.

What is decisive for our problem is that, at one point or another, there was an evolutional branch, that of the prehuman hominids, which was gradually extinguished, and another, that of the humanized hominids diverging from the other. And it is in this point of divergence, no matter where it is found in the philetic line, that the problem arises for our consideration of what the very constitution of the human phylum is, within the line of the hominids. It constitutes the "hominization problem," a problem prior to that of typification with which we have been occupied until now.

Is hominization evolution? The answer to this question depends on a precise concept of evolution. Evolution, in fact, should not be confused with the causal mechanisms of evolution, neither in the somatic order nor in the psychic order. Evolution and the evolutionary mechanisms are two perfectly distinct things.

Evolution is, formally, a genetic process in which specifically new forms are produced from previous forms, in intrinsic and determining function with the transformation of those forms. But we must understand these expressions correctly. First of all, evolution is the genetic production of specifically new forms. Evolution is not only morphological but also psychical innovation. This does not mean that the innovation must be progressive. On the contrary, it can be, and is in the immense majority of cases, a dead-end road of very little evolutionary potential (because of too strict a specialization or for other reasons). This new form proceeds from another, or others (polyphyleticism), prior to it and very precisely determined. Birds, for example, can proceed only from reptiles, not directly from echinoderms. And this is true as much for morphological structures as for psychical structures. The psychic constitution of each animal species springs from the psychic constitution of a precisely determined, prior species, and from it only. In this genetic process, not only is the progenitor precisely determined but the new form proceeds from it genetically and determinately in intrinsic function with it. If this were not so, we would have a systematic causal series, but this series, this system, would not be evolutionary.

The concrete function of the specific form of the progenitors consists in this that they intrinsically determine, by transformation of some of their intrinsic structural factors, the structure of the new species, so that the new species conserves those same basic structures in a transformed way. Only then do we have strict evolution. And this intrinsic factor of determination by transformation concerns the morphological as well as the psychical. At the heart of the new morphological structure a psychic constitution begins to take shape which conserves the basic, transformed, intrinsic factors of the psychic constitution of the previous species. The new species has, for example, many of the instincts of the previous one. It has lost some, but the loss, as well as the conservation, is a transformation within the line of the new psychic constitution, and so forth. Taking all these diverse aspects into account together, we say that evolution is a genetic process in which specifically new psychosomatic forms are produced from other previous ones in intrinsic, transforming, and determining function with them.

Now, in this formal and precise sense, hominization is the evolution of the prehuman hominids to the hominized hominids. It is a genetic process in which the latter proceeds and can proceed only as determined by a transformation of the basic morphological prehuman structures. And in this new transformed structure, and only in it and from it, does there arise a psychic constitution which could not have arisen from the psychic constitution of an echinoderm or of a bird. This psychic constitution conserves, as one of its own transformed intrinsic factors, the basic characteristics of the psychic constitution of its immediate hominid ancestor. For example, the whole of prehuman instinct finds itself transformed, by elevation, in man.

Man has, in a way, far fewer instincts than the prehuman hominid (in this sense, and in many others, including somatic ones, he is the more defenseless animal); and even those which he has conserved are transformed, in the sense of being less "mechanical," so to speak, and open to superior tendencies. But this transformation, whether by elimination of what was useless or by a readjustment of what was conserved, is always a true transformation; and thus transformed, the instinctive sphere of the prehominid is an intrinsic structural factor of the human psychic constitution. We may say the same of the fabrication of tools. Man begins making the same tools as the prehuman hominid, even having learned from him, surely, how to make them. He keeps this animal, fabricating ability, but now transformed into the line of a creative progress.

Intelligence itself grows intrinsically from within these structures, and its growth is determined by the transformation of the structures. Only with the psychic constitution of the prehuman hominid as its basis is intelligence possible and real. A human intelligence could not have come from a bird. Calling the totality of the human psychic constitution an "intellective psyche," in contrast to the nonintellective animal psyche, we would say that the intellective psyche arises intrinsically from the psychosomatic structures of the prehuman hominid in determining and transforming function with them, so that the new species, the human species, includes as its essential, intrinsic factor the transformed conservation of the morphological and psychical structures of that hominid. Man as a whole, then, is psychosomatically an evolutionary outgrowth; he springs evolutionally from a prehuman hominid.

But this evolution still leaves standing the other question: the question of the causal mechanism of evolution. From this other point of view, evolution is the expression of the causal evolutionary mechanism. It is an exceedingly complex problem in which there are profound discrepancies, both in what refers to the causes of the evolution and in what refers to their manner of acting (whether very gradual or abrupt). Thus, for example, we cannot deny the influence of its medium which leads either to the adaptation or the disappearance of a species. There are other factors: the mode of life, ecological isolation, competition or struggle, selection, genic mutation of the chromosomes which sometimes produces processes of neoteny, and soon. In the case of the medium and of the genic mutations, the cause of evolution is physical. In the case of other factors, such as the mode of life, competition, etc., the evolutional causes are at least partially psychical. A mode of life, competition, and the like involve undeniably psychical dimensions, and in this sense the psychic constitution itself is a cause of the evolution.

But the merely physical causes as well as the psychical ones must affect physically the germinal structures, the germinal plasm, if the change that these causes produce is to be stable. A species is not only a living individual but also an individual which generates others of the same structure, that is, the changes must be hereditarily transmissible. As such, these changes must be produced physically in the structures of the germinal plasm, above all in the genes; it is in them that the "genetic code" of a living being is enclosed.

It is possible also that these factors might have to influence other intrinsic structural factors of the germinal plasm. To avoid prejudging anything that pertains to the merely scientific side of the question, let us call these changes of the germinal plasm, germinal changes. In general, these changes are lethal. But if they are not and if there is an adequate medium for the new living being, we have the constitution of a new specific form, morphologically as well as psychically, since the psychic constitution of the new species arises from the morphological structures. This explains why the new species conserves in a transformed way the psychical structures of the previous species.

In the case of animals the transformation determines the morphology and the psychic constitution of the new species, and it determines them by producing them itself. The determination here is effective causation. But this is not the only type of evolutional cause because all effective causation is transforming determination, but not all transforming determination is necessarily effective action. An effective transformation certainly intervenes in the origin of the human phylum. The morphology of the first humanized hominid (Australopithecus or Arcanthropus) is not only determined by transformation of the germinal structures but is also effectively produced by them.

But this is not the case with the human psychic constitution. The human psychic constitution is determined in its evolutional origin by the germinal transformations, but it is not produced by them only. Here the causal determination is not effectuation. Mere sensation cannot produce of itself an intelligence: there exists between the two an essential, not a gradual, difference. No matter how complicated the mere stimuli and their form of apprehension are, they can never arrive at constituting stimulating realities and intellective apprehension. At this point the appearance of an intellective psyche is not only a matter of degree but is essentially something new. In this sense, but *only in this one,* we say that the appearance of an intellective psyche is an absolute innovation.

This does not mean that there is a discontinuity between the life of a prehuman animal type and the life of a human type such as the hominized hominid. Nor does it mean a psychic structural discontinuity. The intellective psyche conserves as its essential intrinsic factor the transformed sense dimension of the prehuman hominid. But the human psyche involves another intrinsic factor which is based intrinsically on the sentient factor but which transcends it. It is the intrinsic factor which we call the intellective factor. Where it is concerned, there is no discontinuity, only transcendence—if one wishes, a continuity in the line of creative transcendence. And since the psyche is not a sum of sensation and intelligence but is intrinsically one psyche, the result is that the human psyche as a whole, the psyche of the first hominized hominid, is essentially distinct from the animal psyche of the hominid ancestor of man. As such, the human psyche is determined by the transformation (by the germinal changes) of the mere hominid into man but is not brought about by the transformation. Because of this it can only be an effect of the first cause, just as at its time the appearance of matter was: it is the effect of a creation *ex nihilo.*

But it is necessary to understand this statement together with what we have said before, that is, that it must be a creation determined by the transformation of the germinal structures. This is as essential as that it be *ex nihilo.* Too often one tends to imagine this creation literally, as an external interference on the part of the first cause, God, with the animal series. The intellective psyche would be an external insufflation of spirit into the animal, which by this addition would be converted into a man.

In our case this is a naive anthropomorphism. The creation of an intellective psyche *ex nihilo* is not an external addition to the somatic structures because it is neither mere addition nor is it external. And precisely for this reason, in spite of this creation, or, better said, *because of this creation,* there is that genetic origin of man, determined from structures and in intrinsic function with their transformation, which we call evolution. Creation is not an interruption of evolution but is, on the contrary, an intrinsic factor, a causal "mechanism" intrinsic to it. Since this same thing occurs in the generation of every human individual at any level, we would not be diverging from the question by considering this generation and later transposing our considerations to the phylogenetic process.

1. I was saying, then, that the creation *ex nihilo* of an intellective psyche is not formally a mere addition. The human individual is already integrally constituted in the germinal cell. All that is going to be his individual human substantivity is already in his germinal cell: the somatic germinal structures and his intellective psyche. Looking at the first of these, one might think at first sight that the intellective psyche is a mere addition to the said structures because these structures are purely biochemical and, as such, have nothing to do with the intellective psyche. They would be, at most, materials disposed to receive the intellective psyche in the creative act. But I think that it is not true that the biochemical structures are a mere *dispositional cause*. They are something more profound. For in the genetic development of that cell there comes a postnatal moment at which *those same* biochemical structures, now many-celled and functionally organized, will demand *for their own viability* the use of intelligence, that is, the actuation of the intellective psyche. Now this exigent character is germinally prefigured in the germinal cell.

In this phase there is certainly no actual demand for the intellective psyche, but there is a biochemical structure which in its due time will lead to this demand. Consequently, the very biochemical structure of the germinal cell is not actually but virtually exigent of an intellective psyche. It is a virtual demand, formally included in the potentialities for development of the biochemical structures, that is, it is a virtual but real demand. In consequence, the biochemical structure of the germinal cell is not a mere *dispositional cause* but something deeper: it is an *exigent cause* of the human psyche. This psyche is not only a psyche of this *body* but is a psyche which, because it is demanded by this body, must have as its essential intrinsic factor the type of *sentient psychic constitution* that this body itself determines. In its turn, the intellective psyche of itself demands a body, and not just any body, but precisely this body with this type of structure and, therefore, with this determined type of animal psychic constitution.

This demand is not a mere addition to the intellective psyche, but an essential of it. Intelligence, for example, is not found oriented from itself toward sensibility but toward this precise type of sensibility determined by somatic structures. The intellective psyche is not pure "spirit," but "soul." This is why it is found determined by the body. This exigent intrinsic factor is *numerically* identical in the soul and in the body, and in this numerical, exigent identity consists the essential unity of human substantivity. This is why the creation of an intellective psyche in the germinal cell is not mere addition, but fulfillment of a biological demand. This fulfillment is certainly creative. We have already said why it is. Creatively, it is a fulfillment of a biological demand of the germinal cell, the contrary of that breach we spoke of at the beginning.

This is what takes place in the hominization of the first infra- or prehuman hominid prior to man. The germinal changes of this immediate predecessor of man are biological exigent causes of the creation of an intellective psyche, of hominization. And, as we have seen, since these structures are somatically qualified, it turns out that they qualify *eo ipso** the psyche created to meet their demand. The psyche of the first humanized hominid must have been of a very precisely determined sentient psychic constitution, that is, the transformed psychic constitution of the infra- or prehuman hominid. There cannot be a human psyche derived from a transformed echinoderm or bird. It can come only from a transformed hominid because it is this psychic constitution and not another which demands an intellective psyche. A species is

* Translator's note: By that very fact.

not only a living organism but also a living organism such that it can subsist vitally and genetically in a stable manner. Now, the echinoderm is in this condition, but the transformed hominid is not unless it does not have an intellective psyche. Let us explain.

It is certain that the echinoderms have an immense evolutionary potentiality of progressive character: they are the origin of the vertebrates. But not all of the evolutional lines of the vertebrates are truly progressive. There are collateral branches, such as that of the birds, that possess only slight evolutionary potentiality and do not progress because, being a specializing evolution, they follow a dead-end path. Their psychic constitution, as their morphology, is closed and stable because of this. There is no meaning, then, in speaking of an intellective psyche because it would form no part in the life of the bird. Other branches of the vertebrates are, on the other hand, of great evolutionary potentiality and as such of a richer psychic constitution: they are the mammals. Among them there are also many collateral branches.

Progress continues only, we might say, in the central branch. But this progress is also formed of evolutional steps. Each stage is morphologically and psychically richer. However, even though full of promise, each stage taken by itself is a closed and stable system in itself. This is why its psychic constitution is only the mere transformation of the sentient psychic constitution of the previous stage. It does not demand an intellective psyche. Only on reaching the stage of hominid does it reach a point at which its further transformation no longer constitutes a stable system in itself.

It is at this point, and only at this one, that the evolutionary potentiality of the echinoderm comes to demand a distinct psyche for its biological stability. A species having the transformed somatic structures that the hominized hominid has, and not possessing an intellective psyche, could not have subsisted biologically with full genetic stability. It would have quickly been extinguished on earth. In its state as pure echinoderm, the echinoderm does not demand an intellective psyche but potentially could very easily come to demand it, though it would come to demand it only, in fact, when it achieved the state of transformed hominid. This potentiality gradually elaborated in evolutionary stages the sentient psychic constitution of the hominid, a psychic constitution which is the work of evolution.

It is only when the hominid is transformed that this sentient psychic constitution, conserved in a transformed way, demands an intellective psychic constitution. And precisely because the sentient psychic constitution of the transformed hominid evolved gradually was there yet no demand for an intellective psyche in the previous stages, nor any reason why it should arise. Hominization, then, is a biological demand. Reciprocally, only a hominid can and must be hominized if it is to subsist as a species. Its sentient psychic constitution is a product of an evolution which starts, at least, with the psychic constitution of the echinoderm but which only in the transformed hominid becomes actually exigent of an intellective psyche.

This permits us to give a concrete content, from the gentico-evolutionary point of view, to the definition of man. In saying that man is the intelligent animal, we must fill these terms with a precise content. In my opinion, intelligence is the capacity to perceive things as realities, as things which are something "in themselves," and man grasps this reality intellectively by sensing it. Human intelligence is constitutively sentient: it senses reality; it senses it as the hominid senses his stimuli: by impression. On the other hand, what is animal in the intelligent animal—the animal which intellects sentiently—is not just any animality but a very precise and formal animality: the *morphological* and *psychosensate,* transformed animality of the hominid immediately prior to man. Man, then, is the reality-conscious hominid, the hominid that senses reality. His animality is determined by the transformation of the germinal structures of his forebearer.

This causal transformation is effective in what concerns morphology and the intrinsic sentient factor of the psychic constitution, but it is only exigent and not effective in what concerns the intellective factor. This psyche is intrinsically one, but it has an intrinsic sentient factor, that of the transformed hominid, and an intrinsic intellective factor by which it transcends sensation, though relying on it and receiving intrinsically its mental formation from it. This would mean that Australopithecus (if hominized) or Arcanthropus would be the fulfillment demanded by the phyletic evolution of the hominids. For this reason, because of the creative action—by the creation itself—there is an evolution in this first dimension. This is not the only dimension. For the creation of an intellective psyche, no matter how *ex nihilo* it is— and it is *ex nihilo*—is not only not mere addition but is also not extrinsic creation. The exigent fulfillment is, on the contrary, an *intrinsic* exigent fulfillment. This is the second point we must clear up.

2. According to what we have said, in fact, the intellective psyche would have been created as a determining function of the structures which demanded it, that is, the result would have been only a psyche which was *in* the structures. But the reality is more profound than only this: the psyche is created from the very biological structures, it *springs from the heart of life itself*, because the exigent causality of the somatic structures is an intrinsic demand. For this reason, the creative action is not only not merely additive but also is not extrinsic; it is not a mere fulfillment but an intrinsic efflorescence. It is an action that acts intrinsically (*ab intrinseco*) from within the very entity of the somatic structures; it is a *natura naturans*, a generating nature. It is not an action juxtaposed with the nature but is what makes a psyche come forth "naturally" from within the somatic structures in the generational act and blossom into life from them.

Because of this anyone who contemplated only the terminal effect, the *natura naturata*, the nature such as it arises before our eyes, would see the psyche spring forth intrinsically and vitally from the heart of the very somatic structures. It is not an illusion; it is a reality. The scientist's point of view is correct. And, moreover, it is all that science claims to see and can claim to see: how from determined structures a psyche intrinsically determined by them comes into being. Let us repeat this with precision. The psyche is not transmitted from fathers to sons. The psyche is not

produced by progenitors. It springs forth vitally in the generational act from within the transmission and exigent constitution
of the somatic structures and is completely determined in its first
state by them.

Even though the psyche is not transmitted, its first state is formally determined by the progenitors because the somatic structures are transmitted, and these are what determine the first
mental state. This efflorescence proceeds in its ultimate root from
a creative action which is intrinsic to the genetic action of the
progenitors. The progenitors are responsible for the fact that
there is an intrinsic creative act. They are the ones who, by their
act, vitally and intrinsically determine the creative action. This
creative action forms a radical unity with the vital action of the
progenitors and makes this action intrinsically one sole, integral,
generative, psychosomatic action. For this reason, if generation
is understood as intrinsically determined by and from the progenitors, then it is rigorously true that man in his psychosomatic
unity, that is, in body and soul, is a genetic outgrowth. In no way
can generation be identified with effectuation.

This occurs in each human individual and, therefore, in hominized individuals from the infrahuman ancestors on. In the germinal change that produces the hominization of the somatic
structures, there springs forth intrinsically, there arises "naturally" from them by an intrinsic creative action, an intellective
psyche. Australopithecus and Arcanthropus spring intrinsically
and genetically from the infrahuman hominid. If we contemplated from within the formation of the first hominized hominid,
we would see his psyche and his psychic constitution spring up
intrinsically from the transformed structures of his prehominid
ancestor. This is what the scientist does, or at least, and with
complete justification, tries to do. As I said before, it is not an
illusion but a reality. And because of this, this psychic constitution conserves the transformed psychic constitution of the previous
hominid.

There is, then, a psychosomatic outgrowth which has an intellective psyche. This is what constitutes a new phylum, the phylum

of the *homines*. That is why, if, as we must, we call evolution the vital process in which new specific forms are genetically constituted from other earlier ones, by a transformation which determines them intrinsically, we must then affirm that hominization is evolution.

The transformation determines the arrival of the first hominized hominid. But in what concerns the psyche, this determination is not effectuation but intrinsic exigency. The creative action in our case is only an evolutionary mechanism. It is a factor integrated with the germinal transformation. It is the intrinsic fulfillment this transformation demands. For this reason the creative action not only does not interrupt the course of the evolution but is the mechanism which finally brings it to completion. As I said before, species which had the transformed somatic structures that the hominized hominid possesses and did not have an intellective psyche, could not have subsisted biologically. It would have rapidly been extinguished on earth.

Let us review what we have said. Evolution is a fact reasonably established by science. Admitting evolution does not mean that we admit, on the one hand, the fact of the transformation of the somatic structures and maintain, on the other hand, that the psyche remains unaffected by evolution. No. Evolution affects the psyche. It affects it above all in its "typification." Humanity is gradually constituted evolutionally throughout diverse stages which are qualitatively different not only in their morphology but also in their psychic constitution. And evolution also affects the psyche in the first "hominization." The human psyche can only spring forth from very precise morphological structures, those brought about by the transformation of the germinal plasm of the unhominized hominid. Moreover, the human psyche can only be human by including the animal psychic constitution as its essential intrinsic factor, not just any animalistic psychic constitution, but precisely and constitutively the transformed psychic constitution of its immediate hominid ancestor. And this psychosomatic unity is intrinsically determined of and by the transformation of the structures.

Correlatively, evolution must integrate with itself the advent of an intellective psyche which is essentially irreducible to pure sensation. If evolution is within the competence of science, the characteristic of intelligence is within the competence of philosophy. In recurring to the creative cause, philosophy does so by integrating the creation of the psyche with the evolutional mechanism. The germinal transformation determines the morphology in an effective way, but it determines the intellective psyche in an intrinsically exigent way. In virtue of this, the hominization and typification of humanity is not "creative evolution" but "evolving creation." From the point of view of the first cause, God, his creative will for an intellective psyche is a will for genetic evolution.

V

At the beginning I said that the problem of the origin of man had been proposed until now only in its theological dimension. And it might be asked how this conception of human origins with which science and philosophy present us can be fitted into theology.

The first thing to say is that the man theology occupies itself with is not necessarily the man which concerns paleontology, prehistory, and philosophy. As I understand it, man is, for science and for philosophy, as we have just seen, the intelligent animal in regard to which the rational animal, the Homo sapiens, is only the final evolutional stage. Now, from the theological point of view only the state of Homo sapiens counts. The man of whom theology speaks belongs only to that stage. The rational animal was raised to a state which we might call "theologal," one described by Genesis and St. Paul. He is no longer a mere rational animal but a rational "theologal" animal. It is not a required elevation, but it is an intrinsic one (*ab intrinseco*). This is why we say it is only elevation.

Consequently, the whole question is reduced to asking where to place the rational animal in the evolution of humanity and where to situate within the line of rational animal his elevation to the "theologal" state. Now, neither with evolution nor without evolution has the Church ever pronounced anything in regard to these two points. From a theological point of view the prerational types of humanity, whatever in fact they were, would only be evolutionary stages which nature, subject to the partial action of the intellective principle, of the intellective psyche created by God from within the transformed structures of the prefigured hominid, had developed from a mere intelligent animal to be a rational animal. Once this level had been achieved, its elevation to the "theologal" state did not have to coincide necessarily with the appearance of the first rational animal. The Church has never imposed this chronological coincidence between rationality and its "theologal" elevation. *When his time came,* the rational animal, the *Homo sapiens,* was elevated to the "theologal" state, so constituting the man of whom Genesis speaks and from whom all present humanity descends.

José Gaos

Don José Gaos (b.1900), a student of Ortega y Gasset, was appointed professor of philosophy at the University of Madrid and later became its rector. In 1939 Professor Gaos emigrated to Mexico to teach at the National University. His own interest lies in metaphysics and logic, and he has aided the introduction into Spain and South America of important European philosophical currents through his translation efforts. Among his major writings are Dos ideas de la filosofia *(1940),* Origenes de la filosofia y de la historia *(1960), and* De la filosofia *(1963).*

"Negation" appeared in *De la filosofia* (Mexico City: Fondo de Cultura Economica, 1963) 320–358. © 1963 by José Gaos. Grateful acknowledgment is made to the author for permission to reprint.

III. NEGATION

Existence is a relative mode of presence of beings, and as such it is essentially correlated with the other phenomena par excellence, the appearance, the disappearance, and the reappearance of beings. We conceive the appearances and disappearances of beings as relations between an anterior *inexistence* and a posterior *existence,* or between an anterior *existence* and a posterior *inexistence,* existence being regarded as posterior to one inexistence and anterior to another and as *finite* between them. It is the *incomprehensibility* of such relations that has given rise to the concept of an *infinite* existence. Thus it is that we modalize existence as essentially finite or infinite. Now the expressions "inexistence" and "infiniteness" are negative, being composed with "in," a prefix of negative "meaning." The *expression* "finiteness" is positive, but the *concept* it denotes, "finiteness," may be negative. It is our intention here to subject such negative expressions or concepts to a systematic analysis—analyzing the whole theme of which they are only a part, that, namely, of negation or the negative in general. We shall proceed from the categories of reason as thought conscious of itself expressed verbally and, particularly, as a conception of the existence of existing things in whose objectification we polarize thought, to the *negative* categories of reason in which we find united, paradoxical as it seems, the highest and the lowest levels of reason.

The importance of negation and the negative has been pointed up more than once in the history of philosophy but, perhaps, never as in the "existentialist" philosophies of our day. However, to my knowledge, no exhaustive phenomenological and systematic investigation of the phenomena of negation or the negative has ever been made. And it would appear that such an investigation should be made before undertaking other work which refers to, or utilizes, these phenomena. I am going to present in this essay the results of such an investigation.

In the first place, there is the question whether the theme should be *negation* or *the negative*. The latter seems to be broader in scope. For we can conceive negation as something negative in a certain "sense." However, there seem to be cases of the negative which do not consist properly in negation but in some *other* "activity" or "relation." Nevertheless, the theme I am going to develop is that of negation, and this for two reasons. First, verbal negation, which is negation in its proper sense, is doubtless a phenomenon endowed with a precision and an apprehensibility which the vaguely multiple phenomena of the negative do not have. And secondly, it is the phenomenon of the negative which most concerns us precisely because of our interest in the phenomenology of verbal expression in general, and in particular that of certain concepts made known by verbal expressions. Elsewhere we have dedicated our efforts to the phenomenology of verbal expression, but we confined our attention there to "affirmative" or "positive" expressions (as we may call them, by correlation with those traditionally and commonly called "negatives"). Here, however, we will consider the other half of that phenomenology. Not a less important half, either, for without it the whole would be *more* than *incomplete*. I prefer the term "positive" because it seems to me more suitably broad than that of "affirmative," which evokes for me *especially* affirmative expressions, such as adverbs of affirmation or those expressions of which these adverbs are a part.

In spite of what I have just said, I have to begin by making the following references—precisely in order to "define" the theme with the greatest possible rigor.

Not all negation is *verbal*. There is also the *gesticulatory* negation which is made by moving the head—or the hand, or the index finger—from one side to the other. And there is also a negation which we can call "practical" negation. By the latter we mean that there are negative attitudes, acts, postures, or manners of conduct which cannot be expressed verbally or with gestures; thus the *attitude* or *behavior* of a person from whom something is requested can reject that request without uttering a word or moving a muscle, simply by not doing what was requested or anything else to give satisfaction to the person who made the request.

But it seems that gesticulatory negation is such solely by association with verbal negation—that it supposes verbal negation as something primary to it. There are gestural expressions, indeed those that are most characteristically such, which, *of themselves,* express that which they are intended to express, for example, the unequivocal gestures of joy or sadness, or those of anger or discouragement. But certain other expressions can be regarded as gestural because they consist in movements equatable with or comparable to those of gestural expressions in the stricter sense, and by their essence they belong, properly speaking, to the species of "conventional signs": gestures of greeting—and those of negation. This seems to be shown and confirmed by the difference between the not merely human but even animal universality of the gestures of greeting—with their comprehensibility or immediate comprehension, which, too, is universal even on the animal level—and the cultural, ethnic, and historical variability and variation of the gestures of negation. Indeed, Ortega says somewhere that the Chinese move their head up and down to say "no" and shake it from side to side to say "yes," which is, in other words, the reverse of our custom. But if we were to see a Chinese coming toward us with a frown and with violent passion in his eyes, gnashing his teeth and shaking his fists, perhaps it would not be wise to wait for him while thinking that such would be the Chinese version of the expression of tender affection.

It seems to be, then, that because the lateral movement of the head, the hand, or the index finger became associated with the verbal expression of "no," the movement itself amounted to saying the same thing whether or not accompanied by any words. For that matter, the association may have begun in the gestural part of the negative expression "no," as it may *with all oral expression:* its "meaningful" factor of oral expression, the *tone* with which the "denoting thing" is emitted (which, like articulated sounds, have their own *graphic signs*), those of interrogation and admiration or in the lack of these, as we have explained in other writings. The emission of the voice is normally made—though possibly "abnormally"—with more gesticulation than the *acoustics* of the *tone*, rather with an *optic gesticulation* of the facial and physiognomical lineaments, or that of a movement of other parts of the body, or even of the whole body. And the fact that the negative expression calls attention to this concomitant gesture is just as normal as the general fact that phenomena of deficiency, absence, or negation indicate the presence of the positive phenomena which condition them but which remain unnoticed as long as they are not interrupted, or eliminated, or prove to be lacking. In short, the gesticulatory negations appear to be reducible to verbal negation, and it seems sound to treat of the verbal negation without treating of gesticulatory negation as a *separate* consideration.

The same is true of practical negation. A negative attitude or behavior, being, as we have said, verbally and gesturally "inexpressive," is doubtless a very exceptional border case. For the case of an attitude or conduct of any sort which does not express itself verbally or gesturally at all is very rare.

The gestural and verbal expression of the psychical is the normal, the human, the "living" way, as is confirmed by the entire extension of the phenomenon of gestural expression which we have treated elsewhere. However, there seems to be an important difference between the relation of verbal negation to gesticulatory negation and its relation to practical negation. As a part of the repertory of gestural expression, gesticulatory negation appears to be quite poor in comparison with the richness, if not of the negative verbal expressions, at least of the constructions into which they enter and of the situations they constitute. Hence it appears that as multiform as it is, practical negation is not as reducible to verbal negation in spite of the multiformity of this verbal negation, as was uniform gesticulatory negation.

Nevertheless, I am going to treat of practical negation together with verbal negation. And this for the following reasons. Not only is the practical negation normally expressed with words and with gestures, or accompanies or is accompanied by verbal or gestural expressions, but also (which is the reverse of this) verbal negation "contains" a negative attitude, posture, behavior, or conduct. It contains it from the side of "signification" in the states of the mind or spirit, with its emotions and movements; these states are signified by the negative expression as well as by the positive expression and by all verbal expression—as I have shown elsewhere, treating of positive expression, and as I shall show later on in this essay, treating of negative expression. Therefore, the analysis of verbal negation leads to the analysis of practical negation, with the advantage of a precision which we would lack if we were to undertake the investigation of the practical negation directly. And if verbal negation did not lead to practical negation in all its various forms or if there were other practical negations besides those contained by verbal negations—a supposition which we tend to reject because of the direct and inverse relations indicated between verbal negations and practical negations—it would be easy, and perhaps even more methodical, simply to annex to the investigations of practical negations, contained in verbal negations, the investigation of the remaining practical negations.

Let us begin, then, the investigation of verbal negation.

As a start let us consider the phenomenological fact of verbal—positive—expression. Negation could not fail to present *some* of the ingredients or concomitants of positive expression, else it would cease to be, and could not be, "verbal expression." But were it to present *them all* and *no others,* it would likewise cease to be and could not be "negative" expression, but would have to be a "positive" expression. The only thing possible is that positive and negative expressions present partly the same phenomena and partly different, and the most probable is that they present the same phenomena in the main, while they differ in the lesser part. In any of the possible cases the most methodical manner of proceeding will be to analyze negative expressions point for point according to the evident phenomena which are furnished by the phenomena of the phenomenology of the positive expressions.

But first it seems convenient, and even indispensable, to draw up an inventory of negative expressions. For as soon as we take one of the points alluded to, we have to apply it to some negative expression. And is it of no consequence if we apply it simply to the first negative expression we encounter? Are not all negative expressions of equal importance for our purposes? We cannot even answer this question without first making an inventory of negative expressions. It is certain that what is proper to the negative expression *in general* must be found in *each and every* negative expression—just as what is proper to verbal expression *in general* must be found in *any and every* verbal expression. But it seems to be possible, and even probable, that if negative expressions have a *special* importance within verbal expressions *in general,* their importance becomes even more "specialized," being graduated, within negative expressions themselves. Furthermore, when we treat of expression *in general,* we are not trying to remake the dictionary. But in treating of a *species* of expressions, it appears to be advisable, if not necessary, that we know the *extension* of what species—precisely *in order to* know what is *included* in it—or what part of the dictionary it is. In any case we lose nothing in making an inventory of negative expressions in advance, and we may even save time.

Having reviewed all the parts of speech, and having collected all the corresponding negative expressions in every possible *sense,* we find that we must classify them under specific titles or concepts.

Let us compare the expressions: "this leaf is not yellow" and "I deny that this leaf is yellow." The "not" of the first is construed as an adverb modifying the copulative verb of the sentence. The "deny" of the second is construed as an active transitive verb which has for its object or predicate the substantive clause introduced by the conjunction "that." The "not" denotes a concept which modifies the activation of relation denoted by the copulative verb. The "deny" denotes the objectifying concept of activity which modifies *me.* The "deny" *designates* this activity, this *object.* The "not" *does not designate* anything like this—as will become perfectly clear when we make this phenomenology. What I am saying here is an anticipation of such phenomenology, and this anticipation is implied by the classification of negative expressions which is based—as it has to be—on the peculiarities of these negative expressions. There is a certain relationship between phenomenology and classification, although not between phenomenology and simple inventory. The "deny" "denominates" and "objectivizes" the denying itself in a way that the "not" does not do. With the "not" I *simply negate* the fact that this leaf is yellow; I am directly and simply executing, to put it thus, the activity itself of denying—from a direct position. With the "deny" I not only execute the activity of denying; *I also say that I deny,* that I execute such an activity—from a reflective position. For we call "deny" a negative expression in the sense that it "designates," "denominates," or "objectivizes" the negating while executing it, and we call the "not" a negative expression in the sense that it "does not designate," or "determine," or "objectivize" the negating while executing it, but simply "executes" it. And this will bring us to the following.

Expressions *designating* the activity of negating include *negative* substantives, *negative* qualifying adjectives, and *negative* verbs, such as negation, abnegation, denial, refusal, negative;

negative, abnegated, denied, negating, annihilating, reducing
   to nothing;

to negate, to deny, to refuse, to annihilate, to reduce to nothing.

Expressions *not designating* the activity of negating are the
negative demonstrative adjectives and pronouns, the *negative*
numeral, *negative* adverbs of place and time, the negative pre-
fixes, and the adverb of negation

non, in-, *nusquam* (English has only certain synonymous adverbial phrases for this), never, not ever, no longer, no one,
   nobody, nothing, zero.

Some of these negations *not designating* the activity of negating are *universal* or *total,* and others are *partial,* in the sense that
the former negate or can negate *everything* existing, while the
latter negate or are able to negate only *some* existing *things,* or
things of a certain species or kind.

Total: non, in-, no one, nothing.

Partial: nobody, *nusquam,* never, not ever, no longer, zero
   (which negate exclusively and respectively persons or subjects, places, times, and numbers).

Thus certain prepositions and conjunctions denote negative
relations in some *"sense,"* standing ambiguously between the
designation and the nondesignation of the negating itself.

Prepositions: without, against.

Conjunctions—the *adversatives:* but, etc.; the *concessives:* although, etc.; the *disjunctives:* or, etc. But the copulative "nei-
   ther-nor" breakes down into "and not."

All these phenomena will fall into place in the phenomenology
that will follow.

Thus it seems evident that the most properly negative expressions are those with which one negates directly and simply, and
not those which (although one negates with them, too) above all
denominate the negating. And it seems that of the first, the most
"important" are the "total" negations, or the expressions "not,"
"in-," "no one," "nothing," and so on. But of these expressions
   "in-," and the synonym of "not" which we shall see;

"no one" and "nothing," and the cases of "not" which
we shall also see.

Thus there remains the expression "not" as the negative expression par excellence, literally the archetype in the twofold sense of primitive and principal. We could have anticipated this result by pure impression or intuition from the use of language. But in philosophy all results have to be justified or established methodically and systematically, to make of them expressed, tested, and demonstrated theses.

The practical conclusion of all this is that we must initiate here the *phenomenology of the "not."*

The "not" can be construed with all the parts of speech. But all of these constructions are ultimately reducible to two, although these are subdivisible, as I shall show.

First, there is the "not" which can be called "relative" in that it negates the relations denoted by the verb "to be" in its copulative construction.

And it is especially this relative "not" that we can call "direct" because it negates relations denoted by the verb "to be" of which the relation designated by the predicate with the copula, or the attribute, is an object of the sort objectivized in a direct position: an object which is neither an expression nor a concept.

We have here the case of the construction of the "not" with the verb "to be" as the copula of a subject with an attribute: the case of all sentences of the form "x is not z." This "not" negates the relation denoted by the "is" between x and z, which can be any of the relations listed in studying the copulative verb "to be":

identity in the terms themselves: "this leaf is not this leaf";

identity in different terms: "the leaf is not an article of paper which is used for writing";

specification, or transcendentalization: "this leaf is not a substance," "is not an existing thing";

generalization or quasi-universalization: "the leaf is not substance," "the leaf is not one of the lowest species";

modification, whether qualitative, relative, or quantitative:

"this leaf is not white," "the leaf is not made of paper," "God is not infinite."

The fact that the negation of the relation turns out to be *false* if the relation or its affirmation was *true* does not necessarily mean that the "no" does not negate the relation.

But as was the case of the *relative direct* "no," so also is that of the "no" construed with

the substantive noun, as in the "non-man" of Unamuno:

"A man that is neither of this or that place, nor of this or that age, a man that has neither sex nor country, but is only an idea. In other words, a non-man";

the adjective of quality as in "non-white" of Aristotle:

"let us say, for example, that there exists the non-white";

the personal pronoun, as in the "non-I" of Fichte: "The I is opposed to itself, and, in virtue of this opposition, it will engender the non-I";

the adverb of manner, of quantity, of place, or of time, as in the "not thus," "no more," "not here," "not today," which are such common expressions that there are no major authorities for them.

All of these constructions are simply *eliptical* constructions of the copulative verb. It is, in fact, obvious that Unamuno is speaking of "the man that is not a man," Aristotle is speaking of "a white, a color, or something which is not white or whiteness," Fichte is speaking of "everything that is not the I," and humanity means "it is not thus" that it is what it might be, "let it not be, nor should it be, more" than it is, "it is not here" that it is or was to be found, "it is not today" that it is or should be.

However, another case of the *relative* "not" is that which can be called "reflex" or reflexive because it negates relations eliptically or not eliptically denoted by the verb "to be," of which the relation, designated by the predicate with the copula or the attribute, is an object of the sort objectivized in a reflex position, and it may be either an expression or a concept.

We have here the case of the construction of the "not" with articles, demonstrative adjectives, impersonal pronouns, adverbs of affirmation, negation, and doubt, prepositions and conjunctions. It is perfectly possible to use the sentence "not because of, but following upon" as a correction of the well-known formula of causality *post hoc, ergo propter hoc*, in the sense of not being a determined relation, a relation of causality, but simply the relation of succession. In this case we negate the idea that the "just" *concept* is that of causality and not that of succession. Not even a case like "this leaf is not here" is different because either one negates *the leaf* as determined by the relation of nearness to the first person or one negates it *as determined by this relation*. If what is negated is *the leaf*, it is simply a case of the anterior relative direct eliptical "not." If what we negate is the leaf *as determined by the relation*, it is no longer the same case; it can only be a question of the negation of *the determination by such a relation* or of *this relation itself*, or the relation which it is, or should be, may be that denoted by "this" and not by "that" or some other demonstrative expression. Finally, phrases like "not yes" and "it is not no" obviously cannot have any other meaning than that of negating the very *expression* "yes" or "no" or the *concept* these denote.

This analysis of phrases or cases is confirmed by the general explanation of all the listings of this group: the parts of speech that constitute them, the articles, demonstrative adjectives, impersonal pronouns, adverbs of affirmation, negation and doubt, prepositions and conjunctions—all have the characteristic of being *determinant of others*, of denoting concepts of relations modifying or modalizing their references, in such a way that the negating of these relations, or concepts, or the expressions which denote them, ends up negating, through them so to speak, not only the relations or concepts, and such, but also that which is determined by them. Or, conversely, it does not prove practicable to negate, except in a reflex manner, these expressions or the concepts denoted by them because these expressions or concepts do not have other objects distinct from themselves than those which they modify relatively. . . . However, the substantives, the adjectives of quality, the personal pronouns, and, as we shall see, the verbs, are expressions which essentially designate substances, qualities, activities: the negation of these expressions can be a direct negation of the objects distinct from the expressions themselves, objects designated by them and distinct from the concepts denoted by them.

But what of adverbs of manner, quantity, place, and time—and, possibly together with these, the *numerical* adjectives and pronouns? Adverbs of "manner" are the adverbs of *qualities* of the active modes designated by verbs; with them, then, it is the same as with the "qualifying" adjectives or adjectives of *qualities* of substances or of other modes. Adverbs of quantity, place, and time as well as numerals are the expressions of *quantitative* modes: it is as if the *quantitative* relations were separated, once more, from *relations* in general by a certain character which is less purely relative, less purely determinative, something more substantive.

But there still remains the second major case, that of the "not" which can be called "active" because it negates the *activities* designated by verbs in their personal forms, including the verb "to be" in its *existential* construction and its synonyms.

This "not" which *negates existence* can be partial or total. It is partial when it negates the existence of a single existing thing or several existing things, provided they are not all that exist; and when it negates all of them, it is total: "there is no God"; "God does not exist"; "nothing does not exist." Nothingness is the negative concept of the existence of all existing things, the negative concept of the existence, which is peculiarly substantivized and which deserves to be considered separately, as I shall do presently.

First I wish here to point out that in the negation, with "not," of the activities designated by nonsubstantive verbs, as in "this leaf does not turn yellow," we must single out the negation of the activity of *to want:* "I do not want," "he does not want."

The negation of the existence of all that exists is so singular and superlative a case that "nothingness" also merits singular, if not superlative, consideration. What I am going to do with it is

the same that I did with "not" in the beginning of this essay,
namely, to initiate the *phenomenology of nothingness.*

We have constructions using the expression itself, "nothing,"
and those using related expressions; "nothing" can also be construed with all the parts of speech.

substantive: "nothing man" (no-man);

adjective of quality: "nothing white";

article: "the nothing," "a nothing";

personal pronoun: "nothing he" (by no means he);

demonstrative and impersonal pronoun: "nothing first," "nothing mine";

copulative verb: "nothing is infinite," "less is nothing," "it is
nothing," "nothing is there";

existential verb: "nothing exists," "there is nothing," "nothing
does not exist";

nonsubstantive verb: "nothing turns yellow," "I want nothing,"
"it is worth nothing";

adverb of manner: "nothing well";

adverb of quantity: "nothing more," "nothing less";

adverb of place: "nothing far";

adverb of time: "nothing early";

adverb of doubt: "perhaps nothing";

preposition: "it is made with nothing," "a matter of nothing,"
"nothing of that," "in nothing flat," "nothing in excess," "so
much noise for nothing," "nothing for me," "do it for nothing," "left with nothing";

conjunction: "and nothing."

Now, some observations.

I did not include the construction of "nothing" with the adverb
of affirmation. An expression like "yes, nothing" in response to a
question like "is it true that it is nothing?" is not natural. On the
contrary, the natural response is "no, nothing." And furthermore,
it would not be a construction of "yes" and "nothing" in the
sense of all the other constructions of "nothing" considered here,
although this could be due, more than to the "nothing," to the

"yes," which is an expression *sui generis,* as I shall attempt to show later on in this essay.

In the construction listed, then, "nothing" is sometimes an adjectival or adverbial expression, that is, an expression which determines another substantive, objectival, pronominal, verbal, or adverbial expression: "nothing human," "nothing white," "nothing he," "nothing first," "nothing mine," "nothing turns yellow" in the sense that something does not yellow at all, "nothing well," "nothing more," "nothing far," "nothing early."

At other times, "nothing" is a pronominal, substantivized expression, that is, *determined* as subject, attribute, or object of verbs, the object governing or complementing prepositions, the term of conjunctions: "the nothing," "nothing is infinite," "it is nothing," "nothing exists," "nothing turns yellow" in the sense that there is nothing that turns yellow, "I want nothing," "nothing is worth anything," "perhaps nothing"—which is eliptical for "perhaps there is nothing"—"it is made out of nothing," and so on, "then nothing"—eliptical for "then nothing happened."

In the same constructions "nothing" has sometimes an *ontological* sense: "nothing human," "there is nothing," "and nothing"; at other times, an "*axiological*" sense: "it is a nothing," "it is nothing."

This twofold sense is confirmed by other expressions related to those above:

  on the one hand: annihilate, annihilated, annihilator, annihilation (which are terms of unequivocal ontological meaning);

  on the other hand: to reduce to nothingness, reduced to nothingness, one who reduces to nothingness, reducing to nothingness, reduction to nothingness; "little or nothing," something of no importance (all of which are more properly and purely axiological terms).

A person reduced to nothingness is not annihilated, in the strict sense, but reduced in the extreme. It is not that he has ceased to exist; it is as if nothing existed any more for him because for him everything has lost its *value.* It is for this that one cannot properly say that a thing is reduced to nothingness.

In the constructions in which "nothing" is *determinant,* one means that *it* is *not,* in any way, the thing determined: "nothing man," a man that is not a man in any way, that does not have the distinctive characteristics of man—even though this is a pure hyperbole. It is a question of a *negation of identity* in the terms themselves which could be called "pleonastic," in relation to that made with the "not."

In the constructions in which "nothing" is the *thing determined,* we mean that there is no existing thing at all or that there is no existing thing that has a certain active, qualitative, relative, quantitative mode, and in particular we mean that there is no value, nothing that has a value or anything that has any value—and without doubt for the particular value of values: "it is a nothing," it is a thing without importance or price; "it is nothing," it is a thing without significance or price; "a matter of nothing" is the same as the latter, or nothing of time; "he dwelt on nothing" means, rather than on nothing at all, on nothing of what was concerned, and so on; "little or nothing," "nonentity" are things of little or no importance.

It is a question of the *negation of the existence* of all existing things, peculiar to "nothing," or of some or some one of them, as that made by the expressions of partial negation which we listed previously. This means that "nothing" is not always used in its proper and strict sense of negation of the existence of all existing things, of absolutely total negation of existence; it is a matter of a logical-grammatical inconsequence without greater consequences.

Included in these constructions are those in which, once the nothing is substantivized, it can be made the "object" or "subject" of all the determinations or modifications to which substances and substantivations are susceptible: a poet can say "black nothing"; a mystic can say "my nothing"; a philosopher can ask "what nothing?" or speak of an "original nothing" and even of "two nothings, one original and one final," and so forth.

Luis Legaz y Lacambra

Don Luis Legaz y Lacambra (b.1906) is Spain's most eminent jurist and professor of the philosophy of law. Among his chief works are Humanismo, estado y derecho *(1960),* Derecho y libertad *(1952),* Horizontes del pensmiento juridico *(1957), and* Filosofia del derecho *(1961).*

"The Juridical Notion of the Human Person and the Rights of Man" appeared in *Humanismo, estado y derecho* (Barcelona: Bosch Casa Editorial, 1960) 107–143. © 1960 by Luis Legas y Lacambra. Grateful acknowledgment is made to the author for permission to reprint.

IV. THE JURIDICAL NOTION OF THE HUMAN PERSON AND THE RIGHTS OF MAN

I

The problem of the juridical notion of the human personality is intrinsically interesting above all because it constitutes one of the most important themes of the science and the philosophy of jurisprudence. But it is also interesting relative to the present situation of man, that is, an interest which goes beyond purely scientific limits to take its place in the area of the specifically human problematic. In this perspective, we are dealing with a problem that is important not only for the jurist or student of jurisprudence but also for man as such, and precisely for this reason attempts have been made to divest it of its importance by eliminating the concept of personality from juridical science itself, under the mantle of a philosophy that began by annihilating the idea and value of man.

There is also the disquieting fact that the European man himself has, by his attitude, contributed to this self-dispossession of his personality. As N. Ramiro[1] wrote, the tyrannies of our time are nothing more than the effect of a flight: man's effort to escape from himself. Just the reverse of Chamiso's character, man sells his substance to content himself with his shadow. Instead of being a man, an actor, more tragic than dramatic, in whose breast an antagonist and protagonist are engaged in dialogue, with the unique peculiarity that the antagonist and the protagonist are one and the same, European man wants to become the puppet of a group that lives through his sacrifice.

The philosophical idea of the person is clearly of Christian origin. In the language of the Greeks, the word person has no application in philosophy because Greek philosophy had no term that meant what we call the person. The Greek never prefixed the I to the verb to be, at least never with any significant value so that such a sentence constituted anything fundamental for religion or philosophy. It was Christ who said of himself that "I am the way, the truth, and the life," synthesizing in the unity of a real and living person this affirmation of a supreme interior life and of absolute independence which were impossible for Parmenides' Being or for Plato's Idea of the Good, and making possible, in a concrete, personal, and historical program, the function of truth, way, and life in the unity of persons.[2]

And if it is true that the whole program of modern philosophy has consisted in a "sublime and desperate attempt to make its own Christ's functions regarding the way (method), the truth, and life,"[3] it behooves us to establish any further juridical concept on the person in a philosophical theory that realizes the program of Christian personalism, one that gives to the person that which belongs to it without permitting the person to usurp what is proper to Christ, to God. We need therefore a theory of the person as liberty and a theory of liberty as the bond of religion. The thought of Zubiri has made essential contributions to this theory, and from it we shall select here those concepts which are of particular interest to our problem.

The primary situation of man with respect to things is to stand "before them." His acts are projects, something which man *throws out* over things from which he stands at his distance while remaining among them, never without them. There is in man a function thought, in virtue of which he does not form part of nature but stands removed from it, and this holds true both for physical nature and for his own psychophysical nature. This ontological condition of his being is what we call liberty: the ontological situation of one who exists from his own being. This does not mean that all the acts of man are free, but that man is free, and only one who is radically free can see himself deprived of liberty in many, perhaps in the greater number of his acts. The reality of human acts does not emerge only from the potencies of nature but also from the "possibilities" which man has at his disposal and to which he must necessarily recur. Thus nature and history are articulate from within. Man transcends nature and history. He is a person who creates his life with his nature and who with his life creates history. Man transcends history, but nature stands this side of history, and between nature and his personal existence man traces the trajectory of his life and his history.[4]

Man finds himself situated in existence. This word is equivocal and can be taken in different senses. If it is taken as referring to the manner in which man *is*, existence means the way in which man ex-sists, *sistit extra causas*, stands outside of causes, which in this case are things; hence we may say that to exist is to transcend and, consequently, to live. However, *is* man his existence? Here we have another sense of the word exist which refers to the being which man has conquered by transcending and living. In this case, we would have to say that man is not his life, but that he lives in order to be. But this, his being, stands in some way beyond his existence in the sense of life. For this reason the scholastics used to say that nature and supposite, and especially nature and person, are not the same even when one understands by nature the individual nature. Personality is the very being of man: *actiones sunt suppositorum*, actions belong to the supposites, because it is the supposite which properly "is." The person finds himself established in being in order to realize himself. To live is to live with things, with other persons, and with ourselves to the extent we are living beings.[5]

Life is mission, because existence has been sent to man. Man receives existence as something imposed upon him. He is bound to life, but this does not mean to be bound by life. Life is what is most completely *ours* since it makes us *be:* at the same time, it is most completely *other* because it *makes* us be. Or, to put it in other terms, in existing man not only finds himself with things which are there and with things with which he has to deal, but he also finds himself with the fact that he must become and that he must be in the state of becoming. In addition to things, there is also that which brings it about that he should be. To that which brings it about that we exist, we are bound: religion is an onto-logical link between human being and something which is not extrinsic but which makes the human being be. It is not a ques-tion of "going to," but of "coming from," or a going which attaches us to that from which we come: to be who one already is. This reveals the foundation of human existence, that which is the cause not of our being in one manner or another but of the fact that we are rather than are not.[6]

It would seem that the religious bond is opposed to liberty. Liberty can signify, to begin with, the use of liberty in life, and in this sense we speak of a free act or one which is not free. Lib-erty also signifies, in a more radical sense, being liberated from things, being turned toward them, being able to understand and modify them. Liberty means liberation, liberated existence. In either of these senses, a bond constitutes a limitation. But both uses of liberty and liberation arise from the radical constitution of an entity for whom to be is to be free. The bond by which man exists confers upon him his liberty, and conversely, man is consti-tuted as a free being in being bound, which thus acquires a posi-tive sense. Taken as the use of liberty, freedom is something interior to life. Taken as liberation, freedom is the radical event of life; it is the beginning of existence in the sense of transcend-ence and life. Taken as free constitution, freedom is the establish-ment of man in being as a person, and liberty is constituted there where the person is constituted: in the religious bond. Freedom is possible only as "freedom to," not only as "freedom from," and in this sense it is possible only as a religious bond. Freedom does not exist except in an entity which is established on the ultimate

basis of his being. There is no freedom without *foundation*. The
ens fundamentale, God, is not an extrinsic limit on freedom, but
the foundation which he confers on the state of being free. Without bond and binder, freedom would be for man his greatest
impotence and his radical despair. With a bond and with God,
man's liberty is his greatest power, so much so that through it
his own person is established, his very being intimate and interior to himself confronting all else, even his own life.[7]

Thus actions belong to supposites, to persons. For this reason,
man is not his existence, but the existence is his own. What man
is does not consist in the effective course of his life, but in this
"being his own" which is in his hands. Man assists at the passing
of everything, even of his own life, and his life transcends the
passing and remaining. Man has it in his power to modify this
"being its own" of life. He can, for example, repent and thus
rectify his being, even to the point of converting it into another.
He also has the power of pardoning his neighbor. None of these
phenomena refers to life as such; they refer to the person. While
life runs on and passes, man is that which remains to him of his
own after everything has happened to him which has to happen
to him. Thanks to this transcendence of the being of man with
respect to his own life, the human person can turn against life and
against himself. That which makes us free makes us effectively
free, and hence able to perform effective acts against ourselves.
Anti-being is essential to the being of man, and this anti-being is
a being-against which supposes, therefore, a bond. Man turns
against himself in the measure that he already exists. Because of
his bond, man, as a person, is in a certain sense an absolute subject, a relative absolute being: absolute, insofar as he is his own;
relative, insofar as his being is acquired, received.[8]

We take our point of departure then in a humanism which is
a personalism because it affirms the value of the person, and this
value consists primarily in being more than in mere existence,
in possessing dominion over one's own life, and this ruling power,
this dominion is the root of the dignity of the person.

When we speak of the juridical notion of the human person we are implying a difference of concepts. The human person is not a person in the juridical sense. If there is a juridical notion of the person, it is because there is another notion of the person which is not juridical but prejuridical and ontologically prior. Yet between the human person and the juridical notion of it, there exists both a relationship of ought and an ontological link. This means that the human person must also be a person in the juridical sense and that the person in the juridical sense is a quality, a mode of being of the human person.

Man consequently must be a juridical person, a subject of rights. But can he cease being this? When a juridical transaction is carried out, or when an action in justice is effected, it sometimes becomes necessary to demonstrate the "personality of the agent." The validity of the transaction or act can be nonexistent because of the absence of this personality. In such a case, the plaintiff is a human person who possesses a juridical subjectivity or personality with the rights to various orders of relations, but not so integral a body of rights that they embrace all possible relationships, since he lacks it, in this supposed case, for this concrete relationship. Always, then, juridical *personality* can be found restricted because of age, citizenship, representation or mandate, and so on.

These restrictions, which are normal and required for juridical security, can be intensified in virtue of considerations of another dimension such as, for example, ideology, and this even to the extreme of total suppression, which results in a person being deprived of the possibility of operating juridically in any order of relations. Hence we would have the case of a human person utterly without juridical personality, which would be the case of the slave. The slave is a human person absolutely without juridical personality, and therefore jurisprudence regards him as only "a thing." However, we are dealing here with an impossibility. Even should this juridical consideration as a thing reach back even to the point of embracing the entire being of the slave as if he were indeed not even a human person (which is incidentally a proof, *a contrario,* of the correlativity of the two notions), the

Romans always acknowledged that this idea of slavery was contrary to natural law,[9] and they regarded ownership over a slave as a form of *potestas*.[10] And even in the positive juridical order this negation of personality was not absolute, for certain rights always continued to be recognized, even though in a lesser degree and in a certain sense surreptitiously.[11]

Thus it is impossible for a man not to be a person in the juridical sense. As a matter of fact, the reasons for restriction of personality depend upon the will of the lawmaker. But juridical personality is a necessary concept, not a contingent one. One may be free to determine who is a person in the juridical sense, but the existence of such juridical personality is not dependent either upon such freedom or upon the lawmaker's will. By ontological necessity, the denying of juridical personality to the human person can be nothing more than an exception which, furthermore, will stumble upon an ineradicable minimum of juridical subjectivity, which demonstrates that the problem of slavery, and in general the problem of the restrictions of the person, is not a problem of personality but of liberty, as was demonstrated by C. Cossío.[12] Every man as such is, up to a certain point, and must be, at least to a minimum extent, a person in the juridical sense. We have here the fundamental and primary exigency, the absolute ethical exigency, which summarizes the truth that exists in all doctrines of natural law. But the determination of the degree and the mode of personality is the affair of legislative statecraft in which, as in all statecraft, the ideas of justice are conditioned by considerations of utility, convenience, and security.

This is a point in which the European and Latin American authors of papers presented at the International Congress on Comparative Law in London were in complete accord, while it was the North Americans who, destroying the objectivity of their own convictions in the area of the person and human rights, assumed relativist positions in disregarding all philosophical bases and adhering to affirmations that are merely political.[13]

Georges Burdeau[14] takes as his point of departure the fact that the different juridical-political systems create a juridical person-

ality in the image of the conception of the human person projected by the ideological vision at the basis of each system. With
this as a base, the problem is posed as to whether the human
person should not be regarded as something prior to any political realization of it, or whether it is not a being endowed with a
dignity of its own which is the foundation of the rights that are
substantial to that person. Lords of human destinies by reason of
the simple presence of their material might, human societies
claim to hold their power legitimately. To justify the present
mode of life they impose upon the individuals which depend upon
them, and to exalt the future they are promising those individuals, they invoke a conception of man. But the tragedy of our age
lies precisely in the claim of the state and extrastate powers to
constrain individuals not only to model themselves outwardly
to the features of the human figure imagined by the official philosophies, but especially that individuals in fact convert themselves into this man constructed for the purposes of a cause, that
they clothe themselves with this political-metaphysical uniform
under penalty of becoming outcasts excluded by society and being condemned, therefore, to disappear. In truth, every positive
juridical ordering of things is the tributary of a certain conception
of man. Man converts himself into a synthesis of juridical situations that totally suffocate his activity and which is oriented by
them according to the ends proposed by the regime. In this way,
contemporary man tends to possess no other meaning than that
of a means which, through the juridical situations arbitrarily
imposed upon him, the powers use as an instrument in the realization of their plans to reorder the social structure.

According to Burdeau this obliges us to inquire whether, beyond the contingent forms given to it by the systems of positive
law, the human person does not imply a value in itself, a nature,
an end, and hence exigencies that cannot be reduced to the
action of state regulations. Burdeau holds that this problem must
be resolved affirmatively, since it would be impossible to treat of
the juridical notion of the human person without primarily admitting its unity and its independence with respect to the concep-

tions of it proposed by various national legislations. At the same time, this initial taking of possession gives meaning to the debate, for there is no reason for the recognition of a human person as having intrinsic validity unless, on the one hand, the person can take a position against the claims of the lawmakers who arbitrarily construct a notion of man according to the political and social ends of the regimes they serve and unless, on the other hand, that notion of the human person can be proposed to these same legislators as that to which the laws they write must conform.

Burdeau voices here the possible objection of "individualism" that can be opposed to his doctrine. In a certain sense, he seems almost to lean toward it. Even if individualism is a dated concept, he contends that it did have a fruitful side: it liberated the human person from the constrictions which nurtured in him an inferiority complex. Breaking the circle of superstitions that were dominating man's life, it opened to him the way to spiritual liberty, and in curing him of all the sequels of his primitive conformism, it permitted him to acquire his true human stature.

But Burdeau is a personalist, not an individualist. He takes the philosophy of Maritain and all the personalist ideologies in which the distinction between the individual and the person was forged as foundation for his conception of the person. Without compromising himself in any personalist orthodoxy, he reasons that it is possible to profit by this double aspect of man: individual on the one hand—a being conditioned by the elements that he draws from a base that is common to all individuals; and person on the other—a consciousness, a being whose liberty escapes social determinism. As an individual, man is the prime matter for the legal theorist, being the infinitely malleable material which the powers shape, by means of juridical regulations, to make of him the constituting element of the type of society they set out to create. The individual is thus the recipient of the rights which make him what he is. The person, on the other hand, is a moral existence not folded back upon himself, but only effective in the realization of a social obligation, a being fully responsible for all of social reality in a constant reciprocity with other persons, but not determined by the social reality. The person is not the passive recipient of the rights that determine the condition of man, but the subject of these rights. Furthermore, these rights are placed in him as in an inviolable receptacle, and they are defined in terms of the exigencies of the person, i.e., as the rights of a being which is committed and bound (*engagé*), as prerogatives which he enjoys only when shared with others.

This personalism offers a certain convenience for the theory of law and of politics. But apart from being disputable, especially when one attempts to derive it directly from St. Thomas,[15] it leads to the inevitably paradoxical thesis whereby man would be a person in the juridical sense to the extent that, as man, he is not a person, but an individual.

In what does personality as a juridical reality consist? How do these manners of being which we call—from various points of view—"personality" line up in the whole reality of the human being? To explain this, we must take recourse to a later development of the theory of existence and of the person in which we find the two ontological planes of personal life differentiated: the private and the social planes or, if one wishes, the personal life *sensu stricto* and the social life.

As Zubiri says,[16] to live is to live with things, with others, and with ourselves insofar as we are living beings. This "with" is one of the formal ontological characteristics of the human person as such. And in virtue of this "with," every human life, because it is the life of one person, is constitutionally either an *impersonal* life, a more or less personal life, or a depersonalized life. In other words, that with which man realizes himself as a person can, and to a certain extent must, conceal his personal being. Zubiri is alluding here to that dimension of human existence which Heidegger[17] expressed with the rigorously impersonal formula of "one," *das Man.* In life, we commonly find man in the form of "one." In Heidegger's terminology, *Dasein* is always a shared being, *Mitsein,* and this is, in its turn, with respect to others, a shared existence: to be together one with the other. In this sharing oneself with others and in delivering oneself to the world which preoccupies it, *Dasein* is not "he himself." Who robbed him of his being in this daily sharing of himself? It was the neuter, the "one," Heidegger tells us. Shared existence dissolves the person's own existence in the mode of being of the others, which tends to present less and less distinct and expressed exigencies. It is in this indifference that the "one" unfolds its absolute rule. We enjoy life as one enjoys life; we read, see, and judge art and literature as one reads, one sees, and one judges; we want to distinguish ourselves from the "masses" as one generally distinguishes oneself from the masses; we regard as excellent that which one regards as excellent. This *one,* which is nothing definite and which is *everybody,* although not as the totality, dictates the being of the commonplace. The mode of being of the "one" is "publicity," which regulates every interpretation of the world and of existence, not upon the foundation of a primary and distinct relation with things but rather on the basis of not entering into them, because it is insensible to differences of level and authenticity. Publicity obscures everything and declares the occult to be known and accessible to all. The "one" is not an existing thing. Nevertheless, it constitutes the most real subject of the banal. It is neither a general subject nor a genus. It is an existential factor which, as the primary phenomenon, forms part of the positive constitution of existence. Existence is "one," and it normally remains therein, hiding from itself. But when it is open to the true sense of the world and of itself, then it passes through an existential modification of the "one" to the authentic identity of existence.

This view of Heidegger presents a strong affinity to Ortega y Gasset's conception of the life of the mass-man compared with authentic or egregious life. But it does not treat of exactly the same thing.[18] The life of the mass-man and the egregious life have the sense of two forms of life of which the one is regarded as ideal and the other as its countertype. They are ideas freighted with value considerations, positive values in the one case, and negative values in the other. For Heidegger, on the other hand, it is a question of existential categories that are present in every existence, and hence they mean only that things are simply thus. The only thing condemned is "remaining" in the mode of being of the "one." For this "remaining" is an act of liberty: the use of liberty to abdicate from liberty. In the "one" there is also liberty, but only that of the possibility of transcending oneself into authenticity. This possibility is continuously renounced, but it hence exists as a positive constituent element, since that renunciation is also free.

It is in the mode of being of the "one" that the phenomenon which we call "social life" has its roots. We should point out here that social life is a much more demanding thing than coexistence. Coexistence is the fact of shared existence, or *Mitdasein*. Every form of life necessarily presupposes this fact, since life, in any of its forms, is the life of beings which coexist, beings which share their existence with others which in turn share theirs with them. If we do not keep this distinction in mind, we can easily fall into certain errors concerning the essence of social life.

For example, if social reality covers the fact of coexistence and coexistence is an essential characteristic of the existing human being, man will be a *social being* not only in the sense that he is by nature destined to live in society but also in the sense that his entire being consists in being social and that, consequently, his entire being, in all of its strata, will be a socialized and socializable being. What is more, not to be fully socialized will be the residuum of an unsociability derived from the tendency of "antisocial" appetites and instincts, and is consequently something which "should not be." The ideal will be the total socialization of man.

A typical example of this error is the philosophy of society of Othmar Spann, who represents the universalist viewpoint.[19] For Spann, all the fundamental questions of social philosophy turn about the "above-yourself": how to determine the metaphysical above-yourself and how this metaphysical above-yourself is transformed into a social above-yourself. The metaphysical above-yourself is not to be conceived, according to Spann, as an atomic coexistence of creative influences over isolated individual men

and things, but as an integral totality of perennial creative influences over the totality of men, so that each man and each thing
manifest themselves to us as members of that one totality, of
which we are members, and of its total creative activity. This
metaphysical above-yourself is the world of ideas, which acts as
a unit, as a kingdom, as the total all, over the unity of men, over
the community. The world of ideas converts into a social above-
yourself, into the total spirit of society, into Hegel's objective
spirit. This objective spirit does not proceed from individuals; on
the contrary, it precedes them. The individual is spiritual only by
means of and in this above-yourself. The individual is filled with
its spiritual contents, not in a mechanical way, but by virtue of
the specific creative force of the individual, so that the personal
life of men—that of being a member—is not denied. This universalism takes its departure from the concept of society as spiritual
totality, of which individuals are only spiritual members (organs).
Since, according to the universalist view, the central nucleus of
human life in common resides in spiritual community or duality,
the growth and development of men living together constitutes a
proper and substantive phenomenon, the phenomenon of society.

Thus this conception makes a spiritual substance of the fact
of coexistence, and since all men necessarily coexist, this fact of
coexistence, ceasing to be metaphysical and becoming social, confers upon them as persons only the condition of members. The
individual remains totally socialized, even though the fact of coexistence is given not an empiricosociological and naturalistic interpretation, but an idealistic and spiritual interpretation.

Social reality exists because there is the previous and radical
fact of coexistence, the fact of existence shared, but we are dealing here with different things. Man lives, and his life necessarily
has to reckon with this fact of sharing. Without it there would be
no meaning in love or hatred, courage or cowardice, nobility or
ignobility, generosity or avarice, or anything that is a mode of
man's being. For his mode of being is expressed in conduct "in
terms of others" or inasmuch as others exist. One loves or hates
someone, one is valiant or cowardly with someone, one bears

oneself in a dignified or base way with someone, and one is mag-
nanimous or pusillanimous with someone. It is because there is
a shared existence that these qualifications have meaning or are
possible for the person. But it is not the shared existence that
constitutes what is peculiar and specific in these qualifications.
On the contrary, it is in these qualifications that a mode of being
of a personality is brought out. Furthermore, it is that mode of
being which, inasmuch as it exists, shares the person's existence
with others. I do not call that life personal which is the life of the
person (for there is no other), but that life of the person which is
plenarily personal, authentically personal, giving here to the term
"personal" a sense of specific difference. I call that life personal
which is constituted on the grounds of the liberty of a bound existence, independent of whether it recognizes, disavows, or impugns
this bond. That life is personal which consists in a free giving of
form to one's own personal being, in the self-creation of a "personality" defined by the integrity one acquires in the recognition
of a fundamental value from which he derives a coherent set of
norms for conduct; that life is personal, consequently, which is
lived from the center of the person, which is religious, moral,
noble, generous, and the like, or the contrary of these, but which
develops outwardly in the whole range of shared existence, of
coexistence, or relations with others, of otherness.

We can say of social life, using Heidegger's terms, that it consists in a "dictatorship of *one*." The "one" is a mode of being that
pertains constitutionally to existence. This permits us to make an
initial distinction. Social life is not "social" because it is called
such. It is not a question of social life as a substantivized entity
(on the contrary, we could ask if a type of life analogous to personal life—Scheler's collective person, for example—is possible in
society or in certain societies). Social life is the life of the human
subject. If its essence consists in dictatorship, it is a dictatorship
of the subject over himself; but it will be dictatorship of the
mode of being of the "one" over the plenarily and authentically
personal reality of the subject. For this reason, in the face of this
rigorously personal dimension of existence, social life lacks this

"authenticity," this radical humanity, and in this sense can be called unauthentic life, dehumanized and impersonalized life. It is life which is not authentic, but not in the sense that it is not "authentic life," that it is more or less life. It is not a question of authenticity with reference to the fullness of being of life as a reality, but of the authenticity of life as the life of the personal being, the being which constitutes the personality. It is not in social life that the being is constituted as a person, although the person must necessarily and constitutionally live within the form of social life.

In social life coexistence is not only the framework within which all life has to be lived. It is also the reality that imposes concrete form and being upon the person. Through this "dictatorial" dimension, the being imposed on the person becomes an "appearance." In social life one "lives on appearances" in the very strictest sense of the word. It is not *life lived,* but *life represented,* according to the phrase of E. Mallea. Representing or appearing is the essence of social life. In social life we have to adapt ourselves to canons that do not emanate from our own personal centers but that we find imposed upon us from without. The more authentic our existence is, and the more rich and intense our personal life is, all the more clear will be our consciousness of that which we "represent" in social life. And the more intense and authentic our personal life is the more authentically social our social life will be. If personal life is lacking, if our existence remains within the dimension of "one," if the whole life of the person is exhausted in social life, becoming thus "insubstantial," social life loses its specific authenticity precisely because it begins to usurp the role of a personal life. And thus the entire being of the person will have turned into an unconscious representing.

Personal life has three fundamental categories: religion, ethics, and art. By religion we mean the bond of man with God (*religatio,* in its root sense, or *religio*). Ethics refers to the fundamental relation of man with other men. And art symbolizes the essential reference of man to things and men inasmuch as men are representable nature. These are final categories that radically

define the being of persons. Rights, we can say without qualification, are not in this vital stratum. Rights are not life, as has
frequently been said; they are only a form of life. They are and
remain in social life; indeed they are the fundamental form of
the social life of man. They are a form which arises from and is
created in life itself, and afterwards they oppose life as a rule.

For this reason, jurisprudence must necessarily deal with the
fact that man is a person also in the social sense. It can ignore or
contradict the fact *in concreto* with respect to one man or a
group of men for reasons which are more or less justifiable from
the ethical or political point of view, but it can never ignore it
purely and simply. For this reason, the concept of person in the
juridical sense is a pure and a priori juridical concept, since no
jurisprudence is possible without the recognition of juridical personality. Since rights presuppose social life or the social dimension
of the human being, they do not enter into the sphere of pure
personal life. But personal life is of the human subject and, consequently, the life of the social being has its roots in personal and
private life, and hence law, as the fundamental form of social
life, must reflect the minimum conditions of personal life that
make social life possible. Thus we say that juridical personality
is in the image and likeness of the human person as such, but
it acquires reality to the extent the human person has a social
dimension and to the extent there is a social life with ontological
structures of its own. One of these structures is the impersonal,
intersubjective regulation, and concretely the juridical regulation.

Social life, in fact, possesses normative structure. This not only
consists in being subjected to or in having to be subjected to
norms. Personal life is also subjected to norms; were it not so,
there would be no obligations for man. These norms are based on
values which are not only valid in general as the categorical
imperative but which also have individual validity. In contradistinction to rights, morality approaches its essence the more it is
individualized in its demands and precepts. But norms are not
present in personal life in the same way they are present in social
life. In personal life, the subject stands before the norms as a free

being. It is liberty that defines the essence of personal life, and the norms make their demands all the more pressing as they lose their meaning for the subject who refuses to accept them freely. For a forced moral life is not a moral life, even when reason is in favor of the demand for the sake of which force is exerted. On the other hand, in social life it is the norm, not liberty, that characterizes it essentially. There is social life because and to the extent there are social norms—the norms of "one"—which impose their dictatorship, denaturalizing or "altering" the personal being of the subject, and denaturalizing it not by chance but necessarily. The subject consequently has to cope with this inevitable denaturalization or alteration if he is to have, in his authentic life, his own authentic personal mode of being.

Hence we say that social life has a normative structure, while it would be preferable to say of personal life that it possesses an axiological or valuative structure. This is because personal life has essential and immanent values that integrate it through the free realization, or nonrealization, of religious, ethical, or esthetic norms. These norms may be more or less general or individualized. And they "have to be present" throughout the diverse and changing situations which, freely determined by man, make up life. In social life, the accent is on the norms, on that which must be. In saying that it possesses normative structure, we are saying not only that the norms are in life, as if there were life and also its norms, but that the norms *are* life. Or we could say that there is only life, which is not the life of man under norms as much as a certain mode of being of men consisting precisely in being a norm. The intersubjectivity proper to social life is a norm because it is a necessary form for living. Not only does it have to be so. Indeed, intersubjectivity imposes authentic demands whose justification roots in their inexorability as a form for living. If social life were only a chance phenomenon, something which happened by accident in the life of man, no demands would have foundation or justification. But the "dictatorship" of social life is justified because it constitutes a necessary dimension of existence.

Since the juridical norm belongs constitutionally to social life, everything in social life constitutes a normative reality and can take on the form of juridical normativity. For this reason, juridical liberty is identical not with the metaphysical liberty of the human person as person, but with the liberty of the social being, the liberty of the human person as a social being. It is the liberty of a being living in society, or living according to the forms and manners proper to that which is social, a being encased in society's structures. One of these structures is the norm. Consequently, the social norm integrates the concept of social liberty in the same way that the juridical norm integrates the concept of juridical liberty. To the extent it is "liberty," juridical liberty is the liberty of the human person. But it is "juridical" in that its concept contains a juridical norm that defines it. As "juridical liberty," therefore, it cannot coincide exactly with the liberty of the human person even if it is constructed in its image and likeness.

If, according to the overworked formula, a person is any man capable of rights and obligations, the essence of personality will consist in the condition of sui juris, in the possession of the self-rule and dignity which make him the subject, never the object of some possible juridical relation. Now, self-rule in the juridical sense can be possessed only by one who, in the full sense of the word, is owner or master of himself, one who is a human person. This is why, for Hegel, to be a person in general means being a person in the juridical sense.[20] Hegel regarded personality as only the formal and abstract aspect of subjectivity, as the affirmation of one's own mastery and one's own right. The counterpart of this is found in the idea of moral obligation (which, for the rest, represents an aspect as one-sided and unauthentic as the sphere of the person and its rights, and both are destined to be overruled in the sphere of the real and concrete ethics culminating, in Hegel's system, in the State).

But the juridical person, even though made in the image and likeness of the human person, is a specific category of social life. For this reason also, the range of juridical liberty, inasmuch as it is a "pared off" liberty, is not as broad as that of the metaphysical liberty of the person. Normally, because of an excess of the latter liberty, they do not coincide. In exceptional cases—but even here it is due to an ontological necessity—the lack is in metaphysical liberty and the excess is in juridical liberty. For the human being, despite his metaphysical and existential liberty, is not always juridically free. And at times the human being is free in the juridical sense, not as an individual human being but because of the formal unity accruing from his relations with others. This brings us to the problem, so important for the doctrine of juridical matters, of the discrepancy between real will and declared will. It also brings us to the problem of the collective juridical personality which presupposes the liberty of a being that is not a human person, or the (juridical) liberty of human beings that live, with special intensity, a relation of society especially defined by law.

Juridical personality pertains essentially to the human person. However, being a category of social life, it is a normative reality, and insofar as it is normative, it is a "construed" reality. The human person is a juridical person to the extent it finds itself in juridical situations, or to the extent it is a "social" person, under which condition it can find itself in juridical situations that are social situations. By reason of its being set in society, the person finds itself in different situations. But it also seeks and creates its own situations. Being set in situations or setting oneself in situations are the two fundamental ontological characteristics of personality. To the first correspond fundamentally one's obligations; to the second, one's privileges or subjective rights, although certain privileges correspond to the first, and obligations can be contracted in the second. And for this reason the essence of juridical personality is juridical liberty. For if in its first aspect liberty is the condition of obligation—insofar as the fulfillment of obligations carries a sanction with it—then in its second aspect it is the condition of privileges in that it implies negatively the nonprohibition and positively the possibility of doing something with juridical efficacy and, above all, the possibility of creating a world of situations in which to set one's own personality.

The intervention of the norm is decisive in that it serves to define what is strictly juridical within the social, and it serves to

cut back to its strict limits the sphere of metaphysical and existential liberty, defining the points beyond which self-rule may not
go.[21] In juridical terms, of what acts is the person master? In
other words, which acts will be imputed to the human person as
a social being, as truly its own and hence endowed with positive
or negative juridical significance, endowed with the recognition
or prohibition of an impediment? Here is where the norm intervenes, defining in each case the concrete juridical personality of
the subject. The human person, which generically has juridical
personality or subjectivity, is according to the specific case "in-
fractor" of a norm, subject of a right, "organ" of the state or of a
collective juridical person, or he lacks personality for a certain
order of relations, and so on. All of this is defined by the norms
which, upon the juridical fact of "imputation," give reality to the
juridical person, be it an individual or a collective person, since
these are analogous juridically. Juridical personality begins and
ends where the imputation, by the Law, of acts materially per-
petrated by a human subject begins and ends. An organ of the
state lacks juridical personality because the juridically efficacious
acts that such a human person realizes (one who acts socially
and juridically as an organ) are not imputed to him as his own by
law, and they neither modify his present juridical situation nor
move him into a new juridical situation, nor do they castigate him
for his omission. But as soon as certain acts are imputed to him as
his own, and fitting personal consequences are attributed to him
(for example, when a functionary or organ of the state responds
personally for the damages caused to a third party through his
having overstepped proper limits in the exercise of his duties),
juridical personality immediately emerges in that same human
subject.

Thus the person in the juridical sense exists, provided certain
acts of the human person are imputed to it by objective Law
and have juridical consequences. Meanwhile, the situation of the
person as organ transforms the person into a "transit station" of
judical imputation, which means that the acts which the person
realizes are not recognized and attributed to the person as its

own, that they have no juridical consequences for the person, and that they are imputed to something real (the case of representation) or ideal (a moral person) which is "out there." The collective person, then, is the ideal center where converge those lines of imputation that cover a number of physical persons. This is how we demonstrate the rigorously juridical character of juridical personality or of the being as an organ, etc. But the necessary substrate of this juridical quality is a human person, inasmuch as it possesses a social dimension.

II

H. Coing[22] has pointed out that, historically, the problem of a juridical concept of the person roots in civil law, as distinguished from the doctrine relative to human rights, which has developed in isolation from the doctrine of personality. With the advent of classical German philosophy, and especially of Kant, the two ideas—person and fundamental rights—receive a new impulse and the connection between them is finally perceived. This connection was also seen very clearly by the law historians, especially Savigny and Puchta, whose doctrine of the fiction is a consequence of the strict link between the ethical concept and the juridical concept of the personality of man. Even the Spanish Krausists saw this connection with great acuity, and it constituted one of the fundamental points of their juridical philosophy, as is clear in Joaquin Costa.[23] It was positivism that initiated the retrocession, causing the two concepts, personality and subjective rights, to be separated again and opening an abyss between private subjective rights and political rights, a separation which, in Coing's judgment, had already perturbed the broad and generous conception of the problem by Savigny.

Perhaps it is a mission of present-day philosophy of law to reestablish the link between the concept of the juridical person and the doctrine of human rights, seeing that both have their foundation in the ethical personality of man. "Since man is called to be an ethical person, he has to be a person for the Law and to possess rights in order to realize his ethical personality in free activity. The necessity of juridical concepts is founded in man's ethical personality; it is this ethical personality which holds them together and causes them to be. *Personas quarum causa* (*ius*) *constitutum est* (*Inst.* I, 2, 12). Law exists for the sake of man. Man is prior to Law; it must serve him. But man possesses a dignity of his own; he is called to give form to his life responsibly, by himself and for himself. This is how the Christian religion views Law. It is also how every superior ethical system views Law. Even the biological structure of man seems to point towards his liberty."[24]

In a similar sense, G. Burdeau affirms that the rights of the person are as remote from the determinisms of collective movements as they are from the arbitrary power of a definition orginating in the state. In fact, this exigency to which the Law responds cannot be manifested better than in an autonomous being, i.e., in a consciousness that cannot be reduced to social conformism and political servility. The person does not exist without the impulse that drives him toward others, without the anxiety that his presence in the world causes him. But this impulse and anxiety have no meaning unless they proceed from a free conscience and from a will that is master of its choices. It is in this autonomy of the person that the rights of the human person have their foundation. Not, indeed, in the form of benefits gained, but as faculties indispensable to man in the fulfillment of his personal vocation.

There is one paradoxical fact in the doctrinal order that has serious consequences in the political and legislative order. The juridical person is possible because the human person possesses a social dimension. And those very ideologies which accent one-sidedly the social character of man, even to the point of reducing him to this sole dimension, oppose the concept and exigencies of juridical personality.

We have already explained that social personality has its roots in human personality as such, and that it would be to mutilate it in its essential reality were we to reduce human personality to its social dimension as covering its entire reality. Juridical personality presupposes the social personality of man, but juridical personality is made in the image and likeness of human personality. If human personality disappears and nothing remains but social personality, then the supposite of juridical personality naturally subsists, but its substance, which is liberty, disappears. There remains the socialized man,[25] which is the man who has lost the substance of his liberty. And the socialized man can be a person in the juridical sense, but almost exclusively in the sense that personality implies responsibilities and obligations.

Without reckoning with this fact of the socialized man, it is difficult to understand much of what is going on today in the world, and especially the tremendous mass of confusion that lies at the base of all this talk of human rights. It is the same confusion that pervades the doctrine of Rousseau which crosses the two ideas—essentially different—of liberalism and democracy and which operates on the concept of an individual dehumanized in order to become socialized and tending to become even more socialized by the demands of the doctrine of *la volonté générale*. The totalitarian meaning of Rousseau's doctrine was seen with absolute clarity in the last century by H. Taine and strictly liberal thinkers like Laboulaye, for whom liberty had perished as "the victim of the principle of popular sovereignty." The theory of Rousseau tends, for this student of the Constitution of the United States, to destroy the will of the individual for the benefit of society: "in a word, the more the citizen sees himself annihilated, the freer he will be."[26] Irremediably totalitarian (or despotic, in nineteenth century terminology) in its tendencies, democracy cannot guarantee the rights of man. "We live for the most part under the rule of the errors sowed by Rousseau. Popular sovereignty for us is the universal will, the sum total of all the individual wills. It extends to all and comprises all. In this sense, the sovereignty is absolute, and hence despotic. Consequently, it can only lend to tyranny."[27] With extraordinary acuity, Laboulaye delineates the difference between these tendencies in French democracy and the strict liberalism of the American Constitution. For the Americans, "the sovereignty of the people is nothing beyond the general will applied to the common interests of the country. But the common interests do not constitute the whole of the country. Besides them, there are individual interests over which the general will exercises no rule at all. Conscience, thought, speech, liberty of movement, and activity are things that pertain to the individual as a man and not as a citizen. No individual, no collectivity, has any right to infringe upon these things."[28] In a very similar sense, Benjamin Constant warned against the illusion of conceding too much importance to the abstract principle of popular sovereignty, as if it could augment the sum of individual liberties. He used to say that the fundamental principle of democracy has frequently contributed to the triumph of the worst despotisms. The true defense against these (despotisms, whether of monarchs or of the people) lies in the division of powers, parliamentarism, the right of resistance, freedom of thought, and so on.[29]

But the sharp thought of de Tocqueville penetrated even more deeply into the sociological substrate of the American political phenomenon. He saw perfectly that democratic egalitarianism and atomism open the door to despotism by weakening the forces of resistance of individuals and groups and by facilitating the formation of large administrative and political concentrations. Though less evident than that of the privileged classes, this despotism is much deeper because it levels even the most insignificant differences and attributes to the collectivity all the power that it removes from the several individuals.[30]

The problem of human personality and of human rights rests today upon the foundation of this sociological and political reality. The so-called totalitarian doctrines are only an acute expression of a broad process of totalization and homogenization which transcends their ideological encasement and which consequently also reaches into democracy, precisely because that process actively shares the same tendencies that are immanent in democracy.[31] For this reason, the "citizen" transcends the "man" more and more, and the problem of individual liberty becomes the problem of political liberty. Liberal liberty is being substituted by democratic liberty. But democratic liberty is a participation in a political totality, and consequently the intangible sphere of the person and his creative center plays a less and less central role. And it is true that the juridical liberty of the person is a "construed" liberty, but the materials employed in construing it are authentic liberty, a metaphysical and existential liberty. As a consequence, if this latter liberty is lacking, no construing of juridical liberty is possible. And it is of little importance in this connection that this metaphysical liberty cannot be destroyed by juridical and political systems. For if, on the one hand, the fact of socialization is continuously depriving it of substance, and if the norms, on the other hand, deny its substantial value and the principle prevails that man only has value as a member of the state or a class or a race, etc., and care is taken that this ideology prevails with efficacy upon individual consciences, then everything has already been done to destroy liberty. Of course, it could go one step further. Indeed, in the most tyrannical and brutal systems, attempts are still being made with medical-pharmaceutical processes against the very reality of free will.

Thus it is not paradoxical that the juridical notion of the person passes onto a secondary level where only the social dimension of the human personality is given importance. In those ideologies, in accenting man's personal insignificance outside of the totality and in tracing the reason of his proper existence and worth to this totality, the personality is broken down into pure social categories, and the most personal matter of all, the fulfillment of one's personal destiny, the "business of salvation," is also converted into a public and social affair, indeed into a political question. The sense of personal responsibility decreases, and with it the sentiment or feeling of liberty, which is abdicated in favor of the masses. This is why certain circles end up distrusting the juridical concept of personality. In the nebulous metaphysics of Hegelian neoidealism, the "community" was the sole reality of personality. The individual was dissolved in this metaphysically interpreted social category, and the only fundamental juridical concept remaining was that of being a "member" of this community.[32]

In the face of these negations, the person and its center, which is the substance of liberty, have to be defended at all costs. The defense can be taken up from the liberal standpoint or from the Christian standpoint. But there are reasons to believe that liberalism can do very little by way of effective defense here. Benedetto Croce, who has good cause to know, affirms this clearly in saying that the usual liberalism is activism, a perversion of the love of liberty, which by the very logic of its process terminates liberty or tends to its contrary, i.e., it tends "to the dominion of individual over individual, to subjection to others, and hence also to subjection to oneself, to the crushing of the personality which at first imagined it would become stronger, but which, unbridling it and taking away its moral consciousness, deprived it, instead, of its inner life and led it thus into ruin."[33]

It is of course true that Croce claims to represent a philosophical liberalism that is more authentic than the usual which is confusedly mixed with democracy and obscurely linked to the interests of the bourgeoisie and so-called economic liberalism. Somewhat in the manner of such thinkers as Benjamin Constant, Laboulaye, and De Tocqueville, Croce professes a certain aristocratism which is integrated into an idealistic philosophical conception of things that separates him from the historical sense of those liberals. According to Croce, liberalism offers nothing to the purposes and methods of the masses; in opposition to the democratic method, liberalism does not claim to call all men to politics and government by putting them all on the same level because this is contrary to the very nature of men, who are not all statesmen any more than all men are by nature poets, philosophers, or heroes. The political ideal of democracy postulates a religion of quantity, of mechanics, of calculating reason, or a religion of nature such as was developed in the seventeenth century. Liberalism, on the other hand, postulates a religion of quality, activity, and spirituality as was being formed at the beginning of the nineteenth century. If democracy lacked the ideal which is the regulating concept of liberty, it would be transformed immediately into tyranny. And this happens when democracy, in the extreme form of Jacobinism, confusing the people with inorganic, frenetic, and impulsive multitudes and exercising its tyranny in the name of the people, attains ends that are opposed to those it proposed to seek. Democratism, radicalism, and freemasonry are also examples of liberal dogmas converted into material things, dogmas which are without flexibility or vitality and which are the instruments of sects and parties, dogmas which do not contribute to elevating intellectual and moral life or to promoting liberty itself.[34]

Insisting upon the purely ethical and philosophical character of liberalism, Croce affirms against Laski that liberal life may have a transitory, but never a permanent, connection with the private ownership of land or industry. It is especially opposed to the falsification of moral life under any form, whether absolutist or democratic, capitalist or proletarian, czarist or bolshevist, the myth of the race or that of the hammer and sickle. The liberal idea has a religious nature which continuously judges and dominates economic history, and it is not economic history making use of religions as masks. Economic liberalism and ethical-political liberalism both find their origins in the immanent and historical conception of life and in the concept of truth, not as something made beforehand but something which is being made continuously, yet economic liberalism cannot be converted into ethical theory and into the supreme norm of social life.[35]

Accordingly—confirming Carl Schmitt's assertion that liberalism is not politics—Croce's liberal conception is a metapolitical liberalism which goes beyond the formal theory of politics, and in a certain sense it also goes beyond the formal theory of ethics, to coincide with a total conception of the world and reality. Historicism and philosophical idealism identify with the liberal conception of life, for which liberty is activity, spirituality, the eternal creation of history.[36]

This philosophical and metapolitical aspect of liberalism confers upon it an irremediable esoteric character; the liberal conception of life can be the conception of only a select few. The problem is how to come down to the level of political efficacy, how to

bring it about that the masses conserve a moral life that constitutes the substance of their personality and their liberty. In this
point, Croce has to have recourse to the dialectics of the historical
process which he regards with radical optimism: out of the thesis
of oppression (in the concrete case of Italy, fascist oppression)
will come forth the antithesis of the passion for liberty. This optimism is probably quite gratuitous and only affirms a commonplace. No one doubts that when man tires of an "oppression," he
seeks "liberty." But what no one has demonstrated, and never
will demonstrate, is that the liberty with which the masses enrich
themselves when emancipated from former bonds is that learned
and philosophical liberty sought for others by the chosen spirits
capable of professing it, such as Croce. For this reason—leaving
aside the intrinsic value of the doctrine and its theological and
dogmatic aspects—from the point of view of political efficacy, the
Christian conception of life constitutes a more solid dike against
socialization and, consequently, a stronger guarantee of liberty
than liberalism. The Christian view of life is not an esoteric conception, but essentially diffusible and communicable. In pro-
claiming the existence of a soul with a destiny of salvation whose
realization is a strictly personal affair, the Christian view creates
the supposites of an inner life that sets up an impenetrable barrier
against any socializing tendency. This establishes the sphere of
the personality on the highest value of life and affirms a primary
fundamental right for man. All the rest will come as a necessary
consequence.

In this necessary consequence, it will be good to avoid the
errors of old individualism and to let Law take a course inclined
to the affirmation of a transcendental order of religious and moral
truths, a course inclined to the maintenance of those other historical truths whose negation would destroy the foundations of
national life, a course inclined to the satisfaction of the demands
of the common good and of social justice. The reasoning of the
new legal currents that tend in this direction can be seen, to
quote A. Borda,[37] in the sense of the moral and the just that nests
in the heart of man. Individualistic liberalism leads to excess in

the exercise of rights; it leads to the use of the Law by those in power to impose themselves on the weak; it leads to the tragic isolation of the individual in his selfishness and his misery, according to Maritain; and it leads to the disappearance of the very idea of the common good and the common responsibility. Thus society races to the rebellion of the parts against the whole, as it was so well put by Auguste Comte. But the contemporary world is tired of injustices and is not disposed to tolerating them *ad infinitum.*

However, we must not exaggerate the anti-individualistic reaction. We do well in denying the absolute and anarchical character of subjective rights. State intervention is also good as long as it is a question of correcting an injustice and of re-establishing equity. But it is necessary to take care that the state does not invade certain rights which man possesses as man and that it does not regard man as nothing more than an economic means. The fundamental problem of modern Law is that of reconciling the interests of man with those of society. The individual cannot operate antisocially, but the State cannot intervene in what touches on human liberty and dignity which, being of divine origin, consequently belong to God before they belong to the State. Men frequently forget that this point of departure is essential in the juridical order. But they turn their attention back to God every time a new absolutism, whether of the right or the left, suppresses liberties and offends the dignity of man. To the omnipotence of man we can oppose only the omnipotence of God. This Christian conception makes it possible to reconcile the person with society, the individual with the State. It permits us to declare with the force they deserve the rights which belong to man as man and which the State cannot fail to recognize, rights which we must conceive as attributes of an essentially social being and which cannot be exercised beyond what is allowed by the conjugation of man with society.

From what we have said, it is inferred that there is an absolute right which is fundamental for man and which is the basis and condition of all other rights. It is the right of always being recog-

nized as a human person. And since the person unfolds quickly in
the ontological sphere of what we have called personal life, which
implies an interior or private dimension, the first right of man is
the right of privacy, the right of having his privacy respected or,
which is the same thing, the right of man that Law claim not to
be anything more than a "form of social life." This respect does
not consist only in abstinence; it implies, besides this negative
(necessary, nonetheless) position, the positive attitude of creating and furthering those religious and moral realities that make
for the enrichment of man's interior personality and which set up
dikes against socializations in all its forms, above all in its spiritual
form. Without personalities rich in interior life, freedom lacks
meaning. It will exist only as external political liberty, but he
alone is genuinely free of whom it can be truly affirmed that
he is a "personality." For this reason, even historically, liberty
and subjective rights had their origin in the actions of vigorous personalities capable of creating resistances—a fact seen as
readily by traditionalist thinkers as by liberal thinkers such as
De Tocqueville or Ortega y Gasset.

But the human person also possesses a social dimension in
which juridical-normative realities, to which juridical personality
belongs, move and have their proper sphere. Hence it is also a
fundamental right of man to be recognized as a juridical personality. Personality in the juridical sense also implies a sphere of
liberty. This liberty is a "construed" liberty in the sense that it
constitutes a "trimming" of the sphere of existential liberty, a
trimming brought about by juridical norms which in fact correspond to a specific ideology. The problem, then, will be to determine what a priori exigencies can be regarded as universally
valid. One runs the risk here of falling into certain excesses (supposed natural law positions) and of elevating a historically conditioned ideology to the position of unassailable dogma. But this
risk must not cause us to justify a relativist distrust for, or to
renounce what corresponds essentially to, the human person. In
the meanwhile, everything depends upon distinguishing carefully between affirmations of ideological or metaphysical nature

(e.g., in the area of religious liberty, the assertion that man has the right to choose freely among religions, on the supposition that any religion is good), the a priori exigencies of juridical liberty (e.g., that man should not be punished juridically for professing one religion and not another), and the concrete exigencies of legislative politics (e.g., whether or not the State can establish, for the accession to certain public responsibilities, distinctions respecting the religion of those aspiring to those responsibilities). This is to say that we must distinguish between theory and simple ideology in order to separate the essential truth about man in his personal and social dimensions from the mere wish to organize Law and the State according to concrete forms that provide wide variability without violating the highest postulates.

Formulating this doctrine in more precise juridical terminology and still maintaining the general character of fundamental assertions, we would say with Coing[38] that the juridical order must recognize the possibility of individuals having subjective rights, but also, we would add, of acquiring them and disposing of them to the maximum, since no juridical order is possible which does not recognize some subjective right. In other words, the juridical order must recognize the juridical personality of men. But it must amplify the concept of juridical personality to comprise both the juridical capacity and the capacity (public and private) of operation, since the juridical capacity is only a minimum of juridical personality, which, to be complete, must also include the capacity of operating with juridical efficacy. Moreover, the juridical order must attribute to man, in conformity with his nature, certain liberties and certain rights that are even antecedent to the State and the political community. These are the so-called human rights which protect human liberty and the possibility of its unfolding in specific relations that correspond to the natural qualities of man. Both of these exigencies have the same foundation: the ethical dignity of man, which imposes itself with invincible and binding force.

These assertions doubtless have the shortcoming of being somewhat abstract and vague. But this is the price of seeking fundamental and universally applicable truth in any area. Yet fundamentals and universals cannot be disregarded if we wish to proceed on a safe path in search of more concrete goals. Indeed, there is need of clarity in fundamentals if we are to achieve any worthwhile concretion in this problem that has engaged humanity so passionately in our time. Perhaps in this light my contribution is not in vain.

Eduardo Nicol

Don Eduardo Nicol (b.1907), a student of Joaquin Xirau and Carreras y Artau at the University of Barcelona and of Ortega y Gasset and Xavier Zubiri at the University of Madrid, became a professor of philosophy at Barcelona. He left Spain after the Civil War and emigrated to Mexico, where he is now teaching at the National University. Professor Nicol, a distinguished writer, is especially versed in psychology and metaphysics. Among his major publications are Historicismo y existentialismo (1950), La vocacion humana (1953), Metafisica de la expresion (1957), and Los principios de la ciencia (1965).

"History and Truth" appeared in Los principios de la ciencia (Mexico City: Fondo de Cultura Economica, 1965) 42–93. © 1965 by Eduardo Nicol. Grateful acknowledgment is made to the author for permission to reprint.

V. HISTORY AND TRUTH

I

The Four Relations of Knowledge

In view of the general crisis of science in our day, it is essential for us to conceptualize and systematically organize in our minds the fact of historicity, which I have identified in other studies as the center from which all the manifestations of the crisis irradiate. The fact itself is not new. Historicity is not a characteristic recently acquired by science, but it belongs to science as a constituent part and, as such, has always been present. Science did not begin to be historical with historicistic philosophy; it is neither the work of this philosophy nor a consequence of the present crisis of physics. What is new is the more or less confused consciousness that men of science have of historicity, those who became aware of it precisely in the unaccustomed acceleration with which their particular disciplines, especially that of physics, are advancing today and in the consequent necessity of constantly reviewing the main categories and theoretical schemes which previously were considered immutable. The conflict presents itself as an apparent incompatibility between the fact of the historicity of science and the timeless value of the truth which was traditionally assigned to its laws. This problem can be resolved only by an-alyzing the modalities of the constituent relations of knowledge.

Since the very origins of science in pre-Socratic philosophy, and even more clearly since Plato, scientific knowledge has been for-mally established upon two fundamental and complementary rela-tions, each of which defined one of the aspects of truth. These were the *epistemological relation* and the *logical relation*.[1]

The epistemological relation is evidently the more primary of the two. It is the relation which is established between the sub-ject of knowledge and the objects in general, and it is precisely through this relation that the subject succeeds in obtaining infor-mation about the ontological and ontic character of those objects. The emergence of science as a special modality of knowledge was not needed for men to realize that the simple noting of things does not constitute complete knowledge. Authentic knowledge is thought. It is an action which the subject concludes on the basis of his immediate apprehensions of objects and with which he attempts to represent to himself not the mere presence of those objects, but also their interdependence. Knowledge is discursive because things themselves are related to one another, depend upon one another, or arise from one another, and in short consti-tute an apparent order which is subdivided into diverse orders and special groupings of objects. In truth, simple perception never reveals only the mere presence of some objects disposed in a static perspective. It reveals a presence and a function. This is why knowledge does not stop in its purely reproductive phase. This phase is nothing more than an abstraction worked out after-wards by psychological analysis. In the reality of life, even primi-tive societies produce a form of thought in which, rudimentary as it is, we find testimony of a desire to respond to the question of *how* and *why*.

The object itself, then, is never a mere presence for the subject. To put this in another way, the presence of the object is a phe-nomenon which includes both being and relation at once, and hence poses a question which is not resolved by mere presence. The isolated thing does not tell us how much of itself must be investigated in order to know it sufficiently; rather, it defers to another present or absent thing without which the being of the first cannot be firmly grasped. Furthermore, being presents itself as dynamic, and its changing is a part of its very being. To know it is to explain its changing. For this reason, even mythical thought is discursive, which means it is causal. It is not satisfied with merely noting things but aspires to explaining them. The origin of things, like the influence which some things exercise over others, also forms a part of the definition of those things, and it must be integrated into our knowledge of them. The question What is this?—which is a question concerning essence— involves the question of origin Where does this come from, what produced it? and this is a causal question. To explain anything, one has to investigate its cause. This is a constant of all thought; it appears even in myth and reappears later in physics. In science the cause is a concept, but physical philosophy does not invent the notion of a "producing agent." It inherits that notion and, to be precise, conceptualizes it. As Cassirer pointed out very well, the first determinism is mythological.[2] In this sense all knowledge is rational, and this includes myth, although this reason (myth) is not yet the logical reason of the *episteme*. That of myth is not a critical reason which, besides examining reality, watches over itself. Nor is it limited to reflecting reality passively, as a mirror. It is itself an active reality. All human reason is νοῦς ποιητικός. Passive reason is a contradiction in terms.

But this lack of critical vigilance in reason is what distinguishes prescientific from scientific thought, what distinguishes the thought in myth and in the common *doxa* from the methodical thought in the rigorous *episteme*. The whole difference lies in method because myth is also systematic, discursive, and causal, as even mere opinion can be. Methodology is the critical action which the *logos* exercises upon itself. It is logic. However, mythical thought also has its own logic. It is not an arbitrary and anarchical discourse, but one which has an inner coherence.

The first pre-Socratic philosophers thought that mythical thought and opinion did not represent things in a way that was worthy of credit, did not represent things as they are *in themselves* independent of subjective belief and traditional conceptions. Although it succeeds in being coherent, the *doxa* does not reflect the objective coherency of things. It does not even aspire to being verified or shared by rational and unemotional motives. With his opinion the subject marks the difference that distinguishes him from others. Thus, the wish "to be right," which is the characteristic attitude of a person who has an opinion, is the contrary of the wish "to explain," in which it is not one's own convictions that impose themselves on others, but realities that impose themselves on one's convictions, Myth, for its part, produces a state of community in belief, but its inner organization contains only an allusive representation of things. Its coherence is that of a new world which the myth itself creates and superimposes upon the real world. And what this symbolic world expresses is rather a collective feeling for life.

The general and even unanimous participation in this belief was not a sufficient guarantee of truth. The social fact of the prevalence of certain opinions is one thing, and the adequation of those opinions to the things themselves is quite another. It may appear that the content of belief expresses some profound modalities of the human condition and of how man conceives his position in the world and his relationship with things. But these modalities and this position are changing. And in truth, when philosophy emerges, the uniformity and vital efficacy of the belief is in the process of being dissolved. The critical sense produces a multiplicity of opinions which are no less subjective than those of mythology but which do not contribute to a community of thought. The intelligence from which the *doxa* emerges is not yet fully rational, but it has lost the binding force of myth. Science then becomes a new form of human bond, the institution of a community of thought based upon reason.

But on what type of reason? Upon logical reason. This *logical* qualification of the *logos* can appear redundant if we forget that myth is not purely irrational but is a specific kind of *logos*. On what is the distinction between these two types of reason based?

We today are inclined to believe that the difference was rooted in the formal and normative character of logic. Without overlooking this character, it must be observed that the primary distinction between the scientific and the prescientific *logos* is more epistemological than formal. The idea which predominated in the mind of the pre-Socratic philosophers was that of method. *Method is a way of dealing with things,* and it is only by derivation that it requires a way of dealing with the thoughts we form of things. To understand this well, the concept which we must bear in mind is that of objectivity. The subjective and mystical community of mythology has been overcome. In its place appears the subjectivity of the individual *doxa.* With the first examinings of a critical and reflective thought, uniformity is lost in anarchy. Science attempts to re-establish the community and uniformity of thought by changing the point of support, founding it for the first time upon the object: only upon the object, and not upon the subject. Objectivity consists in nothing but the subordination of subjectivity. It is not obtained in Greece as it is obtained later in modern philosophy by means of a technique or an artifice of reduction. The methodological reduction of the Greeks is a catharsis, a vital attitude that permits one to attend to the object and to found upon it a thought that is not perturbed by the particular subjectivity. Hence, as the requirement of all science, objectivity is a property of the *thought,* and not of the *perception.* The perception on which myth is based is also objective. It is the mythological thought which is not objective. Thus, in science the thought no longer expresses the impression that things produce in the collective subject or in the individual subject, but it expresses what the things themselves are apart from that appearance which is the mystical and binding *doxa* in myth and which is the arbitrary and dissolving *doxa* in individual thought.

Uniformity and community are then no longer the social phenomenon of an either reflective or unreflective adhesion of subjects to previously formulated opinions and beliefs. It has to be, and the Greek aspires to its being, the inevitable result of a confrontation of thought with the things themselves. And this, naturally, with the condition that the thought has also been purified, much as the attitude of him who thinks rationally is purified. The "guide on the way" is method. And as it is derived from method, logic later becomes the technique of rectitude for the *logos*.

The basic error of Husserl derived, as we shall see later on in this study, from his faulty interpretation of the *doxa*. For him, and indeed for the majority of philosophers, the *doxa* is any form of prescientific knowledge, or any knowledge lacking method. But the *doxa*, even though it has no method, is not prescientific *knowledge* but prescientific *thought*. Primary knowledge is something else: it is the apprehension of the object, not its interpretation, and can have the characters of apodictic evidence which is not found—and this does not surprise us—in mere opinions with which the subject grows into himself in the interested version he offers of things. Hence the overcoming of the *doxa* in no way requires the suspension of the primary data of experience which serve as the basis for the *episteme* as well as for the *doxa*. It does not imply even a preliminary voiding of the world and all that it contains, including one's neighbor. The reality of human and natural objects is not a matter of belief or of subjective opinion.

The method of science is not that which permits it to seek primary and apodictic evidence. It is that which permits the elimination of the irrational opinions that are mounted upon the primary evidence. Science does not create, by means of method, a world apart, a world inaccessible to the uninitiated. The world of science is founded upon sharable evidence. As a result, its rationality is a community. But the community which is lost in the anarchical *doxa* is also lost in the transcendental modality of methodical reduction. The *doxa* permits at least an intercommunication which is partly intellectual and partly emotional or volitive. In the transcendental reduction, however, there is neither a community of evidence nor a common participation in the knowledge.

Another error which also arises from time to time in the historical course of science results from a decline of the methodical spirit, i.e., from a loss of the sense of objectivity. Such has been the case, especially in sophistic periods, with thinkers who attempt to connect philosophy with the modalities of thought which philosophy itself has succeeded in overcoming. Some conceive philosophy as a *Weltanschauung* and thus defer it to the mythological phase which preceded it, as if philosophy, instead of being the *episteme par excellence,* were only a more diversified, but more arid, abstract, and prosaic form of myth. Others confuse it with the *doxa* by conceiving it as the mere personal expression of the philosopher, an expression conditioned by the life and historical situation of the philosopher. Certainly, this expression lays claims to an authority superior to that of the uninitiated. But it is unable to show reasons that confirm its claims.

In none of these cases does philosophy find itself in a position to establish truth. In one case, that of Descartes and Husserl, we would say that it is so because of an excess or abuse of methodology which causes the primary objective and the community to disappear when the truth resides in the subject alone. In the other cases, because of a lack of methodology, the results are much the same. This dissociation of individual thoughts, in whatever form it occurs, has always been, since Protagoras, the gravest symptom that has threatened science beecause it attacks it in its principles and in its very roots as a form of knowledge. But science, either unconcerned with these deviations or crying out against them, always asserts itself as a community of thought, a community held together by methodology and logic. Logic without logicism; form without formalism.

The Greeks observed very well in the birth of science (and that is precisely what it was, a birth) that thought was not secure, as discursive truth, only with the primary cognitive relation. The presence of things is evident. Indeed it is from things that every possible form of thought takes its departure. *To take its departure* means not to be detained there; it means that thought is not limited to registering and reproducing presences which are evident. Thought is *logos*. It is a subjective reason that attempts to find the reason of what is objective. It turns out that it is not enough for this true reason, this truth which is defined as adequation of thought with the reality thought,[3] simply to be in accord with reality. Thought is an action, and although it is sustained by certain positive evidence, it is not enough for thought to recognize and identify these evidences. It has to discourse about them, and for this it requires a regular and uniform procedure. If the *relations of thought* are not regulated *with itself*, there is no guarantee that thought will attain *adequation with reality*. The particular science which is logic is thus born of the necessity of self-vigilance in thought, and it is the methodical form of that introspection or reflection which the critical intelligence already began with the nonmethodical *doxa*.

With logic thus instituted as a science, a science without which science itself in general cannot proceed securely, true thought can be defined as a double adequation: adequation with the real and adequation with itself. To put it in academic terminology, we can say that there are two aspects to truth: a material aspect (in reference to things) and a formal aspect (internal coherency). But we have already indicated that logical science is not the first logic that ever existed. Even without the historical facts that confirm it, it is not difficult to understand *a priori* that the *logos* essentially contains a logic, some logic. The *logos* cannot be alogical. It can be illogical by default, by an inner breakdown of its proper mechanism. Hence the necessity of the precept. Logic, then, is not superimposed upon the *logos* as if it were something foreign to its natural function. The preceptive grows out of this function which is natural, but not infallible. The most elemental intelligibility of discourse, in situations of intersubjective verbal communication, implies a logic. Really and effectively, grammar is a logic. But grammar, as the primary logic of language, exists long before men discover its existence or invent either the name of grammar to designate the formalizations of grammatical facts or the system or rules that permits them from then on to distinguish between good and bad grammar.

Now the philosophical invention of logic is, with respect to scientific thought, something comparable to what grammar represents with respect to common verbal expression. It is neither a pure invention nor the discovery of a new dimension of the *logos*, but the application of a τέχνη, or a regulatory system, to certain functional modalities which the *logos* already possesses by nature. In a strict sense, logic is not a science or *episteme,* since it does not concern itself with real objects. Rather, it is an auxiliary technique of science, as grammar is the τέχνη of verbal expression.

Consequently, when we distinguish between *natural* logic and normative logic, we note immediately that the new logic, that which Greek science worked out in order to facilitate its own task, is not, regardless of how indispensable it is, something primary in the complex of constituent relations of knowledge. The necessity of this artifice, which serves to maintain canonically pure the relation of thought with itself, is only instrumental and hence something derived, secondary, and auxiliary. The basic relation is always the cognitive relation, or that which sustains thought with the things themselves. Thus, just as a science of being, called metaphysics, is not necessary for the human subject to dispose of an evidence of being and to dispose of a knowledge of beings which permits him to conduct his own existence, so is the institution of a logical science or technique not necessary for the *logos* to function logically. Logic only purifies, normalizes, and unifies that function for the specific purposes of a scientific task to which it is subordinated by nature. This originary subordination limits the range of its jurisdiction. It means that, by itself, logic can never solve any problem of knowledge.

The *natural* logical fact is the fact of the internal congruency which we find in any symbolic form, whether it is scientific or whatever. But the particular system of a formal logic is quite another thing. This system is historical, and its evolution depends in its turn upon the progressive refinement in formalism and upon the requirements of positive knowledge. No formal system has autonomous validity. (Validity here means efficacy or cognitive utility.) But it is precisely the progress made in that internal formal refinement that has brought about in our days the notion of a sufficiency of logic. The legitimacy of the purely formal investigations of the specialist permits him to forget the subordination of logic with respect to epistemology, which is like the subordina-

tion of the symbol with respect to the thing symbolized. From
autonomy of science, then, we have passed to a claimed hegem-
ony, as if symbolic formalism were the only criterion of validity
in science in general. The real situation is just the reverse: what
determines the value of formalism is its epistemological utility.
Without the first constituent relation of knowledge, which is the
relation of the knowing subject with the object known, the second
relation, or the logical relation of thought with itself, would be
a vain play of pure symbols without content.

Thus we discover, in examining the history of science, the possibility of there being more than one logic. In the historic course
of thought, the positive knowledge of real objects and the requirements of the theoretical construction can and often do oblige us
to make changes in the logical instrument which we employ for
that knowledge. The primary epistemological relation may also
impose *alterations of modality* in the logical relation. Thus new
logics arise which are equally scientific or useful for scientific
work, even though they may contrast with the traditional logic
based upon the principle of noncontradiction. Hence there is no
way of justifying absolutism in any particular logical system. All
formal systems are capable of being internally transformed by
changing their axioms, and they do not necessarily cease, thereby,
to be systematic or congruent. The most notorious case of this is
that of non-Euclidean geometrical systems. And years before
Lobatchevski and Riemann, Hegel introduced a reform which
was, in the field of logic, comparatively more radical than the
mathematical innovation represented by non-Euclidean geometry.
For non-Parmenidean logic, called dialectics, not only does not
avoid the contradiction but actually implies it, and in fact, in
effecting a type of axiomatic alteration, it puts logic back into that
intimate contact with being which it had lost during its purely
formal development.

This does not mean that the logic of noncontradiction cannot
and should not develop internally, like mathematics, as a pure
abstract system for combining things. The more complex and
purified the formal scheme of logic is, the better it will be able

to serve for scientific work. But it is just this service that determines the measure of its usefulness. Nor is mathematics in itself anything but an *ars combinatoria.* The epistemological value of its formal schemes always depends upon the use that real sciences can make of it. But the positive knowledge of the real, in these sciences, can never bend or diminish in validity because of a requirement of that mathematical system whose role is to serve as an instrument. On the contrary, the mathematical instrument can and often does prove inadequate for representing some already known aspect of nature, with the result that the specific requirements of a science of realities impose upon mathematics the obligation of perfecting and enriching its formal schemes.

A similar thing happens with logic. When it is reality itself— that is, some determinate sector of it—that resists the scheme of noncontradiction logic, the authentic scientific measure will consist in proposing a different logical scheme whose application is adequate to that reality. The *logos* must never be imposed upon being. Logic is a *form* for thinking about being, and hence is to be subordinated to being. In short, though a legitimate and independent formal science, logic nevertheless has no epistemological value of its own. The usefulness of logic is always based upon the onto-logical. It is this that Hegel's discovery demonstrates. It is a conception of being distinct from the Platonic and Aristotelic conception, a conception of being in time that is favored by the constitution of a new logic distinct from that noncontradiction logic which was linked in its origins with Parmenides, Plato, and Aristotle to the ontology of timeless being. Thus a science of realities should never be subjected to the rule of a determinate logical scheme, even when it is a question of the scheme based upon the axiom of noncontradiction, which is also the basis of mathematics (for mathematics is not the sole and universal instrument of scientific knowledge).

Logic and epistemology form, then, one and the same whole body in science, a single functional unit, with two aspects which are complementary. But, whatever its symbolic form, the logical relation, which is a constituent relation of thought, does not necessarily imply the exclusive adoption of any particular formal system.

II

We hold, then, as a principle that the discourse of thought can be adequate to the reality thought when the thought is adequate to itself, when it is congruous with itself.

Since Greece, with an uninterrupted continuity, science has been developing without altering this formula of truth. Indeed this formula seemed so infallible that it came to be regarded as something evident in itself. Thus comparing some systems with others, all the variants of doctrine that were discovered left this common basis untouched. Modern philosophy has not altered this situation. The formal element and the material element of knowledge could be conceived in one way or in another. But in both idealist metaphysics, beginning with Descartes, and the empiricism and critical metaphysics of Kant, those two elements were unanimously considered as the basic and sole elements of knowledge.

It was for the fact of historicity to overthrow this formula. Historicity revealed the existence of *a third relation* of thought. But this new relation could not be simply superadded and integrated into the other two. Indeed, the historical relation overthrew that traditional integration even to the point of *seeming incompatible with the epistemological relation and with the logical relation.* If truth depends upon the situation, how can a pure adequation of thought with its object be expressed in it? Or conversely, if truth is reached by means of the bilateral material and formal adequation, how can it follow the mutations of history? Furthermore, it seems that a formal system must be still more independent of these mutations: its validity depends upon the *a priori* evidence of its axioms. In short, truth cannot be at once temporal and timeless. If it expresses what being is, it cannot change with time; if it changes with time, it will not give a faithful expression of being. Thus one of the constituent elements of thought interferes with the efficacy of the other two.

However, historicity was not a hypothesis or a simple theoretical invention that could be disposed of critically. The historicist philosophies which arose after the Hegelian proposition are susceptible to criticism. But the criticism can work only on the way of conceptualizing and integrating the fact of historicity with other facts of a body of doctrine. No criticism of the historicist systems can deny the fact from which they all take their origin. What that fact reveals is that *history is a component of science, not an extrinsic factor.* Therefore, science has to examine itself as a process of evolution, and not as a pure timeless relation of thought with reality. This means that from now on science itself appears as a proper reality, as an order of phenomena which must itself also be analyzed scientifically (and, naturally, with working tools that no individual science can furnish). As a consequence, *epistemology has to include history.* Putting it in other terms, the traditional distinction between what has been called academically the "historical point of view" and the "systematic point of view" has disappeared from the scene. The systematic viewpoint inevitably embraces whatever can be observed from the historical point of view.

In order to make this scientific analysis of the phenomena implicated in "the fact of the historicity of science," it is necessary to clarify our concept of situation more precisely. In the first place, it is said that a thought somehow depends upon the situation in which it is produced.[4] But what do we understand by the term "situation" in general, or how can a situation be determined formally? If we imagine the historical course of science as the trajectory of an object in motion, we find it convenient to set up a sort of historical referential which will permit us to situate the phases of that process. This is something like the referential of the three coordinates of space and the coordinate of time which the physicist uses to represent an object's successive spacial positions in successive moments of time. If the physical movement is produced on one plane, the object's actual position at the moment "t" is represented geometrically by tracing perpendicular paths from point "o" toward the coordinates "x" and "y." The intersection of the ordinate and the absciss will determine the position of the object within the referential. Now the historical situation of science must be determined analogously by the intersection of two coordinates. The ordinate, in this historical referential, is the line that corresponds to what we would designate as history's *vertical structure;* the absciss would be equivalent to the complementary *horizontal structure.*

These two structures are real, although we can and must use a concept of them as a methodological instrument for the interpretation of the facts. The effective existence of a structure in the historical process is the best defense against scepticism. This means that historical relativity, which is a fact, does not necessarily infer a relativist conclusion. At first impression, the truth seems to be relative to time, each situation seems to have its own truth, and there seems to be no organic connection between one particular truth and those that follow it. Each truth seems to be valid—relatively—in and for the situation which produces it, and it seems to remain circumscribed in that situation. Changing the circumstances, it seems that the truth will also have to change. It would appear that the circumstances impose themselves upon truth, but that no one imposes himself upon the circumstances.

However, the course of the circumstances could be directed, and a sort of internal principle of mutation could occur. If time itself (historical time) has a structure, we can no longer say that the relation of truth with time immerses the truth irrevocably in the confusion resulting from subjective arbitrarity, the basic conveniences of life, the change of perspectives, or the chance factor in personal events. If the structure is evident, these dangers will be avoided. For subjectivism, the perspectivism cannot stand if it is clear that the relativity of thought with respect to historical time is a fact that shows the act of thinking to be integrated in a process which has a rational structure. In defending the objectivity of knowledge, then, it is not necessary to invoke only the first of its constituent relations—which is the relation of the subject with the object—in order to preserve the truth from being circumscribed in the individual subject. If subjective truth is temporal or historical, it remains enclosed in a continuous or not discontinuous process, and its internal structure is as objective as any known "thing" can be. The third relation is also a basis of objectivity.

Since Hegel, some philosophies have reproduced, in historicist terms, the sceptical positions that were traditionally formulated in the terms of empirical subjectivism. The first modern relativism was psychologistic. It regarded truth as relative to the subject, while reducing the subject to the consciousness, and it regarded the consciousness as isolated and out of communication. In making reference to this lack of communication, the subject of knowledge in English empiricism is nothing more than the psychological version of the Cartesian *cogito*. It is, in fact, the *ego cogitans* without the innate ideas. In Descartes, the innate ideas were the bridge by which one could cross over from the consciousness to a being that was not that of the *ego* itself. Without this mediation, the subject of empiricism has no evidence of being beyond the testimony of its own consciousness, and this consciousness consequently finds itself even more isolated than the Cartesian consciousness.

Historicism is apparently going to resolve this isolation of the subject. The subjective consciousness is now a historical consciousness, and this restores the luster, once lost, to the fact of the interdependence between the individual subject—which is regarded no longer as a mere consciousness but as a person with its reality intact—and the situational factor *shared* with others. Historicism tends to bring out not merely the temporality of truth but also the community of the being of the truth, which is man.

But some thinkers, being inclined to relativism, have sought to justify their relativist inclination on grounds encountered, they believe, in the fact of historicity. In so doing, they have reverted to a purely psychologistic or "personalistic" version of historicism. Putting it more schematically, they see the truth as continuing to depend upon the individual consciousness. Therefore, although this consciousness belongs to a subject that is already conceived as an integral and vital unit, and although the subject may be linked now to the external factors of the historical situation, his own vision of things in general—and even of the situation in which he finds himself and which conditions his life—is nevertheless limited by the irreducible perspective of his individual point of view. Thus the conditioning force of the situation is not taken as an objective factor—because objective means shared—and the situation no longer presents the character of a community; the circumstance would thus always be *my* circumstance.

Esse est percipi, says the empiricist formula; and what is perceived is always the intransferable content of an individual consciousness. Historical relativism retains the scheme of that formula but changes its terms; the being becomes the historical, and the perception is historical experience. But this experience is just as individual and just as intransferable as empirical experience. Although the subject's version of his own historical experience is also a historical act, it does not achieve thereby the objective cohesion of an authentic community because it cannot reflect the objective except as it affects the subject. The subject can speak of the situation only inasmuch as he is a protagonist in it. In this "egocentrism," "historical" is what seems to me, as it happens to me. Being depends upon seeming. Only the subject can speak definitively of himself precisely because he is historical. Historicity would confirm the irreducible individuality of knowledge.

Such a position is very similar to that of Protagoras, who continues to have great meaning. Man is again "the measure of all things" because all things change and man himself changes when he tries to know them. Furthermore, he can grasp them only partially; he can say only what they seem to be for him. The universality of change has been reconfirmed by this new modality, historical becoming. We might comment here on the consequent amoralism that inevitably arises from a doctrine such as this, so much like that of sophism. The historical subject is obviously freed of responsibility for his acts if he is intellectually and vitally cut off from the community of being and knowledge. But we are concerned here not with ethics, but with the scientific consequences of this doctrine. Now just as Protagoras failed to understand Heraclitus, likewise have the historical relativists failed to understand that if becoming is a fact, so is *the rational structure of becoming also a fact, and its objectivity makes science possible.* When this structural factor is not taken into account, the result is an amorphous becoming or even the paradox of a discontinuity in becoming, the dispersion of becoming into a number of "vital positions" of the individual or of generation or into a number of perspectives limited by the personal points of view.

The transition from Hegel to historicist relativism is therefore theoretically analogous to the transition from Descartes to Berkeley and Hume. Each transition terminates in a solipsism. This is what results when idealism is carried to its extreme consequences and to all its implications. And this is what we must understand. For in philosophy, it is not enough to attach a name to a doctrine one wishes to discredit, a name which only defines it as contrary to one's own doctrine. But we must define it in order to understand it. In spite of its apparent psychological realism and in spite of its vitalism, subjectivist historicism is a form of idealism, as was the doctrine of Protagoras. It is an idealism which, in order to be logically consistent, must deny the possibility of an ontology of the historical (such as the ontology of Hegel or any other), in the same way that empiricism rejected the ontology of Descartes or that of Leibniz. In a precise sense, for this historicism the "situation" is the subjective situation and not the historical situation. But *without community there is no authentic historicity.* That historicism is false whose proponents hold that the truth will always be an expression of the person who thinks it, that it will be only a product of his own life, and that it will primarily and directly reflect his life situation. It will also reflect the circumstances as they influence the individual situation. But this reflection or expression will not acquire the value of objectivity because the subject is an irreducible "point of view." Of the whole complex of factors prevailing in the historical situation, the isolated subject can reflect only those that enter into his limited perspective and that condition, precisely, his particular "way of seeing."

Thus science is impossible. For *science is transsubjective;* it is, as we shall see, a matter of intercommunication. Science is a fact; and when a doctrine, carried to its ultimate implications, contradicts facts, the formal prescriptions of method alone would suffice to nullify it even if there were no other evidence against it. In this case the decisive evidence is that of an integration of the horizontal structure with the vertical structure in the internal articulation of the historical process. This will suffice to place us on transsubjective terrain.

As a matter of fact, the vertical structure alone would not suffice. Intersubjectivity means *intercommunication across time, and not only simultaneously,* not only in an identical historical situation. I cannot, simply on the grounds that I live in a specific situation, isolate and consider it apart and separated from the course of history. The isolation of the situation carries with it the same consequences as the isolation of the individual subject. Let us regard the subject integrated in the historical situation; let us regard the situation as the community of numerous life situations. The interdependence that exists between the subjective situations within the common situation will permit us to determine the distinctive characteristics of this historic situation. Its cultural products will form a unity of meaning; they will all express their time and will present certain special features or modalities of style that are common to thought and to art, to politics and to religion, to the forms of economic organization, and to the forms of life in general. All of this constitutes the vertical structure of the historical situation. It so happens that this aspect of historicity tends to strengthen the link between truth and life (or "existence") which the previous type of subjectivism, the empiricist type, had already established. Hence the fusion of historicism with vitalism in some thought of our century (that of Ortega, most notably, although the theoretical outlines are confused).

But genuine historicism does not consist in affirming that truth is an expression of the life sense of the age in which it is formulated and that each age, being different, has different truths. A historicist philosophy has to investigate precisely how the transition is made from one truth to another and just what the thread is that connects a given age to the new and different age that follows. The investigation must center upon the internal articulation because the object under study is a process, and not a discontinuous series of differentiated situations. If each historical age or situation is conceived as a tightly closed-off unit, the possibility of historical comprehension is lost, since there is no way of approaching the past from the enclosure of the present.

To be sure, everything is done from or in the present. But if the present is limited to its own distinctive characteristics, there is something which one cannot do, and that is to withdraw from the present so as to actualize the past, so as to bring about that "presence of the past" in which history consists. There is no avenue of communication between one "now" and any other "now." One is deprived of the dialectical articulation between the past and the present, which is the keystone of history itself. One is also deprived, for the same reason, of a projection into the future, of the real factor of the future gestating in the present. Thus the course of history is represented as a series of unconnected presents. But the theme of history is the whole of history, and not merely the historical present, in spite of the vital importance of the latter for each of us. Science is the surpassing of the "point of view." It is historical because of the "point of view." But *without continuity, there is no historicity.* The horizontal structure is complementary to the vertical structure.

It is the situation, therefore, this complex unity of meaning, that constitutes the vertical structure. But the old subjectivisms and relativisms that have taken refuge in historicism, seeking there confirmation of their thesis, emphasize especially the facts contained in this vertical structure without articulating it with the horizontal structure, as if all the aspects of historicity were concentrated in the vertical structure. Although the concept of

situation is a historical concept, it does not seem, then, to belong
to the order of temporality. The situation is removed from this
temporal order if we define each particular situation atomically
by its distinctive characteristics in such a way that the distinction breaks the continuity of the process, leaving a historical hia-
tus between a situation and those that follow or precede it.

In forming a vertical structure, the features that permit us to
characterize a phase of historical development certainly have a
certain permanence without which they could not be identified
as distinctive. We say that the phase *has duration*. But we do
not usually understand this concept in the sense of temporality
or authentic evolutive duration, but rather in the sense of stability. The phase lasts because the features which characterize
it per-sist in it. The situation does not last if these features are
altered, and thus the situation appears to have paralyzed, tran-
sitorily, the course of history.

In any case, the march of time becomes especially perceptible
when new developments appear which destroy or alter precisely
the stability of the vertical structure, or the internal organization
of the historical situation. But this organization always contains
a dynamic factor, a potency capable of determining the future.
That which has duration subsists, but it also changes; that which
is immutable has no duration. When we neglect this factor, the
very characteristics that we attribute to the situation also paralyze
it by imposing on it a stability that it does not have. And then,
when the situation changes, we cannot explain whence the new
development comes that produces the change. The present was
static and could not contain the future virtually. What was to
come was not germinating in the present, and thus the new development appears as something purely gratuitous, unmotivated,
and irrational, something produced by spontaneous generation.

Are all the factors new in the new situation, or does the persistence of some old factors, integrated into the new factors,
maintain the continuity? Is not the presence of the past, and also
the budding of the future, one of the constituent characteristics
of the present? In short, for a full comprehension of historicity,

is not the horizontal structure the necessary complement of the vertical structure? If it is, then the relativism of "personalist" and perspectivist stamp will be eliminated decisively. *The authentic historical perspective embraces not only the situation but also the process.* The limitations of the personal perspective of a perspectivist philosopher cannot be raised to the level of a criterion so as to reduce in general the range of historicity.

A chord is polyphonic, and it is a part of music but not the whole of music. The vertical structure of historicity is similar to a chord. Each isolated note, each independent cultural product has meaning in relation to the other notes or the other cultural products that constitute the harmonic or situational unit. The chord has a certain duration, and it lasts with uniformity just as does the historical situation, but both the chord and the historical situation anticipate the imminent developments, the chords or situations which will introduce some variation and which, in establishing a line of continuity, will reveal the complementary horizontal structure of a melodic or historical unit, complementary to the harmonic or situational vertical structure.

Thus the situation cannot be characterized only by its actual features without taking into account the potential features also present and those inherited from the past. The present is dependent, in the unity and continuity of the process, upon the past and the future. We must insist strongly upon this point because certain easy ideas have gained currency in the thought of our time, ideas which interpret the fact of historicity only as this reference to the present that we have characterized as a vertical structure. Such partiality, though it might be admitted in an English thinker of the eighteenth century, is a contradiction in a historicist philosophy. When the continuity of the historical process is broken, this process is atomized and subdivided into situations distinct from each other, situations which form a series, but a discrete series without connection with one another, *without an internal principle of succession*. In short, they are without structural duration. But history is precisely a functional structure.

When we deny, either implicitly or explicitly, this organic continuity of history, the new features of each situation seem to have emerged from nothing. Once actualized, they can be understood, the ones in relation to the others, for all together they form a unity of meaning. But that understanding is deficient if it does not note whence the new features came and whither they are tending. Because the unit is closed off, it is consequently lacking in meaning. And it lacks meaning not only in the theoretical order but even for existence. Its meaning is revealed only in continuity. To express this with an image, man inevitably feels lonely, and he falls into despair when he ceases to belong to his "historical family." He loses his inheritance, and his only possession is the present, a present which is deformed, however, by the deprivation of the common past and by the literal insignificance of a future in which he will no longer be present and of which he cannot be the determining force.

But vital pessimism, which follows the figure of this fragmentary historicism like its shadow, disappears when the vertical unit of meaning is understood in terms of the horizontal unit. Each specific product of human action has its own horizontal line of evolution. Our fathers implicitly believed that these diverse lines were independent of one another. The consciousness of the "historical fact" has made us aware of the interdependence and unity of meaning of all cultural products. However, this consciousness would be—and is—very deficient and disturbing if it were to tell us of nothing more than the vertical, situational, or present integration of those human creations of each age. This would rupture the horizontal lines of continuity. These lines were regarded as independent of one another because no historical character was attributed to them as proper to them. Nor is this character recognized as belonging to them when we regard them as discontinuous. *If we break the horizontal continuity of each line, we cannot understand how or why the products that form these lines become, in each situation, coordinated vertically.* This explains why the situation—the verticality of the present— produces the experience of the absurd, and is expressed in such terms, as the existentialist philosophy has done. But we do not express the historical sense when we say that "the present has no value because the future will be different," or when we say the contrary, which amounts to the same thing, that "only the present has value because the future will be different." In both cases the present loses its value if it wishes to keep *its own*. It is a paradox of the current crisis that certain historicisms (as well as certain existentialisms) produce this peculiar contraction of the present, this renunciation of the past, and this sterility before the future.

When we recognize the functional connection of the present with the past, we not only avoid historical discontinuity but the present thereby also recovers both its vital and its philosophical meaning. And the lines of evolution of the different cultural products no longer appear as disconnected but as forming a bundle. What is decisive is the fact of the *uniform* evolution, in the horizontal structure, of all those human creations that also correspond to one another vertically or contemporaneously—much as in the orchestra director's score all the sounds are represented in a unit that contains both the harmonic, or vertical, structure and the melodic and rythmic, or horizontal, structure. For this reason, and only for this reason, the situation has historical character, although it sometimes seems to consist in a paralyzation of the process, a static present, a suspension of the changes, the anticipations, and the innovating activity.

But the problem of truth does not appear to have been resolved with this vertical and horizontal structuring of the situation. Indeed, it seems to have become more complicated. For now the truth would not only depend upon the present and everything here and now. It would also depend upon its own past and even upon the past of other cultural manifestations whose object is not to seek truth, as is that of philosophy and positive science, although philosophy and science would maintain such a cohesion with those cultural manifestations that their historical destinies would be in concord. What sense would there be in seeking truth with the means of a science if the evolution of this science had to correspond, no matter what the truth-seeking thinker does, to the evolution of art or of politics?

Although the problem of truth was raised by the fact of the temporality of thought, or the historicity of science, we have already indicated that the solution cannot favor him who claims to restrict the fact or to debate positions within the real field in which the fact is manifested. The fact itself has to be explored even to its most remote limits, without fearing that, in adding still other unsuspected aspects of historicity, this historicity ends up invalidating definitively the ambition for truth that is inherent in all thought. On the contrary, it is only after a complete investigation which emphasizes the difficulties instead of avoiding them that a way to a solution can be found. And that complete exploration must be carried out in the methodological scheme of the vertical and horizontal structure.

The third constituent relation of thought, or the historical relation, compares the truth to an expression and makes it relative only if we consider the situational or vertical structure. What I think expresses what I am, and what I am depends upon the situation in which I find myself. In this sense the truth would not be real because the expressive factor would eliminate the cognitive factor. The truth would not represent reality in a creditable and adequate way, and it would be only the version of a personal, irreducible, and uncontrastable modality of seeing and reacting to things.

The expressive element of thought is not annulled with the horizontal relation, but it is so complicated with that relation that it is a functional dialectical relation.[5] The evidence of a horizontal structure permits us to eliminate the irrationality of subjectivism and the perspectivism that center in the present. But this does not resolve the problem. Supposing that the philosophical-historical analysis had already revealed to us all the dialectical articulations of the process of thought, there would still be a radical antinomy to deal with. If the theoretical situation is, in any phase, a *dialectical derivation* of its antecedents, it does not appear how that theory could attain the truth of adequation. The truth would arise from its dialectical antecedents without ceasing to be expressive. It would depend more upon the past than upon an actual confrontation with the things themselves. When that adequation is effected, in the cognitive relation, the result has to be independent of any historical change even though this change is structural and dialectical. But the aporia of expressivity also has a solution.

III

For the present the problem is in this situation of aporia, and it will have to stay there until it is stated differently. We have been able to present systematically the terms of this extremely complex scheme, or at least the terms in which it has appeared up to the present time. And this alone is a step forward. But it is not enough. The problem of truth and science, raised by the fact of historicity, has no solution as long as we see thought as having three constituent relations and no more: the epistemological relation, the logical relation, and the historical relation (with its vertical and horizontal projection). If there were only these three relations, the integration of the third with the other two would never be possible.

But there is a fourth relation, and the introduction of this last dimension, far from complicating the situation, rather permits the integration of the other three. This fourth constituent relation is the *dialogical relation.*

Thought is *logos.* It is *logos* in the sense of reason and at the same time in the sense of word. These two uses of the term are complementary and reciprocal, as are the head and tail of a coin, and the two should never be separated from each other. Every word is rational, and all reason is symbolic. The analytical function, without which there can be no philosophy, sometimes ignores its limitations and, in separating itself from the reality which was its original object, goes on to produce monsters of abstraction that no longer correspond to any real thing. Every new shading discovered in the abstract seems to justify a different category, and the numerous divisions and subdivisions—all apparently plausible, because fabricated by the understanding

—dissect the object and end up by dissolving its unity.

Something like this happened with the concept of *logos*. Certainly, psychology seems to be unable to give us definite, unequivocal, and clear meanings for the terms reason, understanding, thought, and so on. In the meanwhile, there also seems to be a tacit agreement to consider these three mental functions (to say that there are three functions is, in fact, essentially the same as saying that these are three aspects of the same function) have little or nothing to do with expression. They are silent operations. And it is clear that we can think without saying anything. This leads us to believe that the *logos* as word is an entirely distinct function from the *logos* as reason, thought, or understanding. Accordingly, thoughts can be expressed or unexpressed, but the expression itself is not a constituent part of thinking. The expression would be added *per accidens* to the thought.

Some psychologists, however, have pointed up the fact that we *think verbally* even though we are silent. And without taking recourse here to recent testimony in this direction, Plato had already observed that the νοῦς, which is thought or understanding, is an active function that must be understood as διάνοια, or a "silent dialogue."[6] We will add that thought should not be designated by a substantive, νοῦς, but by a verb, νοεῖν. But the term of the action designated by this transitive verb is not only the object thought by the subject but the *other subject,* the person in general to whom the thing thought is communicated or can be communicated. *Without this possible interlocutor, the terms in which the thought is articulated would lack meaning.* Philosophy did not traditionally realize this, nor do the new semantic directions of logic realize it. The definition of a term is not established only by a relation of the term with the real signified object. Signification is a dialogical fact. If the meaning is not *common,* the term does not signify. Putting it another way, terms are not applied to things in order to communicate a thought formed by an individual in isolation. No thought can be formed or articulated without the cooperation of the symbols, so that "pure" thinking already implies the communicative terms. All *logos* is dialogical. And we repeat that the communication does not necessarily have to be really carried out as a social phenomenon in order for thinking to be a dialogue. Apart from the interior dialogue "of the soul with itself," as Plato puts it, we shall see that the existence of *an other person* in general is a condition for the possibility of thought. To think is to exercise the *logos,* and all *logos* is expression.

For centuries, since Greece, the expressive function of the *logos* was dissociated from the noetic function. Logic itself was not conceived as the regulatory system of verbal expression but as the regulator of the *logos* as "pure" thought. Expression was an impurity because it was external and inferior, derived, accidental, and subjective. The logical relation was the internal relation of thought with itself without dialogical exchange, without an addressee or interlocutor. In short, logical thinking was a sort of intransitive action. If thought was expressed, logic was careful to eliminate all the strictly expressive factors of this *logos.* These factors were regarded, and are still regarded, as compromising conceptual purity which is indispensable to all scientific formulation, and they bring with them the useless residue of subjectivism, inexactness, and lack of method and lack of universality that are proper to the *doxa* or prescientific opinion.

Hence it was disconcerting that this expressive factor or the *logos,* which was so carefully eliminated in the second constituent relation of thought, should reappear later in the third, or historic, relation. The weight of tradition imposes certain conditioned reflexes upon philosophers, and one can understand the repugnance of many toward accepting, with all its consequences, the fact of historicity if accepting it means compromising the value of the logic which was so highly accredited and tested by the millenary task of science. For how could there be, without "pure" reason, objectively, universally, and necessarily valid truths?

But the value of logic does not decline when we re-establish the expressive or dialogical factor of the *logos.* On the contrary, it supports logic. The *logos* is, in fact, expression. But the expressive character of the *logos* only compromises the efficacy of its

rational aspect for him who has previously dissociated the two
aspects from each other and who regards them as incompatible.
The truth does not suffer in being expressive because the *logos,*
as a unity of thought and word, presents a double structure.
As purified as it may be formally—in scientific theory—and as
expressive as it may be subjectively—in an intimate confidence—
*the logos always implies both a communicative intention and a
significative content.*

Method requires that we distinguish between expression and
signification. But the advantage of clarity made possible by
method would be lost if we regarded these two aspects of the
same act, which we distinguish in order to understand better,
as two different acts, as two dissociated, possibly incompatible,
and in any case successive acts. We have to realize that this has
been and still is the predominating opinion, and not only among
logicians. At first sight it seems that the more expressive the
logos is, the less creditable it will be as a representation of the
real. And conversely, the *logos* can be pure and adequate only
when it is neutralized and dehumanized, only when it eliminates
everything that could be vital, personal, and circumstantial.

This dissociation of the two components of the *logos* produces a
correlative opposition of attitudes, each of which is committed to
vindicating one of the aspects against the other. Thought is pure,
some say, and it is only with this impersonal and disinterested
neutrality that it can be legitimately and authentically scientific.
For truth is not expressive. Opposed to these, others hold that
thought is a product of human existence, that it is a vital function.
They hold that the thinking subject does not correspond at all to
that abstract fiction of the "subject in general" elaborated by scientific philosophy, but is the real and concrete man of flesh and
blood, who is vitally and wholly engaged in his act of thought
because he is inescapably centered in himself and cannot assume a disinterested attitude toward things. And the only
value, the only usefulness, the only meaning that the *logos* can
have as thought would come precisely from this vital and total
engagement.[7]

Each of these positions is right, which is as much as to say that neither is right. For half-truth is worse than error, especially when the one half is directed polemically against the other, its complement. Truth cannot dispute with itself.

On the one hand, it is clear that without the purifying force of method and logic, thought's natural claim to truth does not provide the guarantees that objectivity, unequivocal meaning, congruency, and systematic order provide. In this sense, scientific thought is, always has been, and always will be pure thought, pure or *purified* reason. On the other hand, it is equally clear that this thought is not removed from place and time. It is a product of human action. Later on, we shall return to this. But for now, we can see how unfortunate it would be if, in overcoming the rationalist idea of pure reason with an idea of vital and historical reason, we were to regard this vitality as irreducible subjectivity, and this historicity as relativism. To be sure, this confusion can arise only on the margins of philosophy, not in its main stream. But it is a confusion that unites only too readily with a peculiar spontaneous disposition, with a vital and pre-philosophical form of the subjectivism which predominates in the Spanish mind, and this is personalism. The attention centers here upon the person who is speaking rather than upon what he says. Hence the notion of philosophy as a personal statement or confession, with the consequent repugnance for admitting the objective rule of reality and for subjecting oneself to the logical and methodological prescriptions of objectivity and concordance which are proper to scientific work.

Returning now to the essential expressivity (of the *logos*), *everything that signifies expresses, and everything that expresses signifies.* Let us imagine a situation of dialogue between two subjects where the theme of communication is the most subjective and expressive, the least conceptual and abstract possible. For example, each of the two subjects is speaking about himself and confides to the other certain private personal experiences. The first thing that strikes us in this situation is the fact that the interlocutors understand each other. In spite of what poets and

philosophers have held concerning the inaccessible intimacy of
the human subject, concerning the impossibility of communicating or establishing contact with that secret center in the other
being, the fact is that communication does exist. For otherwise
we could not even speak of intimacy, nor would there be confid-
ings of private matters, nor would man have created, with poetry,
a specifically verbal art of subjective expression and, with philosophy and psychology, analytical sciences of the I—and the
thou—in its most secret depths.

The interlocutors understand each other. The level and the
quality of understanding which they attain in the dialogue will
depend either upon accidental factors or upon the essential limitations of the expression itself. But neither of these invalidates the
fact that the dialogue produces understanding, that even not having understood is susceptible to being expressed, and that what
discrepancies exist must be sustained by the basic concordance
in that over which one differs. What then is the basic condition
for this understanding being possible? What is it that makes the
verbal message of the one intelligible for the other? No doubt,
both use an identical instrument of expression, an identical symbolic system. This is evident. But on what does such a system
depend for its efficacy? On the fact that each of the terms of this
language has a meaning that is more or less unequivocal, but
precise enough for the interlocutor to effect, upon hearing it, an
instantaneous mental reference to the object signified by the person speaking. He who is speaking thinks, for his part, about that
same object when he designates it in his expression. To understand is precisely this act of a *common* reference to an identical object, made possible by the use of a word freighted with
meaning. The meaning does not disappear because the word is
expressive.

In the case of an intimate confidence, the experience communicated can strike us as unique, intransferable, irreproducible.
Hence we say that the interior abode of the person expressing
himself is untouchable, inaccessible, irreducibly solitary, radically
foreign and remote. The thou, the deep and authentic being of

the other, would be *cet inconnu*. However, this lyricism of aloneness and incommunicability has no phenomenological basis, however attractive it may be poetically, and no vestige of it must
remain in a scientific theory. For intersubjective communication
is a positive fact, and the *logos* of the confidence would be absolutely unintelligible if the expression did not contain some meanings which permit him who hears it to refer, by means of them,
to some data of *common* experience. No matter how singular and
private the thing communicated is, it cannot be absolutely unique
if it encounters an echo of comprehension. If it were unique,
there would be no term with which to designate it. The symbol
is always a link of community. What counts in this situation of
confidential intimacy is to grasp the vital *sense* of what is expressed. But this sense is grasped, and can only be grasped, by
means of intellection of a *meaning*. The vital expressive relation
implies the co-signative intellectual relation. And to signify is
nothing but to name an object with a verbal symbol which permits one to recognize and identify it dialogically. Thought is
therefore not a solitary and private faculty of the subject, but a
communicative function. It is the very action of understanding—
and of *being* understood—that always presupposes an interlocutor
in general. Understanding is a transitive action.[8]

Hence there can be no special form of the *logos* that is pure
expression without signification. Had the *logos* such a form, the
expression's inherent communicative intention would be frustrated. And the thing expressed in it would be incomprehensible
if there were no signification at all, if the thing communicated
were not a certain significative content. In short, if the expression
did not signify anything, it would not express anything.

Conversely, neither do we encounter the pure signification,
separated from expressiveness or communicability. And not only
because it is impossible to eliminate or neutralize completely this
real and concrete, vital and historical, human subject which the
man himself is in his communicative activity; rather, for a deeper
and more radical reason which touches on the essence of the sig-
nifying activity and not on what a particular subject can or cannot

do when he exercises this function. For, in fact, the necessary condition, *sine qua non,* that every thing signified must realize is that of being intelligible or comprehensible, which means communicable. Even error, even the incorrect signification and the deception must be intelligible. Otherwise, how could they be detected and corrected? However, without going this far, which would already constitute a real dialogical phenomenon, the very subject, who is thinking the real signified object, could not understand it except through the instrumentality of a symbol which, being intelligible, is communicable.

An unintelligible meaning is a contradiction in terms. It is clear that if that meaning were not communicable, it would not be intelligible *even for him who used it by himself alone, before formulating it.* Naturally, the decisive proof of this comes from the communication itself when it becomes effective. For that which is spoken of something that no one can understand contains no significative message, and it expresses only mental derangement, which is the highest degree of aloneness and incommunicability to which a man can come. (And even here, as psychiatry well knows, the sense of life in the expression carries some echo of intelligible significations. For without the interpretation of these, psychiatry would be impossible. In mental medicine, this hermeneutics is analogous to the poetic sense in the comprehension of the lyricism of aloneness.)

Intellection itself, then, is already dialogical in itself even before the meanings it defines are converted into the material or content of an effective verbal expression or exposition. Hence it is not necessary to have the dialogue and to analyze its expression in order to verify, in the midst of the "pure" significations, the undeniable presence there of the concrete man who thought them, with all that this implies. *The expressive factor is already found in the significative function itself* as a necessary condition of intelligibility. There are no concepts without words. Words are not added to significations as tags are attached to a product when it is finished. Words, and symbols in general, form part of the very process of signification or objectification.

Consequently, intelligibility and communicability mean the same thing. A signification is intelligible when the symbol that constitutes it is dia-logically comprehensible or when it has the virtue of making effectively manifest, to the other subject, the objective reality recorded by the subject thinking and ex-posing it in the expression. In short, the "pure" signification, without an expressive symbol, would be purely meaningless and unintelligible. This would break the *communicative link* that is essential to the *logos* because the *cognitive link* between the subject and the object would have been broken. There exists no reality known by a subject that cannot be expressed symbolically. The symbolic relation is formed by these two bonds together. If some one formulated the hypothesis of a private and exclusive reality of a single subject, he could not respond to the question of what that reality is. This question can be answered only with words. The first thing that words reveal is the fact that all reality is shared. Knowing is a co-operation.

Evidently, this statement of the problem of expression—and the corresponding attempt to solve it—places the problem on a more radical plane than that on which psychological, sociological, and historical facts are presented. It is only on this level of a *metaphysics of expression* that we can give an adequate interpretation to those facts upon which both philosophy and science in general base their criticism, judging that subjective expressivity and historical expressivity invalidated completely the claim to truth made by thought.[9] But it was the phenomenological analysis of thought and the revelation of its various relations and structures that indicated how this expressive factor, instead of hindering the acquisition of a truth, rather constitutes the necessary, real, or literally ontological condition for all knowledge, both in the prescientific phase and in the scientific phase.

IV

Expression is not incompatible with truth. On the contrary, there is no truth without expression. But these affirmations may themselves appear dogmatic, or "expressive," in spite of being the conclusions of a wholly phenomenological examination. What they require is the complement of a more exact concept of truth. Much confusion can arise here if we do not realize—which many fail to do—*that the concept of truth is not an unequivocal concept.*

The word truth can have various significations because there are various levels of knowledge in each of which a specific modality of truth is realized. If we fail to distinguish between these levels, we run the risk of attributing and denying to the truth at the same time certain characters which it really presents on one level, but not on others.

Since ancient times, the scientific calling has been characterized primarily as "the search for truth." This notion has spread and indeed has won universal acceptance, both with the learned and with the common man. Indeed, what other characteristic could better mark this calling? The search for truth, with disdain for other interests, is the sign of living nobility in the philosopher and in every man of science. But this formula, "the search for truth," contains more moral meaning than theoretical exactness. In it we detect two correlative implications, both of which are inadmissible. In the first, it is implicitly supposed that, before or apart from this scientific calling, man is deprived of truth and that he neither seeks it nor can he attain it even if he does seek it. In the second, it is suggested that truth is something utopian, or something located in a *terra ignota,* remote and accessible only with difficulty. In order to reach this place, one would have to embark, and only when very well equipped, upon a very arduous trek whose outcome is uncertain but one which is begun whenever the truth is not found as a matter of course.

It was philosophers themselves who fabricated this somewhat romantic version of the scientific calling, and modern men of science have inherited it. It may reflect that calling with some exactness, but only in connection with one of the modalities or levels of truth, namely, scientific truth. However, in order to understand itself, science must begin by recognizing other levels and modalities of truth that are more common, more basic, and more primary. *The way of science is to set out from truth already possessed,* or from one level of truth, in order to arrive at another level. Were truth completely lacking, the passion for seeking it would not even arise. Thus we can say that *man is always and necessarily in possession of the truth.* He cannot exist without truth. He is definable ontologically in terms of truth; indeed, he is the being of truth.

Truth is the recognition of being. We say here re-cognition because this operation implies a *reiterated apprehension of the same object by the same subject* (without which there would be no *identification,* for the being of the object does not remain fixed in its objective *sameness*). But it implies, above all, an *apprehension of the same object by two different subjects.* This recognition is dia-logical, and it is in this recognition that the decisive apodictic evidence of being consists, making it invulnerable to all subsequent criticism and all possible "methodical doubt."

Carrying things to their extremes in order to explain them better, we could say that this dia-logical evidence of being begins in the pre-logical phase. For in the pre-logical phase, the indicative gesture is an antecedent of the significative *logos.* To point to an object with the finger is to make it manifest to someone, and this rudimentary presentation constitutes a true apophansis, which is no less effective for being pre-logical. The object is recognized, at least as *present* before the two subjects, even though, not knowing what type of object it is, neither of them is able to signify and name it. If both subjects already know the object, then the indicative gesture is not an antecedent but a substitute for the significative symbol with which they identify it in speaking.

The analysis of this commonplace situation which all men experience daily is useful because it shows how the simple mute indication of the object, before its conceptualization, already contains a truth and is a pre-logical germ of logical truth. The object indicated becomes manifest to the two subjects by means of the gesture. This common recognition of something real and present is a form of the possession of being. The higher forms of the possession of being, in which it is the *logos* that lays hold of the being,

realize a more eminent type of truth. But there is no truth that
does not come from a primary apprehension of being—however
this primary apprehension is effected—in which the object is
manifested as something real, present, and evident. *Truth is the
manifestation of being.*

Language itself also has modalities that are merely indicative
or pre-conceptual. There is one word which signifies no specific
object and which seems to be the substitute for the gesture. The
demonstrative pronoun when the object indicated has not been
signified by a substantive is verbally equivalent to the mere indicative gesture which is made with the index finger. And it has
the same apophantic or apodictic value, which is to say that it
furnishes the same primary evidence of the presence of something
real. (And let us not forget that this pronoun is called demonstrative, not because it demonstrates, but because it shows. For
the *demonstratio* in Latin signifies the same thing that ἀπόδειξις
signified in Greek, before Aristotle.)

The simple presence of a being, then, is the material of the
most fundamental of truths. It is so fundamental that "the thing"
present does not have to be signified, so fundamental, indeed,
that it discards, with the signification of the substantive, the
literal neutrality and anonymity of the demonstrative pronoun and
of the neuter article. We need not say "this table" to make the
table evident and to make the interlocutor share the evidence of
its real presence. It is enough to say "this" in order to establish
the link of understanding between the interlocutors by means of
the common reference to the object. To establish that link it
would not even be necessary for the two interlocutors to know
what type of object was manifested. When one says "this table,"
the object has already been conceptualized and classified. This
formula clearly contains a truth because it is an abbreviated proposition. "This is a table" would be the complete proposition. This
is confirmed when he who indicates an object verbally commits
an error of signification, in which case the other subject can reply:
"This *table?* But this is not a table. It is a bench." The error of
signification does not destroy the apophantic evidence. Even

though the object is not a table, its real presence is manifest, whatever it is. The error of the substantive does not destroy the truth of the pronoun.

To the extent this presence is literally manifest or manifested, the primary logical evidence is shared, or dia-logical. But even the pre-logical evidence contains, in germ, the primary truth of the *logos*. The apophansis of the gesture is equally dialogical. For even though the symbolic system of the word does not intervene, other symbols do intervene with which the two subjects establish an expressive relation, and the result is that the presentation of the object is a true communication. The gesture is also dialogical. To be sure, the gesture and the demonstrative pronoun lack signification in that they represent no *determinate* object unequivocally. They acquire determination from the situation. They are symbols and, as such, they have in themselves a constant precise signification which is the indication. The indication can serve indiscriminately for any object, but when it is applied to one object, it identifies that object as directly as does the substantive symbol. The thing indicated then becomes evident because it is co-present before the indicator and before him who comprehends the indicative expression.

The apophansis is a presentation. The re-presentation comes afterwards by means of a conceptual and substantively significative symbol. The conceptual representation obviously must also be apophantic. For if the symbol does not make evident something real, it does not fulfill its proper function; it does not signify or represent anything. But in the symbolic representation, there is a subjective component which is superadded to the mere presentation. For the representation is already discursive thought, and the symbol with which we signify and express the thing represented is no longer a mere indication. It no longer says only that the thing is, or that it is present, but it now says *what it is*. Every concept is a concentrated, compressed, and abbreviated judgment. And for this reason, every substantive symbolic representation is ontological. It is a *logos* about the being, a *logos* in which we manifest to what type of being the thing signified belongs, be it table, tree, man, number, virtue, or whatever. We think the concept; it is the work or product of a thinking subject. The word "concept" is a substantive formed by a past participle which indicates *the fulfilled term of the action of conceiving*. This is a human action into which each subject puts something of himself. The *logos* presents very clearly here its two complementary aspects, which are objective representation and subjective expression, the content signified and the communicative intention.

But we must understand well how the act of conceptual representation is produced. *The expression is found in the representation itself*. But to avoid confusion, we must dispense with certain inherited ideas whose authority is based only upon their traditional usefulness. According to these ideas the representation would be, or would aspire to be, a simple literal reproduction of the object, as a copy of the imprint that the object had left impressed in the understanding of the subject. The subject would put nothing of himself into said representation except the reproducing mechanism. The subject would be active but not productive. Thus the expression would be eliminated from the concept.

But the conceptualization is not a *simple* representation, even though it is given this name. It is not limited to reproducing the object. It is not an intuitive spark but the product of relational and discursive thought. This is not noticed at first because the concept is formulated with a single and isolated word, something like the copy of an instantaneous photograph of the object. But the traditional distinction between concept and term cannot be taken literally, for we use the term, the verbal symbol, in order to conceptualize. We must insist that the word is not applied to the concept once the concept has already been thought; nor do we form the concept by depriving the object of all connection with reality, but in a relation with other objects that define or limit the field of the signification. The operation is complex. *It is expressive because it is productive and because the materials of the production are always symbols or dialogical terms*. The symbol "table," with which we represent conceptually a determinate object, concentrates a whole series of symbolic relations that claim to be true, such as the affirmation of the objective reality of a thing; its difference with respect to another thing, such as the chair; the fact that both belong to a common genus, which is that of furniture; the difference between this genus and objects of other genera, etc.

The primary expressiveness of conceptualization roots, then, in the symbolic character of this complex operation. It behooves us to remember this fact. There seems to be no exception to the unanimity with which philosophers have assimilated expressiveness to subjectivity. This assimilation has been illustrated in modern times with detailed analyses. The subject would disturb the objectivity of thought before its production, determining, from an irrational grounding, the orientations and modalities of a peculiar "way of seeing things" which would be more expressive of the person than of the things thought. Later, the subject would intervene expressively in the communication of the thing thought so that it would pursue, also from an irrational grounding, its distinctive "way of speaking of things."

In reality, neither of these interventions of subjectivity can or should be denied. Science has never denied them nor has it regarded them as irremediable or decisive. If thought did not suffer irrational deviations, it would not have been necessary to create instruments of rectification, such as method and logic, which provide the norm for thinking well and which permit us to maintain objectivity. For this reason the idea that expressiveness is essential represents a crisis for science, for it makes the effects of expressiveness seem irreparable. Expression thus becomes the key concept of an irrational subjective determinism. Also, and for this same reason, it has been insisted that the recovery of scientific objectivity would require, not the negation of the fact of expressiveness, but the negation of its essential presence in all thought.

The apparent conflict (incidental to which is the polemic between psychologism and logicism) cannot be resolved if we continue to discuss the efficacy or inefficacy of logical technique for purifying thought of this psychological by-product of expressiveness. This efficacy is a fact, and the fact is called science. We must show, however, that scientific objectivity is possible precisely *because* expressiveness is essential. For this we shall require a more precise concept of expressiveness.

In the polemic over the objective value of thought, both sides agree that the truth is found in the judgment with which we express or formulate an opinion. The concept would present no difficulty. Even subjective determinism implicitly regards the concept as inexpressive. The word "table" correctly designates the object table. And the irrational motivations that would determine the paths of discursive thought or the formation of opinions do not intervene at all in this simple designation. But the basis of objectivity is precisely the conceptualization, not the opinion. And objectivization is clearly a discursive and expressive operation. It is expressive, not because it manifests no peculiarity of the subject, but because it is symbolic. Truth is already in the concept, and the symbol (which does not express the concept but which constitutes it) is not the result only of the thinking subject's relation with the object thought. It is the bond of the symbolic relation which is established between that thinking subject and the other subject in general for whom the symbol must be intelligible. Objectivity consists in this primary common intelligibility. In other words, *the symbolic relation is an objectivizing relation because it is communicative.* What is expressive in the concept is its essential and radical communicability. The expression of the personal positions or dispositions that the dialoguing subjects can assume before the object, or the formulation of their personal opinions, comes later.

Obviously, even the most inconsistent opinion that a man can form about an object presupposes the objectivization of that object. And no other subject could detect an inconsistency which is not so objectively grounded that it permits the identification of the object by the person disagreeing with the opinion in question. To objectivize the object is to identify it, or to possess it in common. This condition in advance of any possible disparity of opinions, or of "considered attitudes," is expressive, not because the subject is inserted in it but because the objectivization is symbolic and dialogical. It will be observed that expressiveness roots in this essentially dialogical character of the *logos* rather than in the particular subjectivity of each individual making use of his *logos*. Hence it is the intersubjectivity inherent in every symbolic function that guarantees objectivity even before the subject can obscure it by manifesting himself to himself with his personal *doxa*. Expressiveness is, above all, communication. And the thing communicated is not primarily a pure personal message but an object. No message is intelligible if it does not make manifest an object of common experience. In other words, *expressiveness is the form of an intersubjective symbolic relation which has as its basis or common reference the objects signified.*

Therefore, those who assert expressiveness at the cost of objectivity are making bad use of a verified fact. This is why we must insist that conceptualization is discursive, that expression (under the species of symbolic communicability) is already found in the objectivizing operation, even though it expresses no opinion, and conceptualization is not to be regarded as containing any personal imprint of the individual formulating the concept. And for the same reason we also insist that these subjective components, which can, and in fact do, enter afterwards into the formulation of a judgment, do not compromise the "fact of truth" in either of its two levels: not in its first level because there the truth is the simple apophansis which culminates in the concept, and not on the level of the judgment because what makes the verification possible is the reality itself of the thing already objectivized. The purifying or corrective efficacy of method and of logic does not depend upon certain intrinsic and formal conditions that these systems possess. Rather, it depends upon the epistemological service that their formalisms render. Without this appeal to the real, logical formalism is empty. But then the contrast of opinions, supported only by the tenacity with which each is defended, also lacks both logical and epistemological meaning. It is only in the case of the omission or denial of objective reality that expressiveness has an irrational foundation. This is the irrationality of him who asserts "This is my truth." But the truth that is true only "for me" is not true for anyone.

This means that all truth, even the concentrated truth of the concept, manifests a reality that is shared dialogically. With the simple affirmation, *ego cogito*, Descartes is re-establishing as effectively symbolic the intersubjective communication that seemed to be cut off with the methodical doubt. When he suppresses or forgets this dialogical or expressive factor of the *logos*, the subject alone can never reconstruct or represent a true world. The world is common. Without intersubjectivity, there is no transsubjectivity.

Although they have not worked out thematically a theory of expression, some directions taken by historicist philosophers are characterized by the attempt to introduce the transsubjective, but not the intersubjective factor, into subjectivism. The subjective would be the "way of seeing things." The transsubjective would be the situational or historical element conditioning this vision. The simple act of seeing is conceived in fact as an "ante-predicative position." And as the "way of opining" is a consequence of that "way of seeing," it follows that opinions, the presumed truths which we formulate about things, have no other meaning than that of expressing our way of being among things, our vital relation with what is around us. And this would occur not only in common thought but also in that thought which lays claim to higher quality and greater purity, namely, philosophy. (If it also occurs in the positive sciences, it is a disputed question which perspectivism takes special care to leave unexamined. The issue seems to be that of denying the scientific value of philosophy, or of emphasizing one's personal value in this negation. For with its rigorous methodology, science imposes too many restrictions and a humility before things which is too cathartic for the subjective personality.) In his own ways the philosopher would express what he is, speaking of what he succeeds in seeing, and he would not be able to give to his testimony concerning what is around him a more creditable and objective signification because no point of view would be sharable.

Even apart from its false premises, this conclusion continues to present a paradox. For precisely the expression, which is essentially communicative, would render the subject incommunicative. The idealist solipsism, which is the uniqueness of the consciousness, is thus transformed into the new solipsism, which is the uniqueness of the circumstance. The new solitary believes it has recovered a world that lies beyond the consciousness, but it has not acquired company. And if this limited world is his alone, in reality he has not gained it at all. What sense would the expression of the only inhabitant of this world have? Or putting it in another way, without taking recourse to this reduction to the absurd, how is expression possible if the thing communicated is a perspective that cannot be shared? Uniqueness and expression are mutually incompatible terms.

There is no objectivity without intersubjectivity. Expressiveness is essential to thought. But, in its turn, what is essential in this expressiveness is neither the modality of the personal relation with objects, that is, with the transsubjective, nor the "manifestation of the I." What is essential is the intercommunication, the intersubjective relation in general, in which every symbolic function consists. This essential expressiveness has often been confused with the circumstantial expressiveness of a determinate subject who formulates his thought in a concrete act of communication. And this confusion gave rise to the false idea of pure reason which tended to neutralize or dehumanize the subject as the necessary condition of scientific thought. But the calling of objectivity, which is proper to science, strives only to purify thought of that part of subjectivity traditionally referred to with the formula "individual interest." It is not even necessary, let alone possible, to eliminate all the expressive characteristics of the subject exercising that calling. This calling is already expressed in the scientist's very choice of science as a vocation, as well as in his style, his preference for certain themes, in his eye for discovering certain truths or in exploring certain sectors of reality, and in his blindness for others. This does not mean, however, that truth is true simply because it is expressed by a subject particularly endowed for finding it, or that it is true only for him. Nor does that cease to be true which is found by another subject who expresses, both in the search and in the discovery, certain different personal characteristics. *Our life does not determine truths; it only conditions our aptitude for finding them.*

We can establish as a main fact, then, that *the expressiveness of thought is independent of the modalities of personal expression which appear even in the purified forms of science.* Whether on the scientific level or on the prescientific level, thought is communicative in itself. Objectivity is dialogical. This becomes more understandable when we give the word "symbol" a meaning close to that which it had originally in Greece. The symbolic relation implies the affinity of the terms that enter into it. And although we say that words symbolize things, this is only to define one aspect of the symbolic relation. For no word possesses *per se* the necessary affinity or congruency with the thing it symbolizes. Nor is the subject congruous with the object. The object is nothing more than the real base for a mediational operation. It is the intermediate term, a common referential for the relation between two terms that *are* affinitive and congruous, and these are the two dialoguing subjects. To symbolize is not the giving of names to things. Or, better said, the giving of names to things is only to communicate with someone by means of the things named. It is the communication, not the naming, that is symbolic. Without the "other" in general, the symbolic relation of the word with the thing is not realized; indeed, it does not even have meaning. In other words, the symbol is significative *because* it is expressive. If it does not express, it does not signify; if it does not signify, it does not express.

This is the essential, the central, significance of the definition of the *logos* as symbolic reason. Expressiveness is a constituent characteristic of reason as such; it is not an accidental and dispensable psychological component of the noetic function. With this conception of expressiveness we can free ourselves of the opposite and false idea that has prevailed for so many centuries, namely, the idea that there is an expressive form of the *logos,* and another that is inexpressive. A symptom of the decadence of this idea is the division it is producing in our days between philosophers advocating pure reason and those advocating vital reason.

But it might be objected that the truth ends up even more compromised by the discovery that the *logos* is essentially, and not accidentally, expressive. And in fact, the thing expressed is expressive, irrespective of how it is expressed. But a metaphysics of expression, or a critique of symbolical reason, obliges us to change the traditional theory of the concept. We have seen that it is in the concept that the objectivization jells, so to speak. It is the form with which the *logos* defines, identifies, or manifests being. Hence the custom of saying that the concept was the "intellectual representation of the object." However, it is not only a representation. Every form of thought, including the concept, is a ἀπόφανσις and, at the same time, a ποίηδις. It is a *representation* of the object and a *creation* of the subject. Putting it in another way, representation is a creation in which, in spite of being a subjective act, with all that this implies, an objective reality becomes clear. This common possession of the being in the manifestation is possible because the concept is symbolic, or communicative. To the extent reality is represented intelligibly, the symbol that represents it contains a truth. This representation can be more or less correct or adequate. But it will be true, in a primary way, if it carries out, in making its significative content comprehensible, the communicative intention of the ἀπόφανσις. For its part, to the extent this objective representation possesses a symbolic character, it is a product of human action. Consequently, apart from the greater or lesser degree of adequation it obtains, it will be essentially expressive because it is dialogical (and it will be expressive *also* because of the particular characteristics revealed in each case by the subject formulating it in a concrete act of communicative relation).

In general, as we can already see, a truth will be the more stable as it approaches the common evidence of the primary ἀπόφανσις. And it will be more instable and hazardous the more it partakes of ποίησις or when it is more theoretical. To the extent that science is theory, and not a simple establishment of facts, it is literally more *poetic*. This means that its conclusions have the value of a hypothesis, that they are historical products which must be corrected and renovated. That is why the purity of reason, which must be preserved in scientific work in order to eliminate all the arbitrarities of subjectivity, cannot seek support in the doctrine of "pure reason" from which precisely expressiveness and historicity are eliminated. This purifying labor itself is a human action and an integral part of the theoretical creation. And it is especially expressive of the scientist's characteristic calling to objectivity.

Nor is it philosophically correct, then, to claim that there is an expressive or historical "vital reason" which can and must be opposed to "pure reason." Rationalism interpreted the indispensable purity of science as the necessity of eliminating the expressive facet of the *logos*. For their part, the vitalisms of reason recover expressiveness, but they regard it as the downfall of objective truth, as a license to prescind from method and system. *Any possible form of reason is expressive, historic, and vital.* Reason does not change its natural mode of being because of a change in the modes of employing it that are dictated by each particular system. But if expressiveness is a fact, so also is truth a fact. Philosophers have been able to present truth and expression as opposite terms because they previously dissociated the two components of the *logos*, which are expression and representation. This gives rise to much confusion. And one of the most important confusions is that which leads us implicitly to regard truth as an "act of affirmation." Such being the case, we would need to consider whether this affirmation had objective value or only a subjective value. The question is badly stated because truth is a *presentation* of the object before it is an *affirmation* concerning that object. Presentation is the condition without which no affirmation or negation is possible. On this radical and primary level, every proposition that is intelligible is true (even the simple concept is true) in the sense of making any real object evident or manifest. The concordance or discrepancy that may arise with respect to what is affirmed or negated in such a proposition comes afterwards, and it can be established only upon the basis of the previous concordance in which the simple intelligibility of what is expressed consists.

The last difficulty before us is that of clarifying how the symbol can represent or make evident real objects in general. But this difficulty disappears in the outline of symbolic reason which we have drawn. For this difficulty is a heritage of the traditional scheme that must be overcome. It was not only difficult but also impossible to sustain objectivity, with the consequent claim to truth in thought, and at the same time to root the objectivizing function in subjectivity alone. We cannot base objectivity in the subject alone. Nor can we explain, having only the subject as our base, the relation of the symbol with the object and the possible comprehensibility of that object. For the key concept is not that of the subject but that of commonness, that of intersubjective relation. At this point the expressive factor reappears, no longer as disturbing objectivity, however, but precisely as its foundation. For objectivity is not obtained in a gnoseological relation of the subject with the object. *Objectivization transcends the individual subjective sphere.* For to objectivize is to manifest or to make a being evident in its proper reality, independent of who knows it, and this is a symbolic operation, which means a logical-dialogical operation. *Truth is objective because it is intersubjective.*

And this is the apparent paradox presented by the critique of symbolic reason, a paradox which may explain the repugnance of some toward accepting its conclusions or toward recognizing the facts on which it is founded. For it now turns out that expressiveness, far from creating a problem, in fact emerges as the very foundation of truth, and this foundation remains unaffected by the subjectivity inherent in the concrete expressions. It was claimed that the *logos* formed truths as pure *logos*, or as apart from expression (apart from the intersubjective relation), and this provoked the crisis of truth whenever the psychological facts in which the expressive subjectivity appears were made manifest. Hence also the consequent prejudice which consists in interpreting the concept of the *commonness of the truth* as a sort of consensus of opinions.[10] But truth is not a plebiscite. Truth can be contingent upon the consensus of others only when it was established previously as the product of one subject alone who would really need outside support in order to convince himself, like the Cartesian *ego*, that his thoughts are not a dream, which he may tend to think, despite their coherency. The concept of the commonness of truth only represents the radical fact of a symbolic co-participation, a common apprehension or possession of being by means of the *logos*. Truth is common because it is communicable.

Once we have restored its dual meaning of thought and word, we see that the *logos* is common or dialogical and that it always contains some form of truth as long as it *presents being*. Only an expression that is *per se* unintelligible would lack truth. In other words, truth is apophantic because it is poetic, active, or expressive. The proof of the truth is called verification, and *verificare* is *facere*, or to make, truth. Truth is a concordant making, and the first and decisive test to which it is subjected is that of its very production, that of its effective communicability.

Thus the more rigorous or scientific it is, the more poetic the truth is. Certainly, this "poet of truth" that the human subject is frequently crosses the frontier which marks the balance between objective representation and personal manifestation. For this frontier can be clearly set off only on the conceptual order. In real life it is undecided, and constant and careful vigilance is required to maintain it even insecurely, which means it requires methodology, the rational guide on the way. Not poetry alone, or the unreal fantasy, or the absolute arbitrariness of the individual is poetic. But science is not poetry for being subjective, as are those other forms of expression, but rather because it is an objectivizing operation, because it is a creation in the modality of strict representative expression.

V

Community is implied in the apparently solitary act of significatively thinking the real. This basic community does not depend upon the concordance of other subjects with the thinking subject, nor can it be compromised by their discrepancy with that subject. Discrepancy is in fact possible, in the sense of being epistemologically legitimate, when it is a question of opinions. In such a case the diverging thoughts all part from a common objective base. This commonness of a basic evidence constituted by "that which is being discussed" is the condition not only of the opinion which proves to be true, but also of that which turns out false.

On the first level of the truth, then, we encounter those simple manifestations of the real whose most purified and precise form is the concept. Since the process of conceptualization is discursive, there is no guarantee beforehand of conceptual truth. The correction of possible error is made by appealing to reality, by trying to give the conceptualized object a better definition. Thus neither does this error in fact compromise commonness, because the verification maintains the common referential. It develops without losing sight of the object itself whose concept requires correction. The concept pertains to "truths in fact." In science, too, it is facts that enable us to determine the truth or the error of an opinion, or to give an explanation of the facts or of a theoretical thesis. Science has no more secure foundation than this. Even principles are truths.

Naturally, there are matters open to opinion, or disputed questions, that cannot always be resolved by means of a direct reference to the facts. Valuations are a very obvious example of this. But neither are the objects corresponding to valuations material for scientific thought. However, valuative thought does not cease, for this reason, to have its proper logic, and even valuative judgments (for example, esthetic judgments), even though they may be questionable, keep their apophantic virtue. They continue to reveal an evidence, although the valuation of what is evident is not itself evident. The critical commentaries on a piece of sculp-

ture may differ with one another, but the statue is itself an object
of common experience, and for this reason it is the base both for
the favorable and for the unfavorable judgment.

Thus the triangular structure of knowledge emerges in all its
clarity: subject-object-subject. For it is not the personal relation
of the subjects with each other that maintains the community of
knowing and thinking, but the previous submission of both subjects to the things in question. Although the attention is directed
to the object, and not to the possible opinion of other subjects,
still the verification or truth-producing action is a concordant
action *in its gestation*. And furthermore, it is so because every
truth of representation essentially contains the possibility of re-
examining, and of letting others examine, that same common
reality to which it gave representation and which constitutes its
significative content. *The commonness of truth depends upon the
commonness of being*. Disagreement in the subjects does not
dissolve the oneness of the real. But being, evidently, does not
become common in its perception, which is individual. It becomes
common in the *logos*.

The truth of opinion is one of the most complex forms in the
scale of levels of truth. In representation, truth is eminently apophantic. The being represented is presented, even though, when
the presentation is a concept, it implies a producing action. In the
truth of opinion, on the contrary, this producing action predominates. Without ceasing to be apophantic (for otherwise it would
not be understood), the opinion is more "poetic." The subject
begins here to occupy a position on the first plane because the
opinion expresses precisely the position taken when it is a question of explaining the object. We are already in the realm of disputes. That about which we form opinions must, of course, be
identified in the opinion expressed. But, above all, it is the subject
who identifies himself and who makes himself known (even
though he is not speaking about himself and the I is not the significative content of his communicative intention, for our opinions
define and characterize *us*). In this type of communication, the
objective representation serves only as a base for a dia-logical

relation in which each of the interlocutors ex-poses himself in pro-posing his opinion. This is why opining is to be exposed or vulnerable.

It is exposed because it implies a responsibility. We have to answer for our own opinions before the opinions of others. As our opinions are personal creations, they represent us. But we have to answer for them also, and especially before the very things they expose. Nor can he dispense with those things who takes a position before them and who formulates his position with that *logos* of the *doxa* which is at once a personal representative and a representation of reality. For this reason the opinion is mutable, as Aristotle already noted (δόξα ἀβέβαιον), even though the thing itself continues to be what it is or stands firm in its being. It is the opinion-holder who is mutable. Hence the institution of science, as a system of immutable truths, represents, not the personal ambition of some subjects who would claim to have more solid truths than others have, but rather the ambition of giving to truths in general the same ontological solidity that things have or the ambition of placing the *logos* in correspondence with the *ontos*. This is onto-logy. All science is ontology in the literal sense.

In opinion we say that the subject begins to occupy the first place. But this does not only occur because the man is so formed or deformed that he cannot temper his involvement in the objective order, nor is it because he always longs to dominate others even at the cost of subjecting things to his interest, even at the cost of an incorrect vision of their real order. That predominance is more radically, if not better, explained in that the very things about which man has primary knowledge stop him from merely reflecting them. Primary knowledge is already an action. But this knowledge invites us to rise to a secondary, more elevated, phase where certain vital questions, which the mere presence of things does not resolve, can be answered. The what, the how, the why, and the wherefore are matter for opinion. The things are there; their real presence is verified. But this is nothing more than the beginning of knowledge, the prime matter which nourishes the innate human vocation of knowing. All knowing contains an unknown, which reveals its insufficiency. It also reveals our insufficiency, which we attempt to fill by advancing further on the way of knowledge. This advance is opinion, and with it we seek to explain things previously recognized, identified, and represented.

For this reason the truth of opinion is more expressive than the truth of representation. Being is better possessed in opinion. But this possession is more insecure because it is more "poetic." It is a work of personal creation. Is there any way of giving security to this possession? Paradoxically, security is obtained in community. *Shared* possession is the more solid and enduring, for while each claims to have the only formula of possession, the being comes out in the midst of the confusion of differing opinions.

Science represents the first attempt—the only attempt, in fact—that man has made to establish a rational community of knowledge. To put it in modern terms, what the Greeks did was to seek a formula of truth in which the community of thought might be consolidated in an effective, universal, and binding way. This could not be achieved on the subjective side, because the new "liberty of thought" which man had acquired in accentuating his ontic individuality gave rise to a variety of discordant opinions. The autonomy of the "I," which is the existential condition of thought, had increased. But, as a consequence, the "I opine" of each one was even more irreducible. Community had to be sought, then, on the objective side, appealing to the things themselves so that it would be the things themselves that decided concerning the truth or error of each opinion. This elimination of everything implied by the natural or spontaneous subjectivism and personalism of men (which sophistic thought always attempts to appropriate as part of philosophy) is what establishes forever the distinction between the *doxa* and the *episteme,* between vulgar prescientific opinion and scientific knowledge. Science sets out to give to its opinions a structure in which the hierarchic primacy of the apophansis over the *poiesis* is re-established as fully as possible. Truth has to be monstrative or demonstrative (apophantic or apodictic); in other words, it must show or represent being as it is, and not represent only the individual who thinks it.

Attained by means of the concordance of objective thought, this commonness of truth aspires also toward producing a conciliation, an attenuation of the bellicosity inherent in the exclusive "I opine." Although the advantage in this is ethical and is superadded to the purely epistemological advantage, it is not incidental or derivative. For the Greek—and it should be thus for everyone—this ethical aspect forms an essential part of the scientific vocation. For this reason the expression "scientific polemic" lacks meaning and is in fact a contradiction in terms. *Epistemé* was divorced from *Polemos* with Tales of Mileto. The only polemics possible are those between persons. Truths cannot be pitted against one another. As representations of reality, they are indifferent to subjective interests. To dispute concerning concepts is to infringe upon the *ethos* of science; it is to return to the level of mere opinion.

However, a modality of opinions which are not scientific, but not vulgar either, was and is still called philosophy. We have said that to opine is to take a position before reality. Whether we like it or not, in living in the midst of things we are vitally and integrally engaged in all our relations with those things, even in that relation which seems the most neutral: the cognitive relation. If the position we adopt is meditated, it deserves credit and has the virtue of being exemplary. Its expression can be that form of *philosophy* which is designated by the name of *sophia* or wisdom. This is a personal philosophy, and for that reason we cannot valuate it objectively, as we can do with the truth of *episteme*, by appealing to the things themselves. What is manifested in it is the attitude, the vital relation of an individual with things, and hence it is not the method but a subtle art like prudence, equanimity, and good sense that permits us to grant or refuse authority to it: more than purely rational science, it is the art of the reasonable.

Sometimes this form of the *doxa* which we call wisdom is articulated internally, embraces more things, and comprehends a greater number of vital relations, so that its complexity forms a fabric of theory. This creates a danger, already noted in Greece, which can never be completely suppressed because it roots in the very nature of things and of human affairs. It is the danger of confusing this natural inclination of theories with the theories of the philosophical *episteme*. In our day, as a matter of fact, men of science regard the *episteme* as concentrated entirely within the precincts of the particular sciences. They implicitly believe that philosophy is and can be nothing more than that uncertain *doxa*, endowed to a greater or lesser degree with wisdom. Some philosophers even think this. Based in this confusion, the attitude of scientists toward philosophy—which is the mother of science and is itself science—comes to be equivalent to the attitude which the first philosophers took toward the vulgar doxa and toward personal opinion.

The confusion disappears when we examine the structure of scientific knowledge and when we see that that structure is identical in both the theory of philosophical science and in the theory of positive science. As distinguished from the nonscientific theory, which is the wise opinion, scientific theory is characterized by the seeking of wisdom *in* the apophansis, in the adequate and disinterested representation of the things themselves, or in truth. But does not nonscientific wisdom contain truth? Indeed it does, but its truth is the truth of comprehension, and such truth is not susceptible to empirical or phenomenological proof. Its proof is of another nature and consists in vital or moral efficacy, an efficacy which is revealed in its persistence as an exemplar, in its integration into the continuity of a cultural tradition that shapes the existence of men and maintains the cohesion of their spiritual community.

This is not a theoretical, but a pragmatic, proof similar to that which natural science exhibits when it rests the truth upon the efficacy of its technical applications. In the case of the *sophia*, however, this proof is not a recourse which indicates a theoretical deficiency because its natural finality is properly in the practical order. The *praxis* here is not utilitarian, but ethical. This is the essential difference. In any case, the *logos* of wisdom is that in which the dialogical character of truth appears most clearly and externally. The exemplariness of ancient wisdom is nothing more than the dialogue which the men of the present maintain, across time, with the wise men of the past. This form of the presence of the past is what we call experience. It is a vital fortune which no individual can accumulate alone and which no community can lose without running serious risks of bankruptcy.

For this reason the man of science and the common man, both of whom tend nowadays to show great disdain and hostility for philosophy, incur thereby a double fault. In the first place, they ignore the fact of the identity of the structure of scientific knowledge in all its forms, a structure which we shall try to describe immediately. Second, they ignore the specific value of nonscientific philosophy. For neither is wisdom a frustrated science, nor can science be genuine science without wisdom. Even if the word philosophy were not used to designate various forms of thought, and even if it could not be anything but *sophia* or wisdom, we would always have to recover it—today more than ever because the particular sciences (the natural sciences, and especially physics) are becoming daily more pragmatic and utilitarian, which is to the detriment of that peculiar modality of the *sophia* which is obtained with the disinterested knowledge of reality. If, besides this loss, the philosophical *sophia* becomes invalidated, what other ethical and vital supports can give man the reason for his individual existence and for the existence of his community?

But the original and most eminent modality of philosophy is precisely the scientific modality. The science of philosophy and the particular sciences have the same internal structure. To make it more understandable, we might represent this structure as a pyramid divided, from the base to the top, into various successive levels. On the bottom level we would find the primary evidences, or the principles. Scientific work is mounted upon this base. The ascending movement does not take its departure, then, from a situation of void or lack of knowledge, or from a total crisis of prescientific knowledge, but is launched with the question suggested by the very things already known when we acquire the capacity of not regarding them as certain. Things are given, or are data for science. Even the possibility of responding to the question they suggest is given in the form of its mere presence before us. This means that science does not go in search of being. On the contrary, it can begin only from the evidence of being. This evidence does not become doubtful. It is the vulgar opinion we have formed about the what, the how, and the why of beings that is placed in doubt. Let us say that beings, all things, present no problem at "first sight."[11] Science is a "second sight" which we direct to things when we realize, with amazement, that the clarity of their simple presence involves an obscurity. It is an interrogating look from which we set out to organize a methodical observation. Thus science tries to reduce mystery to a rational problem. The mystery remains relegated (exalted?) to that edge of existence where mysticism and poetry have their proper meaning and where they treat of the mystery without claiming to make it disappear. This is the realm of the ultimate questions. Science aspires only to answering the penultimate questions.

On this second level of the pyramid, which is that of observation, science gathers and criticizes the facts of common experience and seeks others, pursuing a task which never ends. It is a task of endless gathering and correction. And although we designate it today with a name which has acquired great solemnity, that namely of "scientific investigation," it obviously corresponds to the most rudimentary and elementary level of science, which is the proletarian activity of carting materials.

The true constructive activity, which is the scientific aristocracy, as it were, begins on the third level of the pyramid, the level of laws. The data have no importance in themselves, which is as much as to say that mere erudition is sterile. The search for data and the examination of things and their relations were guided only by the desire to prove the internal laws in those things and relations, to verify their functional uniformities and regularities. Laws are also experienced facts, and their application depends upon a factual verification. This proof pertains, not to the pres-

ence of the thing, however, which is the object of common experience, but to its proper reason. This reason of the thing itself
has to be investigated methodically, and this is why the *doxa* or
vulgar thought was unable to reach it.

This characterization of the levels is schematic, and although
scientific work produces deformations as a result of the isolating
practice of specialization, we can already understand that the
levels of work do not correspond literally to subdivisions of the
body of scientists or to their classification into isolated depart-
ments. And it is so, apart from the variety in individual capacities,
because the levels themselves are not separated from each other
by the barriers of their respective characterizations but are inter-
communicated. The same scientist frequently passes from one
level to another. If he does not do it, others must because the
very organization of the body of science requires it. The mere
assembling of data is effected, or should be effected, by obeying
an intention of more or less definite inquiry. When we come to
formulating a law, it must first of all be tested, and the experi-
mental or other verification obliges us to return to the primary
level of the data from which we started. It is even necessary to
return to the facts from the top of the pyramid or from the highest level of science where we find the theories. The movement
from the bottom up, and from the top down, is incessant.

We have established, then, the fact of the intercommunication
between the levels. Now we must note that the work of science is
not concluded when the investigator succeeds in formulating a
law. The law allows us to group together or integrate a number
or definite field of individual facts. But in their turn, within the
same science, the individual laws also require integration. The
coherent grouping together, or synthesis of laws, is called a
theory and is the systematic culmination of the pyramid in any
science.

In order to understand the fact of the historicity of all science,
the scheme of the pyramid can help us because it brings out the
structural features of scientific thought. To be sure, as we ascend
from level to level, the creation factor augments in force, while

the representation factor remains constant. This is obvious even psychologically. It is not necessary to reason discursively for the simple observation and erudite gathering of separate facts. If the facts are correctly registered, the truth which this register contains is inalterable. Since there is almost no intervention of thought in this gathering activity, we can see that its results, in the same measure, are not historical. The task is more apophantic than "poetic."

Although the fact we have just pointed out is clear and seems elementary, we must underline the fact that it means the negation of the most accredited presumptions of scientific tradition. Men have always believed that the greatest truths, in the sense of being the most certain or definitive, were the culminating truths of theory. On the contrary, the culminating truths are the most precarious, while the most certain truths are the most elementary truths, the modest truths of fact. But these latter are the most certain precisely because they are the least significative. They signify nothing more than a perfection of the common prescientific observation. But they do not constitute science in the strict sense. They are only the material used in constructing science.

Science is construction, and it begins, strictly speaking, on the level of laws. These laws unquestionably possess the same apophantic force—or almost the same—as was possessed by the observation of the facts these laws comprehend. But the formulation of a law imposes upon us the obligation of reasoning discursively. Hence, in the same measure that the law is a work, a *poiesis*, is subject to historical variation as are all human works (and not only because of the external advances of the observation but because of the internal mutations of thought). The truth of the law is both true and historical at once. It is historical as a creation and true as an objective representation.

The theory is to the law what the law is with respect to observation. The theory defines categories, integrates laws, and presents systematic schemes in which the results of the scientific work effected on lower levels are summarized and in which at the same time guidelines for the methodical pursuit of this work are established. Obliging us to discursive reasoning even more than the laws do, however, the theories have a hypothetical meaning or value, even though they are formally presented as conclusions. They are even more historical than laws. And thus we see that the more rigorously and exaltedly scientific a truth is, the more precarious it will also be, because inevitably it will be more "poetic" than apophantic, more the work of active thought than the almost passive representation of pure facts.

Incidentally, this adventurous character of thought in the synthesis of theory is even more notable in physics than in metaphysics. A metaphysical theory which aspires in our age to possess any value and utility has to be phenomenological. This exigency of method does not permit metaphysics to ascend in so free a flight of theory as that of physical theory. And we see this not only in the declarations of the theoretical physicists themselves but also in the epistemological examination of their hypotheses. Not much is said of the theoretical hypotheses that had to be rejected because the analysis of the phenomena failed to confirm them. Natural science goes its way, and its history disdains to mention the paths that remained closed to it. But even the hypotheses that did obtain that confirmation were formulated in many cases by chance, that is, not as the synthesis of a body of previously established laws, but as a hypothesis in the usual sense of the word, as an anticipation that *postulates* a verification.

Phenomenological theories in philosophy can appear more "poetic" than physical theories, not because they are such by constitution and in their structure, but because their expression is such. The formulation of a physical theory is bound to conciseness by the symbolic system in which it is expressed, which is the mathematical system. The symbolic system of metaphysics, on the other hand, is the common language of men, and the same necessity of precision in terms, with a rigor that those terms usually do not obtain, permits and almost forces us to that greater expressive amplitude which manifests, with style, the creative participation of the thinker. But never would it be permitted in philosophy, as it is in physics, to risk a hypothesis in the expectation that some unknown facts may still appear to confirm it or oblige us to reject it. The philosophical theory will prove to be unfounded, according to either the interpretation it gives to the facts or the way of integrating them systematically. But it will have had to bow in advance before the methodological exigency of taking its departure from those facts.

VI

To sum up, in dealing with the problem of integrating the first three constituent relations of thought—or the epistemological, the logical, and the historical relations—we have seen that the problem can be resolved only by introducing a fourth relation, the dialogical relation, which is equally basic. In analyzing the structures of this dialogical relation, we have seen that the antimony between truth and historicity, which was the immediate cause of the crisis, has no basis in reality.

We have seen that every form of thought is symbolic and dialogical, and hence expressive, "poetic," or historical. This does not frustrate thought's search for truth. There are diverse or successive levels of truth from the primary apprehension of being as something present and evident to the complex and summarizing truths of theory. Truth is expressive. But not only is it expressive in its actual formulation, in which certain characterological and situational features of the subject communicating it are unquestionably manifested; the truth is congenitally and essentially expressive because it is produced with the *logos*, or with symbolic reason. This production of the *logos*, this opus of thought and of verbal expression, presents at once a communicative intention and a significative content. A significative content is an apophansis, which means that it succeeds in making a reality effectively patent and evident. If a thought is authentically significative or intelligible, it is true to the extent it is apophantic. But only primary truths, those of simple indication, can be merely apophantic. Upon this base, thought is the *logos* of an apophansis over which

we form a *poiesis*. All of which means that all discursive truth is
a *claim* to truth, something more than a mere exhibition of being.

The claim will turn out to be more or less fulfilled according as
the thought is more or less adequate, according as the thinker's
"poetic" opus is nearer to or further from the basic level of the
apophansis. When this fulfillment is obtained, the personal participation of the thinker seems to disappear because it is an
appeal to the things as they are in themselves, which permits
him to verify or make true his discourse. But in science, truth
inevitably becomes more historical or "poetic" as its level is more
elevated. From the facts to theories by way of laws, truth ascends
without losing its inherent apophantic truth. But it implies, as it
is higher in rank and more broad in scope, a greater contribution of creative activity. The highest truth is not, however, consequently spotted by arbitrariness, subjectivity, and relativity. The
theoretical creation was effected in accord with certain common
logical and methodological precepts, and always with due attention to the things, which constitute in themselves a common
reality. This ontological commonness, that of being and reason, is
what keeps science from being arbitrary. Thus the truth of science is dialogical, or expressive and historical, without being consequently reducible to the characteristics and intentions of the
subjective expressiveness which we always discover when a determinate individual communicates it. It is always a concrete individual, concrete in a determinate here and now, that pronounces
truth. This is a situation of fact. But the *right* of truth is independent of the situation and is founded in the effective fulfillment
of its inherent claim to being an adequate representation of being.

On the other hand, historicity itself has its own structure. It
does not express only the trivial fact that the thoughts of one
epoch are different from those of a previous epoch, but rather
the fact that this diversity constitutes a continuous and organic
line of evolution and reflects a mutation that is realized in accord
with an internal principle. This history of science—like every
change occurring in the universe—must be thought in categories,
must be conceived as a phenomenon obeying a law. The concepts

of horizontal and vertical structure are universal and binding. This means that they represent real and permanent forms of the process. It means that without these structures the process cannot be understood and that the third relation of knowledge therefore creates a problem of truth, rather than clarifying its meaning. And finally, it means that these concepts serve at the same time as methodological instruments for the positive investigation of all the facets of that historical process.

As in earlier ages, we need a science of science, and today it is possibly more pressing than ever before. This was traditionally called the theory of knowledge, and as such it was and remains a part of metaphysics. In a basic way, epistemology posed the question of the possibility and legitimacy of science in general, in the terms of the cognitive relation between the subject and the object. This relation was located outside of historical time. It was thought that the possible validity of a knowledge had to be *completely* independent of any historical mutation. With the awakening of the historical consciousness, however, that validity was compromised. But more than this, the examination of the new problematical situation that had been created tempted men to discard metaphysics; for metaphysics seemed to be indissolubly and constitutionally linked to the ahistorical modality of epistemology. As "a theory of science," metaphysics itself was in crisis. Although it had already discarded ontology, as had the metaphysics of Kant, what had broken down was also this form of "pure" epistemology. The transcendental subject had to be substituted by the historical subject, which is the real man.

If it was not to be limited to being a simple methodology of some particular science, philosophy had to center its investigations on that historical, real, and concrete subject. And that is what in fact happened. But that concentration can be interpreted as a retraction, as an evasion before the original theoretical problem, which was the problem of the principles of science and of knowledge in general. As a result, anthropological studies abounded. However, even though they were legitimate, they gave the false impression that philosophy was fortifying itself in anthropology as in a last refuge before the advance of the sciences. Paradoxically, the intensification of interest in human things made men forget that the study of man could and should yield the key for resolving the question of the conditions of possibility and legitimacy of science.

In any case, the new forms of anthropology became metaphysical, and this no longer represented a gain. As a matter of fact, it is not clear how philosophy, in the wake of the historicisms, could regard man as a *real* subject without reverting to metaphysics, that is, without developing an ontology of the human. One would have only to integrate the new epistemology into this ontology, which had to be the ontology of knowledge, or the ontology of man as the being of knowledge and as the historical producer of science. Thus ontology and epistemology now appeared to be as closely linked as they were before. If this is possible, the crisis has served, after the Kantian episode, to reveal that linking even more clearly than it was previously.[12]

The return to metaphysics was inevitable in order to overcome the crisis. In other words, the general problem of the crisis could be resolved only by means of a renovation of metaphysics which would permit metaphysics to overcome its own crisis. The new epistemology has to take its departure from the evidence that the *factum* of science is a historical *factum*. This is the data, the mass of historical phenomena which is constitued by the diverse sciences in their evolution. These phenomena must themselves be subject to scientific treatment, and this now means a historico-critical treatment, and not merely critical. As the history of science is also an order like any other reality, the work-program of this science of science establishes the necessity of investigating the internal structure of that order, the laws which regulate as a unit the formation and evolution of the diverse symbolic systems that constitute the particular sciences.

But this historico-critical epistemology must also be ontological. Science is historical because it is a human creation. This being the case, what is the ontological condition for the possibility of the act of knowledge? The analysis, at the end of which we can find an answer to this question, must fall back primordially upon the "verifying" or truth-making subject, upon the artifex or creator of science. Science is part of the human calling. It is an ontological potency which man realizes or actualizes in his historical existence. But this means that man is historical in his very being. And consequently the ontological and existential analysis must be, reciprocally, a historical analysis. Ontology cannot, any more than epistemology, be constructed "outside time."

This obviously necessitates a profound readjustment in the picture of traditional metaphysics. Now if the new metaphysics can legitimately be called *metaphysics of expression,* it is not only because it seeks to constitute an ontology of man as "the being of expression" but also because expression can no longer be regarded—as it has been regarded since Greece—as a human phenomenon independent of knowledge and thought. On the contrary, the phenomenological analysis has revealed that expression is a constitutive and essential factor in every act of knowledge that presents apodictic evidences and in every type and level of thought, no matter how purified it is formally. A *metaphysics of expression* is a phenomenological theory of reason. It is a metaphysics of symbolic or dia-logical reason, and it therefore assumes the task of uncovering the universal and common principles of science.[13]

Juan José López Ibor

Don Juan José López Ibor (b.1908) is Spain's foremost clinical and theoretical psychiatrist. Critic of Freud, author of the theory and concept of "vital anguish," he has given forceful expression to his clinical findings. His principal works include La angustia vital: patologia psicosomatica *(1950),* El descubrimiento de la intimidad *(4th ed. 1960), and* Las neurosis como enfermedades del ánimo *(1966).*

"Vital Anxiety" appeared in *Atlantide* Vol. III, No. 14 (March–April 1965) 115–134. © 1965 by Juan José López Ibor. Grateful acknowledgment is made to the author for permission to reprint.

VI. VITAL ANXIETY

A few years ago I published a book with this title. The qualifier "vital" has a precise meaning in that book. I was referring to anxiety that had an internal, *endotimic* origin, one not produced (though at times touched off) by the events of life. The expression "vital anxiety" has passed into colloquial language, and one understands by it the anxiety that the events of life produce, that is, that state of worry which belongs to daily life and today seems aggravated, or at least proves to be more evident, to the average man.

Anxiety is the great theme of contemporary philosophy and literature. Human existence runs its course from birth to death. Its limits are natural and irrevocable. Looked at from this angle, existence is like a bright ray of light standing out against the void. That state of being surrounded by nothingness constitutes the fundamental experience of human existence. That is what is called *anxiety*.

In the hospital receiving rooms we treat sick people. Often they are simple people whose capacity for introspection is slight and whose knowledge of ontological and metaphysical problems is *nil*. At times the patients speak of anxiety, and at times of fear. Very often they use neither of these two words but describe other sensations and disturbances. The word disturbance (*molestia*) proves more suitable here. *Molestia, malestar* (ill-being, indisposition). Their "estar" (condition of being) in life has changed. Existential philosophy speaks of being (ser) in the world. In Spanish there exist two words, "ser" (essential being) and "estar (conditional being). The latter has a concrete and definite meaning that is found in other languages absorbed into the word "ser" (being). In the "comprehensive anthropology" of Zutt, *Stand* is spoken of as a fundamental characteristic of human existence. Its meaning has a certain analogy with the "estar" of the Spanish language. One is (estar) in the world, in life, in a concrete way, with the life one *manifests*. One is (estar) well or ill. One is (estar) sick. One is (estar) happy or sad. One is (estar) anxious. One is hurt or in a bad mood. These are variations in the way in which one encounters oneself in the world; not in the world as objective reality, but as vital reality.

The fundamental core of neuroses is anxiety. Does the anxiety which neurotics experience have anything to do with the anxiety of existential philosophy? To what degree can we say the anxiety of the neurotic is anxiety toward nothingness, without being unfaithful to reality, by using this formula?

I

ANXIETY AND FEAR

The distinction between *anxiety* and *fear* is becoming quite common now. Anxiety occurs when one is faced with the unknown, and fear when one is faced with the known. The known always produces a lesser emotional impact because, insofar as it is known, there exists the possibility of avoiding the danger, of avoiding being dominated by it. For this reason the threat involved in anxiety is distinct from the threat involved in fear. *The transformation of anxiety into fear is a defense mechanism.* When a danger is objectivized, one is less afraid. What moves one profoundly is the unknown because it carries an immediate message from the nothingness that surrounds us.

The transitions between anxiety and fear are evident. Language crystallizes and solidifies fluid states of mind, but in the use of these words we do not follow philosophical rigor.

Sandor Rado reproaches Freud for imprecision in the use of the terms *Angst* (anxiety) and *Furcht* (fear). Fear always has an object, which anxiety lacks. This reproach, which may have some literal basis, fails to have any basis when the expressions are taken in their right sense. Psychoanalysis gives its favorite expressions a symbolic value. Castration anxiety is not a fear of being *actually castrated.* I believe that this anxiety exists only rarely with this character of actuality, that it rather *expresses* a fear of being castrated in one's personality, of the free development of personality being found amputated by repressions of the super-ego, that is, of the moral conscience. In such a case the fear is no longer fear of a concrete object but of an indeterminate restraint acting upon everyone at any given moment. Its indefinite character justifies the use of the word anxiety. Freud perceived the matter clearly on this point.

In another respect, one cannot establish an absolute distinction between anxiety and fear. In reality—on the psychological level, it is understood—there exist transitions between both: very often it is a question of an "anxious fear" and a "fear upon which anxiety supervenes," two different expressions. *Panic* is a fear of everything, of a danger that threatens from every side, and, at bottom, from no side. Language has a wealth of words showing how many nuances exist among similar states of mind. Between fear and anxiety we could situate *dread*, in which the impact of the unknown is more evident than in fear.

Nicolai Hartmann criticizes the differences established between anxiety and fear (fear having a concrete object and anxiety an indefinite object). Anxiety is also felt in the face of something concrete. What is concrete in anxiety is its character of *all-pervading threat*. If one wishes to call this a concrete experience, then anxiety does have an object. The reality, however, is that such an all-pervading threat is of a diffuse character. It is something that approaches a person and hovers over him without his knowing what it is. This is why the patient may often break into flight, as happens in crises of running amuck. But even though the experience is threatening and all-pervading, there is no need to imagine that it is too closely bound up with a spatial scheme. At other times, the subject feels the threat as if something were missing under his feet, as if he could not go on subsisting. They are distinct forms of experiencing nothingness.

At the present time the significant perimeter of anxiety has been disproportionately extended. Freud speaks of *Realangst*, of real anxiety, referring to the emotion that is experienced in a concrete situation, in the face of a definite danger which comes from outside. On the other hand, Kant speaks of anxiety as a degree of fear, and Nietzsche says, "Furcht vor dem Tode als europaische Krankheit," in a situation in which we would now speak of anxiety. And Kierkegaard himself, who gave the word anxiety its new expressive potentiality, says, in *The Concept of Dread*, "that fear, that horror before the abyss of our consciousness."

That anxiety is found in the basis of human existence is the postulate of existential philosophy. Heidegger calls attention to the ontological and metaphysical character of his works. For him the psychological applications are illegitimate; however, they have been made by different authors, and rightly so. When philosophers attempt to uncover the mysteries of the human being in thought and in will, a psychology also arises. And now it has turned out that, from the point of view of existential anthropology, thought, the instincts, or any other human peculiarity give us an inadequate perspective on man. It is necessary to look for that perspective in something more central, in moods, dispositions, and states of mind.

II
ANXIETY, ANXIOUSNESS, TEDIUM, WORRY, NAUSEA

Dictionaries define anxiety, in another respect, referring to "affliction," and relating "affliction" to "grief" and to "sadness." Thus, common language recognizes the transitions that exist between anxiety and sadness as states of mind.

It has been discussed a great deal whether *anxiety* and *anxiousness* are the same. For me they are facets of the same experience. We can consider them in our imagination as situated on different planes: anxiety is deeper, more visceral, more physical, and more constrictive. Anxiousness is higher, more noetic, and freer. When one analyzes well what the experience of anxiety is, one runs up against the two aspects of this gradation: a) *dread* of a dissolution of the unity and continuity of self; b) a "vertigo of freedom," which appears when dissolution threatens.

They are two phases of the same lived-out event, the first expressed by the word *anxiety* and the second by the word *anxiousness*. In the first, there is a kind of distention of the existential *ecstasis*. In the anxious experience the subject comes to the border of the first phase, so to speak, of his being. (A step from non-being to being, from inertia to movement.) He never arrives at it because that would be the very dissolution of being. But that proximity gives it the characteristics of an experience of arresting lived-out time.

When everything is possible, on the other hand, time runs along more quickly because interior time is not a physical time nor a biological time, but an expression of passage from the present to the future. This passage is made in the form of a project. As has been said so many times, the self lives so far as it is worked out, and this working out is, in turn, the projection of lived-out time. When the crisis of anxiety goes beyond its second phase and the whole spread of possibilities appears before being, there is something like an inflation of interior time and a lack of time to realize all that could be realized. In the daily life of the normal man—outside the stellar moments of existence—we speak of time which passes. It is as if time objectivized itself into something external to ourselves. The approximation of this experience to the experience of physical time is evident. In anxiety, it is not time which passes but the subject himself. This transient character of subjectivity is clearly revealed in the crisis.

This is the link of anxiety with *tedium* or *boredom,* another basic state of mind. In boredom the note of novelty which every moment of our life offers us, in respect to the moment before, disappears. The present moment is different from the past. That distinction may reveal itself in two forms, one *extrinsic,* that is, based on the different content, and another *intrinsic,* given by the succession itself of moments. The first is based on the existing differences occupying each moment: I can exist either reading or taking a walk or thinking. I can think about my patients, about my books, or about my children. When this occupation does not appear as distinct, having something novel about it in regard to the previous occupation, a boredom arises which we could call *exogenic.* To defend himself from this kind of boredom, the subject attempts to "kill time," revealing an ultimate sense of privateness, since being—while one lives—has no reason for perceiving time as such a unit of living.

The second, the *intrinsic* novelty given by the succession itself of moments, consists in the following: if we were faced with physical time, we could not speak about novelty. In a straight line the points are equal to each other, but in the straight line of life it does not happen this way; instead, the points succeed one another as generated one by the other. There is no mathematical relation between them but, instead, a *filial relationship.* The fact is clear: in a project, each moment of its realization depends on the previous one and is the seed of the next. Life is, in itself, a project, and each moment comes with a new charge, with a *quantum* of novelty. When this does not happen, a boredom appears which, in contrast to the previous one, we could call *endogenic.* It is existential boredom, the experience of the *emptiness* of life.

Anxiety, anxiousness, boredom, are states of mind which, in spite of their clear differences, have wide zones of confluence. A state of mind, such as we live it, is a totality that takes on different colors but whose substance is the same.

Worry is another attitude of mind close to the previous ones. Here one notes more the active aspect of the mind. Worry, pre-occupation, is (it is obvious as soon as we say it) what precedes occupation but what precedes it in a special way, as a projection of what is going to be done. When one does not know what road to take, one is worried. Worry supposes the freedom that is found at the bottom of the experience of anxiety except that when the active level transforms itself, in contrast to the extreme passivity of anxiety, we come closer to the world of the concrete. It is the same with doubt, perplexity and uneasiness. They are aspects of the same experience realized on different planes of the person. Doubt falls on the noetic plane even when it is doubt about act-ing. One doubts when he makes one decision instead of another, when he thinks this or that. Uneasiness edges toward the psycho-motor plane. It is an interiorization of the reactive watchfulness of being, ready to leap from one action to another. Perplexity is manifested doubt, and at the same time insecurity about the interpretation of what is perceived as a message from the outside world.

When we turn to the vegetative plane instead of to the plane of collectivity, other facets of the lived-out experience of anxiety appear. Suffocation is the oppression of anxiousness that goes to the point of making free contact between the being and the out-side world difficult. Suffocation supposes the stoppage of this interchange and for that reason is associated with the sensation of lack of air. In the suffocating sensation of the "hysterical knot" the sensation refers more to the digestive apparatus but at bot-tom is equivalent. In longing we find ourselves with two signifi-cant pointers. Sometimes it expresses the desire of doing, but an excruciating desire, like one impelled by a living time and con-suming itself. In their cases, "being anxious" means something similar to nausea.

The sensation of *nausea* is equivalent to that of *disgust* or *repugnance* except that these latter move on a more imaginary plane and the former on a more real plane, and for this reason its vegetative accompaniments are more numerous. Nausea is found close to vomiting and often designates no more than the vegetative crisis that precedes it. Since the crisis takes place in the form of vegetative oscillations, it is usually spoken of (in Spanish) in the plural.

Nausea was the title chosen by Sartre to designate the fundamental experience of the character in his novel. What is it that nauseates Roquetin? The inconsistency of existence. There is nothing stable except what we have brought into existence. This experience reveals to us something that remains hidden or unpublicized in daily life: that anything can happen to us; but this possibility is formulated not as abstract but as lived-out. There are no rules or fixed frames of reference. Chance, space, and time exist and are elastic, soft. "The everyday world becomes evanescent; we sink into nausea." This crisis is anxiety projected onto the surrounding world. This is why "anything can happen to us." Arising in this way, the crisis is *vertigo*. Nausea of existence is existential *vertigo*.

But in these considerations I have decided to maintain myself on the psychological plane in as pure a way as possible. The analogy between nausea and vertigo is not revealed by the common usage of both words in Spanish but by the vegetative disturbance which underlies both phenomena.

Nausea is, on the vital plane, like disgust, an attitude toward life itself. It indicates a form of existence close to lower nature, close to chaos, dissolution. Rotten, corrupted objects nauseate and disgust us. In order for a food to permeate us it should maintain its proper being; as soon as it loses that and discomposes, it disgusts us. The same happens with vital experience. Life disgusts us when it loses its proper being or, as is usually said, its reason for being. What is a life without a reason for being? It is life reduced to the chaos of the instincts, to personal and infra-personal biology. What keeps life free from corruption, what keeps it from discomposing, is what connects it and imposes its project upon it: we call that the *person*. Without personal tension, life falls into the anonymity of everyday life.

Another of the terms in which we speak of states of mind is *grief*, which constitutes a bridge or transition between fatigue and sadness. In St. Teresa grief is found as a synonym for fatigue. These states of mind are found to be closer to the emotions, that is, to states of mind determined by external impacts.

Another term in the series is *agony*, which, in the common language, signifies the grief of the dying person. From this it has taken on the image of the animal and vegetative disorder (that occur) when consciousness disappears. "Agony" is the vegetative disturbance of nausea and disgust. The deeper significance led Unamuno to choose this word in *The Agony of Christianity*. I also used it referring to psychoanalysis. Agony means struggle. A man agonizes who lives struggling against life itself and against death. St. Teresa said: "I am dying because I do not die." Anxiety presents us with the same agonized depth. The crisis appears to be a dialectic between the personal and apersonal in man, between the self and the thing. But it is not only this: basically the dialectic is established in the very depths of anxious experience, which fluctuates like a wave that rises threateningly and subsides peacefully until the end comes.

Bollnow says that human existence can be interpreted by starting from any state of mind, and he tries to do it by starting with the states of *exaltation:* the experience of "high noon," of ecstasy, etc. Heidegger chose anxiety, but really the same could have been achieved with another point of departure. The hermeneutics of pathological states of mind shows that anxiety is chosen because it permits us to see more fundamentally what there is at the heart of being. The more pathological they are, the more the states of mind of the same character show their anxious texture, probably because their pathological state arises from deeper layers. In the limit of the depth of existence there is found non-existence, nothingness. Emptiness, tedium, and disgust become existential when they plunge deeper toward that boundary. When more superficial, they are assimilated to daily life and fill it with contents.

III
Normal and Abnormal Anxiety

The pattern is the following one: a *normal* subject can experience fear when faced with concrete situations. A *normal* subject also knows anxiety when he manages to come close to the deepest plane of existence, in a true process of existential enlightenment. Of all the experiences of everyday life, the one which most often produces anxiety is the consideration of death, that is, the experience of the *intrinsically finite character of existence*. The situations in which that experience comes through are full of anxiety, but so also, in general, are all the situations that cause the human creature to sense his helplessness. A normal man feels stripped of value before the unencompassable and incomprehensible. But these words have to be given very special nuances in order that they may indicate the characteristics of the situation plastically.

The situations of the patient in which anxiety presents itself can be concrete. There exist crises of global, panic-filled anxiety which are suffered before everything and in respect to everything. In its acuteness and violence, global anxiety leaves no room for the one who suffers from it to analyze his experience. But, along with this global anxiety there always appear the two specters that basically threaten the patient: madness and death. Apart from the global crises of anxiety there exist crises released by a definite situation. Without going now into a more minute analysis, I do wish to remark that such concrete situations acquire the character of revelations. What the patient feels, then, is his basic anxiety made patent by a concrete experience. *It is a true "aletheia" of the anguished depths of the human being.* A patient will feel anxiety when confronted with snakes or open squares or the necessity of entering a railway car. The situation has, not a general meaning for the subject, but a *specific* one. A woman patient will feel anxiety when confronted by spiders. She felt it for the first time when she was searching in a small-town cemetery for her father's remains; he had been murdered during the war and his body thrown into the common ditch. The spider revealed to the patient, through the experience of the death of her father, the experience of her own finitude. Anxiety, when faced with the spider, was the same as anxiety in the face of death. This is precisely what is abnormal: that situations and experiences of everyday life plunge from the everyday plane of normal life to the profound plane of existence.

The most banal object can be *anxiogenetic;* but it generates anxiety, not in a primary way, but in a secondary way, by the *revelation* of the *primordial* anxiety-filled situation. This revelation can take different paths: the evocation of a memory, the ascription of a value to a definite object or animal (for example, snakes or spiders). What is abnormal is the anxiogenic importance given to trivial objects, entities, or situations. There exist certain categorial orders among these anxiogenic stimuli. The typification of the forms of anxiety depends on these orders, and thus its forms prove to be frequent or habitual: agoraphobia, claustrophobia, and so on.

Morbid anxiety offers another differential characteristic. Anxiety is the expression of a way one encounters oneself in the world, and so we should speak of a *basic fundamental anxiety* rather than of a reactive anxiety. As a consequence, there remains fixed in this expression the constitutive bipolarity of the experience which a being situated in the world actually has. In morbid anxiety the "subject" pole acquires dominance. *Anxiety occurs because of what happens in him,* not because of what really happens outside him in the exterior world. This internal, intra-historical happening can be analyzed from different points of view.

According to Freud, anxiety occurs as dread in the face of the cyclonic movements of one's impulses or, even better, as a repression of the true object of anxiety. This dread has its genesis in the childhood situation when the child feels himself incapable of consciously admitting the source of a feeling of threat, for example, paternal repression (castration anxiety). Mowrer says that any repressed fear can crop up again in the form of anxiety. The repression itself makes the subject more vulnerable when faced with threats and so augments his neurotic anxiety. My point of view differs from those I have cited, but for the immediate analysis of this problem it does not matter whether one maintains one interpretation or the other. One always arrives at the conclusion that the dominating factor in morbid anxiety is what occurs in the interior of the subject. The role of the external event is that of revealer, a release or crystallizer of the anxiety-filled situation. The world of the patient suffering anxiety is not the same as that of the normal man. It is a morbidly "privatized" world with personal landmarks, with promontories and straits very different from those of the normal man, which can go to the unlikely degrees of which psychiatry is aware.

We should analyze what types of conflicts provoke anxiety. It is often stated that conflicts of anxiety are of an instinctive nature. In fact, in crises a patient is filled with anxiety when faced with his own instincts. Why? Because their release threatens to dissolve the personality. Fear of the instincts, whichever they may be, is fear of the monster a being carries within itself. Sometimes it is fear of the liberation of the aggression instinct (the possibility of becoming a criminal, phobia for knives, for sharp-pointed objects, for being alone and so being able to carry out the aggression, and so on). At other times it is fear of the liberation of the sexual instinct—normal or abnormal. An unmarried female patient had a homosexual experience. She is very religious; however, what fills her with anxiety is not the idea of guilt, on the normal plane, even though this also grieves her. The most important thing for her is the idea of having been able to commit an abnormal action. What is monstrous is, not the sin in the religious sense, but the sin against herself, having let, or having been able to let (what was anomalous in her) manifest itself. It seems to her that normal persons are not like that, that they do not have any monster inside themselves. Two months earlier the patient had had her first heterosexual experience. She was sorry for having broken God's law, but she was also happy about what had happened because she realized she was like others, that she could enjoy sex as they did. Here the difference is clearly seen between the lapse on the normal plane and the lapse on the plane of anxiety. Both can be lapses, objectively, but the anxiety which adheres to one or to the other is different in quality. In the first case confession freed her from her feeling of guilt. In the second it did not free her because what was important was not that she was pardoned but that she had become an abnormal being.

Fear of the unleashed instincts is fear of ceasing to be oneself, of alienating oneself. The innermost structure of the ego, in its unity and in its continuity, is threatened. Such an innermost structure, normally, is not capable of being lived out.

A frequent thesis is that anxiety is abnormal when it cannot be endured. Escape from anxiety is neurosis. One escapes by means of certain mechanisms of discharge, alleviation, or defense; by means of these the anxiety does not reach consciousness but is repressed. This discharge of anxiety, says Hafner, is found not only in neuroses but also in the constitution of many social structures and ways of thinking. In the very structure of everyday life one finds the fact that the boundary of anxiety becomes impassable and so keeps the anxiety from breaking out into consciousness. Anonymous life is a life without conscious anxiety. The contrary occurs in authentic existence, which goes along by leaps, by spasms. Anxiety contributes to the anthropogenesis of each one of us and in this sense shows its positive valences.

The positive value of normal anxiety develops around a new way of establishing relations with the world which becomes more acceptable. This mutation should not be understood in an egoistic or narcissistic sense, but in a sense of purifying existence of so much useless ballast that is added to it in the course of life. Habits are necessary, but not to the point of drowning daily life in pure automatism. On the plane of being carried along by everydayness, a person should maintain himself by his creative capacity. A fitting existence does not suppose a break with the world, nor does it suppose an impersonal surrender to the world of things and persons.

W. Schulte asks if anxiety should not belong to the region of the *pudenda,* of that about which one should not speak. Contemporary society forces an opening and does not tolerate any concealment and reserve. From the psychological point of view the liberation of interior pressures is considered healthy. To what point precisely this is true is something that should be submitted to examination. Maturity of personality is not achieved by this process of discharging interior pressures. On the contrary. It proves interesting to oneself whether learning to keep anxiety in the zone of the *pudenda* is something the personality needs for its maturity.

On the other hand, anxiety in the neurotic impedes this normal anthropogenetic growth. The development of the personality is frustrated. Neuroses are sicknesses that keep a man from "being a man." Boss speaks of neuroses as diminutions of existential possibilities, and von Gebsattel as inhibitions in development.

But, in my opinion, in all these explanations of anxiety one assumes a mistaken point of departure, the identity of normal and abnormal anxiety. What is different, it is said, is the means of defense. The fact is that the means of defense are abnormal because anxiety is primarily abnormal. It is abnormal, to begin with, in the way the subject perceives it, that is, in its very presence. Patients often say this. Being abnormal in their genesis and in their manifestation, it is natural that the means of defense that the organism deploys should be abnormal in themselves or abnormally used. I am referring to alcohol and toxins in general. Humanity has always had recourse to them as means of alleviating anxiety. The euphoria that appears at times is a euphoria brought about by liberation from anxiety; but in many people suffering from anxiety the use of such a means of defense goes beyond normal limits, and a toxicomania arises which is not in the products that remedy the pain but in the person who takes them. The toxin turns out to be an agent that is destructive of the personality, secondary to the primary destructive impulse of an insatiable anxiety.

Action also calms anxiety. In instinctive action there are mechanisms of defense against anxiety. A desire for power tends to give confidence to the one who possesses the desire and so to hide, from himself, the fissures and cracks in his personality. Sexuality tends to communication, but when power and sexuality infiltrate anxiety, instead of contributing to the development of the human person they contribute to its undoing. Anxiety-filled sexuality loses its capacity for being a bridge of communication. What is primary, in this case, is not a disturbance of sexuality but an anxiety-filled alteration that infiltrates sexuality; thus, on the one hand, it exalts sexuality, confusing it with the whole idea of the person, and, on the other hand, perturbs it, paralyzes it, closes it in on itself, keeping it from unfolding as a personal means of communication. The fundamental note in sexual perversions consists in their inhibitory and destructive character. One speaks in Freudian language of "masochistic" or "autopunitive tendencies," expressions which allude to the negative dynamics of abnormal anxiety.

IV
THE SOMATIZATION OF ANXIETY

In a normal man the impact of anxiety or of any other emotional state upon his somatic registers has certain molds through which it runs. When Tom, the well-known patient with a gastric fistula studied so minutely by Wolff, found himself faced with a dangerous situation—consisting in the fact that the doctor was able to discover one of his errors, and he became disturbed over this—his gastric activity was suspended, and his state became that of preparation for flight. When Tom fell into a state of anxiety because he did not know what would happen to him once he left the hospital, his gastric activity speeded up. In the second case his conflict was more personal. It may be that, strictly speaking, both types of reaction in this case cannot be qualified as fear and anxiety; but the case constitutes a good example of how each emotion has a prearranged physiological path, within certain limits, along which it flows. It is not a question of fixed patterns or of patterns without individual variations. The same happens in reactions to physical stimuli. In the face of certain efforts, some subjects respond by accelerating their respiratory rhythm, others with high blood pressure, others with perspiratory secretions. What is pathological begins when they jump their limits quantitatively and qualitatively. For it is a question along general lines of reactions that are inappropriate not only because exaggerated but also because they are deviate. A patient with a weak heart has not only tachycardia but also edematic. Analogous events occur in the expression of crises or the state of anxiety.

The first difference, in contrast to normal anxiety, is found in this: that normal anxiety is lived out almost exclusively on the psychic plane. This "almost" does not mean to allude to anything more than the necessity of always taking the body into account when we speak of man. A healthy man finds himself so well regulated that the physiological repercussion of his emotions is minimal and always suited to the degree of the emotion. The more somatized anxiety is, the more morbid it becomes. The anxiety crisis which is translated into a brilliant and bitter vegetative symphony is an abnormal crisis. But it is not only this. The repercussion upon the organic keyboard does not coincide with the habitual patterns of reaction. The reaction flows along other paths, leaps boundaries, isolates itself, becomes independent and persistent. The deviation, the leap, the independence, and the fixation are characteristics which appear in all states of morbid anxiety.

Morbid anxiety takes place on a more profound plane than normal anxiety. This is why its description is often deeper. The patient does not say he has *anxiety:* yet he *does.* The patient speaks vaguely of headaches or tremors or palpitations, and those vague symptoms which are always expressed by means of circumlocutions, "it is as if," which allude to an inner experience of anxiety—*logopheny.* Often when the patient recognizes that these phenomena which occur in him are phenomena of anxiety, he is already on the way to being cured.

I would like to call attention now to a peculiarity which may, perhaps, be the most important one in pathological anxiety. Anxiety is a vital feeling and, as such, is an immediate mode of perception of corporeality; but pathological vital feelings, in contrast to normal ones, are not pure vital feelings in Scheler's sense, but sensorial feelings. We see this same peculiarity in vital sadness as a key symptom of depressions. The patient feels pathological anxiety not only as a diffuse indisposition associated with the primary experience of corporeality, but as anchored in definite places in his body. Abnormal anxiety is concentrated not only in the somatic geography (a dull pain in the epigastrium, precordial oppression, a lump in the throat, migraine, neuralgia, and so on) but also in the psychic geography in the form of phobias. The symptom emerges in the place where the abnormal anxiety appears somatized. In conclusion, vital anxiety is a hybrid of sensorial feeling and vital feeling which provokes in turn reactive or, rather, psychic feelings and attitudes, in Scheler's sense.

V

REPETITION AS DEFENSE

Kubie sees in repetition what is specifically neurotic in a determinate act. "Whether an act is healthy or neurotic depends solely on the constellation of forces that determine it. If such forces, whether they are purely psychological or combinedly psychological and organic, are of such a nature that they predetermine the automatic repetition of the act, independently of any consideration, this act is neurotic, and the forces that determine it generate neurosis. This is the essence of what is psychopathological in human conduct."

We find ourselves faced with one of the most important questions of psychopathologically abnormal life. At a definite moment in the evolution of his thought, Freud brought to light, in his own way, the relations existing between the impulse of repetition and the instinct of death. There is something in organic matter that impels it to seek the state anterior to its appearance, something "that carries life inexorably toward death," he said.

There appears in the constitution of neurosis, also inexorably, this tendency to repetition. Reiteration is found included, moreover, in the dynamic of many psychotic disturbances. When a crisis of anxiety passes, its *passing* is no more than its mutation into a series of phobias or obsessions, subject to imperative change of repetition. In my book, *Vital Anxiety,* I was inclined to admit a dual genesis of both phenomena. Repetition, I then thought, is found anchored in what is biological.

But the heart of the phenomenon is much more complex. The experience of anxiety is, in reality, an experience of a limit-situation which one does not succeed in possessing in its fullness. To the extent that the experience approaches its *acme,* it is more unbearable. In its very internal dialectic there appear the regulatory impulses that keep it from reaching its limit. For this reason the subject who is close to falling into the unbearable fullness of anxiety, into the flooding of his being with nothingness, adheres to *something,* a psychic content. The anxiety then ceases to expand and crystallizes itself around a content which presents itself as a "motive" for the anxiety. This is how phobias are constituted. The defensive role they have in the dynamic of the anxiety-process is evident. The appearance of phobias supposes an "enchronization" (temporalization) of anxiety. The *multum* is transformed into the *multa.* Repetition is a way of giving temporal form to the infinite dimension of anxiety.

This upsetting of the temporal structure of anxiety appears in the life of primitive peoples, indicating the distinction between *cyclical time* and *historical time.* The cosmic, primary anxiety of the primitive man engenders the idea of cyclical time as a defense. What will happen, what will come later? Historical advance is an advance toward death, toward nothingness. Newness is a category that makes the primitive man shudder. What is new must be integrated with what is known, so that it does not cause anxiety. The negation of history, the mechanical repetition of the cosmic cycles or of social or individual life, defend him against the "terror of history." In life "what is new" frightens us because it shows the possibility that there is something hidden

behind what is known and because it is a rush toward death. Man
saves himself from that terror by thinking that it was "like the
other time." The first night must have been dreadful for the first
man. When the new day came and he saw it was like the day
before, he felt calm. Night continues to be, for many victims of
anxiety, the replica of nothingness. Man's acceptance of historical
time, of becoming, is a considerable achievement; it is an acceptance which cannot take place without a certain amount of anxiety.
To the extent that the velocity of historical time increases, the
quantum of anxiety increases. Contemporary man finds himself
exhausted by this experience. To consume the stages of history is
a feat that is accomplished by one's being consumed in one's turn,
in one's innermost being, by the devouring fire of anxiety. The
person suffering from phobia, in what refers to his phobia, lives
in cyclical time instead of historical time. The "eternal return" of
the phobia is a defense against the experience of anxiety, which
does not make it disappear but which minimizes it. It is a vacci-
nation against anxiety, at the cost of spreading out in time the
presence of that fissure in the personality which is the experience
of anxiety.

VI
FREEDOM AND FIDELITY IN EXISTENCE

What separates normal anxiety from pathological anxiety is not
the themes of each. Tillich enumerates three directions from
which nothingness threatens being. Nothingness threatens the
ontic affirmation of being, relative to its destiny: this threat is
death. Nothingness threatens man insofar as he affirms himself
spiritually before emptiness: it is the threat of the absurd in
existence. Nothingness threatens the self-affirmation of man with
respect to guilt: it is the threat of condemnation.

The clinic offers us these same themes: anxiety in the face of
death, the justification of death by the lack of meaning in life,
and the feeling of guilt which is so vividly expressed in endoge-
nous depressions. But does there exist any difference in the way

such themes are presented in a normal man and in a sick man?

The question is always reduced to the experience of nothingness. Guilt is nothing but the infiltration of nothingness into the past. The feeling of normal guilt adheres to facts that the person experiences as morally unlawful. The sense of guilt of sick persons, in a first examination, also appears inserted in past actions of doubtful morality or frankly immoral. That there is a difference between both cases proves to be evident. A normal fault can be expiated in one way or another. In normal life one frees oneself from guilt by means of new acts of life itself: reparation, confession, self-conquest, etc. The abnormal fault is inextinguishable, unless the sick person is cured. There has often been a great deal of irony expressed about the value of morality in human life, based precisely on the melancholiac's sense of guilt which disappears by means of a few electro-shocks or pills. Conscience wiped out by a few convulsions or by pharmacology! People who are ironic about such subjects show a certain shortsightedness in their knowledge of the inner life of man. The feeling of morbid guilt, if it is analyzed deeply, appears to adhere not to this or that act in past life, *but to the very act of living*. The sick person expresses his experience in concrete form for the same reason as always: the experience of anxiety is unbearable. The very fact of living is what produces the feeling of guilt. It is life itself which is worthless because it is impregnated with nothingness. Guilt, emptiness, and death are no more than historico-collective or historico-individual versions of the threat of nothingness. This threat is presented without justification before the sick person, not by a reflective process, but in a sudden way, making obvious the absurdity of existence. And it does not appear on the philosophical plane but in one's innermost life.

The fundamental question left to examine now is whether *in its very interiority* normal anxiety is different from pathological anxiety, or at least one can manage to catch sight of the moment in which both forms of anxiety separate. Let us try to penetrate into the very structure of the vital act. At the very heart of existence, the experience of freedom is found: not of freedom as a motivated decision and reflected act, but as a primordial form of decision which is the same as existing. Every choice is a decision about oneself; in every choice the existence of the being is committed. Jaspers points to an ultimate establishment of the free act in the very existence which decides. That primary decision carries implicitly in it a *fidelity to existence:* this is why the decision is always creative—because existence flows from it.

Something different takes place in the world of pathology. The *fidelity to existence* that the primary decision supposes is found shaken to a greater or lesser degree, and a gap appears in the innermost creative heart of being—a gap in which it is not possible for the creative decision to take place. *That gap is what indicates the presence of sickness.* One cannot speak of a "conscious nihilism of the personality" as a secret will of the person which leads him to surrender, as von Gebsattel says. If there is a nihilist gap, it is unconscious, but it does not affect the plane of will as a choice between motives; it affects an anterior structure, that depth in which the existing subject, still without the light of consciousness, affirms his existence. The affirmation of existence in the sick person shows a lack which is made apparent to us in the neurotic products.

It is very important to know whether there is an affectation of the disposition of freedom and will in the neurotic. It is not that the neurotic freely decides to be a neurotic, but that he is dragged into being a neurotic, though there may come a *second moment* in which he lets himself be carried along, more or less, by that force (*neurotic surrender*). Neurotic will appears only in simulation.

In the psychotherapeutic task it is essentially important that there be clarity about the supposed nihilism of the personality, a nihilism to which the neurotic is compelled by the nothingness in his innermost sphere of being.

In the opening of possibilities in the anxiety crisis there also exists a differential note between normal anxiety and pathological anxiety. The possibilities in normal anxiety float in the future. *Everything can happen:* this or that danger threatens the subject, but the threat is experienced with a feeling of distance, as the future is. The future is a continuation of the present; it is a developing of temporality, but its quality is different. In the very structure of the future there is something qualitatively distinct from the present. The future acts upon the present without ceasing to be future.

On the other hand, in morbid anxiety the future has approached the present. It is not yet present, but it is experienced as such. A person suffering from anxiety may do so because of a real danger, for example, the danger of world war. The difference between the person suffering from normal anxiety and the one suffering from pathological anxiety is established at the heart of the lived-out experience itself. The danger which in the case of the normal subject stands at the door (anxiety "before"), in that of the sick person is already in the house. The future becomes the present, that is, it takes on the qualities of the present. What threatened from the future is now here, as a threat which spreads its imprisoning nets around the sick person. Naturally, it is not the whole of the future, only that around which the anxiety concentrates in the form of phobias and obsessions. Possibility is experienced in one way by a healthy man and in another way by a man suffering from anxiety. Possibility in morbid anxiety is alienogenous because it carries implicitly in it the threat that the being may be converted into another being (alienated being) or into non-being (death as the image of nothingness). Any possibility in real life, for example, the danger of a war or of a sickness, is experienced very differently by the healthy man and by the man suffering from anxiety. In the latter such a possibility carries within itself something ominous, strange, incomprehensible, a secret possibility of transforming him.

However, there must be something more at the heart of it. We can speak of nothingness without being frightened because the positive affirmation of being, in a state of health, can allow us to do it. It is not that one needs "the courage to be," as Tillich says, but that this courage is implicit in life itself without requiring any effort. The positive forces of life act as a current which rushes forward and finds its way as it advances. This is called "a sense of being alive." Health is not defined by quantitative variations, but by this implicit sense of affirmation of being which is found in every human life. The very presence of death needs to be recalled every day so that we do not forget it.

This positive affirmation of life is what is shaken in sickness. On the psychological plane, the sickness carries with it a perturbation of the vital feelings which are enveloped in this diffuse enjoyment of healthy vitality. Anxiety is, psychopathologically, an altered vital feeling, like the sadness of the melancholiac. Pathological anxiety appears in the concrete situation of the living man. It is not a speculation about being. It is a feeling which imposes itself and which, analyzed in its inner being, gives us a presentiment of nothingness. If such an experience is possible, it is because the vital force is sick; and if this is so, it is because in man the soul is found incarnated in the body.

The coalescence in *primordial anxiety* between the normal and the pathological perspective is what makes possible, taking an experience of abnormal anxiety as a starting point, to elaborate a metaphysical theory of anxiety, as Kierkegaard did.

Anxiety is the threat of nothingness, but anxiety leads to being or to nothingness. In the second case we find ourselves before pathological anxiety. Neurotic and psychotic disturbances and symptoms are enclaves of nothingness in the edifice of the personality. It is necessary to make another limitation: these enclaves come from alterations in the lived corporality. They appear insofar as man, in his facticity, is found tied to a body. They are recognized in certain distinctive notes, certain signs which we call symptoms. Their general character consists in the prevalence in the dynamic of anxiety of its somatotropic ingredients. The mechanism of repetition, the so-called conversion reaction, the diminution of the vital level, the disintegration or threat of disintegration of the unity of the self by the revolt of the instinctive phantasms, the transformation of the relations of the

self with the world as its home, such as occurs in claustrophobia or agoraphobia, and such—all these are manifestations of
pathological anxiety.

This insistence on the difference between normal and pathological anxiety seems to contradict a fact that seems to pertain
to clinical experience and even to general human experience. I
am referring to the gradual transition from neurosis to normality.
Where is the boundary line? Here it is necessary to distinguish
two problems: one which concerns the conceptual boundary; and
the other, the real boundary, the one we have to mark out every
day in each of the cases the clinic offers us. In respect to the conceptual boundary the previous pages attempt to give an answer
by pointing out the qualitative differences between normal and
abnormal anxiety. Such differences refer, in turn, to a genetic
fact, the physiogenesis of abnormal anxiety. Corporality, inasmuch as it is *physis,* inasmuch as it is a presence, is what is
altered. This alteration is manifested on the psychic and somatic
planes, but it invades the personal plane of being and reduces its
disposability. G. Marcel points to disposability as coming from
freedom. In neuroses there is a rebellion of the cathonic structures which increases their area of action. Between the personal
and apersonal planes there is established a dialectic, a living-
together, a dialogue, which are the symptoms, the visage which
the disturbance presents to us.

The root of the distinction is found, clinically, in two points:
one, in the recognition of the presence of neurotic symptoms; the
other, in the estimation of the possibilities for development of
the personality. They are two distinct planes: the first more
objective, the second more evaluative. The presence of the second one makes the boundary more difficult to determine. Every
value judgment is made in a context of personal relations, and
hence in a historical atmosphere. This is identical with what
always happens in medicine. Until now, as far as I know, and in
spite of the progress in statistical calculation of correlations and
the use of calculating machines, we do not have in somatic medicine a definition of sickness to rely on that is exempt from value-
laden criteria.

To sum up, existential anxiety is anxiety in the face of nothingness. Vital anxiety is also, in my opinion, anxiety in the face of nothingness, born of an endotimic imbalance. Anxiety is always a presentiment of nothingness. In this mode of presentiment there exists a difference between normal and morbid anxiety. Existence is anticipation. In morbid anxiety the future which the anticipation supposes has been incarnated into the present. Morbid anxiety, in itself, is not only the threat of a break in the unity of the self but an anticipated actualization of a threat. For this reason morbid anxiety is somatotropic. The body-psyche unity is dislocated in the sickness, and there is a displacement toward corporality in this state of mind which is anxiety. Morbid anxiety is an incarnated anxiety, the same as the sadness of the melancholiac. It is not that anxiety expresses itself more on the corporeal plane, as in the conversion reaction, but that it is originally there. Nothingness, death, or madness is anchored in the very corporality. The special mode of anticipating the future alluded to before has its root here. For this reason, the psychodynamic of morbid anxiety is not, nor can it be, only a psychogenetic problem. Any object can be anxiogenic, but for each neurotic only definite objects are. The specific, triggering character of anxiety proceeds not only from historico-individual circumstances but also from the very structure of being. Its personal coefficient is revealed by this. Anxiety lays bare the heart of personal being and its gaps.

Anxiety does not appear in the face of a definite object but in the face of everything and in the face of nothing. This first indeterminacy calls attention to a fact: one should not speak of an anxiety reaction but of an anxiety situation. One *has* fear, but one is *in* anguish. Anxiety is not a mere "relation to an object"; it is a "situation in the world." Anxiety has as its principle a basic character and not a purely reactive character. Situations trigger anxiety, but they do not generate it. In reality, what happens is that anxiety is revealed in a determined situation. The dynamic of anxiety consists in an *aletheia*.

Is abnormal anxiety a revelation of the anxiety that exists in the depths of each being, as an aid to its very existence? In such case, why does it appear so concentrated in the sick and not in the healthy? Why is it so different in its clinical manifestations?

Every form of neurotic anxiety is anxiety in the face of death or madness. Death and madness mean the annihilation of being, of the self in the world. If the patient is afraid of having a cerebral tumor or cancer, or of becoming infected, and so on, it is all personal, historical forms of living out that fear of the annihilation of being. The situation is analogous in the building-up phase of a schizophrenic outbreak. Being feels itself not only threatened but handed over helpless to the annihilating threat.

Nothingness is inapprehensible. Incomprehensible. Nothingness can never be an object of knowledge. We can have only a presentiment of nothingness, the impression that emanates from it, that comes from it. Nothingness pertains to the unconscious, it is found always masked and needs a certain hermeneutics. Since it is ambiguous in its manifestation, its interpretation is not easy. Neurotic symptoms are echos of nothingness, but this echo of the great and permanent absence appears to us imbricated with defenses against it.

This thesis concerning vital anxiety supposes an enrichment of the interpretations of the anxiety crisis. Earlier I stated that the fundamental thing in it is that the self feels threatened in its unity. But, why must the self lose its cohesive and unitary force? Whence must come that "weakness of the self-ego" of which Alexander spoke? That a constitutional weakness of the self exists is evident. But there are also circumstantial losses of that functional energy of the self, and one of them is a decreasing of vitality, in the wide sense. Anxiety is thus anchored in the purest biological dynamism. This should not surprise us if we think a moment about the fact that the human being is constituted of *soma* and *psyche*, body and soul.

Vital anxiety means that man experiences it, and man is bound substantially to his corporality. In this servitude lies his finitude and his facticity because he is tied to his corporality and can die. I speak of *vital* anxiety. Because man has an awareness of experience of his corporality as condemned to disintegration.

José Luis L. Aranguren

Don José Luis Aranguren (b.1908) was until 1965 professor of ethics at the University of Madrid. He is one of Spain's most acute social and philosophical critics, as well as a constructive critic of the position of Catholicism in the modern world, and is widely influential among younger thinkers and writers. Professor Aranguren stands for the opening of Spain to Europe and the West. His writings include Catolocismo y protestantismo como formas de existencia *(1957),* La juventud europea *(1961), and* Etica y politica *(1963).*

"The Moralization of Power Through Its Self-Limitation" appeared in *Etica y politica* (Madrid: Ediciones Guadarrama, 1963) 219–251. © 1963 by José Luis Aranguren. Grateful acknowledgment is made to the author for permission to reprint.

VII. THE MORALIZATION OF POWER THROUGH ITS SELF-LIMITATION

THE STATE AND POWER:
THE STATE AS A PRIMORDIAL STRUCTURE

Until now, in the analysis of the moralization of the State from below, from its citizens, considered individually or in groups, we have relied on the assumption that the State is a "result," that is, the product of a pact, the *social contract*, and, also according to another direction of thought, the product of a plurality of powers which produce despotism only when they join.

But, is this conception of democracy and liberalism—according to which the State would be a mere function of the empirical human will, an artefact constructed by it—exact? No. What is political, as well as what is moral, constitutes a *structure* that is prior to a man's, each man's, deciding to conduct himself morally or politically. The State or, more strictly speaking, the *Staatlichkeit*, the state institution as such, constitutes an *Urphänomen*, a primordial phenomenon, a *Faktum* (to say it with Kant's word, which, however, proves weak here), a reality that is the result neither of the will of the individuals nor of a combination or fusion of other communities, so that only historico-genetically, and never according to its essence, can it be "deduced," for example, from the family or the tribe.

Naturally, this state institution, or essential structure of the State, takes on different empirical forms throughout history; and these are produced by concrete men. How? It depends on the situation and its contingencies. It may happen, as in the case of the American independence, that a *new* State is *founded*—through a community will for emancipation and by a war. This new State arose by means of a "pact," the Constitution, not among individuals, as in Rousseau's theory, but among communities, the different states of the Union. Here, rather than a "separation," there has been a "union" of powers; their confusion. It is understandable how, from such a situation, there arose a presidential regime. In Spain between 1808 and 1812, even though the historical legitimacy of the State, incarnated in the king, had failed because of the cowardly betrayal of Carlos IV and Fernando VII, the constituents preferred to believe, piously, in the situation of a throne vacated because of circumstances beyond control. Since, in any case, there was no real, effective, and armed power other than the nation, this *de facto* reality had to be reflected in the Constitution—on a deeper plane than that of its exterior imitation of other foreign constitutions—by means of the recognition of a distinction between powers, the actual power of the nation in arms and the historico-traditional power of the dynasty: powers which had already been separated in reality before being separated by law. In England, the only nation in which the modern State is arrived at without a break in continuity, the fundamental trust is the one formed between political realities, between distinct, but not separate, "powers." The separation occurs rather in those countries in which, without overthrowing the monarchy, the powers it had concentrated during the development of absolutism are "torn" away from it; but these powers, which are apparently torn from it, it had, in reality, already been losing to the degree that new social powers with political pretensions were arising in the country.

The Nature of Power

We see, then, that not only the State as a structure but also its
function or exercise as power constitute primordial phenomena.
This unitary political power, on the historical and empirical plane,
may be organized either as an institutionalization of social powers
that have arisen in the heart of the community or, vice versa, as
a dismemberment, a separation of the powers which constituted
a political unity. On the real, historical plane there may be found
union or dismemberment, distinction or separation of powers.
But what is primordial is the State and the unity of power.

Power, considered psychologically, is force—not blind force, but
a force oriented rationally to the attainment of an end. This end
should be exterior to it, in the sense that it constitutes an objective at whose service the power places itself. But it *may* happen
that *power for power's sake* becomes an end. We are then faced
with the naked impulse for domination, with the pure "will to
power" or the affirmation of oneself over others. This substantial-
izing of power does not necessarily make it blind; on the contrary,
it can make it take on the form of a "voluntarism" that uses intelligence in order to grow. For this reason, Guardini was able to
speak of the demonic character of power in the Greek sense, that
is, its ambiguous and morally ambivalent character. From the
demonic to the *demoniac* there is not, semantically, much of a
jump. This is why often throughout history power has been considered an evil, at least a temptation, and, at times, a sin: a necessary sin, one which, for that very reason, should be reduced to
a *minimum* by the limitation of power. (Remember Lord Acton's
well-known remark: "Power corrupts; absolute power corrupts
absolutely.") Another Catholic writer, Werner Bergengrun, wrote
these words: "The great contradiction in the world: clean hands
are not strong; strong hands cannot stay clean." If we concede
that the essence of what is political is power, the theme of this
book, the problem of the relation between politics and ethics
becomes the problem of the relation between *Kratos* and *Ethos*.

And it was for this reason, as we saw, that anarchism wanted to suppress power. But let us not anticipate, let us not yet place ourselves within the ethical point of view.

We wrote a moment ago that power, like naked force—that is, on the political plane, the utilization of police methods, of physical violence, of compulsion—is multiplied by the use of intelligence. A modern characteristic of this amplification of power is its *technification*, which, apart from making it more powerful, converts it into an apparatus that produces the impression of omnipotence and irresistibility, of power without limits, immense power: it is terror as a creation of a collective *suspense*, of a threat always suspended over the head of each citizen, and absolutely inescapable. This aspect which power takes on in totalitarian States in modern times greatly favors, as we are going to see, its mythification—mythification in a new style.

Actually, political power cannot present itself, for long, as pure force—tyranny, despotism—but needs to justify itself. This justification may be irrationalistic and consist in a mythification which does not limit force; rather, the contrary. Or, it may well tend to the rationalization of power.

THE JUSTIFICATION OF POWER BY MEANS OF ITS MYTHIFICATION

The oldest form of the mythification of power is the divine or quasi-divine claim of the ruler. Hierarchy, the divine cult of the emperor, the claim that a particular dynasty is a descendent of the gods or has been expressly designated by them to reign, are its primitive variations. The "modern" form of such a mythification is the theory of the divine origin of power, when it is conceived as rooted in the monarchic institution: God would have willed monarchy positively, and consequently kings would be kings providentially by divine right.

Tradition, that is, immemoriality as the source of power, is another form of mythification, not too far removed from the previous one. If the previous one presented itself with a "supernatural" claim, this one is "natural" in the strongest sense of the term: as immovable as a cosmic law, as something that has "always been so." For the rest, the traditional justification and the one which appeals to direct divine origin usually present themselves together.

The "sacralization" of power in the forms mentioned above is, so to speak, in the "Catholic" style. Analogously to the way in which divine grace descends upon men through the ecclesiastical institution and the sacramental channels administered by the Church, temporal power and the corrresponding "grace of state" of its titular head, the king, flow through the dynasty. But in contrast to this conception, another, not "ecclesial" but "prophetic," not "Catholic" but "Protestant," conception is possible. It is the one Max Weber calls the charismatic conception. The *charisma* is a grace *gratis data* that comes down directly and vertically upon man, not indirectly and horizontally through a whole dynasty. The charismatic conception is one which, by reason of its more "democratic" character, since the "chosen one" comes from the people instead of proceeding from a caste of lords of the earth, is closer to present-day feeling than is the dynastic one. This messianism can clothe an absolute form in such a way that the providential man appears as the very incarnation of destiny and the personification of the community he must redeem; it may also be experienced as vaguely metaphysical and is then a form of transmission; or rather as the lesser messianism of a man, in principle equal to the rest, though extraordinarily gifted, whom Providence and circumstances have given the opportunity to become the savior of the community.

In another respect, messianism may manifest itself as fascinating and, oppositely, terrifying (remember what we wrote before about terror), or purely as a protector and not a judge, benign and patriarchal. Finally, it may present itself as a governorship justified by an irrationalistic theory of leadership and tied to an ideology (the case with fascism and in particular with national

socialism with its "myth" of the supremacy of the Aryan race),
or it may well be experienced by the community as an immediate "fact" lacking any definite ideological significance. (This is
the case today with DeGaulle who, even though he personally
holds an ideology, is not followed at all because of it, so that
his prestige is totally independent of his philosophico-political
conceptions.)

Evidently, the "circumstantial" and not ideological or "awe-
inspiring" charisma can hardly be considered a religious mythification, except in a defective sense. It serves, then, as a transition to
mythifications that are not religious or, at least, not formally religious. The *prestige* which is accorded a person, but which may
also pertain to an institution, looks more like charisma than geneo-
logical grace because it is more fitting for new-born powers than
for established powers (even though these also can "preserve"
their prestige). It may be based on *leadership,* which has been
so much studied by social psychology in the United States and
which consists in a personal capacity for command (a concept,
as one may see, close to the mitigated form of charismatic authority, of which it is the full "naturalization" and psychologization).
From the according of prestige it is easy to pass to the so-called
cult of personality. There is another concept very much studied
today, that of *glamor,* close to the one of prestige but less dynamic
and more psychoanalytic than the latter, important above all
because, through mass media, it facilitates the personalization
of power.

Among the nonpersonal but social forms of prestige, the prestige of the proletariat (a prestige susceptible of being elevated to
the highest degree of myth) is very operative today among the
intellectuals of the left, as Raymond Aron, more than anyone
else, has emphasized. The prestige of technicians should also be
cited here, and so the prestige of technocracy which in today's
society has replaced the lay prestige of the "secret societies,"
indirect organs of power during the last century. The prestige
which *Opus Dei,* considered as an association for temporal action,
enjoys in certain sectors of the wealthy and semiliterate bur-

geoisie of Spain rests upon the religious ingredient, brought "up-to-date," and upon the, now somewhat anachronistic, prestige of "secrecy."

THE TENDENCY TO THE DEMYTHOLOGIZATION AND FUNCTIONALIZATION OF POWER

If, through the mitigated charismatic forms and through leader-ship, there is perceptible today a tendency to mythification or, at least, to the personalization of power, there are also very visi-ble tendencies in an opposite direction. No one any longer holds, ingenuously, that democracy is government of the people *by* the people. The people cannot govern themselves, not even through "delegates" or "representatives," mere executors of their "man-date." Things happen, rather, and more and more so, inversely: certain specialized persons, less and less "lawyers" and "orators" and more and more "economists," "administrators," "professors," and "technicians," formulate a detailed program which tends to be the project of a true "development plan"; and the other citi-zens, their equals, but not specialists like them in such questions, vote this or that plan. One thus arrives at a *functional* concept of government, according to which there exists only a difference of "function," not of "status," between rulers and ruled. This functional concept may be qualified and, in fact, is qualified with language that comes more or less from Bultmann's theology of "demythologization" or "demythization" of authority.

Along with functionalization there is joined effectiveness, that is, efficacy. Today precisely the criticism most frequently made of parliamentarianism is based on its lack of efficacy, in contrast to the effectiveness—which is taken for granted, not always cor-rectly—of totalitarian regimes. The instrumental value of a sys-tem of government, its good functioning, is an objective necessity, intensified today by the acceleration of history and a psychologi-cal demand of the new generations who have a technicist and not a rhetorical mentality. But efficacy, which in our time is pri-marily efficacy in respect to economic development, should not be confused with the *decisionism*, so often absurd and at least mediocre, of some regimes for which the fundamental objective is maintaining the autocrat in power.

To sum up, we find ourselves, then, in one respect, with the tendency to *rationalism* or rationalization of politics. But in another respect, as we have seen, in our time new forms of *irrationalism* and of mythical or quasi-mythical exaltation of power are appearing. If we accept as an operational concept of man the notion that man is a rational being *in via*—that is, rational, to be sure, and more and more so, but not purely rational—we should look for a transactional formula between the tendency to the "cult" of personality and the tendency to the functionalization of power.

To find the formula that would join the increasing rationalization of politics and the personalization of this "reason" in a human being capable of speaking to people warmly, with a direct, truly democratic, comprehensible language, one which, in spite of the prosaic character of the technico-administrative questions of modern politics, is stimulating and dynamic—this is the problem of government that each nation is faced with, if it wishes to avoid the dangers of technocracy and mythification, apparently opposed to each other, but in reality both opposed to the maintainance of an authentic democracy.

Let us remember that Hegel, in developing his theory of the powers of State, had to deal with the concept of the monarch—the most difficult of all, as he himself admits in his system, because what is highest, the State as subject and plenary reality of the ethical idea, is incarnated in an individual and contingent figure, that is, in what is most precarious. Besides appealing to a unity of decision in an *Anführer,* Hegel wished to see in the prince, as is done in the ontological proof for God, the unity of concept and existence. Of the whole artificial and antidemocratic Hegelian construct, we retain only the synthesis of *concept* and *existence.* This is how power must be: according to a concept, that is, rational and democratic; but also personalize, that is, *existing* to the greatest extent possible.

NEGATIVE ETHICITY OF THE STATE: THE MORALIZATION OF POWER BY ITS SELF-LIMITATION: RELIGION AND MORALITY

In the previous chapter, apart from functionalization and rationalization, which is not of a direct but of an indirect, ethical character, we have studied expressions of power which claimed to justify it without limiting it and even without giving it a form. On the contrary, it was better that power appear, inasmuch as it was sacral, without limits, immense. They were justifications or attempts at justification that were purely irrationalistic. Now we should study the justifications of power that consist, by contrast, in its configuration, that is, in its limitation, and so change the State into a frame and channel of moral activity.

Religion—in the era of absolutism almost uniquely—constitutes or constituted a first limitation. Religion was an operative social force. The Supreme Pontiff, aside from temporal power, possessed an authentic power which was able to be matched with that of kings and emperors—remember Canossa—since even when it was religious, it was recognized and accepted by all. Excommunication, for example, was a terrible weapon. Without having to go so far as to employ these last resorts, the Church (the whole Church, since each priest also participated in religious power—a priest could, as one example, deny absolution) made itself heard and respected. To this exterior pressure we must add the pressure of the internal forum, and so on, that is, the religious conscience of the sovereign. Religion was, then, undoubtedly, a brake, a political limit.

So was morality. It is true that Machiavellianism constituted a serious attempt to subordinate morality and religion to political power. However, Machiavellianism, in order to be efficacious, must not appear to be what it is; otherwise it would cease to be Machiavellianism and become cynicism. Now, political cynicism is not only immoral politics but it is also bad politics. For this reason every State tries to present its objectives as just. Every sensible ruler sets himself to conquer public opinion, interior and

exterior, insofar as it is a moral "tribunal." Thus, for example, all
States declare today that they want peace, and, naturally, a just
peace. Ludwig Freund has insisted on this political "interest"
which morality possesses and on the possibility of exercising an
efficacious "moral pressure." Similar, too, is the function of natural right, halfway between pure morality and positive right, inasmuch as it is an attempt at constituting a new right.

To moralize power, to make it reasonable and just, is, in short,
to endow it with *authority*. Authority, in paternalistic times,
presented itself as superiority. This was the way the *auctoritas* of
the elders in the gerontocracy or patriarchial society was presented: as a superiority in age, in knowledge—that is, in wisdom
and knowledge of life—and so, it was inferred, in government as
well. Even in regimes that no longer consisted in pure gerontocracy, use was made, along with the *edictio* or legislative power
of the people and the *imperium* or *potestas* of the executive mag-
istrates, of the *auctoritas* of the elders assembled in the senate.
Afterwards, *auctoritas* passes, in good part, to the jurisprudents
and philosophers and tends to be, rather, an exterior brake on
power (in spite of the Platonic conception of the philosopher-
kings, at times realized, as in Marcus Aurelius) which the power
counts on, however, and with which it clothes itself as far as
possible.

As historians have pointed out, the evolution of the imperial
institution at the end of the Middle Ages, having lost by then all
power and having conserved only a merely moral *auctoritas*, is
of itself alone unmistakable proof of the end of an era; and, in
the same way, Bodin's "modern" conception, which disassociates
sovereignty or *potestas* from *auctoritas* and places emphasis on
the bare *factum* of power and, correlatively, on the *factum* of its
recognition, disregarding its "basis," signals the beginning of
another era, that of voluntarist absolutism. However, the princes
of the seventeenth and, above all, of the eighteenth centuries,
who brought "philosophers" to their courts, were seeking in this
way an exterior moralization of their power through the prestige
of the Enlightenment. And, in another respect, rulers, in regard

to their social extraction, have always, at least until the advent of communism and of the society of the masses, come from the higher estates, possessors of a greater culture, or from the bourgeoisie which was supposed to have proved its "managerial capacity" by means of the knowledge of life, considered to be privileged according to the liberal mind, that comes from an individual's growing rich by his own effort.

THE LEGAL STATE AND THE INSTITUTIONALIZATION OF THE OPPOSITION

Together with religion and "natural," or rational, morality, but with greater possibilities for institutionalization in the political order and with a limitation which is authentically objective *self-limitation,* law constitutes another form of the moralization of power which, even though it, too, is negative, is less exterior to politics itself than the previous forms. The *Legal State* is, or has been, the great modern creation. Earlier we treated the *division of powers* as a demand made by citizens to defend themselves from despotism. Now it should be considered as a technical form of the self-limitation of power. From this point of view, the division of powers claims to be, as we anticipated, the objective (that is, independent of exercise or nonexercise by the citizens) establishment of liberty as *freedom from* autocracy or the unipersonal possession of *all* the power. Jurists have shown us, however, that the separation of powers is never complete, neither in England, where Montesquieu believed he saw it realized, nor in Montesquieu himself, and even less so in our time. Thus, in the Spanish regime of institutionalized electoral corruption, the legislative power depended entirely on the executive power, but the latter in its turn depended on the royal trust.

In contrast, in regimes of authentic parliamentary majorities, the executive power proceeded from these majorities and was a simple delegation by them. In the present democratic regime of two parties, once these have established themselves in powerful organizational apparatus, the relation between the executive

power and the party, of which the former is simply the directive
committee, is, as Georges Vedel has written, "an episode in the
interior life of the Party," and then the emphasis of the separation is transferred to the separation that exists between the party
in power and the party of the opposition, that is, between "the
power of today" and "the power of tomorrow." The recognized
existence of the *opposition,* with its rights and functions, is, precisely, as the author cited goes on to say, what politically distinguishes Western democracy from the Marxist regimes. "Séparation des pouvoirs? Pas nécessairement. Mais séparation du
pouvoir, a peu prés sûrement, oui."

Decentralization

It has been correctly noted that the introduction of the system of
the so-called separation of powers was, in continental Europe, a
compensation for the centralization of power. But, as de Tocqueville, Lord Acton, and others saw, throughout the nineteenth
century the self-limitation of power demanded its decentraliza-
tion. "Separatist" problems have arisen or, at least, been provoked
because of increasing centralization. Even democracy as such,
when it is centralized and suppresses "intermediate associations"
becomes, as Montesquieu had already warned, a popular tyranny
which, in the name of abstract equality, destroys liberty, that is,
concrete liberties. Social pluralism, intermediate groups, regional
and local communities, professional and labor associations are,
much more than individualism, the true guarantees of liberty in
the face of an absorbing and centralizing absolutism—whether
autocratic or pseudo-democratic.

Supranational Claims

Also, the very existence of the international community, insofar
as it is a "moral tribunal" and a balance of powers, capable of
limiting the power of a State by material and moral pressures,
and its institutionalization by means of the creation of supra-

national organisms which deliberate over international problems and are accompanied by juridical, economic, and even military power, constitute, without doubt, and, above all, will constitute in the future more and more, a claim for the moralization of politics by means of the restriction, subordination or, at least, coordination of State powers.

THE DEMOCRATIZATION OF POWER

The present-day parties, those we referred to before, the parties of the masses, are fundamentally organizational, and so, regimented. However, they do not by any means make up the total electoral population of the country. We thus come upon a new limitation of power, on which its real democratization is based. Democracy, in one respect, is, as we have just seen, recognition of the opposition. Without tension, without difference of opinion, without opposition—based, it is true, upon a common ground of agreement or a constitutional "pact"—there is no democracy, and this is the origin of the "passion for unanimity," as it has been called, of totalitarian regimes which need to "prove" at all costs the nonexistence of opposition. But, if one does not manage to arouse the political interest of the citizens, make them enter the political arena, share reponsibility, and so share the political power, there is also no democracy.

In the political vocabulary of the eighteenth century, democracy is the identification of subject and sovereign in one and the same person, the citizen. The present-day identification, at least as a goal, of rulers and the ruled—excepting a functional differentiation—runs parallel to the present-day identification of producers and consumers. Before, the few who ruled were the same ones, more or less, who were the consumers, while the rest, the majority, obeyed and produced, without consuming more than the minimum necessary for life. Today, the consumer's economy and the democracy of the masses tend to make everyone share consumption and power.

But, how accomplish this, how attain a true democratization of power—that which political science today calls *legitimacy*, in the sociological sense? Evidently, through participation in power by the greatest possible number of citizens. For this there is required, first of all, an extension of political *information* (this was the "preparatory" function of the Enlightenment) and politico-economic information which would permit the people to form a political opinion. Now, it is quite difficult for each individual to form a political opinion without being influenced by the others, and particularly by the political *élite*. As Duverger has shown, "brute opinion" is incomprehensible and cannot consist in more than vague and inarticulate tendencies. Political opinion is always the result of propaganda—no political information is aseptically impartial—and so, to some degree, "manipulated." But, in another respect, the opinion worked out and created by the *élite* has its repercussion on them, and so establishes a true *dialogue, which is precisely democracy.*

Democracy has been described now, in the terms of modern science, as a *system of communications* between the functionally specialized power and the masses, like a mutual game—if it is not a mutual game, we have a political regime of pure manipulation of opinion and not a democracy—of "demands" and "responses." Thus, the scientific problem of democracy consists in making this system of communications as direct and sensitive, and also as generalized, as possible. In short, the questions and answers must reach the receiver rapidly and faithfully; and the entire nation must be incorporated in the power by this net of communications. The first proposal poses the "technical" problem of the elimination of intermediate and deforming elements, about which we will have something to say a little further on. We are going to say a few words now about the second proposal.

Systems of government which exclude from participation in power certain social strata—the proletariat, a population racially discriminated against—tend not only to social illegitimacy but, by the same token, foment political attitudes—anarchism, revolutionary socialism—that break up the wholeness of the community. This has been precisely the weak point in all the regimes of continental Europe, in contrast to the British and Scandinavian capacity to give political responsibility to the whole of the population before communism could acquire social power. Political integration, like social integration in general, is fundamental for stabilization. Individuals or isolated groups—the ones who feel excluded, to the left or the right, socially or regionally, from politics; the ones who consider themselves deprived of rights, public attention, or *status,* such as the social groups in decline; or the ones poorly equipped for adaptation to the demands of a civilization in transition or expansion and who consider themselves without opportunities, condemned to immobility, to the impossibility of social ascension—incline normally to radical non-conformity and so to the rejection of a democracy which for them is no democracy. Good politico-social communications are as necessary as a widely extended and well-cared for net of geographical communications (highways, railways, planes, and so on).

THE TECHNICAL PROBLEMS OF DEMOCRATIC MORALIZATION

For the democratization of power it is not enough that the communications net reach everyone; it is also necessary that the communications "apparatus" not interfere with or deform the communication, not constitute an "interposition," but rather, on the contrary, make easy a faithful and sensitive transmission of the system of demands and responses of which we spoke before. In short, it is necessary that one "hear and speak well" by means of this apparatus.

The apparatus most criticized today as an organ of transmission and expression of true national opinion is the *parliament.* And in reality, except for the parliamentarians themselves, everyone recognizes, in general, that the parliament *represents* and *expresses* the national interest very poorly. A modification of its structure—a problem which it is not necessary for us to enter into here—and a limitation of its functions so that it does not block, as it frequently does, the effectiveness of the government's functioning, seem to be urgent requirements in our time. Parliament, as long as it does not become a syndicate to defend the interest of the parliamentarians, nor submit to parliamentarianism's classic vice of becoming a stage to exhibit oratorical aptitude and "speaking for the sake of speaking," is necessary as an organ of critical dialogue with power, and of a demand for information about questions of government—the "pleas and petitions"—and, finally, of political education. But, evidently, the parliamentarian spirit must transform itself from "rhetorical" to "technical." And, in another respect, even though parliaments continue to exist, parliamentarianism, or the political regime of the supremacy of parliament, has reached its end.

Political parties have also become debatable, not in the sense that we can do without them—(when they are suppressed, they are replaced by coteries, cliques, pressure groups, and parties that are not recognized as such and are therefore irresponsible)—but in the sense that their organizational substantialization, their bureaucratism and their self-enclosure, disables them as organs of communication and mediation. The great contradiction, which is found in the very essence of modern parties, consists in the fact that the competition for power imposes a *superorganization* upon them, and this superorganization has its own structural laws which have an antidemocratic tendency. In fact, since Robert Michels' book was published in 1911, it is well-known that an organizational bureaucracy, which constitutes the source of the power of the mass parties, is found inherently bound up with oligarchy, an invincible oligarchy, because it becomes institutional; and that the popular and democratic origin of the leaders and "functionaries" of the party is in no way a guarantee of a democratic spirit because the functions they carry out transform them psychologically and because the "discipline" is an "objective" demand that, as such, is imposed upon all, whether they like it or not, under pain of ineffectiveness.

The mentality of socioeconomically inferior classes, which nourish the greater part of the masses, is psycho-social and situationally inclined to intolerance and to direct action—more and more so, as they learn by experience that discipline is what constitutes force; and this, naturally, reinforces the tendential law of the parties to which they belong. Even more than the proletarian classes, social groups in decline, the ones who feel insecure or impeded in their integration with the new conditions of a society in transformation, are belligerently antidemocratic and constitute the principal clientele of the fascist or pro-fascist parties. Democracy, in the Western sense, is a function of the economic development of the nation and adequate participation in the national income by all the citizens. When entire groups of these citizens feel economically exploited or insecure and when the country is poor or undeveloped, democracy (always in the Western sense) is impossible or unstable.

A certain type of religiosity, more traditionalist than enlightened—which, as such, feels threatened by the "secularization" characteristic of our times—also constitutes, by its fanaticism (which, as psychoanalysts have shown, is the expression of an inner insecurity) an antidemocratic force which is added to certain mass parties and which contributes without doubt to corroborating the tendency to the right on the part of every Christian-democratic party, as "leftish" as it might appear in its beginnings. This is the reason for the importance, in the sense of democratic and liberal action, of what political sociology, and especially American electoral sociology, calls *cross-pressures*. Individuals or groups subject to affiliations, convictions, propaganda, or pressures that push them in different directions tend to adopt democratic attitudes, attitudes of respect for general opinion, and of understanding for the points of view of others, which are in part theirs also. This is the normal political behavior of the person who is at the same time a Catholic and a worker, a bourgeois and an intellectual, a progressive and a farmer, and so on. The political tension which builds up within these persons or groups reflects well the moderated difference of opinion that is fundamental for the stabilization of democracy. The danger in

the predominance of such a situation is the opposite of that of
radicalism, that is, disinterest in politics and abstention from
voting.

The most important structural "burden" that weighs upon democracy is, without doubt, techno-bureaucracy. We have already
seen it in relation to parties. Technical intervention in politics
supposes not only a specialization and rationalization of power
but also a tendency to form oligarchic "teams." Only a new type
education, less "metaphysical," literary, and humanistic and more
oriented toward economics, sociology, and, in general, the so-
called human sciences, positivistic in their methods, can make
possible a democratic dialogue between the "specialists" and
public opinion so that the latter become capable of understanding
the former and the former not yield to the temptation to political
absenteeism.

THE POLITICS OF IDEOLOGIES AND THE POLITICS OF ECONOMIC INTERESTS

It is indubitable that there is a correspondence between the
decrease in importance of parliament and an increase in the importance of the techno-bureaucracy and that, beyond the dangers
in the latter to which we have just alluded, such a change is correlative to the decadence of abstract *law*, the product of jurists,
to the increasing importance of the technico-economic *plan*,
worked out by specialized study commissions and work teams,
and finally to the substitution of real socio-economic problems
for *ideologies*.

What is the extent of this decadence of ideologies? Politics has
consisted, fundamentally—at least in appearance—in a confrontation of ideologies: absolutist and liberal, traditionalist and democratic, fascist, socialist, and communist. It has been a conflict of
Weltanschauungen, of conceptions of the world. Now, the characteristic of our times is that, within the two great blocks, Western and Oriental, ideology is now well stabilized and taken for

granted, and, when it is not argued, ceases to constitute the object of politics.

Politics becomes openly a conflict of *interests:* partial interests which oppose each other and which it is necessary to reconcile; individual and group interests which go against the "public interest" that should become the predominant one. Does such a concept mean that politics must fall into the irrationalism of the pure collision of private interests? On the contrary. Discovering where the deepest interest lies, beneath the apparent or immediate ones; working out plans for development and expansion which eventually favor everyone; finally, making clear to the community what the national interest is, beyond the partial interests, and managing to impose the former by conviction: these are eminently *reasonable* tasks.

No, politics is not inclining to irrationalism but to effectiveness. For this reason it is becoming more sober and technical. Brilliancy, grand invocations of the "metaphysical" essence of the nation, and its spiritual grandeur are ceasing to constitute the content of politics and are being replaced by a positive work which, compared with grand intellectual speculation and impressive ideologico-historical syntheses, proves to be "secondary" and "boring." Politics is tending to become administration. This is why it has been possible to write at the halfway mark of the twentieth century that the characteristic note of the stabilized Western democracies is that they find themselves in a "post-political" phase. The political parties themselves, when the time comes for action and political vindication, leave their "programs" in a discreet second place and act like what they are in reality, organizations defending the interests of the classes and groups they represent.

Bear in mind that even in underdeveloped countries the point of view of interest is superimposed upon the point of view of ideology and that, precisely because of this, socialism is adopted by them as the most rapid and efficacious means of obtaining economic development. "State socialism," then, in which the socialization is not, as in Marxism, a liberation from alienation but a simple instrument applied by the élite with a modern point of view who, replacing the old tribal oligarchies, have taken over power by making the country fully productive. In this sense, our era has become more positive and less "metaphysical," more *Marxist,* so to speak, than historical Marxism.

The most confused and uncertain situation in regard to the future is that of the semideveloped countries. The essential characteristic of these countries, more than the intermediary degree of development, taken in itself, is, I believe, the cultural gap, the enormous difference in level between culture as "a tradition of culture," "spirituality," "humanism," "metaphysics," "self-awareness," and so on, which are high, and economic culture or development, which is meager; or, if one wishes, between *ambition* and *reality*. For this reason their insertion in the community of developed countries is difficult, from the strictly economic point of view, even though it corresponds to the country's *aspiration*. (For example, it is evident that the prospect of Spain's entry into the Common Market has mobilized public opinion in its favor.)

THE CASE OF SPAIN

Certain of our countrymen, intelligent cultivators of a pessimism and even a national masochism, consider that Spain is an *underdeveloped* country where an oligarchy which impedes the meager means of production is content to take routine advantage of them without any really enterprising spirit, with a quasi-feudal way of thinking, with their scant capitalistic sense which is much more financial than industrial and always dependent upon foreign interests.

This frame of mind, which is ultimately catastrophic, at least in its first phase, and is residually existentialist, offers to a part of the youth—(not the most intellectually or technologically gifted, but enthusiastic and utopist)—as paradoxical as it might seem, a stimulating prospect. Actually, if Spain is an underdeveloped country, everything is waiting to be done, and so the task is immense; it is a task which permits the association of the politico-social mystique of revolution as a substantial modification of national structure, with the nationalist myth of a country which must still battle for its true independence.

The "model" for this exalting independence from the outside and revolution inside has been, without doubt, "Castrism," an essentially Latin phenomenon, which its apologist, Sartre, has presented in reality as a Marxism much more mystical than technical: the authentic constitution of a nation as a national "group" from the inertia of its inherited structures. With this mystique which overlaps with the old and symmetrical mystiques of the "red" militia and the Falangists of the left during our civil war, and before with the anarchist, there now is united the Catholico-social mystique of a progressivism which, in these past few years, has taken hold of many young people. It is true that these days the Castrist "model" has worn itself out, once it lost independence in relation to Soviet communism; but there is the new Algerian model, ready now to serve as a replacement, in the sense of the "Africanization" of Spain.

It is clear that the actual "conservative" physiognomy that Europe presents today contributes to strengthen this anti-European feeling among the radical youth. But to reduce Europe to its present governments is unjust. Marx (and Sartre)—through whom the revolutions in Cuba and Algeria are seen—are Europeans.

The attitude we have just described—which prefers integration with Hispano-America or Africa (Africa, for this attitude again begins at the Pyrenees) to integration with Europe, whatever might be its strictly economic reasons (which we cannot go into) —forgets the previously cited important fact of the difference in the level between economic development and cultural development. We do not mind conceding, for the sake of argument, that Spain might be considered economically an underdeveloped country, because that is not the problem. The contradition of our country is comparable, in its internal *décalage*, to that of the lower middle classes. *Economically*, they are proletarianized; their incomes are even lower than those of many workers. But *psychologically* they do not feel they are proletarians. Our country's problem would be simple—if not to solve, at least to pose—*if Spain could consider itself an underdeveloped country. But it cannot.* The ideological superstructure, the weight of its culture, the still-alive memory of its empire, keeps it from being able to. It would be easy, but it is not possible. I even have no objection to recognizing that, at least in certain aspects, it would be convenient. To what point has an almost purely ideological Europeanization and importation of institutions, but not of infrastructures, favored or harmed Spain? A difficult question to answer.

At times one might think we live in a country with *too much* culture in relation to its economy, a country with a head too big for its feeble body. Do we realize, for example, that the skepticism—which is always a result of cultural development—of our country, even thought it is not so radical as that of other developed countries, is sufficient to impede that ingenuous dynamism that the masses of certain underdeveloped countries have so fabulously developed? There is no doubt that here in Spain we must preach *opportune et importune* "realism" and "practicality" because that oversized head of ours is filled with a lot of rhetorical and metaphysical smoke. But this realism and practicality are not incompatible with a judicious awareness of grandeur which many Spaniards have acquired precisely during their years of exile and as a result of objective studies, in spite of the fact that they were not very keen before, and rightly so, on calling up Otumba and Lepanto at the drop of a hat. In any case, nations cannot slough off their history, as snakes do their skin, and start all over again—though it is, perhaps, a pity they cannot.

The Social Justice State: Individual Ethics, Social Ethics, and Personal Ethics

Up to this point we have seen that the totalitarian-state solution is not satisfactory, but neither is the welfare-state solution without objectionable aspects from the ethical point of view. In another respect we have also seen that the individualistic attitude of the pure liberal State is now absolutely anachronistic because of its impotence; precisely because of that it has been replaced by the attitude of the welfare state, which is the present "neo-liberal" version of liberalism. What, in the basic ethical point of view, is the reason for the inadequacy of the two systems, the neo-liberal and the communist? Communism orients human life according to a pure *social ethic*. The "society of abundance," in spite of certain correctives such as the admission of social security, orients existence according to a pure *individual ethic* (which is, in the last analysis, the neo-utilitarianism of a this-worldly welfare). But ethics, like life, is both individual and social, and to amputate either of both these dimensions is to impoverish and falsify it.

The society of abundance, we have already seen, is built up on egoism and upon individualist squandering in an affluent consumer economy which, *structurally*, because of the very way the system is built up, needs, demands, to be fomented. Not only this: it is very probable that due to that structure, and not to a simple deformation, there exists the ethico-political necessity of cultivating *inequality*, or, as is said today, *status, standing,* social "levels." It is not because of consumption, but because of the demands of prestige, of "keeping up with the Jones's," that it is necessary to change cars each year. In the British electoral campaigns of 1959, to which we referred before, the Conservatives, in the face of the worker puritanism of the Laborites (the party of labor, of work), carried out a careful exploitation, in the "differential" sense, of the deproletarianization of a great part of the worker population.

However, in another respect, communism cannot, under penalty of ceasing to be communism, foment the development of a personal morality. In fact, the development of personality, in virtue of the socioeconomic conditioning of morality, requires a kind of private consumption, a possibility of "choosing" and thus giving a "personal" stamp to the things with which each person surrounds himself. The man who lives in his *own* setting, who travels in his *own* ("private") car, and who truly disposes *freely* of so-called free time has become psychologically independent of

the State and the Party, and so *is no longer* a communist. The
socialization of consumption is essential to communism, not simply for economic reasons but for ethical reasons: to obtain its
supreme objective of *a life in common, of collectivization,* of
making the whole of life public.

Real Democratization: Economic, Social and Political

If morality must be both personal and social, this means that the
old *legal state,* without ceasing to be such, will have to constitute
itself as a *justice state,* which, precisely in order to make possible
the access of all the citizens to the material common good, to real
democracy and to freedom, will have to organize production and
will also have to organize democracy and freedom.

The present tendency to socialism on the economic plane,
whatever might be the quantitiative degree and political character of this socialism, seems to be inscribed in reality itself. In
any case, the motive force cannot be—nor should it be—capitalistic
interest determined to give primacy to a superabundance of
consumer goods in order to obtain, as an ethical by-product,
everyone's well-being, but should be rather the organization of
economico-social democratization, inspired by an authentic wish
for justice, for giving each person his due. Similarly, privileged
attention given to public services, instead of to the egoism of
arbitrary private consumption, and the ethical interventionism of
the State are indispensable. The State should limit—not by prohibition but through heavy taxes—the antisocial expenses, the
vulgar and unbridled publicity, the individual squandering, and
favor instead social activities and services, public health, and education, especially for leisure time. In short, what the scholastics
called, in a now outworn expression, the "common good" should
take precedence over profit and loss in the "great societies" and
also over a State conceived as power and domination. In the
same way, the social systems of planning are now absolutely
unrelinquishable even though they carry with them certain use-

less bourgeois virtues and an impersonal institutionalization of other virtues. For the rest, the superfluity of charity and philanthropy as "works" should in no way bring on their disappearance as "spirit": precisely their becoming a professional function will demand a greater professional morality and a greater religious morality in the secular vocation.

Political democracy also—a democracy compatible with efficacious power—must be promoted, that is, organized socially. This should be done by means of the promotion, both theoretical and practical, of an authentic political education and by means of the socialization, without centralization in the State, of teaching and the mass communication media. The university, radio, television, and such must become, not politically but administratively, *public service* (the function of administrative law in the social legislation of the near future will of necessity be enormously important), precisely so that all the citizens with all the groups have access to them instead of their continuing to be monopolized capitalistically and through privilege by a few.

THE ORGANIZATION OF FREEDOM AND ITS REDUCTION TO WHAT IS ESSENTIAL TO IT

That this supposes a limitation of freedom is undeniable. But it is a question of limiting it precisely to safeguard it and to democratize its essential core.

One hundred years ago there existed greater freedom—a practically unlimited freedom, though reserved, in the political and economic fields—to a few at the expense of the rest. It is true that an *ad hoc* rhetoric, which was, furthermore, spontaneous and naive, tried to compensate the poor, showing them the freedom that poverty offered. The romantics are the ones who invented the consolation this attitude affords. Thus, Victor Hugo contrasted to the French *liberté de pensée* the German *liberté de rêverie*, a metaphysico-poetic freedom—that, in his opinion, perfect freedom of the Neapolitan *lazzarone,* a freedom consisting in "existing almost without working, working almost without fatigue, singing

morning and afternoon and being free as the air." And even at
the end of the century a Spanish writer and friend of Ganivet,
Navarro Ledesma, wrote an article entitled "Who's Poor!" wondering whether "a country does not have what it takes to be truly
blessed in which the unfortunate laborors are so rich in spirit
that they prefer four hours in the sun to four pennies a day."

No, today one cannot, or better, one should not, be able to be
free in this way: neither with the freedom of unfettered capital-
ism, which leads to the monopolization of all political and economic freedom by a few privileged persons, nor with the freedom
of vagrancy and destitution proper to those who subsist, gypsy-
like, as parasites on the margins of society.

Freedom must be made general, extended to everyone; but for
this it is necessary to reduce it to its essential (economic, political,
intellectual and cultural, religious) core, to make it compatible
with the freedom of others, and to cut back everyone's freedom
in what is arbitrary and capricious. The regulation of city traffic
is a good prototype, a pilot project, a model, so to speak, of the
future of freedom. From now on, to a greater and greater degree,
we will not be very free in what is accessory. It will be enough
that we succeed in preserving the principal freedom.

The Vitalization of Ethical Structures of the Plane of Aliety by Means of Simultaneous Moralization of the Planes of Individuality and Alterity

To gather up the threads of our discourse, we see that in an era
as rationalized, technified, and complex as ours morality must
be inserted on the plane of what has been called *aliety,* that is,
the political, administrative and technical, and eminently social,
plane. Social moralization cannot be confided to individuals, not
even on the interpersonal plane of *alterity,* but must be institutionalized, converted into a function, into a public service.

Does this mean that the morality of *alterity* and the morality
of *individuality* have lost their meaning? Certainly not. A total

transfer from the ethico-social plane to public administration would turn the entire citizenry into mere consumers of the new "handouts" furnished by the State. What is ethically social, insofar as it is a function, is transferred to the administration. But the functionaries will have to be motivated "from within," so to speak, by a professional moral necessity and by their interpersonal and private virtues. And the beneficiaries of this providence-state must make ethical demands upon themselves and keep alive a fighting spirit of initiative and enthusiasm in order not to fall into inertia, conformism, and sluggishness, which are (I will mention in passing, but in order to make it explicit) the most dangerous enemies of this institutionalized morality. It is precisely in the fight against conformism and sluggishness that the activity of the *intellectuals* takes on its meaning. If "it is good that there be heretics" and if authentic democracy always requires difference of opinion, no one can fulfill this necessary, albeit thankless function, as can the intellectual, the "modern heretic" in society, in every society—Eastern or Western.

It is quite naive to think, as some do in the East and in the West, that morality constitutes a pseudo problem that can easily be eliminated, thanks to a definite, economico-social structuralization of superabundance and collectivism. There are always moral problems, even though they may be different on different levels. In the Eastern bloc they come from coercion and the lack of personal freedom. In the Western countries of the welfare society they come from raising to the level of a "virtue" the egoism of the consumer—the consumer of everything: material goods, culture, youth, love, religion—and from having lost a meaning in life. There are no longer thefts, but there are suicides and senseless crimes. They do not know what to do.

Spain's case is very different. We know quite well what there is to do because there is almost everything to be done. We find ourselves so far from prosperity for everyone, from general welfare, that we will not run the least risk for a long time of falling into the "materialism" of developed countries. For this very reason, achieving this welfare is defined, not as an economic by-product, but as a grand moral task that requires everyone's effort, on the personal ethical plane as well as on the social ethical plane.

This is to say that social moralization must be realized both by personal and by institutional means. To reject the ethico-personal function in social morality would be to disregard the fact that the whole of ethics is primarily personal, that moral acts and virtues, duties and feelings, conscience and responsibility concern the only really existing persons, individuals. But individual persons are powerless before the leviathan of the State and before the powerful pressure groups behind it; and, for this reason, morality must be fixed by institutionalizing it as far as possible in the very structure of the politico-social apparatus. All this, without ever forgetting the intrinsically problematic character of this moralization and the fact that the moral task, personal as well as collective, is in reality a task that is infinite, historical, and unending.

Pedro Laín Entralgo

Don Pedro Laín Entralgo (b.1908), professor of the history of medicine at the University of Madrid, is an example of the fusion of scientific and professional medical interests with humanistic concerns. He has brought to bear keen psychological and human as well as professional insights on the vital problem of the doctor-patient relationship. Among his publications are La espera y la esperanza *(1957),* Theoria y realidad del otro *(1961), and* La relacion medico-enferme *(1964).*

"The Doctor-Patient Relationship in the General Framework of Interhuman Relations" appeared in *La relación medico-enferme* (Madrid: Ediciones de Revista de Occidente, 1964) 235–258. © 1964 by Pedro Laín Entralgo. Grateful acknowledgment is made to the author for permission to reprint.

VIII. THE DOCTOR-PATIENT RELATIONSHIP IN THE GENERAL FRAMEWORK OF INTERHUMAN RELATIONSHIPS

The relationship between doctor and patient is first of all a mutual relationship between two men. The gravest error of anyone who wants to describe correctly and wholly the structure of the relation between doctor and patient would be to overlook or fail to recognize what at another time I have called its "generic basis," that is, the fact that in this relationship there are articulated, with greater or lesser effectiveness and harmony, the need of one man and the capacity of another to remedy a need. Before being this particular state of illness, an illness is a particular and accidental form of the constitutive indigence of the human condition. Before being a diagnostic and therapeutic technique, medicine—by which I mean the condition of being a doctor—is a particular and acquired mode of the human possibility of aiding one of one's own kind who is in need. Generically considered, the doctor-patient relationship is an *interhuman relationship* and a *relationship of giving aid*. Let us try to see with some precision the inner character and structure of this obvious assertion.

251

I

By its intention, form, and content a relationship between two men can take on a practically indefinite number of typical forms. These extend from friendly embrace and friendly conversation to mutual homicidal aggression, the latter by way of the simple glance of indifference or disdain or by the careful avoidance of any glance whatever. However, this inexhaustible number of possibilities can and must be ordered according to the two cardinal modes of the interhuman relation, the *objectifying* relation and the *interpersonal* relation.

I call *objectifying relation* that in which one of the two men whom the relation joins tries to turn the other into a *pure object*. The case is even stronger when they treat each other mutually with this same intention. Intentionally and hypothetically, the other, in such a case, is then reduced to being a *thing*, an exterior reality without personal liberty or goals of its own. Not a few of the most influencial descriptions of the interhuman relation rest upon this hypothetical and mutilating reduction of the other to a thing, a mere natural object. Among these are the well-known descriptions given by Hegel (the famous master-slave schematization) and by Sartre (encounter by way of the objectifying glance).

The intention of the objectifying encounter, however, never consists merely in simple objectification. This intention, as a matter of fact, may seek to make of the other an object of contemplation, a *spectacle* or an object of manipulation, an *instrument*. As a spectacle, the other stands before me offering for my own purposes (esthetic enjoyment, scientific curiosity, professional interest, disdain, etc.) the succession of the aspects which its reality shows—or can show at the moment of contemplation. As an instrument, the other is real for me insofar as it offers me the possibility of modifying it artificially in the service of my own purposes. Pure contemplation, in principle, *lets* the other be what he tends spontaneously to be; the conversion of the other into an instrument makes him become passively something which,

of himself, he would not have been and uses this mode of being
in one way or another.

But the picture is not even now complete because both contemplation and instrumental utilization can be either loving or
hateful. I can contemplate the other person with love (with one
or another of the many forms of love) or with hate (one or another of the many forms of hate). Absolute indifference, the *tertium quid,* does not seem possible if the moral reality of the act
of contemplation is examined with sufficient finesse. In the same
way, I can manipulate another person as an instrument with love
(and so, to help him: thus a mother handles her infant) or with
hate (that is, so as to do him harm: the essence of torture is
precisely this). Loving contemplation, contemplation with hatred,
manipulation with love, hateful manipulation—these are the four
typical forms of the objectifying relation. Perhaps it will not be
useless to add that, in this case, love takes on the form which I
have proposed to call *love at a distance* and that, symmetrically,
hate is now *hate at a distance.*

When I intentionally objectify another, hypothetically and
operatively reducing him to the condition of an object or thing,
do I treat him according to what he is in and for himself? Evidently not, because the other is not a thing but a person; not an
object but—in the modern sense of the term—a subject. One may
recall Unamuno's perceptive practical admonition:

> Que uno es el hombre de todos
> y otro el hombre de secreto,
> y hay que librarse de modos
> de hacer a un sujeto objeto.

(Man in his public character is one thing, and another in his
private character; we must avoid ways of making an object out
of a subject.)

Man is essentially a person. To be an existing person is the
essence of a man. By objectifying the other, placing myself in a
relationship with him *purely and exclusively* to make an object
of him, I mutilate and degrade him even though my intention

may seem to be loving. If therefore I wish to treat another man in accordance with what he is in himself, I must establish an *interpersonal relationship* with him. In what does this consist?

One answer presents itself: my relationship with another man will be interpersonal when he and I consider each other and treat each other as persons—in a word, when we consider and treat each other as individual substances possessing a rational nature (Boethius), as subjects having their own ends (Kant), or as living and intelligent beings with their proper substantivity (Zubiri), even though neither one of us may possess the slightest idea of these three philosophical definitions of what it means to be a person. Or, again, in a more empirical and descriptive way: when he and I consider each other and treat each other as beings to whose individual reality belong life, interiority, intelligence, freedom, and capacity to appropriate. One is a person insofar as he carries out intelligent free actions which are his own. This is equivalent to saying that the activity which defines and constitutes the interpersonal relation will be the joint performance of the actions in which and by which the other performs—realizes, places *in actu exercito*—his condition as a person or, in a more immediate and psychological way, the performance of the living experiences in which such actions become more or less conscious. The interpersonal relationship is a shared experience which is realized as successive and joint performance.

According to what has been said, the principal modes of the interpersonal relation will be these two: *experience lovingly shared,* in which the unitive intention emerges as a particular form of love (friendship, erotic love, etc.) and *experience shared in hatred.* For example, whoever visits a friend who has suffered some misfortune, in order to share his sorrow, does not content himself with contemplating him; certainly, he contemplates him, but he tries further to experience in his own soul the suffering that his friend is undergoing. But anyone who hates another man personally—just as Joaquin Monegro hated Abel Sanchez in Unamuno's well-known novel—wants to share in a dominating way everything that the other person tries to do and feel freely in the intimacy of his own soul. In the last extreme he wants to kill the freedom of the other in its very root.

When the interhuman relationship is truly interpersonal, love or hate impels us to penetrate into the interior of the other, into the life of his soul. One, therefore, is *insistent love* and the other *insistent hate*, in the etymological meaning of the adjective (*instans*). Hatred can go no further. Love, on the other hand, can become *abiding* or *co-effusive love* when the two persons who love each other believe in each other's love and pour themselves out to each other in acts of giving. The unit which the two persons form in such a case ceases to be a simple *duo*, like those who are bound together by the achievement of a common, accidental, and external goal, and becomes a *dyad:* "dual union" becomes "dyadic unity."

II

If the foregoing schematic exposition presents and orders, as I believe it does, all of the typical forms of the relationship between man and man, what place does the medical relationship hold among these forms? Under which of the preceding rubrics can an interhuman relationship whose purpose is help be placed when this relationship has as its active subject the doctor, and as its passive subject the sick man?

It is possible to think that the medical relationship is purely and exclusively objectifying relationship between human beings. At least this is the way the science of pathology in the West, from the time of Alcméon of Kroton to our own century, has tended to think of it. According to this conception, the sick man must be a *pure* object of cognitive contemplation for the doctor (in a word, a spectacle, in the widest and noblest sense of this term) and a *pure* object of therapeutic manipulation (in the end, an *instrument* of the curative process which the therapist carries out). The patient must be, in principle, what the individual plant is for the botanist who identifies it and what the malfunctioning motor is for the engineer who has to repair it: an object to be contemplated in the one case and an object to be manipulated in the other. And when it is necessary in diagonsis and treatment to depart from these schemata, this will be, at the most, a resigned and tactical—not scientific and technical—concession to the reality of the external world which can never be completely dominated. That this mental attitude has had fabulous diagnostic and therapeutic efficacy must in strict justice be emphasized. However, no matter how great this efficacy has been up to the present or may be in the future, can medicine be satisfactory if it theoretically does not recognize that the reality upon which it acts is a person? The sick as well as the doctors of our century have given a resoundingly negative reply to this question. Programmatically to convert the sick man into a pure object—to "reify" him, according to the current term—is to mutilate and degrade the fullness of the human condition. Since the patient is a man, the relationship between him and the doctor must be an interpersonal one: this would seem to be the inescapable norm.

Nevertheless, can the relationship between doctor and patient be a purely and exclusively interpersonal relationship between men? Not at all. For someone who is paying a visit to console an afflicted friend, his friend's transitory physical condition is a relatively secondary concern; the important and decisive concern is the suffering which the one whom he is visiting is at that moment undergoing in his innermost personal consciousness. The doctor, on the other hand, cannot act as a doctor unless he makes the body of the sick man an object of contemplation. For example, to tap a patient's chest—what is this if not to make his chest an object which makes noise? But a friend acts as a friend when he sincerely shares the pain his friend is suffering, while the doctor —who cannot share, even though he may, in sympathy, want to, the visceral pain or vertigo of his patient—must "operate," either with medicine or manual operations, on the physical reality of the person who has sought his help, and therefore he must manipulate this reality, make it the passive instrument of his therapeutic purpose. No, the medical relationship cannot and ought not be a purely and exclusively interpersonal relationship.

The conflict, nevertheless, is not beyond solution. Between the pure objectifying relationship and the pure interpersonal relationship there are intermediate forms of the bond between men. This is not because a type of communication different from objectification and joint performance is established between man and man, but because both elements combine in a different way in the peculiar structure of this bond. The human unit formed by the objectifying relationship, whether the latter be contemplative or operative in character, is found to be made up of a subject (the human individual who objectifies) and an object (the human individual who is objectified). The human unit formed by the interpersonal relationship is, in its perfect form, the dyad, the "we" of an I and a you who are united in love, but without loss of physical identity. Between the subject-object unity formed in objectification and the dyadic unity formed in interpersonal union, there are at least two typical intermediary realities: the *duo* and the *quasi dyad*.

I call *duo* the unit which is formed by two men who are functionally united with each other for the attainment of a goal situated outside them. A commercial contract and camaraderie constitute two clear examples of this relationship between men. Will the medical relation prove to be another instance of this particular kind of dual cooperation? This would seem to be Von Weizsacker's opinion when he calls the therapeutic relation *Weggenossenschaft*, "the comradeship of fellow travelers." However, for reasons soon to be made clear, I think that the unit formed by the doctor and the patient (setting aside for the moment its constitutively social nature and the inevitable incardination of the one and the other in the society of which both form a part) belongs to another type of relationship, the *quasi-dyadic*, whose generic structure will become perfectly clear if we consider in summary manner three of the most characteristic forms of the relationship whose purpose is aid: counsel, teaching, and medical assistance.

In the counseling relation, one man helps another make a *decision* concerning his life. It is the higher form of Heidegger's "procurance" (Fursorge), the preventive procurance" of one who, knowing what the other is and conjecturing what he might possibly be in the future, points out to him the path to this future and leaves him free to take that path or not. It belongs to the one counseled to make the personal decision to follow the counsel given or to turn a deaf ear to it. It is hardly necessary to point out that objectification and joint-execution are integral parts of the act of counseling, while, of these three forms of the relation whose purpose is to give aid, the latter is the nearest to the purely dyadic relation. As a matter of fact, a genuine friendship in which neither of the friends counsels the other is perfectly possible, while it can also be true that the counselor may not be the personal friend of the one whom he counsels. It is no less certain, however, that friendship, in the most intimate and proper sense of this term, must on occasion express itself in the form of counsel. On such occasions counsel takes on, for the moment, the dyadic form. This is why I said above that the counseling relation, which is quasi-dyadic in itself, stands very close to the purely dyadic relation of friendship and of love.

Another cardinal form of the quasi-dyadic relation is *education*. In this relation, the teacher helps the disciple to acquire a *mental habit*, or, as we may say, to learn something. The pedagogic act also demands objectification and joint action; he would be a poor teacher, indeed, did not try to carry out in his own soul, in a conjectural and divinatory manner, what goes on in the soul of the boy he is teaching. And, like objectification and joint-action, so too is friendship necessary: from Socrates and Plato we learn that without an *eros paidagogikos* socially and psychologically realized as *philia paidogogike,* the art of educating would be impossible. This "pedagogic friendship" is not, however, pure interpersonal friendship; for as a friend, and without diminishing his good will toward the other, the friend willingly accepts the other for what he is, while the educator is such insofar as he does not accept his student as he happens to be at that moment but seeks by his art Plato's *techne paidogogike* to modify this provisional and deficient mode of being. This is the case even if the person

being educated is a mature man or even an elderly one. Education, the typical mode of the quasi-dyadic relation of aiding,
stands at a further remove from the pure dyad than does counsel.

There is, in the third place, *medical assistance.* One who aids
the sick in the role of doctor seeks to help the sick person to
acquire a *psychosomatic habit;* for that is precisely what health
is. This purpose, as we shall see step by step, will demand of the
doctor psychic acts of co-execution, though in an even greater
degree it will demand objectifying operations. For illness is
always a condition of the body and, as a consequence, the sentiments which reveal it in the soul of the sick man are primarily
somatic. The friendship of the doctor for his patient, the *philia
iatrike* to which the Hippocratic Aescleipades already alluded,
stands therefore at a still further remove from pure interpersonal
friendship than does pedagogical friendship; and since, to a certain degree, it must be *insistent* love, it is already very close to
that "love at a distance" of friendly objectification which I
mentioned earlier.

To sum up: in the dyadic relationship of pure, interpersonal
friendship, objectification is indeed necessary, but only as a
means (thus the friend regards his friend and the lover the person loved). The decisive and terminal element in it is unitive
co-execution. By contrast, the terms are inverted in the quasi-
dyadic relation of aid: here co-execution is necessary as a means
and objectification—at times under the form of contemplation
and at other times under that of instrumental manipulation—is
elevated to the status of the proper end of the interpersonal relationship because what is now sought by it (even in the most deli-
cate and respectful cases of counsel) is an effective modification
of the reality of the other. Hence, there is an *ascesis* of friendship,
while there can be no technique of friendship; and reciprocally,
the activities of counseling, teaching, and healing should be
ordered—must be ordered if they are to be effective—according
to their respective techniques, which are the more rigorous and
sharp the closer they lie to pure objectification. We shall say,
therefore, that within the framework of relations between human

beings *the medical relation is a quasi-dyadic cooperation of aid directed toward the attainment of the psychosomatic habit which we are accustomed to call health.* We shall say further that among all the relations whose end is aid—without regard for the case of saving a shipwrecked person or some case like it—the medical relation falls nearest to that which I have earlier referred to, generically, as the objectifying relation.

Having said this, I must immediately add that the quasi-dyadic character of the relation between doctor and patient is—in a certain, but not in any simple and absolute, manner—terminative. The medical relation is consummated as a relationship between two persons, the doctor and the sick man, and ill indeed would be that medical assistance which did not end as a quasi-dyadic cooperation between those persons. To affirm this, however, is not to fail to recognize the constitutively social character of that relation and, therefore, the necessity of understanding and carrying out diagnosis, treatment, and the ethical obligations to which doctor and patient alike are subject as socially conditioned acts. The more sharply the social condition of any human relationship is etched and set in relief, the less purely interpersonal its intrinsic character. The dyad relating two friends or two lovers is achieved —so far as this is possible for man—at a trans-social level. The quasi-dyadic unity between counselor and counseled, teacher and pupil, doctor and patient—this unity, above all, can be established only *socially* even though later it must terminate and does, as a matter of fact, terminate as a bond between two persons.

III

Let us examine carefully the internal structure of the bond between doctor and patient, understood as a quasi-dyadic relation. We already know that this relation has a basis, constituted by the conjunction of the motives revealing themselves to doctor and patient, and that this basis is realized in a way which is at the same time cognitive (diagnostic), operative (treatment), affective (transference), and ethico-religious. Now we must take

another step forward and ask ourselves what may be the texture
and the internal dynamic of the process by which that basis is
established. To do this, it would seem necessary to adopt beforehand as our norm a determined type of the relation between the
doctor and the sick man.

The medical relation, in fact, exhibits in both the formal and
the material orders the most diverse aspects. Its social field may
be a polyclinic, a private consultation room, the bedroom of the
sick man in his home, a hospital room, or a battlefield. Its content will differ in the visit of the internist to an acutely ill person,
in surgical intervention, and in psychotherapeutic treatment. The
most diverse basic intention may move the doctor to act or carry
out this role: a genuine medical vocation, a purely scientific interest, a professional duty, a dominating appetite for gain or prestige. The sick man, in his turn, may be moved to approach the
doctor by the most conflicting motives: to regain his health,
the pure desire to "know what he has," the more or less conscious
purpose of securing a respite from work—motives, moreover,
shaped by the most diverse types of mentality (superstitious or
scientific, religious or irreligious) and governed by the most
varied dispositions of soul (confidence or distrust, hope or despair, a will to struggle against his illness or complete prostration
before it). Later I will try to show how, from the mutual implication of this complex net of motives, the different typical modes
of the medical relation arise. But in order to pursue our analysis
profitably, it seems inescapable, as I said before, to refer to an
ideal or canonical mode of this relation: that which establishes
itself between *a doctor who is moved by a true medical vocation
and a sick man who has a genuine will to get well, without any
especially developed magical or superstitious mentality and with
some confidence in the technical capacity and in the person of the
doctor attending him.* What, in such a case, will be the internal
structure of the relation between them?

I think this last question demands that we distinguish four
principal moments or phases in the medical relation: the *proper
end* of such a relation, the goal toward which the quasi-dyadic

bond between doctor and patient really aspires; the specific *modality of the shared experience* which is established in that relation, the central and unitary configuration of the acts by which the quasi dyad, doctor-patient, is established; the *proper bond* of the medical relation, the specific character of the union which is achieved by way of these acts; and, finally, the proper communication between doctor and sick man, the complex of technical resources, in the most ample sense of this term, to which the doctor must have recourse so that these acts of shared experience may take on effective, empirical reality.

1. No minute or subtle reflection is necessary to make us aware that, in the case which has been selected as our norm or model, the *proper* end of the medical relation is the health of the sick man. The immediate purposes of this relation—the purposes which must always be present if the doctor proceeds as a doctor—are the formulation of a diagnosis and the prescription of a treatment; its ultimate purpose, however, cannot be anything other than the *health* of the patient. This apparently obvious statement must be energetically underlined, because contemporary medicine, inebriated at times by the incipient and fascinating success of its techniques for modifying human nature—techniques which are pharmacological, physiotherapeutic, surgical, psychotherapeutic, social, etc.—has come to the point of thinking that the purpose of the doctor as such may be, beyond purely physical health, the *moral goodness* of man (making men good) or the *felicity* of the human condition (making men happy). The utopia of Huxley's *Brave New World* continues and blossoms anew in the West, despite existentialism and *Angst* after World War II. I yield place to no one in devotion to science and belief in its fabulous possibilities, but this illusion I reject wholeheartedly; even more, I consider it a grave aberration of the mind. The proper function of the doctor as such is not to make men good or happy, but healthy. As a doctor, he can and ought to go no farther than this. And since it is certain that the healthy man is much better disposed to becoming good and happy than is the ailing or sick man, it is necessary to conclude—because the human

condition demands we so conclude—that: (a) goodness and happiness are not the necessary consequences of health, a psychosomatic habit of the individual nature, and depend before all else on two conditions—the use which the person in question makes of his liberty for erecting his own existence and that mysterious determination of human life which the ancients called *fortune* and which we today are wont to call, according to our religious beliefs, either *chance* or *providence;* (b) the achievement of these two supreme goals ought not and cannot be the object of the doctor but the particular enterprise of the person himself, since he is the titular and the administrator of his own liberty, and of those persons who have as their charge the ordering of society and the indication of the ultimate end of man's existence (statesmen, priests, and the like). A healthy person may be good or morally bad, very happy or miserable, and will be the one or the other according to the peculiar character of the world which he inhabits, the use he makes of his liberty, and in the end the favorable or unfavorable sign that presides over his fortune.

How then, according to this position, is health—the proper object of the doctor—to be understood? I believe that the right path toward the reply to this question must take its point of departure in two preliminary assertions: (a) the *reality* of health has a complex structure; (b) the *idea* of health possesses a configuration and a content which depend, to a certain degree, on the point of view of the one considering them and are, in a certain way, socially and historically variable.

The complexity of that condition of life which we are accustomed to call "health" is made patent by the multiplicity of the criteria according to which, in practice, health is defined. The *subjective* or *sentimental* criterion is the one to which the individual human being most immediately and spontaneously appeals. According to him, every man who can sincerely say "I feel healthy" enjoys health. The sentiment that the individual man entertains toward his own life is in this case the decisive factor; health is conceived as a diffused and generical "sense of well-being." Can a subject who feels well, but in whose body there is a tumoral, tubercular, or syphilitic lesion which can be observed, really be called healthy?

An enemy to subjectivities on principle, Western medicine has, from its birth, preferred to employ an *objective criterion*. The ruling norm (metron) of medical knowledge ought to be, according to the Hippocratic writing *De prisca medicina,* "the sensation of the body," the sensorial perception of the patient's body. Therefore, in order to declare a man healthy it is necessary to consider him as a "perceptible object." But with this, not everything has been said because the objective character of health can be established from four points of view which differ very much among themselves: *morphology, functional activity, vital fatigue,* and *behavior.*

From a morphological point of view, a man is healthy whose body reveals no directly or indirectly observable deformation (that is, an alteration in its macroscopic or microscopic structure) nor a material character different from that which this body normally exhibits. Health, according to this norm, is the morphologically normal state of the living body, and normalcy is technically understood as the absence of "malformations" (an equine foot, a bifurcated spine, "lesions" (the "anatomical lesion" of Morgagni, the "cellular lesion" of Virchow, the "biochemical lesion" of Peters), or "foreign bodies" (a stone, a poison, a pathogenic seed). Group radiographic examinations (volunteers, students, etc.) are perhaps the most demonstrative example of this manner of understanding health. Matters alter, however, when the point of view taken is that of *functional activity.* In this case the healthy man is the man whose vital functions follow a pattern which is judged normal because it falls within the limits that define the "functional norm" of the species. The numerical measurements and the graphic projections to which the various "functional tests" (circulatory, respiratory, kidney, metabolic) now provide the matter of judgment. The *vital stress* of the individual can also in itself be the objective criterion of health. Anyone who adopts this criterion will consider healthy any man who can conquer without excessive fatigue and without apparent damage to himself what the society to which he belongs and what he himself hopes to get from his life: professional work, military service, intellectual or artistic creation, etc. Finally, there is *behavior* to be considered insofar as it becomes socially and objectively perceptible. Without a "normal" behavior—without behavior in conformity with the "normal" rules of the society to which one belongs—one cannot speak of health even though the morphology, the functional activity, and the vital fatigue of the individual do not appear "anormal"; this is the case in certain psychopathic cases.

In the complex *reality* of health, therefore, there are brought together a subjective and an objective moment, while the latter of these is differentiated into the four points of view which we have just examined. As a consequence, the idea of health which will be entertained will vary according to the measure used in examining and defining it, and from this point of view the same condition of life may be held "healthy" in one historical-social situation and "morbid" in another. In certain primitive societies of Siberia, the shamanistic trance fell within the "normal" pattern of life of the shaman; the latter was, in the eyes of his fellow tribesmen, an exceptional man, but not an ill man. Yet in the civilized society of Europe or America what would be the judgment passed on an individual who seriously, and not by imposture, claimed to have traveled to distant lands and to have dominated the spirits during his ecstatic trances? And in any civilized society whatever, is it not possible that, in a situation of public enthusiasm, certain men may appear subjectively and objectively healthy, while in a different situation they would be considered sick? There is no complete health for a man, as R. Siebeck has written, without a satisfactory reply to the question "Health for what?" And this "for what?"—belonging to it, however, inasmuch as it is a demand of personal life, not determined by it alone—has a decisive influence over our idea of health and even upon its reality.

These considerations make it possible to establish the following assertions: (a) The doctor must distinguish between perfect health and relative health. (b) *Perfect health* is that state in

which a subjective sentiment of well-being coincides with a morphology, a functional activity, a vital expenditure of energy, and a
behavior which are manifestly normal. (c) Perfect health is a
limit-condition to which the different actual conditions of human
life approximate. What we habitually call "good health," therefore, is a *relative health,* and this constitutively relative character
of human health may depend on: (i) a light, though sensible,
subjective or objective displacement of life in the direction of a
condition of infirmity—therefore, toward a state in which the individual ceases to be entirely healthy and yet is not truly sick (the
corpus neutrum of the medieval Galenists); (ii) the point of
view which the one considering the matter has chosen, since it
is possible that the same individual may appear healthy when
viewed from one point of view and ill when viewed from another;
and (iii) the greater or lesser resistance of the individual—when
his organism has been altered by an external cause—to the loss
of his functional pattern, the security and the elastic equilibrium
with which his normal life is lived. (d) From a general anthropological point of view, and as constituting the "objective and
subjective normalcy" of the individual nature, health is a psychosomatic habit in the service of the life and of the liberty of the
person; it therefore consists in the physical capacity of realizing,
with minimal malaise, and if possible with pleasure, the vital
projects of the subject in question. Thus, this capacity must constitute the proper end of the relation between doctor and patient.

2. Since this is the true end of medical care, it should be the
proper mode of the shared experience which is established in
the relation between doctor and patient. So far as the acts that
constitute it psychologically are concerned, shared experience
between human beings may be either contemplative or manipu-
latory objectification, or more or less friendly or odious co-execution. *Tertium non datur.* Since that is the case and since the
medical relation, as we have seen, ought not to resolve itself into
pure objectification nor into pure co-execution, what should the
doctor do to live with his patient? Can he limit himself to objectifying, as a doctor, the psychosomatic reality of the patient (to

discovering in him a collapsed lung or a mental aberration) and, as a compassionate person, to sharing the experience of the afflic- tion which the illness has caused in the intimate sensibility of the patient? As I see it, *the doctor must share the patient's experience by systematically completing objectification with co-execution and co-execution with objectification.* In the chapters dedicated to diagnosis and treatment, I will study in some detail how this methodic rule may be adequately fulfilled. This rule is the correl- ative, in anthropological and personalistic medicine, of that "sen- sation of the body" described in the work *De prisca medicina* and exercises the same role which the latter has exercised in the purely cosmological and physicalistic pathology that has been traditional in the West. I will try to explain its meaning in a brief introductory manner.

A number of times I have said that the doctor must objectify the reality of the sick man both cognitively and operatively. By means of the exploratory techniques which the treatises on somatic semeiology describe (inspection, palpitation, percussion, auscultation, endoscopic and radiographic explorations, graphs, chemical analyses, etc.), he observes by means of the senses of his own body the anatomical or biochemical lesions of the body of the patient and objectifies them in an intuitive manner. By means of the nosognostic rules which the manuals of psychiatric semeiology teach (psychiatric interview, psychological tests, and so on), he objectifies and contemplates with the eyes of the mind the living alterations of the patient: hallucinations, delirious ideas, obsessive ideas, disordered affections, and many others. A cavern diagnosed acoustically or radiographically is for the explorer a *somatic object,* auditive in the first case and visual in the second. A delirious idea correctly diagnosed is for the doctor a *mental object* in a twofold sense: because he has come to know it by the use of his own mind and because he places it as an objective reality in the mind of the sick man. In both cases, the reality of the patient is objectified by the doctor.

However, does the diagnostic and therapeutic objectification of the sick man by the doctor exhaust the possibilities of shared experience between them? Even more, can the doctor, even if he so desires, limit himself to a pure action of objectification in his relation of shared experience with the patient. Whether he wants to or not, whether he knows it or not, does he not always find himself obliged, *as a doctor,* to perform psychic actions which are not solely objectifying in their purpose? This constitutes, in my opinion, the nub of the problem.

Let us consider a limit-case—in appearance, a pure case: the activity of the surgeon when he operates on an anesthetized body on the surgical table. Rather than a person, there is before him—or so it seems—a simple living object, distinct, only in its anatomical form, from the horse or the dog on which the veterinarian might operate: a pure object, which he looks at, feels, cuts, and manipulates as a pure object. But even in this case can medical aid be pure objectification? In the process of surgical intervention can the surgeon, more precisely the good surgeon, limit himself to objectifying the reality of the sick man contemplatively and operatively? Not at all. Lériche has more than once emphasized the obligation of imagining the kind of scar the operation will leave on the body of the patient. In each case, it is necessary to select the type of incision whose scar will be most tolerable for the person who must bear it as his own for the rest of his life. And this of course demands that the surgeon know the personality of the person on the operating table, foresee his future life, conjecture how he will react to the various eventualities of that life, and therefore to co-execute in a divinatory manner the possible attitudes and responses of the person whose insensible and unconscious body the scalpel is falling upon. A surgical operation is, therefore, a particular form of an objectifying interhuman relation, but it is also a manifestation—no matter how tenuous—of a co-executive and interpersonal relation. The same might be said, *mutatis mutandis,* of the diagnosis and treatment of a person in a comatose state. Despite what Goldstein, drawing on the full weight of his authority, has been able to say, a human individual is never, not even in the most profound state of unconsciousness, a pure organism.

Even less will he be such when his personal condition is expressed consciously and in act, as in the case of the diagnosis and treatment of a subject who is neither under anesthetic or in a state of coma. It is true that a doctrinaire person with a doctrinaire anatomy-clinic mentality, as an example, will try systematically to reduce the body of the sick man to the condition of a cadaver undergoing autopsy; however, in spite of this effort the actual diagnostic activity of the most one-sided of clinical anatomists cannot avoid not only an objectifying but also a co-executive and interpersonal contact with the living reality of the subject whose illness he is seeking to diagnose. And what is said of diagnosis must be said no less of treatment. The sick man is a person and must be viewed as a person and treated as such by the doctor. The way to treat a person personally is, as we know, the co-execution of the psychic acts which define and constitute him as a person: his "very own" psychic acts.

What are the personal acts of the sick man which the doctor, in his role as doctor, can and must co-execute? Obviously, those relating to his illness. If the affective relation of a sick man with his wife has nothing to do with the suffering he is now undergoing, to describe and share the living experience of that relation would be, on the doctor's part, not an exploratory act but reprehensible curiosity. However, this is saying very little because a fundamental distinction must be made in the personal experience of the sick man with respect to his illness.

Husserl has called *das Mir-Eigene*, "the for-my-very-self," the phenomenological sphere of the lived experiences belonging to the proper reality of the subject. The lived experiences of my thoughts and the feelings that my body arouses in my consciousness are integral phases of the "being-for-my-very-self"; the sensation of the table which I have before me and the glance of one who impertinently observes me are, by supposition, lived experiences of mine, but such that belong not to the "being-for-myself" but to the "being-for-another," the sphere of *das Mir-Fremde*. I think that this Husserlian concept is very valuable, though still insufficient, because this sphere of the "for-my-very-self" is not homogenous and is found united to two others, phenomenologically and psychologically very clearly marked off from each other: the sphere of the *in me* and the sphere of the *mine*.

Let us suppose that at this moment a pain in the molars assaults me. Unquestionably, this pain emanates from a part of my body and, no less indubitably, it is in me, in my consciousness. Can I say, nevertheless, that it is mine? By no means. I live through it as something brutal and incomprehensible which has risen up in me; for me, it is something that supervenes upon me, which assaults me "from without." Even more, I do not accept it into my life: I rise up against it; I try to eliminate it from my consciousness by taking an analgesic or, more radically and significantly, by suppressing that part of my body from which it proceeds and in which it resides. The toothache is *in me*, but it is not *mine;* at least, it begins by not being mine even though, lacking a more precise and discriminatory verbal expression, I must call it "*my* toothache" when I want to talk about it.

What then is the *mine?* Obviously that which I live as an integral part of selfhood; that which belongs to my person as a property; that which in the most secret and intimate portion of my being, I feel is necessary if I am to be and to continue to be "I myself." *The mine* may be an element pleasing or displeasing to me even though in virtue of the most profound anthropological and metaphysical reasons it may always be easier for me to consider *mine* those ingredients—whether they be acts or sentiments—of my own life that are pleasing to me. Not infrequently we fall into the deceptive illusion of holding as *ours* modes of being or lived experiences that really do not take place in us or give us any pleasure, and of judging as *not ours,* that is, alien to the selfhood of our person, those experiences that quite properly, though unhappily and regretfully for us, belong as a matter of fact to the real constitution of our "I myself." To say of something that it is *mine* (its *myness*, if I may use the expression) what is decisive, therefore, is not the pleasing or unpleasing character of its affective action on my person, not the biological or judicial titles by which it is ascribed to my life, but the authenticity and the ultimate certitude of its belonging to that intimate redoubt in which really and truly I am "I myself" and in which I can speak of "myself."

A psychic act, idea, belief, volition or sentiment can be *mine* in three ways. And these three principal ways by which I come to establish the "selfness" of my person are assumption, creation, and donation.

Everything is *mine by assumption,* which, coming into my life from without me, is actively incorporated by me into my personal reality, assumed in it. Thus, for example, my love for my children has come to be "mine"; this love, once established, becomes a substantially integral part of the reality of my "I myself" and continues to belong to it even though my sons may die or I might at times become forgetful of them. In the same way something that transpires in my body may succeed in becoming *mine.* In the following pages we shall study in a summary manner the structure of this appropriating assumption which is so important for understanding with any precision the personal attitude of the sick man toward his illness.

That is *mine by creation* which arises in my life through the work of my creative liberty and which, as a really and truly proper possession, is incorporated thereafter into the selfness of my person. Without this further appropriation of his personal creations, the creator will not succeed in having them truly and definitively as *his own* though they have, beyond doubt, issued from him. "This is not mine" is what the poet and the painter say of a work which they repudiate as stillborn or ill-begotten, in other words, a work which, though it has been produced by them, they do not accept as their own. As assumption makes its own that which originally was alien, repudiation and rejection make alien that which began by being one's own. None of this, it should be clear, prevents creation, insofar as man can be a creator, from being the most important part of the self-formation of the personality.

Finally, that which is *mine by donation* enters my life from outside it and is what I accept into the intimacy of my being as something destined for me. By assumption I conquer actively as my own something that in the beginning was not for me; by way of donation I receive that which an act of belief makes me see as dedicated to me, something that a principle outside of me, whatever it may be, presents and offers to me. My vocation is mine by donation, and likewise my inventions and successes prove to be, effectively, mine by donation. Every act of creation, and even every discovery, begins and ends by being—for him who carries them out and achieves them—an offering, a gift, a donative.

What then is there in my life that has begun by being radically and originatively *mine*? Very little. Almost nothing: an incipient freedom, limited and obscure, with no other patrimony save its forced or weak will to be, which, by reason of acceptance, assumption, and creation, has little by little constructed my "very own self" and has gone into the building of my personal selfhood, constructing, in a word, the sphere of the *mine*. My body, for example, by its nature belongs to my reality, and in this sense I can and must say "I am my body"; at the same time, however, it is part of my being by acceptation, and it is this, precisely this, that permits me to call it mine or to feel, in its regard, the different experiences which the incomprehensible and strange may arouse in me: strangeness, admiration, or, in the Sartrean sense, "nausea."

Here then is the result of this necessary and informal phenomenological digression. Those psychic acts are truly my own which go to make up the selfness of the person, the sphere of the *mine*, and increase it by assumption, creation, and acceptance but limit it by exclusion or repudiation. The "human acts," a scholastic would say, are formed in this way in the ontological and psychological habits of the assumed personal or hypothetical personal principle. The parts which the subconscious or the unconscious zones of the personality respectively play in this process matter little here. The only thing to be noted at this point is that co-executive shared experience (this is its *aporia* or, if one wishes, its drama) must have as its material the act with which the other establishes and affirms his own personal self, that which for him is most intimate and reserved, that which is most "his own."

What then must be, in this light, the co-executive activity of the doctor in his relationship with the patient? I shall reply to this question by distinguishing two extreme and opposed cases, the acutely ill and the neurotically ill, and another which falls between them, the chronically ill person. More than once we shall have to appeal to this way of ordering the modes of illness, very near, in a certain way, to the well-known schema of Weizsacher's "neurosis," "biosis," "scolerosis."

In *acute illness*—a case of pneumonia, a sudden onset of nephritic colic—the possibility and the medical importance of interpersonal shared experience are minimal. The sentiments which appear in the state of illness—physical pain, vertigo, fatigue, or swelling—belong originally to the sphere of the *in-me*, not to the sphere of the *mine*, and are radically incapable of becoming shared experiences. The toothache belongs to the one who suffers it and to no one else; insofar as it is a morbid condition of one's own body, illness isolates, and this is the reason why, in such cases, a diagnosis and a treatment which look only to objectification may be technically sufficient.

However, is the acute illness *only in me?* Indubitably, no. In a certain degree and in a certain way an acute illness can become, even though I do not prolong it, *mine*—either because, having to suffer it, I more or less consciously give it a meaning in my personal existence (merit for eternal life; an excuse for not fulfilling a duty I find burdensome) or because the affliction has not arisen in my earthly life by pure chance but rather in virtue of a more or less conscious genetic process to which is assigned, in the course of this life, a psychologically comprehensible meaning (we may cite as examples the "psychosomatic" anginas of which Weizsacker speaks. And when this happens—when the acute illness is really and truly the ill person's own, in addition to being *in him* —the co-executive activity of the doctor will be not only a possibility but also a technical imperative. Co-execution in such a case tries to grasp, by conjecture, the personal meaning, conscious or subconscious, of a reality previously known by objectification.

It is, we may say, the exploratory activity which completes the diagnosis.

The case of *neurotic illness* is quite different. Let us imagine, for the sake of greater clarity, that it is a question of a psychoneurosis: an obsessive neurosis, for example. The doctor begins by hearing the neurotic person relate his suffering, and while hearing him, he understands and experiences in a certain way in his soul what the ill person is undergoing in his own. What characterizes these patients, among other things, is that they feel compelled to live out as "their own" (which they do violently according to a tormenting manner imbedded in the structures of their "personality," even though at one time or another they do struggle against them) the doubts and obsessions which torment them. However, this co-executive or comprehensive diagnostic process will not prove complete if the doctor does not bring to completion a double process of objectification: the contemplation of the obsessive ideas of the sick man as true "mental objects" (psychological diagnosis in the strict sense) and (since the illness is always an illness of the body, even though at times the concrete somatic disorder escapes our observation) the discovery of the bodily alteration or "physical object" in which that neurosis has its immediate cause. What the diagnostician is not completing is objectification—which, as has been said, must be successively achieved with the eyes of the mind as well as those of the flesh.

Between acute illness and neurotic illness—(it would be more correct and exact to say "preponderantly neurotic" because all illnesses contain some neurotic element) falls the *chronic illness*, the illness with which the sick man sees himself obliged to deal in order to plan and to work out a life which is *his own*. In regard to it, the mode of shared living between the doctor and the patient has to be most imperatively and most clearly a systematic transition from objectification to co-execution and from co-execution to objectification; here, therefore, medical assistance takes on its greatest complexity. There will be occasion to examine this statement more fully; here I cannot go beyond the summary terms of this preliminary indication. My purpose was only to show that from the very form of my analysis the shared living between the doctor and the patient must always be the mutual and well-ordered technical implication of an objectifying relation and a co-executive relation.

3. Here I can only examine briefly the problem of the *special bond* of the medical relation. What is the specific character of the union which, by means of this double activity of objectification and co-execution, is established between the doctor and the sick man? What is it that really unites them in the therapeutic act?

The answer cannot be univocal because the character of this uniting bond will depend, at least, on what the intention of the doctor and the attitude of the sick man may be when they meet on this ground. In the following chapter we will consider the spectrum of the different concrete modes which the therapeutic bond may assume. However, without diminishing this real diversity, it is certain that from the time of the Hippocratics to our own day the same opinion has been repeated whenever the doctor has tried to express what he considers desirable and normative in his relationship with the patient. This opinion holds that, *when medical assistance is what it ought to be, the bond which unites doctor and patient is love.* Among the many forms of the bond of love, the one determined simultaneously by the specific need of the patient (his illness) and the specific capacity for giving of the doctor (his technical knowledge) will be *medical love.*

The preceding historical investigation has made us see the successive modulation of this *leitmotiv* of medical asssistance. Through Plato (the sick man is the friend of the doctor by reason of his illness, *Lysis* 217 a) and the Hippocratic *Praecepta* (where there is love for man, there is love for art), the Greeks always taught that the primary nexus between the doctor and the sick man ought to be friendship, *philia,* in the specific form of *medical friendship.* Christianity inherited this teaching, though it understood and practiced it according to the Christian idea of friendship and love, and thus transcended personally and supernaturally the radical naturalism of Greek thought. The unitive bond between doctor and patient ought to be technical charity: the outgoing love of the doctor toward the needful man, the sick man, technically realized as diagnosis and treatment. The professionalization of the Christian doctor, with its necessary economic consequences, ought not to alter in principle this fundamental rule of medical assistance. The conception of "medical friendship" in the modern secularized world differs according as the doctor has remained faithful to the vision of man as person, or, renouncing it, has again subscribed, though, clearly, no longer in the Hellenic manner, to a purely and exclusively naturalistic anthropology. In the first case, the nerve center of the ideal bond between the doctor and the patient continues to be, though secularized with respect to its fundamental perspectives, *technical friendship,* a relation diagnostically and therapeutically friendly with a being endowed with autonomous ends; in the second, the relation between doctor and patient has been conceived as a specific form of camaraderie; without any reduction of his more or less professional or scientific interests, the doctor helps the patient so that he may, within the society to which he belongs, contribute normally to the historical realization of human nature.

The increasing vigor of psychoanalysis has led some to give a new name to and to understand in an unusual manner the character of the bond which relates doctor and patient: the old *philia* has been changed into *transference.* Here is the Freudian text where for the first time, 1895, allusion is made to transference: "In the sick persons who decide to submit themselves to the doctor and to place their confidence in him, understanding of course that they do so willingly and without being required to do so by him, it cannot be avoided that, at least for a certain time, a personal relationship with the doctor should appear inconveniently in the foreground, and it would even seem that such an influence on the part of the doctor would be an indispensable condition for the resolution of the [therapeutic] problem (*Studien über Hysterie* [1909] 132). The faith which the sick man places in the doctor (the peculiar form which medical friendship takes in him) is now conceived as a "transference" at once disturbing and necessary; and the doctor's will to help is the technical response (friendly, of course, but according to a new idea of friendship) to the "transferential" relation which the patient, without seeking it, has established with him. (In a later chapter, when we shall study thematically, the affective moment in the relation between doctor and patient, this very important contribution of psychoanalysis to the theory and practice of this relation will appear again and be amply considered.)

4. The fourth structural moment of the medical relation is, finally, the proper *communication* between those who constitute that relation, the complex of the principal technical resources to which the doctor must appeal so that his acts of objectification and co-execution may prove really effective, that is to say, the glance, the word, and the silence; manual contact and instrumental relation. In order to communicate with his patient the doctor observes him, speaks to him, listens to him, puts his hands on him, employs the most diverse exploratory and therapeutic instruments. We shall have to study what all these means of communication represent in relation to the technical and human bond between the doctor and the patient. But to this end I think that it is necessary to examine beforehand the motives which determine the meeting of the one and the other; in other words, what the medical relation *can* be, before it effectively *exists*.

Luis Díez del Corral

Don *Luis Diéz del Corral (b.1911), professor of the history of political philosophy at the University of Madrid, is a prominent historian of political ideas and philosopher of history. His writings include* El liberalismo doctrinario *(1954),* El rapto de europa *(1954),* De historia y de political *(1956), and* Ensayos sobre arte y sociedad *(1955).*

"On the Singular Character of the Historical Destiny of Europe" appeared in *De historia y politica* (Madrid: Instituto de Estudios Politicos, 1956) 235–264. © 1956 by Luis Díez del Corral. Grateful acknowledgment is made to the author for permission to reprint.

IX. ON THE SINGULAR CHARACTER OF THE HISTORICAL DESTINY OF EUROPE

THE MODES OF HISTORICAL ACTIVITY

Europe differs from other great civilizations not only in virtue of a special direction of its historical destiny or of a special fecundity of this destiny, of a refined awareness it has had of this destiny, but also in something prior and more substantial. The difference between the destiny of Europe and that of India, China, or the great civilizations of the past does not consist merely in some adjective attributable to a common substantive: the homogeneous historical destiny of these peoples or civilizations. It consists in the substantive itself. Historical life, such as the West has possessed and possesses, is not something that is commonly found among human beings or among their most advanced societies, at least, but is something that belongs to the West in a particular and exclusive way.

That is the reason and the cause for the prodigious development of European civilization. Because the Europeans understood and practiced life, individually as well as collectively, socially as well as historically, in an active and creative manner, they were able to develop the vast world of objective forms of their culture, forms that spread from their old home ground to inundate the entire face of the earth.

In order to understand the historical heart of a people or of a civilization, it is not as important to analyze the objective products of its science, of its politics or its art, as to lay bare the vital root from which all these have emerged. We say vital root, not understanding vital root as something clouded, instinctive, and irrational, but as something clear and rational. At this point we may invoke the support of Ortega's idea of vital or historical reason.

Historical examination should penetrate to the intimate forces which impel peoples and civilizations in their march through history. It should investigate, with an attempt at conceptual clarity, the fundamental principles and the basic attitudes, the most primary value-judgments of the great subjects of history, in order to understand their concrete cultural forms *ab origine*. Most especially—this is the question that interests us here—how a people feels when placed before the undertaking in which historical life consists: whether it feels it as something inevitable and forced upon it, from which it is best to flee, or as something attractive, enjoyable; whether it looks upon it as a routine or as a new and adventurous enterprise; whether it considers itself called, with a vocation, to follow a definite course which leads to the highest peaks, or whether it lets itself be led along any course whatever; or perhaps it follows no exact course either because it finds no paths or because the paths do not seem to lead to any worthwhile goal.

In order to comprehend these differences in the many diverse ways in which the different peoples or civilizations of the earth understand historical life, it is best to go back analogically to the many diverse ways individual men have of looking upon their life task. In this way the general problems are easier to view. This is an old procedure employed by the thinker who, perhaps, most influenced the history of Western thought, Plato. In order to know what the civil community, the *polis*, was in its essence, in its idea, he began by analyzing individual man, how his faculties were distinguished, what functions they served, how each is articulated in relation to the others, etc. It then proves easy to prolong or project the dimensions of the object studies and pass from individual man to social man, to man "writ large."

EUROPE'S DESTINY

The individuals we deal with possess a series of similar characteristics or circumstances: they beget sons, they possess wealth, they practice a profession, they exhibit a certain repertory of ideas. They naturally vary in the extent of their participation in those common denominators: some are poor, others rich; some practice an intellectual profession, others manual, and so on. In this way each one acquires a definite profile. But, even though we may have determined all the exterior points that constitute that profile, we shall not have exhausted the characterization of the individual in question; rather we will have sketched a hollow figure, one without substance, without a heart. It would be necessary to find out what this man is like seen from within: what his fundamental attitude is toward life; whether he actually believes in it or shuns it and looks for a refuge in prejudices, habits, blind obediences; whether he feels he is adrift in existence with no port to go to; or whether he considers that he is driven by a call, by an authentic vocation which would give a unifying sense and motivating principle to his life.

In America, where inheritance, social position, class, and rank count for less than in old Europe, one is accustomed to value a man for himself, without social ornaments, and most especially one esteems his existential attitude toward the tasks of life, his capacity for creation, for adjusting and for controlling life, more than inherited wealth or a work already completed but liable to be lost, one which, in any case, refers to and is dependent upon the person who produced it. For this reason the New World is a good place to reflect on the problem which is the object of this essay: what has been the internal nerve beneath the muscle, the guideline through the tangle that the vast and proliferous cultural creations of Europe represent; that is, how those cultures understand their historical destiny, how they feel about the course of life, whether or not they feel called to the fulfilling of a mission.

Within Europe itself it is perhaps more difficult to pose the problem because the Old World finds itself too burdened with urgent problems, too laden with concrete tasks, euphoria and depression, pride and regret, even desperation. The European man who a few decades ago was sure of his destiny and gave it almost no thought (it seemed so manifest to him) is now very ill at ease. He thinks he has come down quite a bit after the two world wars he had unleashed and because of the menacing employment of his creations by the great extra-European protagonists. He cannot quite put in focus, as he should, the question of his historical meaning, of the destiny it has fallen to him to fulfill.

One current in historiography which has been in vogue since World War I proclaims loudly that Europe's destiny has no specific singularity, that it is like the destiny of any other civilization, as much in its term as in the rhythm or inner modality of its development. Each civilization has had its historical destiny, and by following it out has produced its integrated patrimony of science, art, techniques, law, social forms, etc., which, taken as a whole, is equivalent to the patrimony of the other civilizations. A democratic equality thus extends itself over the planet between all kinds of existing or past civilizations, insofar as each offers a certain substantive character. What is curious is that it is a question not only of an equality demanded by way of revolution by the members of civilizations which for decades have been held to be inferior but also of one gratuitously conceded by outstanding historians and philosophers who belong to that civilization which a very short time ago considered itself the queen of the whole planet.

We have here a gesture of generosity, a gesture of charity, rising out of the Christian conscience of Europe. But it is also true that it contradicts one of the most characteristic motive forces of European history, to wit: the serene quest for truth, since the destiny of European civilization differs—we repeat—from others, those of India or China, for example, not by being better or

worse, more productive or less productive, more nationalist or
less, but by being destiny in a specific and almost exclusive way.
Implied opinions, discouragements and self-accusations, grudges
between different European nations, and ideological prejudices
obscure the cold truth. A cold, naked truth, relative to objective
structures without any kind of possible axiological nuances. To
say that the historical destiny of Europe is destiny in a specific
way does not mean to say that it is better than the particular way
of doing and living out their history that the Chinese, the Indi-
ans, or the Mohammedans have had. Rather, there are quite serious indications that would predispose us to make a negative
judgment because this specific destiny of Europe means a historical life that is tense, passionate, exhausting, and dramatic.

THE CONCEPT OF DESTINY IN THE FAR EAST

The term that the Chinese use which is similar to destiny, *ming,*
means something very different and certainly much more tran-
quil. The Chinese feels no anxiety in realizing his destiny. "If the
wise man completes something," writes Confucius, "that is good;
if he does not complete anything, that also is good: he acknowl-
edges destiny." "The perfect man perceives danger and bows
before destiny." Confucius indicates some vague prescriptions
for him, prescriptions which are not taken as moral command-
ments but as imperatives of nature.

The order of these imperatives will be conceptualized by Lao-
tse in the metaphysical form which he calls *Tao. Tao* is the principle, anterior to all beings, from which all beings are derived. It
is something like the absolute in Western philosophy, but conceived naturalistically. *Tao* is not an intelligent principle but a
law of fate; it is not something spiritual but something material,
imperceptible because of its tenuousness, simple, without form,
omnipresent, without desire or effort, something entirely full and
calm, in spite of the fact that sentient beings come from it and
return to it in a circular evolution of growth, decay, death, rebirth,
etc. The ideal man, the wise man, must mold his life on *Tao;* he

must prolong his life by temperance, peace of mind, abstinence from anything that fatigues and wears, doing as little as possible, and, if possible doing nothing, so as not to interfere with the rotation of the cosmic wheel, universal evolution.

In very definite terms, Lao-tse counsels inhibition as an attitude toward the world: "Do not act. I have come to understand that to wish to conquer the world by action is a project doomed to failure. . . . Exercise yourselves in inaction and everything will put itself in order." An immanent, inexorable order to which man should conform himself humbly. Lietse emphasizes even more than Lao-tse the fatalistic character of such an order and the consequent passivity of the wise man: "The mystery which cannot be explained is fatedness. It is composed of impenetrable obscurities, of complications which accumulate day after day. Those who are persuaded of the existence of this fatedness do not believe in the possibility of reaching a goal . . . they count on nothing, feeling they are playthings in the hands of blind destiny. Upright and filled with integrity they tend toward no goal; they neither grieve nor rejoice over anything; they do not act but permit things to follow their course. . . . The following reflection of Hoang-Ti sums up very well the conduct to be followed by the enlightened man: the super-man must remain motionless as a corpse and move only passively, because something makes him move. . . ."

On the basis of such a concept of destiny in the great Chinese thinkers, who reveal the mentality of their people (and to which later there was added the decidedly different, though no more dynamic, concept of Buddhism), the special characteristics of the history of the Far East become explicable. It is a history characterized in the first place by a monumental stability. "We early find China," wrote Hegel, "elevated to the state in which we find her today. For, since the antithesis between objective being and subjective movement toward this being are still lacking, variability is impossible and the static which reappears eternally replaces what we would call historical." The German philosopher will sententiously declare: "The States of the East are dead and stay upright only because they are bound to nature."

It is a declaration that today sounds exaggerated and petulant, swelled by a European superiority complex, above all because it is extended to all the countries of the Far East including India as well, although India, evidently, is distinguished by an intense spiritual life, by a profound metaphysical religious sense. In fact, the Indian concept of destiny, which is designated by the word *Karma* and which, perfectly formulated in Manu, persists throughout centuries with hardly any modifications, is quite different from the Chinese as well as from the Greco-Latin conception. *Karma* is not any independent or abstract force which works upon human acts in an irresistible way. It is something immanent in their execution. It is the internal moral causality of the acts realized by the individual. Every act causes an effect which will be realized sooner or later in the form of a reward or a punishment, joy or suffering, a rise or a fall in one's condition in life. Death is powerless against this law because acts outlast it. Acts beget acts, each one being the product of an earlier act and the seed of another, later act. Nor does this succession suppose any other sustaining force than an undefined, individual selfhood which can be maintained at the most diverse levels in the scale of living beings, as the belief in the transmigration of souls demands. Thus, as Mircea Eliade has written, the universe, including the gods themselves, is "penetrated with *karmic* potential."

With this concept of destiny as a basis, it seems that an intense historical life could, and even should, have been developed. If the individual creates his own fate, if his existence runs along rails which he himself had laid down, it is possible to think that the sum of individuals, that is, the Indian people, would have traced, in the course of time, a path of aspiring and ambitious creation. But the virtues of the doctrine of *karma* were limited to the scope of a purely individual morality which (whatever its qualification might be from the ethical point of view) found no reflection in a creative activity of the community. The vaguely vital and impersonal character of the doctrine, the abstract and indiscriminate meaning of soul, whose selfhood, in some interpretations, means nothing more than an abstract center of imputation, of actions objectively connected with one another over and above the different forms of existence, the spontaneous tendency to conformism and resignation, and so on—all this has had as a consequence the evident inefficacy of the Indian man, from the individual as well as the collective point of view.

"The doctrine of *karma*," writes Louis Renou, "has encouraged inaction for the fear of acting badly. This concept has profoundly marked the conduct of the Indian people, coinciding with the pessimistic reflection which, in another respect, engendered the doctrine of *sansara* (the transmigration of souls). All gnomic literature testifies to the virtue of not acting. Every affection takes on the form of a punishment, every act that of an error or of suffering." From a purely moral and spiritual point of view this attitude may contain high values, but from the social and cultural point of view it produces fundamentally negative values. *Nirvana* (which liberates the individual from the binding power of *karma*, as a state in which actions are realized without desire and attachment, and therefore do not produce possible consequences in a future life) certainly does not mean mere negativity in the moral and religious order, but a state of perfection reached by means of long and scrupulous efforts. However, as a collective ideal of happiness, it paralyzes historical life. In any case it is not a factor that promotes the construction of a positive science, a dynamic state, or of a progressive economy.

The Wise Man's Attitude Toward Destiny

How far from *nirvana* the wise man and the cultured man of Europe in our times finds himself! How far, too, from the *apathy* with which the wise man of old watched the decline of classic civilization! The true Stoic was right in locking himself up in his ivory tower, from which he watched the advance of events that were so often catastrophic, as one watches the current of a river which, even though it hurls itself over shattering cataracts, presents itself to an observer as a mere spectacle. But, before the advance of the historical events of our time the attitude of mere observer is impossible, for there are no bridges, nor riverside towers, nor bluffs rising above the waters to serve as an observation point. These waters have burst all bounds and inundated everything, sweeping before them household goods and our very raiment.

Nor is there any place for the attitude of one who maintains his post imperturbably like that Pompeian sentinel whom the volcanic ashes enveloped and suffocated, without moving him to abandon the duty he was carrying out, and whom Spengler at the end of *Years of Decision* sets up as a model for the Europeans of his time. Such a Stoic attitude might have been valid at the decline of ancient civilization but cannot be maintained in the crisis of ours, and the attempt to preach it must prove inauthentic and ineffective. This is not to say that we must not remain at our posts and not abandon them, even though clouds of ashes and fire threaten us, following the example of that good Pompeian. The fact is that the internal motives and the circumstances of such an attitude have changed so much in the course of centuries that the proposed exemplar is no longer valid. It is simply and purely invalid, since the ashes and fire which can exterminate us in the first place were not phenomena of a natural order but eruptions of man-made Vesuviuses, mechanical and even social giants manufactured by the portentous human intelligence, by the wise men of our time, who, instead of remaining at the margin of the historical current, as they did in China, in India, or during the last centuries of antiquity, accelerate that current and hurl it forward with the unparalleled and powerful personal effort of their minds.

No. The decisive factors which threaten our civilization are not a kind of waning and retrogressive sign, as in the case of the decadence of the ancient world: fall of birth rate, barbarian inundation, the breakdown of the economic system, the rebellion of the countryside against the city, a lack of vigor in scientific and technical thought, and so on, but very concrete and hypercivilized factors: a surfeit of invention, excess of population, vast material efficiency, disproportionate knowledge, and control of the most secret forces in Nature. For this reason, Berdyaev's thesis of a new Middle Age cannot be maintained, at least in its name. Western civilization and Western man have forged their own crisis, their alleged decadence; they are not its passive subjects but its active protagonists. To be sure, one cannot forget the part which the barbarians have in our present situation. However, the danger they offer does not lie in their rudimentary state of barbarism, as was the case with the barbarians who broke through the Roman *limes*. Rather, it is the mastery which in a few short decades they have been capable of acquiring over the technology invented by the European West, especially its war techniques. In this way the West comes up against itself in the barbarians which threaten it, against the products of its industrial technique, its science of war, its social ideas assimilated by other peoples after having been suitably transformed and adapted.

It is impossible, then, for the European to extricate himself from the trammels of his historical destiny, free himself from its implications, to situate himself outside its limits, even though it be by way of resignation like that of the ancient Stoic sage. We may consider the attitude of the philosophers most in vogue in our time, not only the philosophers of mathematics and scientific logic but even those most removed from these disciplines, those who fall under the problematic designation of existentialists: there is no attitude more opposed to the attitude of the philosophy and the philosophers of the period of the decadence of the ancient world. Even the philosophers most cited in our day are in the midst of the historical stream and accelerate and hurl it forward with their ideas just as do mathematicians, physicists, biologists, and engineers. Consider also the attitude, so unlike that of Stoicism, displayed by that social ideology which, according to Spengler's comparison of the decadence of the ancient world with that of the West, most resembles Stoicism—socialism. Socialism, at least in its most extreme forms, is very far from the static, passive, resigned, and long-suffering attitude of ancient Stoicism; rather, in the form of communism it has become the lever and the fomenting agent for the rebellion of the non-Western peoples against the West.

A PHILOLOGICAL EXCURSUS

However, there is occasion for us here to ask whether the term "destiny" is not perhaps unsuited to designate the specific way in which the European people live out their historical lot; whether it does not carry, at least in its current acceptance, a sense of pre-determination, of the inexorable concatenation of events, of fatedness, contrary to the one we have just placed in relief. Evidently, this is to a great extent the case, and for this reason it will be necessary to determine in what concrete, though perhaps extraordinary and marginal sense, we understand the word "destiny" when we add to it the adjective "historical" and refer it to Europe as something which is essential and exclusive.

It will be necessary to define our term and our concept with regard to its vulgar usage and to the scientific usage which is so frequently made of it, even though the most responsible writers generally indicate the diversity of acceptances the term is given. Thus, for example, A. Dorner, in the introductory article to the series of entries dedicated to the term *fate* in the *Encyclopedia of Religion and Ethics*, edited by James Hastings, makes the point: "Destiny, as a matter of fact, being in a certain way an undefined concept, may involve an ethical vocation and may in that case be applied to the goal which a superior will has placed before a moral personality as an ideal that has to be realized through an ethical effort."

This is certainly not the usual meaning of the term, and even less the one attributed to it by the philosophico-historical conception which in our time has stamped it with more or less pseudo-scientific rigor, but with indubitable success and an unquestionable expenditure of talent. We are referring to the notion of destiny which is the nerve center of that strange work, at once so equivocal and so penetrating, so equally arbitrary and enlightening, *The Decline of the West* by Spengler. A dialogue with this work must be undertaken when one starts out with a title like that of our essay.

For Spengler, as is well known, the idea of destiny is radically opposed to the principle of causality. Destiny is a symbol which refers to the Universe of History and the comprehension of which is intuitive, while the idea of causality refers to the Universe of Nature and is logical and rational. Destiny is related to life, causality to death. For this reason destiny, which is to causality what time is to space, represents the "inescapable necessity of life," and for this reason also "real history is freighted with destiny though it has no law." Spengler takes this position with respect to the materialistically determinist concept of destiny characteristic of many thinkers of the preceding century but comes to substitute for it another kind of blind determination, biological in character, which functions as the inexorable, inflexible axis of historical life. Historical life grows, reaches maturity, and declines with an inexorable rhythm in the biological development of each culture.

The relationship in which the Spenglerian conception of destiny stands to the conception of historical cycles, its blind biological unfolding and its intimate connection with the thesis of decadence, readily supplies us with the clue that, subject to personal modifications, Spengler's concept is simply that of the ancient world reborn. It is another example of the way in which the ideas of antiquity have been reborn in the course of Western history, especially the idea of fate and the cyclical conception of history. This German thinker, following the footsteps of Machiavelli, Vico, and, above all, Goethe and Nietzsche, has revived this idea of fate and injected into it the Germanic conception of destiny. Or, it might better be said, he has developed the seed of the idea of destiny which has always been latent in that of fate and has exploited the virtualities which have always been vestigially present in it. For, in a curious way, the different conceptions of destiny, although they lose their force, never completely disappear but, in some way, linger in obscure regions of popular beliefs, in learned reminders, in the heart of words which maintain their primitive philogical configuration, even though their ancient meaning is attenuated.

Thus, in our language the word *"hado"* comes from the word *fatum,* and when we employ it we revive the spark of old ideas now more or less moribund, which nevertheless may spring back to life if, in propitious historical circumstances, the breath of a perceptive intelligence breathes upon their embers. We do, in fact, bring them back to life when we employ adjectives like *"fatidico"* or *"fatal"* or the noun *"fatalidad."* As to the word *"sino,"* its roots are still more ancient. *"Sino,"* according to the Academy's dictionary, is "fate or destiny determined by the influence of the stars." It comes from the word "sign," that is, from the signs of the zodiac, where the *simtu* came to have its dwelling. *Simtu* is the special destiny of the Babylonians, a destiny which presented itself in the form of a decree, the concrete and individual sentence handed down by the supreme tribunal of the gods. We also see the pessimistic conception of the Germans—their conception of the *Gotterdammerung,* the twilight of the gods, which during the optimistic centuries of Christianity had gone underground—flower again in Wagner's art, in Spengler's philosophy, and in the politics of the Third Reich. With reference to the conception of fate characteristic of Islam, *quadar,* an Américo Castro will show us unquestionable traces of it in Spanish beliefs, idioms, and forms of thought. Sometimes we reach down to the stratum of a more primitive mentality, as when we speak of "suerte," a notion antecedent to that of destiny in the forms in which have referred to it, and our use of it comes to indicate a kind of "retrogression toward fetishism," as Auguste Comte said.

In contrast to the conceptions implicit in the terms stated above, another concept appears in the course of the Middle Ages based on the term "destiny," derived from the Latin verb *destinare,* which did not produce the substantive form *destinum,* equivalent to the term which figures in the title of our essay. In Latin only late and rarely do we find the word *destina, -ae,* which means support, aid, link, in a decidedly static sense, as derived from the verb *destinare,* which—proceeding from *sto, stare* (*estar,* to be in a certain condition) by way of the form *stano* with the prefix *de*—means, in its proper sense, to bind, prevail upon, fix, affirm, or establish. Thus, Caesar writes, *"destinare antemnas ad malos"* ("to fix the crossbar to the ship's masts"). In a cognate sense, the word comes to have a more active meaning: to direct one's sight toward (*collineare*), to propose an end for oneself, to reach out toward a goal, to strive toward some purpose, and so on, and thus we come upon the neuter noun *destinatum*, equivalent to *"propositum, finis, certum consilium necnon scopus praestitutus."* There also exists in classical Latin the word *destinatio, -onis*, with a similar meaning; there is completely lacking, however, a word derived from the verb *destinare* which would designate a superior power in the active sense of the modern term destiny, or in the passive sense of that which has been destined by destiny.

Only after the Middle Ages are well advanced, after the active sense of the verb *destinare* has been emphasized in middle and lower Latin, do we come upon the noun destiny. Littré in his dictionary selects a twelfth-century text, *"Et tel destin m'ont doné li felon,"* and several others in which the term *destinée* (*the effect of destiny*) appears. In the poetry of the troubadors the use of the noun in an active sense is clear and frequent; Beranger de Palasol writes, *"Ie us am, qualque danse m'en sia/ Destinatz ni a venir."*

As far as the Castilian language is concerned, the texts which may be adduced are not very old. The word appears in the Marques de Santillana, *". . . sea destino o cur so fatal,"* and in Garcilaso, its use becoming more general in the sixteenth century. It is curious that in Castilian Spanish the Christian sense of the term appears very accentuated. Thus, Fray Luis de Léon writes, *"Pues desde el sacro asiento/ . . . el firmamento gobiernas, y camino/ das solo a lo que quiere tu destino."* Solís, in his *Historia de la conquista de México*, gives the following definition: "We call destiny, speaking as Christians, that sovereign and supreme disposition of the first cause which permits the secondary causes to operate as its dependent causes and the mediating principles of nature."

The new, active, and finalistic meaning of the word in the end imposes itself to the point that the *Dictionary* of the Royal Academy thus defines the verb *destinar: "ordenar, señalar y determinar una cosa para algún fin o efecto. Viene del latino destinare, que significa lo mismo"* (to order, to indicate, to determine something for some end or effect; it comes from the Latin *destinare,* which has the same meaning). That is to say, the new acceptance projects itself onto the original meaning of the classical Latin, falsifying it, in spite of the erudition of the authors of the great Spanish dictionary. In a curious fashion a word which had begun with a predominantly static meaning changes that meaning in the course of the centuries until it presents itself in the Romance languages with another meaning, eminently dynamic and teleological. We bring this meaning into play as often in ordinary life as we speak of *"el destinatario"* (the addressee) of a letter, of *"la destinación"* (the destination) of merchandise or of a ship, or in speaking of destiny in the sense of consigning, indicating, or applying a thing or a place to a determined end.

Precisely because of the active and teleological sense of the word destiny, the adjective "historical" suits it so well. This is not the case with *moira, fatum,* the Chinese *ming,* or the Indian *karma.* This is evident also in the residues of the first words in the Castilian language: we may speak of the historical destiny of France but not, in a strict sense, of the historical *"sino,"* the *"suerte,"* the *"fatalidad,"* or the *"hado"* of France. These nouns have a meaning of inflexible and mechanical consequence, or rather of discontinuity, of momentary and inconsequent occurrence, which is far from the particular meaning of the word destiny, one that fits so well with the adjective "historical" to the point that whenever we speak of the destiny of a people, there comes to our lips the complete expression "the historical destiny of this or that people." In contrast to this expression, we very frequently say *"¡Que fatalidad!"*—exhausting its meaning in the single event to which it refers.

Destiny in Classical Antiquity

The classical conception of destiny underlying the word *"fatali-dad,"* "fatedness," is not favorable to the development of an active, creative, truly historical sense of history. The Homeric "moira," with all its simplicity, imposed unbreachable barriers, not only to men but for the supreme agents as well, for the gods themselves. Under another aspect, the gods are presented as powers invested with a mythical religious sense, purely natural-istic in character. For its part, the notion of *"heimarmene"* which originated among the Ionian philosophers, while more systematic and far-reaching than the concept of *"moira,"* will envelop human action to the point of strangulation in its extricable nets; this will be true even when, as at the end of the period of antiquity, it presents itself, in purified form, as divine providence. "Man," Martin P. Nielsson writes, "realizes his puny stature and bows humbly before the divine omnipotence and wisdom, but there is no place for the trust of a son toward his father. For is is a matter of a god who is nothing else than the law of causality, the law of nature. In this way, such a religious sense, though felt very profoundly, remained without effect."

This inoperativeness spreads throughout the long process of the decadence of the ancient world, a decadence which proves to be the natural terminus of a fearful, despairing attitude toward the future. The horizon of the future always remained closed for the Greek. "The future," the chorus of Aeschylus' *Agamemnon* cries out, "there will be time enough to know it when its day arrives. Until that time let it take its course. To try to know the future would be to want to lament before due time. It will reveal itself in sufficient clarity under the sun which will witness its birth." The future held no attraction for the man of antiquity; it was something fearful, and its vehicle of expression, the oracle, is always sad and prone to evoke despair: "Does there ever come from the oracles any word which gives joy to mortals?" the same tragedy of Aeschylus demands. The verbal art of the prophets makes use of woeful events in order to make us understand the true meaning of the terror which it inspires.

The man of antiquity does not feel himself driven toward the future either by any impulse within him or by any superior urging; the latter, rather, in the form of *"moira"* of *"heimarmene"* reins in and debilitates action, no matter how impressive it may appear to be. The tremendous tension which marks so many chapters of ancient history is not, strictly speaking, a temporal unfolding, a projection into the future, but, rather, a kind of explosion of the present. Time is felt, by the Greek, as present, and temporal succession as a succession of juxtaposed presents, as the theory presented in Aristotle's *Physics* makes us aware. In like manner, when historians consider the great series of events, they project onto them a presential, static, categorical conception of time. The thesis of historical cycles seeks exactly to annul the historical character, to paralyze, to "eternize" history, suppressing the singular, innovating, irreversible character of events. Every event no matter how novel it may appear, is nothing more than the repetition of another which has happened before, absolutely identical with it, and it will repeat itself again later when the wheel of time shall, in its rotation, again have reached the same position. The historical cycles repeat themselves again and again with absolute fidelity, like the seasons of the year and the phenomena of the vegetal world. Basically, the cyclical conception of history is an attempt to subsume historical movement under quietistic categories, which take their origin in the vegetal world, and corresponds to naturalistic legalism of the ancient conception of destiny.

CHRISTIAN PROVIDENCE AND THE MEANING OF HISTORY

In a word, it is the legalism of a destiny which is not truly destiny or is destiny only in the ancient sense of fixed and static concatenation, of "destina," and not in the active and impelling, finalistic sense of destiny in its modern acceptance. What was the path traveled by the primitive meaning of this term that it would lead it eventually to take on such a different twist and aspect? That

path was none other than that of Christian spirituality, which
liberated man from the confining chains of "fatum" and at the
same time opened infinite horizons to the sense of the future and
of authentic historicity.

The process was long and complicated. Here we can only point
out its most salient milestones. It has its beginning long before,
in the Old Testament, in virtue of its monotheistic and transcendent conception of the divinity, its radical denial of all sacred character to nature, and the specifically historicist meaning of the
Hebrew religion, with its tension between a promise made in a
concrete moment of time and the realization of that promise in
a determined future, vehemently desired. These stages are found
to be internally articulated. Only the denial of all sacred character to nature could open the gates to a consciousness of true historicity. So long as man feels himself chained by a divinized
nature, he is not able to entertain the possibility of discovering
the peculiar link between human actions and historical events;
his own specific structure lay buried beneath the weight of an
inexorable causal law, natural in character, such as characterizes
"*ming,*" "*heimarmene,*" and "*fatum*" and, in the last analysis,
that "*karma*" which reaches even to the most elemental levels
of biology.

Only when the sacral roots which human life plunged down in
nature have been cut and when human life has committed itself
to the supreme claim of a transcendent divinity, creative and personal, could it reorientate itself with renewing hope toward the
future. The good now no longer depends upon the countenance
which things turn to man, according to the favor or disfavor of
destiny; now the goodness that shines out in them is nothing but
the reflection of the light which emanates from an Ultimate Good.
The man who considers it his task to realize an ethico-religious
ideal established by God will judge all things by taking into
account their possible usefulness toward this ideal end, and they
will thus become concatenated in a unitary and dynamic manner.
For this man there exists no blind "fatum," no arbitrary will which
paralyzes his own energies; for him all things are ordered by God

so that they may serve the ultimate end, and precisely because it is God who has ordered the world in this way, all notion of a destiny without goal or of an arbitrary will disappears. For such a man no actual situation is unalterably determined; rather, every new situation is a spur to a more complete realization of this ethico-religious purpose, to which the mechanical uniformity of nature provides the most effective means.

With these vast and unified religious and moral perspectives, history takes on a totally new meaning. Its development is man's continuous march toward the completion of his special mission along a route traced out not by a blind "fatum" but by the providence of a personal God, the advent of whose reign constitutes the culmination of all existence. Only a religious eschatology could lay bare the peculiar character of historicity, which for its full manifestation, however, still required the hyperhistorical impact of the mystery of the Redemption. The New Testament completes and perfects the historicistic meaning of the Old with the coming of the Messiah. The beyond, or hereafter, not only determines history with respect to its beginning and to its end but breaks into the center of it as well, charging it with a supreme and supernatural historicity in the figure of the Son of Man who was born, suffered, and died at the determined time, in a determined place. The coming of Christ, as St. Augustine again and again stresses, completes the rupture of the cyclical theory of history, and spreads out its reiterative cycle and reveals the singularity of each event in virtue of the supreme historical uniqueness of the life of Christ.

On the other hand, the eschatological tension increases with the effort to fix the end of time in the second coming of Christ. The longing for this end is enkindled and made stronger by the historical knowledge of the Savior who comes to be a kind of concrete and portentous electric force which hurls the hearts of Christians toward the consummation of history in the kingdom of God and also enkindles them with the desire for the greatest possible realization of this kingdom in the course of this temporal pilgrimage, as medieval Christianity exemplifies.

SECULARIZATION AND DESTINY

The goal of Christianity lies beyond the world; the path to be traversed, however, lies through the world, and perfection for the *homo viator* of the Middle Ages is reached, not through a mystical assumption by a leap over the here and now, but rather by way of the greatest possible realization of the demands which the beyond lays on the present, the here and now. Civil society and the life of the individual have to be remolded, reshaped in their every fiber, but in a precise and vigorous way, to take into account their worldly presuppositions, with a concrete desire to carnate Christian ideals on the model of the supreme mystery of the Incarnation. In this manner Christian hope inserts itself as a dynamic historical tension into the field of the moral life, of thought, of politics, of art, of economy, etc., dramatizing and fructifying, despite many obstacles, the most diverse sectors of Western culture. The categorical spiritual demands of Christianity "irradiate, as do those of no other religion, human existence, shape life, and awaken in us," as Alfred Weber writes, "the energies and activities which in the depth of the soul desire the unconditioned and which are capable of moving mountains."

The modern talents which move mountains also have their origin, in the last analysis, in the infinite spiritual aspirations of Christianity, as we have sought to throw into relief in a recent book *El Rapto de Europa.** If, beginning with the Middle Ages, the Western peoples have pursued with untiring eye the improvement of the conditions of life, of their material well-being, never being satisfied with the level already reached, this has not come about merely through longing for material goods, as men are wont to say, but by reasons of other aspirations of the most distinguished lineage. The artisan, the architect, the artist, the engineer, the entrepreneur have always sought to impress and mold into their work some rays of this supreme ideal of integral,

---

* Luis Díez del Corral, *The Rape of Europe* (London: George Allen and Unwin Ltd., 1959).

completely positive well-being of Christian beatitude, so completely opposed to the empty blessedness of *nirvana* and to the meaningless finalism of ancient *fatum*, from whence it was not possible to derive the last exemplar for the reconfiguration of historical reality according to supreme canons.

The same thing comes to pass in the case of Western science, which was set in motion by theological science (though no comparison with the aspiration of the latter toward conceptual construction is possible), and of European art and politics as well. However, it is not a matter of different directions, of independent developments, but of different manifestations of one central historical tendency, of branches which spring out of one single trunk. This trunk, the axis and backbone of European historical life, has grown vigorous and strong, and all its members have developed in unison with it. European mankind has felt itself called to realize a portentous and unending supernatural task even here on earth, to give a unified and all-inclusive meaning to the dispersed and localized existence of man, to serve supreme ideals of culture which, without ceasing, elevate the human condition. Thus, European history proves fruitful, creative, and universal in a completely incomparable measure.

Certain it is that in the course of the centuries, in the general process of the secularization of European life, the religious forces were driven underground and were to a great extent tergiversated or replaced by another order of motivations.

It is necessay as well to take into account the effects of the resurgence of other concepts of destiny, such as that of *fatum* and the *eternal return*, which appears in such outstanding writers as Machiavelli and Guicciardini. It is a matter of secondary and intellectual phenomena and not of the displacement of one concept by another. The fundamental component of the ancient concept of history—to wit, that there is no true advance, or progress, in history, that all ostensible progress terminates in a regression which leads back to the point of departure—could not achieve the status of a true *idea-belief* (in Ortega y Gasset's sense of the term) as the modern era of culture became defined. At most it could figure in the repertory of ideas of some isolated thinker or groups of thinkers and, in the last analysis, would end up employing the Western conception of destiny and accelerating its process of secularization in the sense of considering the event, or events, as ruled by an immanent, rational, worldly principle of order. The cyclical conception could prove only partially admissible: only in its ascending and not in its descending curve, for which consideration would no more be necessary than to imagine a circle, very ample in radius, whose line gradually ascends, rising slowly but surely toward a zenith which is placed far in the distant future; and the Christian idea of destiny itself urged the concept toward development in this direction, including the slant toward secularization.

From another angle of vision also the Renaissance made use of antiquity and of its concept of time and of history to delineate the idea of progress in the Western world by establishing antiquity as the point of reference for the measurement of the height in time at which the Renaissance itself stood. The dispute between the ancients and the moderns would culminate not only in the victory of the latter but also in the strengthening of the historical consciousness of modern man, since the comparison of his art and science with those of antiquity confirmed the increment of knowledge and other cultural values with the passage of time. The Renaissance of an antique world in the modern epoch had begun by giving European man an awareness of superiority over his immediate predecessor, medieval man; the latter was reduced in stature by comparison with the excellencies which appeared in classical antiquity and with which modern man experiences a feeling of solidarity. It ended, however, by giving also to modern man a sense of superiority over the man of classical antiquity and his cultural world, which modern man so much admired. The admiration which he felt for that ancient world and its great figures did not diminish, but it remained submerged in the admiration which modern man began to feel for himself, for the world which he was in the process of creating and which appeared to him as something new, much more valuable and worthy of enthusiasm than all that had appeared in the past.

During the course of the eighteenth century, belief in providence was transformed among European peoples into a belief in a progressive destiny; within this concept of progressive destiny, the dramatic, demanding, transcendent movement characteristic of the Christian conception of history was converted into an immanent, automatic, ingenuously optimistic movement. The goals which European man pursued descended from their elevated plane, became more mundane, more readily attainable, and envisioned a less spiritual mode of happiness, though the old formal schemes endured; these goals of beatitude continued to be surrounded by an aura, a nimbus of infinity, presenting themselves with the demands of a final and sacred goal; and individuals, societies, and peoples hurled themselves in pursuit of them with a decided sense of vocation.

At times, the process of secularization reached farther and terminated in rebellious, superpromethean activities, which seemed to contradict their point of departure. For the historian who understands how to penetrate the great symbols and forms in which historical life moves or expresses itself, this contradiction is only apparent. This problem of secularization within the intimate life of European history is most complex. Though the tension and the religious potential of Christianity were so high, though they made their fructifying effects felt in all the sectors of life, yet Christianity was able, paradoxically, to yield place to supersecularized forms of life; and these latter forms vastly exceed those produced in the wake of other, more naturalistic, more worldly religions, such as those of classical civilization or of the Far East, or those more abstract, less concerned with the remolding of life, namely, the religion of Islam.

For if we were to analyze the concept of destiny characteristic of Islam, *quadar* (an undertaking which space does not allow us) we would find, to our surprise, that because of an excessive monotheism, because of the absolute character of a transcendence which knows no mediation or incarnation because of the complete subjugation of the creature, destiny comes to "eat its own tail." By way of the absolute will of a hypermonistic God, it comes to have a fatalistic and passive meaning which yields no fruits for earthly life. The Islamic world ended, as a matter of fact, by falling into a state of historical and cultural lassitude, which was already adumbrated in the name "Islam" (meaning submission), while Western Christianity—enkindled by a divine hope, made enthusiastic, in the literal Greek sense of that term, because it felt itself to be the mystical body of the Mediator— launched itself into a prodigious historical adventure, impelled by a sense, filled with hope and dynamic to the highest degree, of the singular character of its destiny.

José Ferrater Mora

Don José Ferrater Mora (b.1912), trained at the University of Barcelona under Joaquin Xirau, left Spain after the Civil War and is presently professor of philosophy at Bryn Mawr. He has done much to amalgamate Spanish and Anglo-Saxon philosophical themes, especially linguistic analysis. Among his writings are El hombre en la encrucijada (1952), El ser y la muerte (1962), and El ser y el sentido (forthcoming).

"On Taking Things for Granted" appeared in Volume II of *Obras selectas* (Madrid: Revista de Occidente, 1967). © by José Ferrater Mora. Grateful acknowledgment is made to the author for permission to reprint.

X. ON TAKING THINGS
FOR GRANTED

I

It has often been held that a philosopher is one who takes nothing for granted. Philosophers, like everyone else, live in a world containing stars, mountains, trees, and black cats, but they are supposed to wonder whether such a world really exists. Being a philosopher, I follow suit, and ask: Does it exist? My senses are unreliable, and so are those of my neighbors, and even my next of kin. Am I then to appeal to God? Let us assume that I do and even that I accept some well-known views on God's nature. I could wonder then whether God is not more than enough. Everything but he will become superfluous. Why then any stars or black cats at all? It may be argued that stars, black cats, and what not exist because they have been created by God—indeed, that the very expression "exists" means "has been created by God." Since this argument is no more convincing than any other of the same type, we are in a quandary unless God himself comes to the rescue and reveals his creation to us, or to whom it may concern. Now, if philosophers are not to take anything for granted, they should discard revelations along with everything else. To take nothing for granted is utterly incompatible with taking for granted nothing less than the Alpha and the Omega.

It has been contended that God does not need to reveal anything to us, including his own existence, for his existence gloriously shines through his creation. We are now back to our point of departure except that we are more bewildered than ever. Stars and black cats, many have surmised, are creatures of God. Could they exist and, for that matter, persist without a creator? For time out of mind black cats have been begotten by other cats, black or white or some color in between. Yet, who begot the first black cats? Or is there an infinite number of cats? Let us retreat from cats to other less sophisticated beings: to amoebae, to amino acids, to atoms, to electrons, to protons, neutrons and other seemingly innumerable particles; the fact that all of them have been caused might seem to presuppose that there is a First uncaused Cause. Now, until we succeed in discovering, or proving, the reality of the First Cause of so many second causes, who can guarantee the reality of the latter? Second causes prove that there is a First Cause, and the First Cause proves that there are second causes. A perfect circle, as vicious as all such circles are.

Some philosophers will come to the rescue at this point and will assure us that we do not need to worry about circles, including vicious ones. Circles of the type considered must be somewhere, and the obvious place for them to be is a mind which thinks of them. Assuming that we should take nothing for granted, should we not at least take for granted that we should take nothing for granted? What does it mean to take nothing for granted except that someone thinks that there is nothing to be taken for granted? We can thus begin from scratch without necessarily sinking into nothingness; the mind, or rather some activity which we tend to reify as "the mind," saves us from complete philosophical shipwreck. Whereas everything else seems to wane and fritter away, the mind persists. While we were wondering about whether stars or black cats really existed, we were thinking of them. These disturbing entities may be nowhere and thus prove not to be entities at all. In any case, however, they seem to be firmly rooted in the mind *as* thoughts. Something has been found at last which is reliable enough—more reliable than senses, neighbors, and even God: the mind.

Is not the mind, then, a befitting starting point? It is certainly a starting point, but the problem is to know what else it is. The mind can think of anything, but it cannot substantiate that what it thinks exists, as it were, outside of the mind. Thoughts lead to other thoughts, but all ends here. If the way leading from thought to reality were only tedious, we might put up with it for at one point or another we would eventually reach our destination. The trouble is that the way leading from thought to reality is neither tedious nor exciting because there is no way at all. The only way to reach reality from thought is to take a plunge and leave thought behind. But then, why start with thought? No such start is needed when from the very beginning we are in the midst of realities and, so to speak, in the thick of things. Reality is where everything, including thought, is.

Much ado about nothing. It does not seem worthwhile to boast of being a philosopher if, in the end, all of us, philosophers or not, reach the very same conclusion: we are, or rather live, in a world which contains many things, including black cats, trees, stones, mountains, and stars. No one can give us complete assurance that such a world exists, but we are in no need of assurance; as a matter of fact, it is more painful to disregard the world than to acknowledge it. Rather than receding from us, the world exerts a constant, and at times overwhelming, pressure on us. "The world" is, of course, a paltry name to stand for an infinitely complex network of all kinds and shapes of realities. Thus far I have referred to what may be called "the natural world," a world containing such things as stars and black cats. But other worlds—or, if one wishes, other sides of the world—exist which are not, strictly speaking, "natural," but which are real. I am typing words on a sheet of paper which has been produced from natural materials but which has not grown, as Aristotle would say, "spontaneously." This sheet of paper has been manufactured by men using machines which are also man-made; it has been transported by vehicles which do not grow on trees; sold in stationery stores which are strategically located in cities containing houses, sidewalks, and traffic signs. On this sheet of paper words are written which men have devised within the frame of a language.

All these artifacts do not stand isolated from "Nature" but more properly belong to what is named "culture." When I say that we are living in the world, as realities among realities, I am referring both to natural objects and to cultural products. Actually, to say, or write, that we live in a real world presupposes the existence of a cultural universe to which language and ideas expressed through language belong. It may be doubted whether there would be any ideas without brains, which are natural realities, but the fact is that ideas themselves are not, or are not exclusively, natural realities; like machines and words, ideas are "artifacts" of sorts. I am not intimating that the natural world and the cultural world are mutually independent and, still less, that they are mutually hostile; what I have been saying about both conveys the idea that they form a kind of "continuum." In any case, when we speak of the world in which we live and to which we belong, we cannot help acknowledging that it contains things of many kinds, and not only the type of entities of which trees and black cats are said to be instances.

II

In fact, the richness of the world, and thus of what I may be allowed to call, rather sweepingly, "reality," is much greater than is often suspected by desert-loving philosophers. I have been talking about "objects," whether natural or cultural, which are, as a rule, quite familiar to most men and which are, furthermore, easily accessible to our perception or to our ordinary experience. Trees, stones, and black cats, as well as sheets of paper, machines, and houses, are exposed to view. Some other objects, on the other hand, can be perceived, or detected, only by means of instruments capable of recording whatever signals they may emit. Such is the case with galactic clouds or distant stars. Some extremely fine textures of inanimate or of animate beings are visible only through a microscope. Some much finer textures or elements are not, strictly speaking, even visible; they remain invisible and are detected only through their (visible) effects. Such happens with traces of particles in a Wilson chamber. We may even come to the point of talking about "inferred entities." This is not, of course, the end of the story, for this story has no end. I can perceive directly the sheet of paper which I am now using. In the same manner I could perceive the machines employed to manufacture it. Yet, I cannot perceive the economic system which has made possible the production, distribution, and sale of this sheet of paper because an economic system is not a thing, not even a collection of things, but a set of rules, conventions, habits, traditions, and such. Nevertheless, an economic system pertains to the same world of which I have been speaking and is not independent from, but rather intimately tied up with, material objects such as sheets of paper; after all, economic systems have been described as systems of material relations even if such relations are material in a sense somewhat different from the physical one.

That many things, including some which can hardly be characterized as "things," are needed to make up a world, not to say the world, can be shown as soon as we cease to be too discriminating in our inventories. There may not be more things on earth and heaven than those we can catch a glimpse of, but there are still enough to make our list quite impressive. My neighbor amuses me or else he annoys me; as soon as I am through with this bulky manuscript, I will submit it to a publisher; when, and if, it is accepted and produced, I will then be in touch, directly or indirectly, with a limited, though hopefully alert, group of readers. The world, or at any rate the world in which we live, also "contains" feelings, persons, and human relations. There are pleasant dreams and nightmares; moments of exultation and fits of depression; periods of calm and neurotic spasms. My relation with the world, or with what is left of it without me, is not limited to knowing, perceiving, and inferring; I am in the world also in the sense that I care about it, or could not care less, or commit myself to some of its features, or try to stand aloof, and so on. The world is *also* the human *praxis*. Whether action precedes contemplation, or the other way around, and whether we are supposed to understand the world or try to put it upside down are fascinating but, at present, quite irrelevant issues. The fact is that neither thought nor action can be brushed aside if we want our inventory of the world to be reasonably complete.

What about seeing, or dealing with, the same things in many different ways? Even plain, ordinary objects are many-sided. The world is bursting with possibilities in a manner different from, but not altogether unrelated to, Leibniz's idea that many possibles tend to actualize themselves. A painter, or at any rate one who is still conservative enough to consider colors as an essential ingredient of his craft, sees not only the color yellow but also, and sometimes above all, the possibilities with which this color is endowed before he actually spreads it on the canvas. To common sensations some less common impressions must be added; things, as well as qualities, seem to have skin and flesh—roughness, smoothness, abruptness, viscosity. We imagine things, and thus we can conclude that they are only imagined and by no means real; yet, not only does our imagination have a reality of its own but also its contents may prove to be unyielding, if not obnoxious. Imagination often duplicates reality; in any case, it never completely departs from some real, solid ground.

III

Far from taking nothing for granted, should we then not take everything for granted? In a way, we should. Everything is, of course, a great deal: it includes what is and what is not; what has been and what will be; what could have been but never was; what is necessary and what is contingent; what is possible and what is impossible; the physical, the psychical, the ideal, the good, the bad, the beautiful, the curious, the attractive, the hideous, and so on. In this sense, or senses, of "everything," it would be preposterous to maintain that philosophers should take everything for granted. There is another sense, however, in which it can be said that philosophers should take everything for granted: they must begin with the world rather than with nothing. To take nothing for granted means to begin with nothing, and thus to use the term "nothing" as if it designated a something out of which would eventually emerge the very same world which we had cautiously bracketed. It must be remembered that philosophers who take nothing for granted have taken for granted the very thought that nothing should be taken for granted. We have seen, however, that their intellectual prudence does not lead them very far. Rather than providing them with a point of departure with which to reach reality, it has locked them up in the rarefied atmosphere of a pure and naked thought which can think only of itself and of nothing else. "Thought of thought" is one of Aristotle's definitions of the Unmoved Mover, but whereas that venerable entity was supposed to move something—indeed, everything—pure and naked thought taken as a point of departure does not move anything, including itself.

Pure thought understood as thought, or thinking, without any presuppositions suffers from a chronic and perhaps incurable disease: the purer it becomes, the more difficult it is for it to perform the only activity which might justify its (otherwise assumed) existence. Pure thinking is pure only insofar as it does not think. As soon as it does, it has to think of something which differs from itself and which is, or so it seems, "impure." To avoid the "impure" character of reality, thought permeates everything with itself—which is what it means to assume that things are only insofar as they are thought. Now, if things are only insofar as they are thought, then they must be exactly as they are thought. We have not budged an inch; indeed, no sooner do we try to budge an inch than we are ensnared in the "impure," namely, the un-thought, and un-thinkable, character of reality.

IV

What I have been saying thus far seems to be not only unquestionable but also wasteful, for it was intended to give the kiss of death to a doctrine which many judge to be a mere ghost long since buried under a thick layer of dust—the ghost of idealism. Why not let it sleep peacefully in death? The poor thing was harming no one; why then insist on reviving it? Is it only for kicks? Let us make no mistake—idealism may, in its traditional garb, be quite dead—assuming, of course, that a basic philosophic doctrine can ever die, or even slowly fade away, which is more than I am ready to admit. But nowadays there are ways of doing philosophy which, without in the least claiming to be idealistic, are at one with idealism in leaving things and realities out in the cold. To those initiated in these new ways of doing philosophy, things and realities seem to be considerably less appealing than the words that are used to talk about, or handle, them. To be sure, no one swears by ideas any longer. Many, however, seem to be ready to swear by words even if only to end by crucifying them. Thus idealism, the philosophy of ideas, seems to have given place to a most peculiar kind of "verbalism"—the philosophy of words.

The above description is, certainly, rather unfair to the new ways of doing philosophy. These ways are many, and they are all excruciatingly subtle. To begin with, philosophers interested in words are by no means "verbalists," at least in the ordinary sense of this term. Indeed, how could they be "verbalists" when they maintain that philosophy is, or should be, an instrument for verbal deflation? Furthermore, no matter how fond these philosophers seem to be of words, they stubbornly refuse to be confused with mere lexicographers. They are dealing, or so they claim, not with words, but rather with concepts; it just happens that concepts are expressed by words and not, say, by things or even actions. These philosophers therefore seem to make sense; at any rate, that is what they are most eager to make.

Philosophers of every school have a great deal to learn from them, in particular when they indefatigably warn us to be on our guard against the traps set by the very same language which they are said (often unjustifiably) to worship. "Cats are real"; "Is sugar really sweet?"; "What is the real structure of a molecule of calcium?"; "Is this wine real Malaga or imitation Malaga?" Here are four ways of using the word "real" (including, in one case, its adverbial form). So-called traditional philosophers, free from immoderate linguistic misgivings, have raised questions such as "What is reality?"; "What is it for a thing to be real?" Less traditionally-minded thinkers, more cautious or perhaps less imaginative, have confined themselves to asking, for instance, "What does the predicate 'is real' mean?" or "Is 'is real' a predicate?"

So-called linguistic philosophers get rather impatient with questions concerning reality or meaning, or both; what matters to them—I was about to say "what really matters"—is neither reality nor meaning, but use: the use, or rather uses, of terms. In order to promote their aims they advise us again and again to stop, look, and listen—above all to stop and listen. They may not be great road builders, but they are very industrious sign posters even to the point of obstructing the way with warnings. "Slow," "Winding Road," "Detour," and, more often than not, "Caution: Philosophers Crossing." As a consequence our trips are likely to become somewhat parochial, but there is little doubt that they prove much safer than the former philosophers' grand tour. For the sake of safety it seems wise to worry about language without, however, bothering to ask what language is, for the point is to scrutinize and rescrutinize the many curious ways in which language works.

When all is said, however, the fact remains that all ways of doing philosophy, not excluding the best ones, have a prize and that it is extravagant to pay more for them than they are worth. Warnings posted by linguistic philosophers would be most welcome if they helped us to proceed a little further. Unfortunately, a great many of their signs only make us realize that there are still more signs coming; much too often they are not of the type

"Steep Hill Ahead" but rather "Signals Ahead." As a consequence, they tend to become somewhat repetitious. "Are atoms real?" Here is a warning in order to indicate that the term 'real' in "Are atoms real?" is not used in exactly the same way as that used in, say, "Is this wine real Malaga?" This difference in use has often been recognized, at least implicitly, by many of the traditional philosophers who have dared to talk about "reality"; it happens, however, that they did not emphasize this point as the only important item on their agenda.

If traditional philosophers are to be blamed, it is not because they have been touchingly naive; they are to be indicted, and not merely blamed, on more serious counts which linguistic philosophers seem to overlook. On the other hand, some linguistic philosophers seem to take little notice of the fact that the term 'real' in "Are atoms real?" is, or can be, used in a very precise manner, and with a well-defined meaning, within the frame of a language contrived to that effect: the language of physics. It may, of course, be argued that such is the case with the language of physics but not with that of common sense. And since both languages differ considerably one from the other, it would seem reasonable to conclude that we are dealing not only with a term having different uses but with two different concepts for which it is only confusing to use the same term.

Unfortunately, the problem cannot be obliterated so swiftly. For one thing, although we can speak about the world in many different ways, and in various languages, the fact remains that the world is one, or, less metaphysically expressed, that there is just one world. We can and occasionally should speak of "the world of physics," "the world of common sense," and so forth, but it would be preposterous to conclude that they are different worlds in the sense in which it is said, for example, that Mars and Venus are different planets. To discuss the uses of terms is, therefore, at the same time to discuss those realities for which these terms stand.

Linguistic philosophers have not merely dismissed realities and types of realities. They have often emphasized that "reality" exerts its demands on "language"; things being what they are, we talk the way we talk. Now if reality commands respect from the most talkative of linguistic philosophers, it would seem that by finding fault with some of their claims I am doing what I did with some of the tenets of the idealists: conjuring up a ghost just to have the fun of exorcising it. The ghost I have now conjured up may be christened "linguistic idealism." There is, of course, no such thing, and there are no such ghosts. Yet, I do not believe that I am wasting my time by bludgeoning at ghosts for the following almost poetic reason: ghosts may haunt us just because they do not exist.

The ghost of linguistic idealism materializes as soon as a philosopher tries to do with words what traditional idealists did with thoughts: to take them as points of departure in order to return to them without bothering to wade through reality, while he thinks in good faith that reality is being thoroughly explored. Since both thoughts and words have taken shape during man's long intercourse with reality, traditionalistic as well as linguistic idealists are "more realistic" than some of them would care to confess. The fact, however, that thoughts and words are, so to speak, permeated with reality is not a sufficient reason to follow them blindly. When the latter course is taken, thoughts or words, or both, tend to operate *in vacuo*—and thus point to thoughts or words, or both.

Linguistic philosophers would, of course, strongly (and justifiably) object to the above description.[1] Do we mean to intimate that linguistic philosophers might succumb to even the slightest degree to the temptation of using words *in vacuo*? This should be the last thing to say of philosophers whose main, and perhaps sole, task is to scrutinize the machinery of language with the purpose of ascertaining whether or not it is out of order. It would be more sensible to indict nonlinguistic philosophers for allowing language "to go idle"—or "to take a holiday." On the other hand, linguistic philosophers are well aware of the fact that the same word can perform different jobs, that several words can perform the same job, or that one or many words seem to perform one or more jobs while doing no job at all. The words "truth" and "true" serve to make it clear that I am not fabricating or that I am not dreaming. "It's true that I have read the *Odyssey*" is intended to convey the idea that I have actually read the *Odyssey*. Yes, I've held the venerable text in my hands, and my eyes have run over the lines as I tried to understand, and often to visualize, what the bard describes. I have even wondered about the abundance, not to say the squandering, of epithets; I have had good, clean fun with sirens and cyclops, while growing bored to death with Penelope. "Truth" and "true" can also perform replacement jobs. "He is a true teacher"—he is a dedicated teacher; "Essence is the truth of Being"—essence is the basic and ultimate nature of what there is; "Vermeer paintings: how true to life!"—the paintings of the Dutch master reproduce life faithfully even to the point of making, in a sense, "real" what is "only painted," and so on. Well and good, but once the uses of words have been thoroughly explored, and even neatly classified, is there nothing else to be done? Have things not been left untouched? It may be argued that things have been adequately dealt with through words; we have disclosed in this manner not only how rich, varied, and auspicious language is but also how diverse and complex reality is. Furthermore, we have been philosophically modest. Nauseated by lofty speculations, we have simply and nimbly played a game that can be called "Coming Down to Earth" where things are.

Linguistic philosophers may thus claim that far from shunning things, they have looked at them squarely in the eye—through language, of course. They may also and perhaps above all maintain that their strenuous effort to grasp the machinery of language has provided them with a shield against philosophical anxieties. When philosophers step into the labyrinth of language without realizing where they are, they are likely to feel overwhelmed by intellectual anxieties and even by a peculiar kind of insanity. They can be compared to bulls in a china shop in that they shatter everything to pieces while still hoping that what remains standing will deserve to be called "reality." Needless to say, nothing is left unbroken, and so the whole of reality goes down the drain.

Unfortunately, linguistic philosophers verging on what I have called "linguistic idealism" have a fine madness of their own. Contrary to so-called speculative philosophers, however, linguistic philosophers produce a different kind of damage. Whereas the former break everything that can be expressed in some ordinary language, the latter smash everything that is expressed in an extraordinary language. Leaving metaphors aside, let me now come to the point: following in the steps of other philosophers, linguistic idealists emphasize certain aspects of reality to the detriment of many others. Real is, and is only, what can be handled in a plain language which is reasonably flexible and copious.

There are a number of words that do not seem to work properly within the context of an ordinary language, as is the case not only with a great majority of philosophic words, such as 'substratum,' 'substance,' 'essence,' and perhaps 'idea,' but also, at least in certain conditions, with some para-philosophic words, such as 'space,' 'time,' 'meaning.' So much the better, some will retort; it was high time to stop using the wrong pack of linguistic cards. "I will meet you at seven o'clock sharp": this is perfectly all right and raises no problems; at any rate, it raises no problems about the nature of time. Time, or whatever it is to which we give this name, is, so to speak, exorcised and thus mastered. But, what does it mean to say 'sharp' when talking of seven o'clock? Is there anything like seven o'clock sharp? As soon as we begin brooding over it, we are beset by perplexities, for seven o'clock sharp is neither a little nor even an "infinitesimal" little before seven, nor is it a little, however small, after seven, but precisely and exactly seven. Thus, it is an instant so fleeting and volatile that it takes no time and is, therefore, outside of time. Time outside of time: what a silly thing to think or say! To have mastered time to the extent that we could even anticipate what we were going to do at seven o'clock was refreshing. Yet we do not even know what "seven o'clock" is. Shall we then abstain from meeting the one we have promised to meet at seven? By no means. We do not know what "seven o'clock" means, but we are quite familiar with sentences where the expression 'seven o'clock' occurs. We will be strictly punctual, and when we arrive we will point to our watch and say: "Just as I told you, it's seven."

Thus we will shake off our perplexity. In fact, we will have proved that it was a perplexity to be dissolved rather than a problem which we and countless others have unsuccessfully tried to solve.

A new problem presently creeps in. Can we be completely sure that there was no problem? In order to be relieved from this supplementary burden, we must convince ourselves that problems such as the one raised by saying "It's seven o'clock sharp" are not about language; if they were, we would not even have to start walking in order to get wherever we were supposed to be on time, for talking would have sufficed. These problems have been engendered by language, and so they cease to be problems and become perplexities.

How can we reach such a reassuring conviction? Only by assuming that we no longer need to get out of language. And this is quite another matter. "Seven o'clock sharp" is an expression describing time. If we stick to the recommendations of the linguistic philosophers, the thing to do is clear: let's not waste time talking about it. Too much time has been spent trying to answer the question "What is time?" We cannot, or should not, resort to Augustine's famous *boutade* "When I am asked, I do not know; when I am not asked, I know." For I do not even know whether I know or not, so please do not ask me. As a linguistic philosopher I do not claim to know or not to know what time is; I am simply intent on eradicating all confusions arising out of any talk concerning the nature of time or the meaning of "time." In this sense, linguistic philosophy is irrefutable. But then so are all other philosophies provided that we ask only what they are meant to answer.

Traditional idealism, existentialism, Thomism, to mention only a few, are in this respect equally convincing; their followers refuse to answer, or even to grasp, questions having no meaning

outside of the corresponding doctrine. Could I ever prove that
a Thomist is misguided unless I stepped out of Thomistic philosophy? Linguistic philosophy is in this respect even stricter
than Thomism, existentialism, or traditional idealism, for such
a philosophy stubbornly refuses to answer any question about
any thing. Indeed, linguistic philosophy, and *a fortiori* linguistic
idealism, is still more radical than traditional idealism. The latter
takes, or tries to take, nothing for granted. The former does not
limit itself to taking nothing for granted; it surmises that no
reality should ever be allowed to creep in since, if they did, questions would be raised about its nature. How could that be toler-
ated when it is contended, to begin with, that we are wasting our
time from the very moment we try to explain what any reality,
not to say reality as such, is? When someone loses his way in a
labyrinth, he soon becomes impatient with stories about what
kind of labyrinth it is, and often no doubt grows irritated with
elaborate explanations about labyrinths in general. He will be
only too glad when a more practical-minded friend comes to his
rescue and shows him a way out.

V

Linguistic idealism, and *a fortiori* linguistic philosophy, has of
course a point. It is an undeniable fact that we live in a ready-
made world—a world overflowing with different ways of life and
hence with the languages and linguistic games inherent in such
ways. It is a fact that we live not only in a natural world but
also within a cultural universe permeated with words and ideas.
We live, in fine, in a world previously ordered and classified by
thought and by language. Wittgenstein's books are filled with
accounts of such a world, and Sartre's *The Words* gives a moving
picture of it. Above this world, perplexities float. Most of them
have been begotten by the very same language which has aided
men to order and classify the world. Yet, this is only the beginning
of the story; under the vast, wandering clouds of perplexities,
problems lie in ambush. Under the perplexity revealed by the

expression "I will meet you at seven o'clock sharp" lies a most obdurate problem, the problem of time. To say that time is, at bottom, an activity of consciousness may be an error, a fallacy, a misrepresentation, or a misunderstanding, or all these things combined. It may happen that time is not the activity of any consciousness, or even of consciousness in general, but an absolute reality, whatever that means. Perhaps time is some property of things or a network of relations. Perhaps time is not made of instants but of patterns. Linguistic philosophers claim, of course, that any of these theories is a way of rushing headlong against the limits set up by language.

The question is, however, Which language? Twentieth-century English? The Spanish of the Golden Age? Classical Greek? Cantonese, Hindi, Quichuan? It may be retorted that the answer is simple enough: the language that sets up limits is, and can only be, the language which we have inherited or else decided to handle. I agree if all that is stated here is that nothing can be said outside of a language. I disagree, however, if it is added or intimated that the limits set up by language have been preordained forever by some sort of brand new linguistic Demiurge. To rush headlong against the limits set up by language—any language—is by no means a suicidal attempt; rather it is a prerequisite for any attempt to modify language, to stretch it as far as it can go even at the risk of breaking it. Science and, needless to say, philosophy are living testimonies that such attempts are not mere whims nor have they been made in vain. It has sometimes been held that whatever can be said in a science or in a branch of science, for example, physics or physical optics, can also be said in ordinary language provided that it be rich and flexible enough to stand the test. The only important difference is that the very same thing can be said more concisely and rigorously in the language of a science.

Now the question is: What is said? Is it exactly the same? I am aware that I am treading on slippery ground and that I will be unable to prove my point, but I cannot help making a point, namely, that *not* exactly the same thing is said in both languages.

No matter how many words are required to "say" that some physical forces are weaker than others, the fact is that within the context of ordinary language the term 'weak' will never succeed in expressing what it says within the context of the language of physics—wherein, by the way, "saying something" may not be the point at issue. If the term 'weak,' with as many footnotes as needed, sufficed, then we might consider that an ordinary language or a fragment thereof could become an extension of the physical language. On the other hand, the latter could be considered as a kind of shorthand of the former. Now, even if the language of physics were, within certain conditions, "more exact" than any ordinary language, we should not be allowed to conclude that the relational predicate 'is more exact than' is synonymous with the relational predicate 'is an abbreviation of.' "Exactitude" is not necessarily "a closer way of describing"; it is a way different from others.

VI

The point that linguistic philosophy makes is, thus, a point of fact. In the world in which we live we often begin with words; at any rate, words are given to us simultaneously with things and with situations. Many of our needs are adapted to the words we use or could use. What I am doing now, good or bad, I am doing with words. Yet, I feel confident that I am not merely swimming in an ocean of words. Mere words lead only to other words, as thoughts lead to other thoughts. It must be acknowledged that many of the so-called linguistic philosophers would ultimately agree with most of what I have said, at least insofar as they would not consider words as being "mere words." After all, their great pope, Wittgenstein II, made it clear that words constitute a linguistic game, that linguistic games constitute languages, and that languages are not only collections of signs or sounds but also ways of life.

In this sense linguistic philosophy has done its best to avoid falling into the trap of idealism, including "linguistic idealism."

Some of these philosophers have ended by doing almost the same thing as some of the greatest philosophers of all times; they have handled language, and occasionally broken its barriers, in order to hold fast to things. They may still claim that they are primarily concerned with linguistic games and the consequences thereof, but sooner or later they will have to admit that some of these games prove to be more decisive—that is, ontologically more decisive—than others. Aristotle's "linguistic game," or collection of "linguistic games," for instance, is obviously more decisive, ontologically speaking, than the brief linguistic interlude in which we indulge when we occasionally meet for the purpose of wishing each other well without really meaning it.

I have (rather sketchily) presented these subtle points only because I want to emphasize that, although the doctrine—or, if it is preferred, the method—called "linguistic philosophy" turns out well more often than some would admit, it can easily degenerate into what I have christened "linguistic idealism." I will eventually return to this question; for the moment it suffices to note that if linguistic philosophy limited itself to revolving around words, it would go no further than traditional idealism went when the latter revolved around pure thoughts. Not much is gained when we substitute some kind of First Talker for the First Thinker, the silent, thoughtful, hard to move Unmoved Mover.

To go from words to things with nothing in between is like going from knowing to the object known: an idealistic stunt. It does not matter whether such a stunt be Gothic in style, as was the case with traditional idealism, or rococo, as has sometimes been the case with linguistic idealism. In either case we are only juggling realities, and snarling beyond hope the order, or disorder, of realities with the order, or disorder, of our ruminations be they ideas or words, or both. Incidentally, ideas and words are also "realities" with which we have to reckon and which we can take for granted along with everything else.

It is, of course, another question whether we should take statements about things for granted. It will suffice for the moment to point out that we could, in principle, take things for granted without necessarily taking for granted statements about them. After all, this is what phenomenologists claim that they are doing; strictly speaking, phenomenologists do not brush things aside but confine themselves to bracketing statements. Now I suspect that although bracketing statements is methodologically sound, it ceases to be so when statements remain bracketed *per saecula saeculorum.* We do not gain much by bracketing all the statements if at the end we are unable to produce any statement. Bracketing statements indefinitely is like bracketing things forever and ever.

Let us remember our point of departure and the question we raised: Should we take nothing for granted? It seemed at first that we should, but we are beginning to fancy that the less we take for granted the more we talk about it—a rather frustrating state of affairs from a philosopher's point of view.

Julián Marías

Don Julián Marías (b. 1914) is a prominent, vocal disciple of Ortega y Gasset. He has devoted a great deal of attention to his master's thought and has developed the Ortegan notion of rázon vital *into a philosophy of human integrity. A writer and lecturer, he has toured America. Among his important works are* Introduction a la filosofia *(1947),* La estructura social *(1955), and* Ortega I: Circumstancias y vocación *(1960).*

"The Idea of Metaphysics" appeared in *Obras* (Madrid: Ediciones de Revista de Occidente, 1962) 373–414. © 1962 by Julián Marías. Grateful acknowledgment is made to the author for permission to reprint.

XI. THE IDEA OF METAPHYSICS

Prologue

This essay attempts to give the reader an idea of metaphysics. To do so, it must question this very word, the origin of the term "metaphysics," and record some of the vicissitudes it has suffered. However, our purpose is not so much to give the history of a term as to give readers a sense of the reality of metaphysics, a reality which, of course, has a history.

Considerable innovations will also be encountered in the pages that follow, not only in regard to what is usually understood to be metaphysics but also in regard to previous publications by the author. However, we feel we can safely say this *new* idea of metaphysics is, in a certain sense, *traditional:* in the sense that it corresponds rigorously to what the intention of metaphysics has been from its beginning.

The novelty of some of the ideas and the conciseness of this essay have obliged us to make a great effort to be clear. Since these pages are so brief, it is not possible to omit from consideration anything that is said in them. I believe our presentation is

easy to understand and that it requires only an attentive and
alert reading.

I

The Term and the Reality

The strange history of *metaphysics,* one of the most outstanding
terms in modern languages, is well known. When, in the first
century before Christ, Andronicus of Rhodes attempted to classify the writings of Aristotle, he found some books that were
difficult to title and to situate within the body of Aristotle's work.
He finally decided to list these books "after the books on physics."
This expression, which was not really a title, means nothing
philosophical. It was not even a word, and yet it was to become
throughout the course of two thousand years the name for the
most important of philosophical disciplines, the one which is often
simply identified with philosophy itself. How was this possible?
And, above all, what does it mean?

Tà metà tà physiká (τὰ μετὰ τὰ φυσικά)—"those [books] after
the physics [books]." The first thing to say is that this is not one
word but four. In the hands of Andronicus of Rhodes, the most
important books of Aristotle were not *named* but only *designated,*
pointed out: the ones after those that deal with physics. So that
the term "metaphysics" should one day come to exist, it was necessary, first of all, that these four words should become *one* by
the suppression of the articles and the fusion of the preposition
and the substantive. However, we should note that the union
takes place in Latin, not in Greek (later in Arabic, and thus in
Averroes). Nevertheless, what I have just said remains problematical and only half true. For, is the word "metaphysics" really
Latin? Not at all. It is only a transliteration changed into substantive form without any translation of the Greek phrase *tă metà
tà physiká.* It appears in this transliterated form in the Middle
Ages from time to time, and later with frequency when in the
twelfth and thirteenth centuries Aristotle's works were incorporated into scholasticism—both Muslem and Christian.

This is precisely what is so interesting: "metaphysics," which
has had such an exceptional success in the history of ideas, is not
an actual term from Greek science, or even a meaningful word,
but an arbitrary expression of haphazard origin which has hardly
any meaning. In other words, it is not a case of a concept but
of a poetic expression, more exactly a rhetorical and poetic
expression. Let me explain.

"Metaphysical" is an adjective, *metaphysicus*. The form *metaphysica* is the neuter plural of this adjective: the metaphysical
(books); only later did it take on the feminine substantive form
by analogy with other terms. But what is important is that *metaphysica* means nothing in Latin (and nothing interesting in
Greek). It is a word *received* from another language, coined,
which does not function primarily as a meaning but rather as a
strange and somewhat occult sign. This is why I say it has a *rhetorical* function. It also has a poetic aspect because there is without doubt some *vague* meaning injected into it that the Greek
never had or could have had: something *beyond* physics or,
rather, something that refers to that which is *beyond* the natural.
The success of the word metaphysics is due to the fact that it
is experienced, not as a prosaic *post-physics*, but as an echo-
filled, provocative, mysterious *trans-physics*, literally so in St.
Thomas and through him in the whole of the medieval and
modern tradition.

This word, once it had assumed that *vague* meaning, acquired
a special life. It has a double virtue: it promises but does not
compromise. I believe that this essential vagueness of the word
"metaphysics" has been the reason for its long-lasting success and
that it is a characteristic to be carefully preserved and guarded
—a characteristic by the way, shared with the word "philosophy."

If now we were to ask ourselves what metaphysics is, we could
answer by taking two different approaches. The first would consist in examining the *definitions* that have been given of it: either
to select one and accept it as true, or to extract an idea common
to all the definitions, or to show their succession and variation.
But rather than give us an idea of what metaphysics *is*, this

would give us only the series of meanings attributed to the word. The other approach would be from another direction; it would attempt to observe what metaphysicians have done, what has been the actual reality taking place throughout history. Though such an observation may seem easy, there is an unexpected difficulty: the word "metaphysics" is a later designation, not of a discipline, but of one of Aristotle's books. The story of metaphysics cannot limit itself to a history of that which has been called metaphysics. This obliges us to go beyond the name—with the name as point of departure—into a problematic prehistory. Thus, the first question that arises is the origin of metaphysics itself.

II
The Origin of Metaphysics

The one sure criterion in our search, the one we must use as our starting point, is the work of Aristotle—the first work that was called metaphysics. What then, does Aristotle call the chief philosophical science, the one that one day will receive the name we are concerned with? We must distinguish two types of nomenclature in the texts of Aristotle: the terms used in metaphysics and the "definitions" of metaphysics, that is, the concrete formulations of the content of metaphysics. The terms we are here interested in are clearly of the first type. We shall investigate the others later. The four principal terms are wisdom (*sophía*), first philosophy (*próte philosophía*), knowledge gained by inquiry (*zetouméne epistéme*), "theory of truth" (*tés aletheías theoría*). I shall presently explain why I have placed this last phrase in translation between quotation marks.

The differences in these four terms are obvious and highly meaningful: wisdom is an accepted and traditional word which designates the ultimate and supreme form of knowledge, the fundamental ambition of the "wise" man. Aristotle arrives at the conclusion that wisdom consists precisely in the discipline we call metaphysics. This is the purpose of the inquiry made in the first two chapters of Book I. First philosophy is also a "hierarchical" designation, and at the same time a methodological one, which points up the importance and the demands made by the discipline to be instituted and established. This is exactly the meaning behind the third expression, "knowledge gained by inquiry," a problematic knowledge, one that by its requirements, its function, and its primacy is defined only for the time being even though for the time being it does not exist, except as an undertaking and a task still to be accomplished. The fourth expression requires a longer study.

The "theory of truth," in fact, is a completely improper rendering—only a literal copy of the Greek so as to conserve it, and not really to translate or interpret it. When Aristotle says metaphysics is "truth theory," he is speaking of the same thing he refers to when he speaks of men who "philosophized about the truth." He is not referring to a theory of truth, to an inquiry as to what truth is. One does not find this in the pre-Socratics. When he opposes the men who in the beginning theologized (*theologésantes*) to the more recent ones who philosophized "about the truth" (*philosophésantes*), Aristotle emphasizes the idea of *alétheia* as an unveiling or making *evident* of what is real, what there *truly* is, what things are in *truth*, that is, what they always *were* in their originative and primary source—their principium, *arkhé*—and so *are* and *will be* forever.

This ultimate underlying source of things, which one *can* arrive at and which one can make manifest, since there is a way or a method of doing it, is the source or the origin from which things come into being; at the same time it is what things really are at bottom, what, properly speaking, they consist in. These are the two ideas that reside in the notion of *physis* or nature.

When Aristotle treats the background of his own thought at the beginning of his *Metaphysics*, he divides the past into two different parts: a near past, that of those who "philosophized," the pre-Socratics, and a remote past, in a certain sense opposed to the first, though the two share a certain essential common ground. This remote past belongs to those who "theologized" in different forms of mythical thought. In other words, if the theo-

retical discipline which was later to be called metaphysics has a
function in human life, its origin had to be found in a need of
human life that had been satisfied before by some reality "homologous" to metaphysics, that is, by a reality that had occupied a
similar place in a corresponding vital structure. If we start with
this primary reality and introduce the historical movement, metaphysics will appear no longer as a "homologue"—a static and
therefore reversible term—but as the "surrogate" for it, a "vicarious" substitute activity which takes its place, and at the same time
as originating from it as the situation changes.

We cannot now go into this problem in detail. I have spoken
elsewhere with some precision about *moîra* as a "pretheoretical
analogue to *physis*" and about the discovery of a means or method
which allows one to go from the patent to the hidden and convert a capricious and uncontrollable "revelation" of reality as it
is in its origin into an active, human "unveiling" of the truth. One
particularly clear example should be enough to show what I
mean. In the eighth century before Christ, in his *Theogeny,*
Hesiod placed the story of the genesis of the gods on the lips of
the Muses. One is here far from theory or philosophy. In spite of
this, the Muses make a singular declaration in the very prelude
of the poem: "We know how to tell many lies that seem to be
true; but, when we want to, we also know how to tell the truth"
(v. 27-28). The words Hesiod uses are highly significant: lies or
falsehoods (φεύδεα) are contrasted first of all to ἔτυμα, things that
are true or, more exactly, things that are authentic, which they
resemble or seem to be and for which they pass or seek to pass.
Secondly, things that are false are contrasted to ἀλήθεια, truths
which are spoken or proclaimed, that is, things which are made
manifest or become obvious. Truth, or *alétheia,* uncovers authentic
realities, *étyma,* which are usually covered up or disguised simply
by a resemblance to falsehoods, *pseúdea.*

An expression which coincides almost literally with Hesiod's
is found in Homer (*Odyssey,* XIX, 203) when Ulysses says
"many lies quite like the things that are true" (Ψεύδεα πολλὰ λέγων
ἐτύμοισιν ὁμοῖα), that is, verisimilitudes. Notice also that the

epithet Hesiod applies to the Muses is *artiépeiai,* which is usually translated as "truthful" but which means literally "of exact word," that is, they speak rightly and adequately.

"To escape ignorance," says Aristotle, men sought wisdom. The human need to know *how to orient oneself,* not in regard to this or that particular thing, but to that which is fundamental, requires a reference to the hidden foundation beneath that which is obvious. At first, men could do nothing to reach that latent foundation; it had to be that hidden basis itself which revealed itself in one form or another. A man was able to orient himself and knew what to guide himself by to the extent that he believed in these lightning-like revelations of reality—in oracles, divinations, and so forth. When that belief was shaken—by many historical experiences, trials, failures, and knowledge of other worlds —an uncertainty began to take hold of men; and when, finally, among the "seven sages" and, even more, in the school of one of them, in the Milesian group about Thales, there flowered a new belief: that things are "fundamentally" the same, that they derive one from the other by generation and, therefore, possess a certain consistency or coherence which can be investigated— on that day the old radical need changed its meaning and became something which, to a certain point at least, was in man's hands. To search for that reality now would be no longer passive recourse to an oracle; it would be addressing oneself directly to reality and compelling it to respond. It was now man himself who was going to *verify—verificare, verum facere*—what things were. Truth is no longer what is said truthfully to a man; it is what a man does, that is, what he *uncovers.* This is the origin of metaphysics.

III
CLASSICAL METAPHYSICS

I believe it is useful to avail myself of this expression, classical metaphysics, to designate the longest portion of its history, which includes essential diversities but which is defined by an area of common assumptions: I mean the period from Plato until the crisis that was produced in the eighteenth century and culminated in Kant, that is, the time until the very possibility of metaphysics was questioned. If one wishes to mark the two extremes, they are from Plato to Wolff.

Before Plato, actually, metaphysics did not exist as an established discipline, though the problem of metaphysics had been brought to light by a successive series of concepts dating from the very beginning of philosophy, at least from the time of Anaximander. The idea of nature or *physis* was the model for the philosophical interpretation of what was real. If things proceed by generation from each other, and from a primordial source, they can all be reduced to that source in virtue of their fundamental identity. This interpretation came about conceptually only when to the notion of nature was added the interpretation of it as a principium or *arkhé*. A third notion—whose origin would be in Pythagoreanism—was that of constitution; in addition to arising from an originative source or nature, things consist in something, they have a definite constitution. When Parmenides substantialized the idea of constitutiveness—speaking of a being, *tò eón*—the concept he formulated was to underlie the whole of this classical metaphysics and the subsequent quarrel over the very possibility or impossibility of metaphysics.

A body of metaphysical doctrine as such was not yet to be found in Plato. The literary form of Plato's work, which was not at all unintentional, contributed to this. In the division usually made of Plato's thought—dialectics, physics, and ethics—there does not appear a discipline that corresponds to what was later called metaphysics, and a reconstruction of Plato's "metaphysics" would have to draw on distinct elements of the three disciplines. But when we say this, we should also point out that the majority of the metaphysical concepts that characterized the First Philosophy of Aristotle and have been sacred since his time were already formally in Plato, in whom, therefore, the first mature metaphysics is found as a foundation for all later metaphysics, though not in independent literary form.

It is Aristotle who gives it this form, though it should be noted that he never wrote a "tract on metaphysics," since this is not what his fourteen books on First Philosophy were, being written at different times, relatively independent, and never forming a unified and systematic work. The supreme form of knowledge, wisdom or *sophía*, he says, is a science, a demonstrative discipline or *episteme* capable of demonstrating things according to their principles and of observing and contemplating with noetic vision the principles themselves, which, since they are first principles, cannot be demonstrated. Aristotle gives a triple definition of the discipline with these specifications: (1) a science which considers *being as such* universally; (2) a divine science (in two senses—one, that it would be the knowledge God would have, and two, that God is its object); (3) a science of substance. But he is speaking of only one science, not three, and this oneness which requires the convergence of the three definitions was a problem for Aristotle, as it would be for all later tradition.

The various sciences consider only a part of reality—for example, numbers or plants—and from a partial point of view, only for a study of a nonessential quality or attribute, such as for example quantitative properties or the characteristics of vegetable organisms. But metaphysics refers to the totality of things inasmuch as they *are*, not for anything each might have in particular. Upon examining the different ways in which things exist, the diverse types of things that exist,* Aristotle sees himself forced to make a radical intellectual innovation. Opposing both Parmenides'

---

* Translator's note: Anticipating here the distinction Marías will make later, I have translated "ser" and "ente" not by "being," as is customary, but by equivalent phrases, in order to make clearer in English what is being said. As Marías will point out later, Spanish distinguishes with two words, "ente" and "ser," that which is usually indicated by the single English word "being." "Ser," used as a verb, has meanings equivalent to some of those of the English verb "to be"; it is used especially as a logical copulative and used also to indicate identity and existence. In English, only the context distinguishes whether the word "being" indicates a "person or thing that exists," or "all that exists," or "subsistence," or "existence" (in the sense of a state, not of what exists), or the "essence" (fundamental character or content) of something or all that exists. The Spanish use "ente" to mean a "person or thing that exists," or "all that exists," or the "subsistence" of a

idea of all that exists [el ente] as one and unchangeable and the
sophists' proclamation of the basic changeability and lack of constitutiveness of what is real, Aristotle establishes the doctrine of
modes of existing [ser] which are analogous to one another—
what is, is one and many, it is predicated in many ways, but
always in reference to one predication which is primary and is
the foundation of the others. This predicate is "substance" (*ousía*).
Studying what exists [el ente], insofar only as it exists, metaphysics arrives at the theory of subtance; and the supreme form
of substance, that in which the conditions of what exists [el ente]
(*ón*) are fully and sufficiently realized, is God, the "first immovable mover," pure act, in whom everything is actual reality without any mixture of potency or matter. Lastly, the contemplation of
what is real, inasmuch as it exists, this *theory* in which things
become evident and are no longer hidden, is what constitutes
wisdom, *sophía,* and only God possesses it in a stable, permanent,
and proper way. Man can attain it only precariously and at inter-
vals. The most he can hope for is a habit, a form of life defined
by a certain *friendship* with wisdom: this is *philosophy,* the divine
science—divine in the double sense expressed before. Because of
this, man attains a certain likeness to the Divinity in the theoretical life, which reaches its perfection in metaphysics.

Aristotelian metaphysics is closely bound to logic from one
point of view, to physics from another, and finally to ethics. Being
[el ser] was predicated in four ways: (1) to be essentially or

person or thing or all that exists (which implies more than the mere state of
existing); the context must distinguish which. They use "ser" to mean a
"person or thing that exists," or "existence" (in the sense of a state, not of
what exists), or the "essence" (fundamental character or content) of a person or thing that exists; again, the context distinguishes which one is meant.
In an attempt to avoid confusion, from this point on I shall translate "ente"
and "ser" by their principal meaning in context by using the following
phrases rather than the single word "being": (1) "ente" (a) "something that
exists," (b) "all that exists" or "what exists," (c) "subsistence"; (2) "ser"
(a) "something that exists," (b) "existence" or "to exist," or "existing"
(indicating a state only), (c) "essence." Immediately after my translation I
shall include in the text in brackets the Spanish word Marías uses so as to
indicate which set of meanings is connotated.

accidentally; (2) to be, according to the categories; (3) to be true or false; (4) to be in potency or in act. In each case, what was differentiated was what exists [el ente], and the differentiation had diverse modes of enunciation or predication; thus, the "*flections* of being"* were also the predicates or the categories according to which things could be spoken of (substance, quantity, quality, relation, place, time, position, state, action, affection), all of which were based on the first one, on substance, to which all the others refer. The division of what exists [el ente] into true and false presented an analogous relation with logic, since truth and falseness exist primarily in a predication or judgment: "A is B" makes it obvious what a thing really is (the truth, *aléthia*) or disguises it with an illusory essence [ser] (falseness, *pseúdos*). Physics, on the other hand, was the science of natural things or things which are by their nature, and nature (*physis*) was the principle of motion. The Aristotelian theory of potency and act, of matter and form, which describes the structure of substance made it possible to understand motion and therefore to understand what nature really was. Motion (in its general meaning of change) was no longer an impossible passage from not existing [no ser] to existing [ser] or from existing [ser] to not existing [no ser]—as it had been for the Eleatics—but was now a passage from one mode of existing [ser] to another mode of existing [ser], from existing [ser] in potency to existing [ser] in act. This shows that the Aristotelian *Physics,* of which the doctrine of soul forms a part, must be an element of metaphysics in the modern sense of the word. Lastly, metaphysics as a finished form of the *bíos theoretikós* or contemplative life is the key to the Aristotelian ethic, since the contemplative life was for Aristotle the properly human life, the life in which happiness could be found.

The whole later history of metaphysics rested on Aristotle's presentation of the metaphysical problem. The cultivation of metaphysics as such has always been united to the reappearance of Aristotle's work. This is what happened in the Middle Ages,

* Translator's note: "the variations in how things exist [ser]."

as much in the Muslem scholasticism (Avicenna, Averroes) as in Christian scholasticism (St. Thomas, Duns Scotus), and in a certain way in Jewish scholasticism (Maimonides). All of them invoke Aristotle, and a good part of the work they had done in metaphysics was a commentary on Aristotle. However, it is clear that in spite of this intention, the historical situation in which they found themselves and the motive for their intellectual work gave a quite different orientation to a metaphysics that often aspired to be the same as Aristotle's. Do not forget that St. Thomas, for example, was primarily a theologian and that all his intellectual work is oriented toward theology. Gilson has contrasted accurately a theological order, St. Thomas', and a purely "philosophical" order removed from revelation which would be "Thomistic" only in the sense that a philosophy was composed of elements *taken* from Thomas' work. Strictly speaking, scholasticism is not philosophy but a particular combination of theology and philosophy.

This conditions even the details of medieval metaphysics. Keep in mind that in contrast to Greek metaphysics, its chief problem was not motion but creation; that existence [ser] was not so much opposed to not existing [no ser] (*mè ón*) as to nothingness; that the fundamental concern in the problem of analogy was, not that things *are* in different ways, but that they are *created*; that the theological considerations (Trinity, incarnation, original sin, the Eucharist) were the ones that provoked and oriented the statement of problems, such as those of universals or substance. But it is also just as important that we point out the fact that the whole of the metaphysics of the Middle Ages remains within the intellectual boundaries of Aristotelianism, uses its concepts, and only differs from it when it cannot avoid differing.

This metaphysics, which is *distinguished from* the theology of St. Thomas but is united with it, gradually disengaged itself in the fourteenth century and came into its own as an *independent* and autonomous discipline at the end of the sixteenth in the hands of Francesco Suárez (1548–1617). His *Disputationes metaphysicae* (1597) was—if one prescinds from the problematic *Sapientiale* of Thomas of York in the thirteenth century—the first treatment of metaphysics that was worked out "distinctly and separately" (Suárez' own words). Suarez, who was to rethink tradition in view of actualities, worked out a *natural theology* distinct from a supernatural or revealed theology. Metaphysics continued to organize theology, since Suarez was a theologian, but now metaphysics served as a foundation prior to theology. So it acquired autonomy and took on the aspect of a science. It had to question itself, its subject, and its structure.

The *Metaphysical Disputations* begins with a discussion on the object of metaphysics. Suarez examines different opinions and criticizes them in order to arrive at his own definition: the total object of metaphysics is what exists [el ente] in its aspect as really existing. Bearing in mind the degree of abstraction belonging to it, he defines metaphysics as "the science which contemplates what exists [el ente] only in so much as it exists, or in so much as it prescinds from matter in referring to existence [el ser]" (*Disp.* I, sect. III). Thus understood, metaphysics is a speculative, not a practical, science whose purpose is the contemplation of the truth for its own sake. It is concerned with the knowledge of things and of ultimate causes, with the most noble things that exist [entes] and the most universal and abstract ideas. In sum, it is wisdom and the knowledge most naturally desirable for man insofar as he is man.

Finally, the trajectory of metaphysics took one last turn in the eighteenth century. Descartes had brought back Aristotle's expression in the original Latin title of his *Meditations on First Philosophy* and had centered metaphysics on the question of the existence of God and the immortality of the soul. From this time on, especially with the Cartesian distinction between thinking substance and extended substance, all the metaphysics of the seventeenth century—Malebranche, Spinoza, Leibnitz, Berkeley —was to have as its central theme the problem of the communicability of substances, bound up closely with the question of the reality of the exterior world and the existence of God. When we come to a "scholasticism" of modern philosophy in Wolff (1679–

1754), a program for metaphysics appears that was to influence Thomistic neoscholasticism, especially beginning in the second half of the nineteenth century. For Wolff, metaphysics was divided into general metaphysics, or *ontology,* and special metaphysics which included three disciplines: rational cosmology, rational psychology, and natural theology. This scheme was the last form of what we may call "classical metaphysics" before the crisis initiated in English philosophy in the seventeenth century had attained its mature form in Kant's *Critique of Pure Reason.* When doubt was sown about the very possibility of metaphysics, a different and much deeper reflection about its assumptions and justification became necessary. All metaphysics following the Kantian crisis is conditioned by having come after it, by having been established and defended with it in mind, and consequently metaphysics has absorbed the Kantian problem, taking it to heart as its very own.

IV
Metaphysics and Antimetaphysics

From the Renaissance on, a certain hostility toward metaphysics set in. At first the hostility was toward only certain aspects of metaphysics. This was the case with the humanists who reproached the scholastics for their abstract and sterile debates. In Descartes, who practiced metaphysics and used the name, there are passages with hints of aversion for the word. Expressions with similar suggestions are found in Hobbes and in Locke. There was a double basis for these reproaches: first, the inaccessibility and questionability of the objects metaphysics studies—when one insists on their incorporeal and suprasensible character—and, second, the obscurity of the concepts it uses, which makes it possible to develop very clear and strict chains of reasoning without knowing what one is talking about. The hostility and reproach increased during the eighteenth century in three different areas. The French Encyclopedists dwelt on the many differences in opinion between metaphysicians and the little attention they paid one another (d'Alembert) or they wrote with irony, as Voltaire did, about the "transnatural" and "immaterial" character of the objects metaphysics studies, about what Voltaire often called "the novel of the spirit." Hume, for his part, pursuing empiricism and sensualism's position to its ultimate consequences, criticized the concepts of substance, soul, and cause in general and destroyed the body of traditional metaphysics at the same time that his elimination of the ontological argument destroyed the bridge that God established between the mind and things, according to the idealism of the seventeenth century, which Hume classified as "dogmatism." Finally, at this point came Kant's "Copernican revolution," the gravest event in the history of metaphysics.

The idea Kant had of knowledge brought about an inversion of the usual perspective: instead of thought adapting itself to things, things must adapt themselves to the structure of thought. This paradoxical "Copernican revolution" was based on Kant's discovery that what man knows is not the "thing in itself," which is necessarily inaccessible, but the "phenomenon" which is constituted by the subject with the "given" and the "posited," that is, by the very structure of subjectivity (space and time being pure intuitions or *a priori* forms of sensation and categories or *a priori* forms of understanding). Kant believed, on the one hand, that to be universal and necessary knowledge must be *a priori*, that is, not *based* on experience. But, on the other hand, in order that the knowledge be real, sensation or experience must be added to the formal aprioristic forms. The Kantian critique of metaphysics bases itself on these assumptions.

Kant had a double point of departure: positively, Wolff's idea of metaphysics, with its division into general metaphysics, or ontology, and special metaphysics, divided into rational cosmology, rational psychology, and rational or natural theology; and negatively, Hume's criticism, which, as Kant said himself in his famous phrase, "aroused him from his dogmatic slumber." Upon being accepted, Wolff's outline of metaphysics appeared to Kant to represent *pure* knowledge, that is, an *a priori* knowledge of three objects: the world as a totality, the soul, and God. Now Kant shows in his *Critique of Pure Reason* that those three objects are beyond all possible experience. They are "infinite syntheses," that is, one is not able to establish the necessary conditions to have an *intuition* of them; the knowledge one obtains by reasoning has no real foundation, that is, it is not authentic knowledge. From this point of view, metaphysics appears to be impossible if it is taken as a speculative discipline, and that is why it had not yet got onto "the sure path of science," nor can it ever do so. Metaphysics exists as a "natural tendency," as a *Naturanlage* that carries men toward the absolute, but its role within Kant's system is to be very precise: it is to be a science of regulatory Ideas that have unconditioned validity only within the scope of *practical reason,* as postulates of this reason; or, rather, it is the name given to the pure portion (the aprioristic portion) of the philosophical disciplines (the metaphysics of nature, the metaphysics of customs).

It is not necessary here to explain in detail Kant's doctrine nor to pass judgment on its foundations. What we are interested in is pointing out that all philosophical thought since the end of the eighteenth century more or less formally accepts Kant's point of view and denies, or more or less argues, the legitimacy of metaphysics. In some cases this is united to a metaphysical speculation that goes a little out of control, as German idealism does; and at other times this is an embryonic metaphysics without our realizing it—what could be called the metaphysics of the antimetaphysicians—like that of the positivists. The predominant situation in the nineteenth century was that metaphysics was despised and forbidden; a doctrine or a line of reasoning was disqualified simply by being labeled metaphysical. The few who attempted to use metaphysics in the last century often displayed a curious attitude: they pretended not to have heard of Kant, and they turned their backs on him; it is as if he had never been born nor had written the *Critique of Pure Reason*. Some other efforts, the newest and most original ones which were to prepare the ground for present-day philosophy, argued against Kant's thesis. But it should be noted that they were weakened internally by one or the other of the two following defects: one, they refuted some of Kant's arguments against metaphysics yet left intact the general implication of his criticism and so its principal force; or, two, they attacked Kantianism as a total error, as a deviation in philosophical thought, without paying attention to the large portion that is true or to its irreplaceable role in philosophy. This means that they did not do justice to the philosophy of Kant, to its truth or to its error. Because of this, the attempts at metaphysics in the nineteenth century were undermined either by not understanding Kant or by excluding what he contributed to philosophy, even to a metaphysics opposed to his fundamental assumptions.

The antimetaphysical attitude does not belong to the past. The "scientistic" inclinations of present-day thought, above all those of logical empiricism, deny the possibility of metaphysics. Its point of view is tied up with that of Comte and concentrates on the logical analysis of language. For the most extreme empiricists, metaphysical statements simply make no sense. This is the last form, the most radical one, of the movement whose steps we have traced so far.

V
THE "RETURN TO METAPHYSICS"

Metaphysics became a "disputed question" in the nineteenth century. Those who rejected it, such as the positivists, practiced it. When they declared that reality was sense data, they were building up a metaphysics without knowing it. This made their rejection of metaphysics all the more deplorable, that is, they irresponsibly confused an interpretation with reality itself. Comte's attitude was justified by the excesses of the idealist speculation in the first third of the century, by the systematic spirit, and by the idea of philosophy as constructive thought. The wish to address oneself directly to reality without adding mental constructs to it was legitimate, but it was not as legitimate to identify what was *real* with what was *given,* and the given with what was given in *sense experience*. With the realization of the excess there was in this, a reaction set in against Kantianism and positivism, and with that a "return to metaphysics."

Revolutions are usually followed by a "spirit of restoration." An analogous attitude followed the Copernican revolution of Kant, with the typical assumption that "nothing has really changed." We cannot forget that a good part of the philosophical movements which proposed a return to metaphysics were based on the pure and simple omission of Kantianism, of its background—in English philosophy—and of its positivistic consequences. Even many present-day philosophical currents are prejudiced by this. But I must make it clear that by saying this I do not mean to imply that today's philosophy is less Kantian or positivistic than it is. Precisely the contrary. I find that it is too Kantian and positivistic precisely because it has *not* been efficaciously Kantian or positivistic. To the extent that a school of thought is "pre-Kantian," for example, it is exposed to being Kantian, to coinciding again with the Kantian point of view and, consequently, to having its evident partial justification involve it in the error there was in Kantianism, an outdated error we have long ago corrected.

Let us not forget that the variations that take place in a doctrine thoughout its history depend in great part on the attention given its various parts. Problems are discovered or abandoned. They are abandoned not so much because they have been solved as because they cease to be problems, because men cease to feel themselves obliged to inquire about them or to have to orient themselves in relation to what they are about. The history of philosophy is conditioned by what we might call the horizon of problems. The loss of metaphysics in the eighteenth and nineteenth centuries had as its principal origin a change in the direction of attention: the primary concern became one for the problems of the origin of ideas, knowledge, and the natural sciences.

The fact that certain groups maintained an interest in past problems was one of the causes that made possible a return to metaphysics. I am referring to the theologians, especially Catholic theologians. Even though metaphysical speculation declined rapidly after Suárez and lacked a creative impulse, it remained "preserved." The very promising attempt at a modern theology, to some extent Cartesian, which took place at the end of the seventeenth century— Bossuet, Fénelon, etc.—in which the Augustinian and scholastic traditions were united with the thought of Descartes and Leibnitz, was soon interrupted for complex reasons. But, in any case, the cultivation of theology, even in its less lively forms, maintained contact with the great metaphysicians. Thus the first seeds of the restoration of metaphysics are found in the Catholic scholastics: Bolzano, Rosmini, Gioberti, Gratry, Brentano, and naturally those who at that same time or a little later began the neo-Thomistic movement, Liberatore, Sanseverine, Kleutgen.

Metaphysics became current again in several areas and regained the operative force it had lost. However, we should not forget that this was a slow, resisted process. Most of the thinkers of the second half of the nineteenth century, and even of the first decades of our century, were saturated with an antimetaphysics attitude. This lasted until Dilthey and Husserl. We remember with what suspicion and even hostility Husserl accepted the metaphysical derivation of phenomenology. Similar reservations are found in Bergson. But since the end of the last century the universal belief that metaphysics is an impossible anachronism has been shaken, and an atmosphere has developed which has allowed metaphysics to take root again. I am insisting on the negative aspect because it is essential: it is not so much that on a certain day the problem of metaphysics was newly established for sufficient reasons, such as that the antimetaphysical attitude was seen to be questionable and insufficiently justified. The ultimate inconsistency of positivism was a decisive factor. Remember that Husserl tried to develop, in the face of a partial but dominant positivism, a total and effective positivism and that his faithfulness to that attitude led him, more than anyone else, to reaffirm the ground from which metaphysics was again to spring in spite of Husserl's desires.

We may distinguish three groups of motives which led to this restoration. The first motives were initially extraphilosophical, particularly the theological ones; they were a desire to revindicate and justify metaphysics, almost always in its scholastic forms, as a reaction against modern philosophy, not only the part of modern philosophy opposed to metaphysics but the totality of modern philosophy. The second group of motives, the first example of which is found in Bolzano and then fully developed in Brentano, was a desire to regain objectivity; through Marty, Meinong, von Ehrenfels, and above all Husserl, it led to a philosophy which again took on the theme of reality, having overcome all subjectivism and psychologism. The third group of motives was particularly subtle; the motivation sprang from the discovery of certain realities or aspects of reality whose general character is *irreducibility:* the "primitive fact" of Maine de Brian, "existence" in Kierkegaard, the triple reality of "sense" in Gratry, "life" and "history" in Dilthey. These realities, which to a certain extent provoked an irrationalist crisis in philosophy, have made it transcend explanatory, positivistic, scientistic assumptions and face philosophy with fundamental problems. This triple origin conditions the characteristics that present-day metaphysics presents and is the reason for not a few of its internal difficulties.

VI
METAPHYSICS AND ONTOLOGY

Having arrived at this point, we begin to suspect that it is not entirely clear as to exactly what is to be understood by metaphysics. Since the seventeenth century, and more frequently since the eighteenth, metaphysics has been designated by a name which is usually taken as a synonym for it, at least for the greater part of it: *ontology.* This term dates, as far as we can tell, from 1646 and was used by the German Cartesian and occasionalist Johann Clauberg in his book *Elementa philosophiae sive ontosophia.* In the prologues he uses the term *Ontology,* along with that of *Ontosophy,* to mean a *scientia, quae contemplatur ens quatenus ens est.** This name, which appears again in the second edition (1681) of the *Philosophia vetus et nova* of J. B. du Hamel, is the title of one of the books of Jean Le Clerc, *Ontologia sive de ente in genere* (1692), much before Wolff's work *Philosophia prima sive ontologia*, first issued in 1792, which is usually considered to be the first tract on ontology under this title.

All these authors believe they are being faithful to Aristotle. Le Clerc says this very explicitly and calls the science *ontology*, with the thought that he is merely reviving Aristotle's definition. But let us not forget that Aristotle's definition is a triple one. In Aristotle there is no *one* sufficient definition of it as the science of what exists [el ente] only in its aspect of existing, nor is there question of three definitions which correspond to three *parts* of the science, as occurs in Wolff and in some of the neoscholastics. The discipline *itself* is at the same time and for the same reason the science of what exists [el ente], of substance and of God, that is, the three "definitions" are more *a posteriori* ideas, internal theses. What is involved is knowing reality, a reality which motion makes inconsistent; one must go from natural things or by way of nature (*physei ónta*) to nature itself (*physis*). The earlier Greek tradition had placed motion outside what exists [el ente] (Parmenides, and to a certain extent the idea of element, or *stoikheîon*), or rather it had placed constitutiveness outside things so that they had only a participated constitutiveness (Plato). Aristotle was to found the theory of what exists [el ente] on the idea that the *eîdos* is in the thing itself, informing it as *morphé;* he considered each real thing as something that had an "estate" or "domain" of its own out of which its possibilities blossomed as a nature. This is the idea of *ousía*, substance, whose full realization is *theós*, God. Now the internal difficulties of Aristotle's idea of substance and of the conceptual schemes with which he tries to describe it—matter and form, potency and

* Translator's note: "A science which contemplates what exists only in its aspect of existing."

act—show, precisely when they are applied to true substances (living beings, man, God), that "substance" is the title of a problem rather than a solution.

Earlier I said that revolutions are usually followed by a spirit of restoration and that the "Copernican revolution" of Kantianism was not an exception to the rule. I meant that the return to metaphysics was obviously a return to ontology, much more so than before Kant. There were many reasons for this, apart from inertia, and it is not easy to probe them all. Let us look at these three: 1) the *terminus a quo** of Kantianism was an ontological metaphysics (Wolff), 2) there was a strong scholastic ingredient in the "return to metaphysics," 3) in view of all the forms of subjectivism, there was a need to regain "objectivity," and ontology appeared the best form for a theory of "objects."

But something new occurred some twenty-five years ago: the distinction between *ens* and *esse*. The two had been traditionally mistaken one for the other to such a degree that in the majority of languages only one word is used: *être* in French, *being* in English. In Spanish the distinction is clear between *ente* and *ser,* and Heidegger had no difficulty in making the distinction in German, *Seiendes* and *Sein*. In Heidegger's opinion, philosophy had persistently forgotten the problem of existence [el ser] because it had been concerned only with the *things* that existed [el ente]. The meaning of existence [el ser] in general, *der Sinn de Seins überhaupt,* is Heidegger's problem. The problem has thus been transplanted from what exists [el ente] to what makes it [el ente] exist, that is, *existence* [el ser].

However, the relations between existence [el ser] and what exists [el ente] are not ever sufficiently clear. Heidegger himself has essentially modified some of his theses from one edition to the next in his *What is Metaphysics?* In his book *An Introduction to Metaphysics* (1953), he complains that his question has not received enough attention and that an "ontology" in the traditional sense of the word is being cultivated. Because of this, he

---

* Translator's note: "The starting point."

adds, it may be for the best in the future to throw out terms such as "ontology" and "ontological." Heidegger is probably thinking about the notorious, and the rather significant, fact that existentialism has fallen back on the idea of existence [el ser] and inherited all the consequences that implies: to exist [ser] and not to exist, to exist [ser] in oneself, to exist [ser] for oneself, essence and existence, ontology.

However, more fundamental than these difficulties is another more important and radical one. Is it licit to identify ontology and metaphysics? One cannot begin with existence [el ser] only. It is necessary to derive it and to justify it because existence [el ser] is an *interpretation* of reality, that is, of "what there is." Ortega demonstrated something decisive; inquiring about existence [el ser], searching for what things "are," has an assumption as its basis: *the belief in existence* [el ser], a pretheoretical belief, and —so far as it is pretheoretical—an unjustified belief that things "are." This belief has its own essence [ser] and constitution which we can investigate and discover. Existence [el ser] is not the same as reality; it is, I repeat, an interpretation of it, of "what there is," an expression which seems to us quite vague and which in fact is so because it is prior to all interpretations. What there is is a constituent of me because I am *myself* insofar as I have to deal with what there is.

The universality of existence [el ser] which philosophy has traditionally insisted upon (Aristotle, St. Thomas) has a clear basis: once I have arrived at the interpretation that existence [el ser] is, that is, once I am of the belief that "there is existence [ser]" and I adopt the position of questioning myself about it and searching for it—that is, once I have adopted the posture of what we call knowledge—*everything* (everything *there is*, the whole of reality) appears to me *sub specie entis** as something that *exists*. The universality comes from the fact that *everything* is considered from that point of view, is submitted to this new interpretation. Existence [el ser] is no less a *derived* concept

* Translator's note: "With the aspect of something that exists."

for this. One has to be very careful about a possible error that threatens us; if one says "being is what already was," one has the impression that the present situation is transcended and an "absolute" character of being has been discovered; but it is enough to replace the word "being" with what it means: in saying *"what exists* is what has already been," one notices that what is affected by the determination "already" is not the "exists" but the "what," in other words, the reality—the *very same* thing that exists is that which has already been; that is, I interpret as existence, now that I have placed myself in the attitude of knower, the *same* reality which *was* before I arrived at this interpretation.

It seems to us that the world is composed of "things that exist [entes]," perhaps that the world itself is something that exists [un ente]; but all this is consequent upon the interpretation called *existence* [ser]. It is not true that the man who does not theorize (in an extreme case the primitive savage) is surrounded by things that exist [entes] and handles them, deals with them and utilizes them. What happens is that what *for me* are things that exist [entes]—not always but only when I adopt an attitude defined by a belief in existence [el ser]—are the *same* realities that must be contended with by the man who does not theorize (which includes myself in my basic dimension).

If the purpose of metaphysics is to tell us how to orient ourselves to reality, the *a priori* and obvious identification of metaphysics with ontology cannot be permitted. The expression *metaphysica sive ontologia* is inadmissible because it makes the content of metaphysics already supposed, and so deprives it of its basic character. Metaphysics cannot be "defined" by its presupposed content because that automatically invalidates it in respect to its very aim. The only possible "definition" consists in determining its function, what we demand of it. Every other definition of it in relation to its content or structure must be an *internal thesis* of metaphysics and therefore can never be prior to metaphysics. I mean to say that it is metaphysics itself, once it has gotten under way, that has to find out and justify what kind of discipline it is and tell us what the condition is of that reality about which it is going to give us basic certitude. If metaphysics were ontology, the identity could not be stated in its own name; it would have to be an assertion contained within metaphysics, and metaphysics would then discover some day this assumed identity. But the identification of metaphysics and ontology is not even acceptable *a posteriori,* since, as we have seen, existence [el ser] is an interpretation of what is real, an interpretation one arrives at in virtue of certain suppositions, one which must be "derived" and justified. Any metaphysics which begins with existence [el ser], which takes it as its point of departure, turns its back on the basic problem—precisely the derivation of the concept of existence [el ser]—and renounces *basic* certitude; that is, it is not metaphysics. Notice that from our point of view it does not matter whether ontology be understood as the science of what exists [el ente] or the science of existence [el ser] because this cannot be used as a starting point any more than can the "comprehension of existence [el ser]" be used as something fundamental which assumes nothing.

However, do not forget something essential: reality is thought out according to a certain interpretation, not only thought out but also lived out. An attempt to ignore this would be unrealistic and illusory. When one speaks of a science which "assumes nothing," one must be extremely cautious if only for the fact that the idea that such a science might exist may be a blindly accepted assumption. For this reason metaphysics cannot begin with a doctrine of existence [el ser], and even less with a "neglect" or "omission" of existence [el ser] or any of the other interpretations of reality. Beneath an ambition to simplify, there often lurks an ancient and anachronistic primitivism which is completely contrary to being truly fundamental. I mean to say by this that in trying to give an account of reality, to know how to orient ourselves in respect to it, we find its interpretations as absolutes, and *among* these absolute interpretations we find existence [el ser], the one which constitutes our intellectual tradition. It is necessary, therefore, that we go beyond interpretations to stark reality, as it is in what we can now call with full meaning its *fundamental truth.* Metaphysics, then, has more than a little to do with ontology: it has to account for ontology and for existence [el ser], taking as its *start fundamental reality.* One must transcend existence [el ser] to reach reality. But we should not think this is easy and that saying it is enough to enable us to do it. Traditionally, the instrument of knowledge, the *lógos,* had been identified with the attributes of existence [el ser], and vice versa. But that makes doubtful the method and, therefore, the very possibility of metaphysics.

VII
Metaphysics as the Science of
Fundamental Reality

Fundamental reality is that in which all other realities are grounded, that is, in which they appear in any way to be realities, and that is why I "find" them and must cope with them. In this sense all realities that are not the fundamental reality are "grounded' realities; they are constituted as realities within the boundary of fundamental reality, in the "whatness" fundamental reality is, no matter what the nature might be of what is real in each particular case. Looked at from another point of view, fundamental reality is what remains after I eliminate all my ideas, theories, or interpretations; it is what is left when I direct my attention to what I find to be irreducible, whether I like it or not, and what obliges me to forge ideas, theories, and interpretations. The fundamental reality is human life. This is a central thesis in Ortega's thought. Speaking more exactly, it is *my life,* the life of each individual person. When I prescind from everything that my thought adds to reality, when I am left with stark reality, I find: things and myself, myself with things; I mean, myself doing something with things. This is *living;* this is *my life.* Every reality, whatever it is, appears or is presented to me *within my life.* This is the boundary or area where every reality is constituted *as a reality,* that is, over and above whatever might occur to "what it is that is real." If, for example, something is independent of my life, it is independent *of my life*, and I find it in my life as independent. If something transcends my life, my "encounter" with it occurs in my life. This is the only thing that permits me to talk about it and discover its transcendence. If, lastly, something is impossible, and so does not exist in any sense, neither in my life nor outside it, it is nevertheless in my life that my "encounter" with its reality (in this case its impossibility) takes place.

However, we must emphasize from the start that we are not speaking of *Dasein* or of *existence*, nor of *man*. The path Heidegger takes is the inverse of ours. Though his problem is the meaning in general of existence [el ser], he is forced to base ontology on prior existential analysis of existing (*existenziale Analytik des Daseins*), in which, by the way, he has lingered so long that it constitutes the principal portion of his published work. In other words, this means Heidegger goes from *Dasein* to existence [el ser]; we, however, go from existence [el ser] to life, from existence [el ser] as an interpretation of reality to fundamental reality, prescinding from all interpretations. This itself shows that *Dasein* is not the same as *human life*. "Human life" is not man, and the theory of human life is not at all anthropology. Nor is it, certainly, Heidegger's analysis of existing; for him, anthropology studies the existing individual which is man, and the existential analysis of existing inquires into the "mode of existing [el ser]" or that which exists [el ente], which is called *Dasein* and which is what we are. Our point of view is essentially different: my life is the fundamental reality which includes things and myself ("I am myself and my circumstances," Ortega, 1914) and which is anterior to both terms; that is, it is the reality on which depend the two abstract terms "I" and "thing," and these two terms are diametrically opposed in a dynamic coexistence which consists in a *task:* my need to do something with circumstances in order to live.

Man is not at all fundamental reality; he is a grounded reality which I discover in my life, just as I find other realities. Even the man I am, insofar as I am *man*, is an interpretation of what I am, a theoretical elaboration of a certain portion of reality which I find as I go on living. Strictly speaking, "man," far from being a reality, is a theory.

My life, then, is not man, nor is it the I, nor is it the mode of existing [el ser] of something privileged that exists [un ente], which is what we are. Life is not exhausted in the I—which is only an ingredient or abstract intrinsic factor of life—nor in any thing because things are found somewhere, and life is, on the contrary, the very "where" of things. It is the area in which realities as such are constituted, in which my encounter with them occurs, my having to contend with them. To the extent that this takes place, all these things are ingredients of my life. My life, then, comprises *with me* the things that surround me, my circumstances or world, including, naturally, their horizon, the hidden world beyond it, its farthest reaches.

For this reason, the theory of human life is not a preparation or propedeutics for metaphysics, nor even a foundation for metaphysics, but is clearly *metaphysics itself*, that is, the search for fundamental certainty about fundamental reality.

But precisely here is where the problem begins because if the words I have just written are not taken in their strictest sense, if one skims over them or understands them inertially or with different assumptions, so prescinding then from what is essentially new in their meaning, they become a colossal triviality. I used the word "fundamental" twice, first as an adjective modifying "certainty" and then modifying "reality." This whole idea of metaphysics depends on the precise meaning of this adjective.

Let us consider first of all its reference to certainty. Certainty is not mere knowledge or "information"; it is knowing how to orient oneself. To begin with, this supposes that it refers to something in relation to which I *must* know how to orient myself. If someone tells me that the name of the person who passed in front of the Frauenkirche of Munich at eight-sixteen this morning is Weber, even if it is true, can it be called a certainty? The information that the temperature of the beer Mr. Weber will drink is exactly 6.72 degrees centigrade is not certitude, unless for some reason I need to know it. It is, then, my necessity that gives the information the character of certitude, not its simple "truth" or exactitude. Ignorance of an innumerable number of things leaves us indifferent; an infinite amount of information leaves us in uncertainty in regard to what matters to us. Even more: many actual certainties are not sufficient for us; even they themselves, for their incompleteness or because they are not clearly reconcilable with other certitudes, provoke uncertainty. This is why I previously recommended caution in regard to a science that "assumed nothing." Every science assumes something; what is important is what it does with its assumptions, that is, what function they have in respect to that discipline.

Life is full of questions with respect to which we have no certainty. On the other hand, we *are* certain about innumerable things, and this is why there are many realities that are not questions for us and never have been. When finally something is a question for us and we *arrive* at certainty about it, then we reach a *truth* in the strict sense. When I have *fundamental* certainty, life is not *in* question, though it may be *full* of questions. All the partial certainties about what is in life are not sufficient for me to know how to orient myself in respect to it. When I need to know how to orient myself to *life,* then fundamental certainty is *imperative;* I must *search* for it or *contrive* it if I believe that it is possible, that is, that at least to some extent it is within my power to obtain it.

The adjective "fundamental" was also used to describe reality. In saying that fundamental reality is my life, I have been very careful to add that my life is not me, nor man, but that "I am myself and my circumstances," and every reality that in any way can, enters into my circumstances. To consider the idea of life in this way, is it not the same as introducing into it all that is imaginable, as making it all of reality, the sum of all that is real? If my life is identified with all reality, does it add anything to call it "life"? And is it not falling back into an abstract, Fichtean "I and not-I" type of schematization, this cramming of the whole of reality into the notion of life, under the pretext that all that is real is either I or is not I? This is the problem.

We must take the expression *fundamental* reality seriously, that is, we must take seriously the distinction between fundamental reality and grounded reality. This distinction, in contrast to what took place in Descartes with *res cogitans* and *res extensa,* is operative—I mean it affects reality itself. What we are saying should show that there is no question here of taking "all" reality as being the same, as a sum or set. But there is another risk we have to guard against: understanding fundamentality to be a synonym for simplification. We are not talking about going back to an "elemental" situation, for example, to the functioning of the human organism among bare, physical things. Who is to assure us that going in a hypothetical "backward" direction is to lead to a beginning? Who is to tell us that the "destruction" of what we really find is not as much a "construction" as beginning with all the knowledge accumulated in history would be? We know very little of Adam, and what in him was human life was conditioned by its supernatural relations; thus, far from being direct experience, Adam is a theory.

In saying that I need to know how to orient myself in respect to fundamental reality and that in this reality, that is, in my life, all reality is included *in some way,* it must be pointed out that what is important about that "all" is that nothing is excluded, not even the sum of "all real things." I need to know how to orient myself in respect to the character and structure of reality *as such.* But let us not stumble again. What does that "as such" mean? It is a circumstantial expression whose meaning is different in each separate case since it reduplicates whatever it is applied to. In this case it means "insofar as it is reality." And since reality is that which I encounter, reality as such means: *reality insofar as I encounter it.* It is necessary to overcome once and for all the thousand-year-old attempt to omit a reference to me in reality, either that attempt or the one to "subjectivize" reality. I am an ingredient of reality, not in a surreptitious or shameful way, but as a constituent of the *realitas** of all that is real, though I am not a component or part of that which is real.

* Translator's note: "Realness."

My encounter in reality with reality is not inert or merely theoretical: I find myself *living*. I find reality in the role of a setting for my life or *world* in the widest sense of the term. In other words, any portion, aspect, or interpretation of reality presupposes *my life,* the area in which it is found and constituted. Thus, life is the *real organization of reality*—over and above all theory, such as the idea of the "whole of reality"—and therefore it is fundamental reality in the literal sense of these words.

It is a question, then, of not replacing reality *itself* with interpretative systems, especially with those which, in virtue of their simplicity, are the most difficult to make clear: things, all, universe. The meaning of reality depends on the pristine discovery of it, which is none other than my encounter with it as I *live*. Living—not existing [ser]—is the fundamental meaning of reality. It is in living that the constitution of the real as such takes place. Only the examination of the structures of my life uncovers for me the area of fundamental reality in which all grounded reality appears and takes on its *real* character. Thus, metaphysics, when it gets under way and tries to fulfill its function of finding a fundamental certainty, finds that it is *a theory of human life.*

VIII
The Theory of Human Life

Metaphysics is not a certainty one "has"; it is a certainty one "arrives at," and so it supposes a prior state of uncertainty, that is, it is derived and has an origin. It must justify itself; it must give an account of each one of its truths. In this sense, but only in this one, it has no assumptions. This is because Adamism is not possible; one cannot begin metaphysics from scratch; only from within a situation which obliges one to begin it. This situation is defined by different certainties, and, in spite of them, by a fundamental uncertainty. Metaphysics counts on these certainties; it takes its departure from them, but as realities, not as certainties, that is, it does not derive its own certainty from them—on the contrary, these certainties demand and postulate metaphysics.

When the vital situation takes root and man begins to search for fundamental certainty, he is practicing metaphysics, whatever idea he might have of it. This is why one can speak with full meaning of the metaphysics of the antimetaphysicians, of the metaphysics they have practiced by denying its possibility, that is, by denying a certain form of knowledge they found in its recent tradition.

However, having said that metaphysics is a theory of human life, it is well that we give a few precise ideas about the character of this theory. We say this because a difficulty arises: we have said that we are talking about fundamental reality and that this reality is precisely what remains when I eliminate all ideas, theories, and interpretations, when I am left with what, because it is the stark reality that I have to deal with, obliges me to make these theories and interpretations; and the question comes to mind: Is not "human life" a theory?

Without any doubt it is. What is strict reality is *my life,* that is, myself with things, myself doing something with my circumstances. To speak in general about "human life" is already to form an interpretation, a theory or doctrine—as justified and true as you may please, but not for that any the less theoretical. Human life "in general" does not exist; it is not real. Real human life is *my life:* the life of each person, in the measure in which each one gives his own meaning to this circumstantial expression. My life is a life that is not only *this* particular one, in the sense of being an individual life, but also in a more profound and decisive sense in that it is an absolute status of *irreducible,* circumstantial, and concrete reality. If there were no more than this, there would not even be any meaning in speaking of "human life." This notion of "human life" is an interpretation I arrive at because of certain very precise reasons.

Here I cannot describe these reasons formally. It is enough that I indicate the first one which is sufficient in itself alone to force me to elaborate the interpretation. My life appears to me as *shared living;* I mean that I find in it, in my circumstances, as ingredients of it, certain realities in which I recognize other "I's" which are for their part subjects of other lives, so that they function as centers of circumstances of which I form a part. This is to say that my life—the unique, irreducible, and immediate reality—includes a reference to something I see myself obliged to consider as "other lives." This has two consequences: first, it brings me to discover myself as an *I* face to face with a *you*—secondarily with a *he* or *she*—and so confers a first meaning upon the expression "*my* life"; second, it shows me the "disjunctive" character of life (its being this life *or* this one *or* this one), and in this way it offers me a new notion, "life," which has a decisive peculiarity: it is not so much a universal, a species or genus, shall we say—not so much life in general as it is the concrete form in which that strange "universal," "life," appears as *each person's life*.

The result is, then, that *my* life, *fundamental* reality, appears to me secondarily but inexorably as *this* concrete life, a circumstantial disjunction of *life;* however, *life* is, for its part, and also inexorably, the life *of each person.* This means that the relation between "my life" and "life" does not seem very much like the relation of an individual with its species. In the latter, once the species is given—sufficient in itself, at least as an ideal object—it may happen that by a "principle of individuation" the species is individualized into diverse individuals which are in a certain respect interchangeable in respect to the species. Or, on the other hand, given a plurality of individuals, some common "notes" are found in them so that if one directs his attention to those notes only and prescinds from the rest of the reality of the individuals, they offer him a coincident *aspect* which is precisely that of the species. This is not the case with life. My own life is conditioned by shared living; in it there occurs the inescapable fact of *others,* and its intrinsic reality is constituted by the historico-social element of inherited interpretations which I call "things." In my life, then, there is found a reference to other lives, and so to *human life.* On the contrary, though I can rely on a normal type of universal, the notion "human life" is unthinkable without circumstantializing it, without basing it on the direct intuition of *this* life, more concretely, *my* life, the only one which is directly accessible

for me, and without which "life in general" is purely and simply
unintelligible. Contrary to nonessential attribution in individualization and species forming, there is an absolutely intrinsic and
necessary relation, the *ultimate* justification of metaphysics. If
we keep in mind only the vital function of metaphysics, remem-
bering what we said about "homologous" and "vicarious" function, and so prescind from what metaphysics has of precise
philosophical theory, we find that this vital function is inexorably
and necessarily intrinsic to human life. In other words, metaphysics is only a concrete historical form of realizing one of the
constitutive requirements of human life.

IX
THE METAPHYSICAL METHOD

We must keep this last consequence in mind because, as we shall
soon see, the metaphysical method is derived from it. It should
be pointed out at once that this expression should be understood,
not in the sense that metaphysics *has* a method, but rather in the
sense that it *is* a method, since it is a way toward reality itself.
What we want, then, is to pinpoint precisely what this method,
which metaphysics is, consists in.

The principal difficulty, pointed out at the end of section VII,
is the traditional identification of existence [el ser] with *logos*.
From Plato on, or if one wants to be strict, from Parmenides on,
these terms have been defined reciprocally, in a more or less surreptitious way. But how is it possible for thought to transcend
existence [el ser], to derive existence [el ser]? The predication
of existence [el ser] is based on identity and permanence. As I
have demonstrated elsewhere in detail, when I say A *is* B, A functions twice: first when I say A and then when I say about it that
it is B because this B is the B of A; in other words, the first A has
to be the same one that is B—A has to be *one* and *permanent*.
Hence the difficulty in predicating about any living thing and,
strictly speaking, about everything that is real, since every reality, and in a pre-eminent way every living reality, is essentially
inexact.

Reality appears as constitutiveness or "suchness": to be real means to be *such and such* a reality. Now the traditional form of obtaining knowledge has been by explanation, *explicatio,* taking apart the elemental components of a reality. Since what has interested us for centuries has been *handling* things—handling with the hands, in a literal sense (technique) or mental handling (science)—our notion of knowledge has been based on *reduction:* the reduction of a compound to its simple elements, the reduction of an effect to its causes, or, at best, the reduction of something that has a source to its principal source, its principle. When I know the mechanism of this reduction, I can, inversely, put the complex thing together from its elements, deduce the effect from its cause, derive what has a source from its first principle, in a word, handle these realities any way I want.

If only this were sufficient. In any case, reduction carries me from the thing I want to know to *another* thing. One might say that this other is more important because it is an element, a cause, or a principle. Yes, but it is a different thing, that is, I am left with it instead of the first thing—I am left without the *primary* thing. If I am not interested in the first thing for itself, but only, for example, in handling it, in producing it, directing it, foreseeing it, measuring it, and so on, there is no problem. The difficulty begins when I cannot *renounce* the primary reality, when it is presented to me as unexchangeable, irreplaceable, in sum, *irreducible.* To take a very simple example, think about a color: the green of the tunic in El Greco's *San Juan.* The wave-length of all the chromatic vibrations that produce it can be explained to me optically; also, the mixtures of chemical elements that are used on the palette to achieve it can be explained; and that is all excellent if what interests me is to "localize" that color, to place it with precision on a scale, to reproduce it; all those explanations are valid for a blind man. But, if what matters to me is the *color itself,* as it does to the painter or the one who contemplates the painting, all that is worthless. The only thing to do is open my eyes and see it. Then I have that color before me in its very self-sameness, in its own irreducible reality as such a color.

The discovery of the irreducible—existence, life, history—made the fundamental insufficiency of all explanatory knowledge obvious; and since this knowledge had been precipitately identified with the function of reason, irrationalism was very reasonably the result and has been the history of philosophy for two-thirds of a century, persisting throughout the remainder on the part of certain stragglers behind the times.

There was a moment when it was believed that the problem had been solved in *description*. With description we hold on to the thing itself, the irreducible, that reality which we cannot abandon. That is true, without doubt; it is simply that, for very fundamental reasons, description is not enough. Its insufficiency is not derived from the fact that knowledge demands more but from the fact that it is not possible to *live* without going beyond description. Irrationalism has only one important drawback: it is impossible. Life is given for me but not given as an accomplished fact, which is a long-standing and essential thesis of Ortega: I find myself in a situation with things, and I have to do something to live; I have to form projects in respect to the facilities and difficulties I find myself faced with, a certain project or ambition I imagine, which is in turn possible only in function with the whole program, ambition, or vocation that constitutes myself. In forming this project, the circumstances appear to me as possibilities, or impossibilities, from among which I must choose. How is choice possible? If I had only that which description can give me, I would have no more than unconnected notes or data and would never be able to decide. To decide, I must know how to orient myself in respect to the *total* situation I find myself in, realize what it is, apprehend it in its totality and in its connection. This is what we call meaning or *reason*.* Years

---

* Translator's note: The Spanish word "razón" has meanings equivalent to all those of the English word "reason" but has also another which concerns us here: *meaning*, not only in the sense of justification or explanation but also in the sense of *intelligibility*. The overall connotation, then, of "razón" is of whatever is the basis of meaning, logic, justification, or balance, including soundness of mind. This is why, when Ortega or Marías speak

ago, in order to give a definition of reason, I limited myself to an analysis of what the word meant in its usage, which involves no less than ten acceptances where it functions; the resulting formula was simply *the apprehension of reality in its connectedness.* This means that in order to live, it is necessary to go beyond description; it is necessary to arrive at a reason or a theory (which does not have to be the theory that preceded the descriptive theory), one which is demanded and imposed upon us by itself and by the vital necessity we have of deciding and choosing.

At this point we have only begun. It is necessary to go over the idea of reason quite strictly because the "relatedness" proves to be problematic; it is not enough to take the notes all together, nor bound up as a mere sum, nor even as united by a purely logical bond. The relation of *Fundierung* which Husserl claims for the integrating notes of an essence is an unreal one, and, moreover, finds its application only with certain very special kinds of essences. It would be necessary for us to determine why certain notes are notes *of* a reality. Apprehension of reality in *its* connection, I said before. Which connection is this?

"What is real," "the world," "things," "consciousness" are only abstractions, as we know, from the real unity in which they are constituted. The actual connection of reality is the system of itself, that is, of *living.* Reality in its *concrete* form is my life. Only the word "live," or better yet, the word "live" as it is used *personally—I live—*is concrete. It is only in this word that both the *connectedness* and the *concreteness* of reality become apparent. To live is to find oneself in a concrete situation, which becomes transparent and connected in the sense that its components are really bound into a figure we call the *world.* The decision in which life consists at each moment, that doing something with things in my circumstances, with *purpose*—without which, as

---

of *vital reason (razón vital),* they are not implying, as the sense of the English might suggest, that reality reasons itself out as a conscious subject would but that reality as we find it going on is the basis for all the meaning we see in it.

Ortega has shown, there is only "activity," not human *perform-ance*—takes place when I apprehend the real situation in which I find myself, *myself with things*. To live, then, is to apprehend reality intrinsically, in its actual connection, in the connection it has in spite of me, apart from my ideas, as a situation in which I find myself and of which I, together with my projects, am an essential ingredient. In a word, life is the concrete form of reason.

However, looking at things from another point of view, life is never automatic, though without automatic mechanisms it would not be possible. I mean that the action of life does not simply break out in an obvious or, I repeat, an automatic way but sup-poses an essential, prior *pause* that keeps human activity from being simply reaction and converts it, in its relation to other things, into initiative activity which issues from within myself. I cannot live without knowing how to orient myself because life is precisely doing this thing and not that thing, according to the circumstances and in view of what I intend to do. But, in order to orient myself, I have to do something, realize what my situation is, apprehend what is real in its actual connection, the connection I find it in as I live. And this is precisely *reasoning, thinking*. If life is reason, that is, the concrete form of reason, as I said before, then life is possible for me only if I reason.*

We saw before that fundamental reality, *my* life, is not pos-sible without my apprehension of it, without a projection of its figure, and, consequently, without that minimum "intrinsic the-ory"—if I may be permitted the expression—which is "life." We find, now, that living demands reason and that reason, the appre-hension of reality in its actual and concrete connection, func-tions only in *living*. Forty years ago Ortega called this necessary co-implication, or complication, of reason and life *vital reason*, with its double significance: first of all, reason as that without which life is not possible; and second, reason as that which life is, that is, reason in its function of apprehending reality. If the fun-

---

* Translator's note: What is understood here by the phrase "if I reason" is "if I look for and find a basis for intelligibility in the actual structure of reality."

damental reality is life, and metaphysics is an attempt to find
fundamental certainty about that reality, its method—I mean the
method in which it consists, the actual path toward apprehending, possessing, and mastering that reality as a reality, that is,
as I find it and find myself faced with it, in living—that method
can be none other than vital reason.

X
LIFE AND REASON

The fundamental reality prior to theories or interpretations is *my*
life: the concrete, single, circumstantial life of each person. But
that life must necessarily be represented to itself because it must
project itself imaginatively to work itself out, since it is not an
already accomplished fact. Life is, as Ortega used to say, futuriza-
tion and a poetic task. Consequently, my life is not possible except
when it is understood as "life," that is, when I find a meaning for
it. Life is finding meaning, and I can find meaning for something
only by living, that is, by making it really function within the
ambit or area of my life.

This means that human reality presents dual, inseparable
aspects. The only real life, individual life, is something that happens to me, here and now, in these precise circumstances, and
the means of having access to it is to *relate* it, to tell someone
about it. The form of "statement" that corresponds to it is a
report, a narration; and because of this, vital reason is a narrative
reason. However, I can only report or narrate something; I can
only understand *my* life, in reference to a scheme in which the
structure of *life in general* is manifest. Do not forget, though,
what I said before: "life in general" has no reality, it does not
exist anywhere, it is not "sufficient" even as an ideal object, that
is, the scheme we are speaking of can only be obtained by an
analysis of individual life, primarily mine, thanks to which I discover *in my life* certain structures, conditions, or demands without
which my life would not be possible. We are not, then, speaking
about a general theory independent of my life that could be

conceived or formulated apart from it; the theory is extracted or abstracted from the singular concreteness of my own life. And notice that for the moment the theory has no "generic" character; we are dealing with a constitutive formulation of my individual life. I find in my life and I extract from it that structure or "theory" which I call "life" and without which my life could not take place. However, it would be just as inexact to attribute a directly generic character to that structure as it would be to suppose that other lives had nothing to do with it. The case is that I find those other lives radically *within my life* as secondary realities in respect to it, that is, as grounded in it.

The universality of this interpretation "life" is derived: it proceeds from the fact that since it contains the requirements and conditions without which there is no life; upon finding that every other person also has his life, I infer that there must be the same structures within those lives, structures that would be unreal of themselves but are grounded in the individual concreteness that corresponds to the circumstantiality of each one of those lives. This is the only reason that the notion "human life" is converted into "human life in general."

The narration of individual life is possible, then, only because of an abstract theory which is universal secondarily, and it itself is possible, even as a theory, only as a complex ideal object grounded in that concrete life which is my life. In other words, the theory is analytic, obtained by an analysis of the actual reality of my living; but this living, in its fundamental immediacy, is possible only in a carrying out, even in rudimentary form, of that analysis which every man makes, permitting him to understand himself and project himself imaginatively into the future.

It should be made clear that that "carrying out" of the analysis of human life is not executed originally by each man, at least for the most part. The historical and social condition of each man makes concrete life function always at a certain *level;* this means that my life and its contents are already interpreted for me by the social circumstances which surround me, that is, I live out these elaborated, theorized contents, and as I continue living there is naturally forced upon me a very precise interpretation, conditioned circumstantially, of human life. The way others act, language, the system of customs, the function prescribed in advance for the things around me, the artificial environment around me, the emotional and evaluational nuances with which things are presented to me—all this makes reality *such as I find it* (apparently, therefore, the true reality) already interpreted and makes it correspond to one idea of human life. This is what I mean when I say that life is *intrinsically* historical and social. At the same time, it is clear that all "Adamism" is an abstraction and, to the extent that it attempts to present itself as a fundamentalization of things, is false.

We still need to take into account a third, intermediate zone between the individual and concrete reality of my life and the necessary structures (which *because* they are necessary are universal) that this analytic and abstract theory reveals, a zone obstinately disregarded by thinkers, one which I have called the *empiric structure* of human life. The empiric structure of life embraces those formulations of it which are not *sine quibus non*** conditions; nor are they constitutive requisites for every life, therefore not appearing in the mere analysis of a life or being contained in the abstract theory; nor are they purely empirical and individual formulations of this or that concrete life. The fact that the world is precisely this world with the definite structure it has, apart from the circumstantial or worldly condition of life; the fact that in addition to being corporeal man has this concrete form of corporealness and not another which in principle would be possible; the fact that the duration of human life, besides being limited has a certain average and foreseeable quantity; the fact that the categorizing of lived-out time into ages has a certain periodicity; the fact that human life has a sexual condition: all this that does not pertain to constitutive requisites for "life," that is not *a priori* but empirical, and that in principle could be otherwise is, however, structural and stable. *Empirical structure* is

---

* Translator's note: "Indispensable"; literally, "without which no."

the concrete form of circumstantiality and leaves room for *possible* historical variation. Individual and concrete life appears cut out and realized within the frame not only of the necessary and purely analytical formulations of all life but also within the frame of the formulations of the empirical structure in which it is found inserted.

This exhibits some important characteristics of the idea of metaphysics which I am treating here, probably with excessive brevity: first of all, the meaning in metaphysics of the term "life." Life has been discussed quite a bit—under this name, or the name of existence, or again with Heidegger's *Dasein*, "existing"—especially from Dilthey on. But I am not speaking of the same thing or of anything approaching it. This makes some justified criticisms of these forms of thought turn out to be totally inapplicable to an intellectual position that goes beyond those objections and reaches its aim from its very outset. Human life, in its concrete form of *my life*, does not mean man, and even less, "subjectivity." It is fundamental reality, between the *functional and nonreal* construct "human life" and the singular, circumstantial, and concrete reality "my life."

If we had not gone through this long description, the consequence of all we have been talking about might be an unexpected surprise, that is, if it is really true that "life" is not a strict reality but is a theory, this theory is in no way arbitrary, unnecessary, or gratuitous but is imposed by the apprehension of that irreducible reality which is *my life*. This is not all; this apprehension is necessary, too: it belongs to the very reality of life. In other words, life is not *possible*—understanding the word possible carefully—without an apprehension of itself, without an imaginative projection of its figure to itself, that is, without the presence before it of its structure as such and such a "human life."* A peculiar "transparency" belongs intrinsically to life. In this transparency

---

* Translator's note: Marías does not mean to suggest, as the framing of this sentence might, that "life" is something that has a reality and subjectivity apart from individual lives; he means that "life" as it is found in *individual* human lives necessarily involves self-representation.

the very constitution of life shows itself, in order to allow life to work itself out. This constitutes the area in which all reality as such is constituted, in which that character which we call reality accrues to something. As I said before, it is the real organization of reality in contrast to any abstract mode of referring to it and ordering it. And that organization is not merely "localization"; it is not exhausted by one's simply "being in it"; rather, the real mode of "being" is to be *living*. Living, not "existing [ser]" or even "conditional existing,"* is the fundamental meaning of reality, the foundation of all existing [ser] or "conditional existing," the foundation of every discovery of "things"—among them, man—and of myself as an "I."

We could say that though my life is not the *implication* of all reality, it is the *complication* of it, to use Ortega's terminology in a context other than his. Thus, not every reality is an ingredient or component of my life, nor does it form a part of it, nor is it an intrinsic factor, a note or portion of it, but it is found essentially bound up with my life to the extent that I am able to relate myself to it as to reality. To say that something is reality means, whether we are aware of it or not, to relate it to my life. This is what "grounding" it in my life means.

If, forty years ago, Ortega had limited himself to studying life, he would have taken the same path that many philosophers took before him, during his time and after him. However, he did something more, from his very first book, which at first sight may seem very little, though in fact it launched metaphysics along a new path, one so different that in spite of unquestioned coincidences—which occurred above all because of the simultaneousness, because of the common level of the same problems—it leads to quite different results, as will be seen more and more clearly

---

* Translator's note: "Conditional existing" is the translation we have used here for "estar." Spanish distinguishes, in general and informally, two modes of being by its two verbs, "ser" and "estar," whereas English uses only one verb, "to be." When it means existence, "ser" indicates a kind of *essential* existence; generally speaking, it is used to indicate *what* a thing is. "Estar" is used to indicate, in general, *how* a thing is, what *condition* it is in.

as time goes by. What Ortega did was to unite the words "life" and "reason" to refer one to the other, to show that far from being opposed and irreconcilable, they are inseparable. In place of a "philosophy of life" or any form of "existentialism," he began something quite distinct: a "metaphysics of vital reason."

This is the decisive issue: vital reason. If it were not for it, philosophy would be phenomenology, phenomenological descriptions—which are admittedly indispensable and often splendid— that do not arrive at apprehending reality in its connection, that do not *find a meaning* for it, that promise but never fulfill the realization of a metaphysics. Or, using other assumptions as a basis, one would rely on abstract reason and form a theory about a reality cut off precisely from its concreteness, its actual constitution in my life, its intrinsic organization as such and such a reality.

Because, only if one has life function as *ratio*,* only if one looks at reality exactly as he encounters it, in the living discovery of oneself within it and of it along with oneself, only in this way can one go beyond the sphere of the actual "living forms," the acts or contents of life; only in this way does one transcend interpretations (above all that decisive interpretation which is existence [ser]) and grasp and understand—*com-prehend*—life itself as fundamental reality. This is possible, of course, only under a double condition: first, that one go beyond phenomenology, beyond all "description" and *consciousness* thinking—which, far from being true reality is not even reality but only a theory or interpretation—to the real system of actual life; and, second, that one go from abstract logic, from the logic of identity based on the idea of existence [el ser], to a logic of concrete thought,

---

* Translator's note: "Ratio" is the Latin word whose meaning corresponds to "razón" or "reason" and from which these words were derived linguistically. However, "ratio" has many additional meanings. Spanish, being closer to Latin than English, conserves much more of the wide range of meanings belonging to "ratio" than does English. We have indicated one meaning in a previous footnote on "reason." Some others are: order, method or means, system, theory or doctrine, conduct, condition, relatedness, vested interest, balance of value (in the sense of an evaluation).

which is the organ of a thinking interchange with reality, along with a theory about the *forms of situations,* a *morphology of thought* in its actual concreteness—not only a catalogue of schematic forms of abstract thought but a theory of the *forms* of connectedness, and so of possibilities of mutual grounding much richer and much more varied than one would suspect.

All this has one final consequence. I have insisted several times that the theory of human life, understood as a theory, is not the propaedeutics of metaphysics; it is not a preparation for it but *is metaphysics.* Since philosophy has a systematic structure, and so a circular one, this would not be the wrong place to renew and reinforce the evidence this thesis should have had in previous pages that a view of it from another of its concentric levels could give us. The theory of human life, in effect, studies the structure of living, more directly of *my living,* and by intrinsic, but secondary necessity, of human life "in general."

It begins, then, in a certain sense, with me. It speaks of things that happen to me, of the "I," of circumstance, performance, insecurity and certitude, disaster, time and history, authenticity, vital frames of mind, absorption in thought or commotion, beliefs and ideas, perhaps of anguish and even, if you wish, of nausea and disgust, and perhaps also of happiness. But if the theory of life is taken seriously, that is, if it is committed to being a *theory* —not a mere description—that is, to *finding a meaning* in its subject, and if this subject is human life in its selfness, not its simple living forms or partial contents, then it is obliged to confront the decisive problem of its structure, of the dynamic polarity between an I or *someone* and a circumstance which constitutes with that abstract I the real and concrete I which *I am* as an actual living reality. At the same time it must inquire about the diverse planes of perspective, about their actual articulation in living, about the corporeality which constitutes me, about the world in which I am living, about the horizon of that world and about its frame in what lies beyond it and gives unity and figure to my life.

With this we come to the essential issue: the theory of life discovers life's property of being a *complication* of all reality; finding

meaning for life requires, therefore, finding a meaning for that
dimension of it in virtue of which it places all that appears as
reality in "complication." The study of that essential structure of
living which is complication demands, then, an inquiry about *all
reality*. But let it be well understood that we mean all reality inasmuch as it is *in complication with* my life. The study of the various
different realities is embodied in separate disciplines corresponding to each reality; the consideration of them insofar as they
appear together in complication with my life belongs to the
theory of life, that is, to metaphysics. Phenomenology hinted at
something of this when it said that intentional objects reappear
whole in reduced conscious thinking as terms of the living forms
or intentional acts of pure conscious thinking. But the difference
between that position and ours is essential: here we are not speaking of intentionality or of conscious thinking but of actual life
and relations of real complication between realities. Thus, since
the theory of human life is the science of fundamental reality, it is
also the science of mutual grounding and, therefore, of grounded
realities, though it studies them only as grounded. This means
that metaphysics—closing a cycle opened by Kant—is relentlessly
driven to transcendence, not because of any decision or capricious
convenience but because transcendence is the very condition
of life.

NOTES

NOTES TO CHAPTER I
Pages 2–40

1. The study of language, and especially of vocabulary, from both the cognitive and the valuative aspects of the meaning of words is very interesting because it fixes the terms of being and value, of the ontological and the axiological, in reality and human life. I have dedicated two works to this theme: "La contribución del lenguaje a la filosofía de los valores," a discourse I delivered upon my entry into the Royal Academy of Moral and Political Sciences in 1920, and "El lenguaje y la filosofía" (edited in 1945 for the Consejo Superior de Investigaciónes Cientificas [Instituto "Luis Vivés" de Filosofía]).

2. See numbers 71 to 76bis in my "Fundamentos de Filosofía" (in collaboration with Manuel García Morente).

3. See, on both of these categories, the chapter "Ontología" of my "Fundamentos de Filosofía," in numbers 130 to 139.

NOTES TO CHAPTER IV
Pages 92–124

1. "El porvenir de los derechos individuales," in the Revista Espanola de Derecho Internacional II, no. 2 (1949) 476.

2. D. García Bacca, "El plan del filosofor medieval y el plan moderno de filosofar," in *Asomante* I (Puerto Rico, 1950) 6. On the idea of person in the Greeks, cf. Amor Ruibal, *Los problemas fundamentales de la filosofía y del dogma* V (Madrid-Barcelona, n.d.), chaps. 2–4, 9–10, see p. 398: "Although Greek philosophy, especially that of Plato and Aristotle, distinguished between nature, essence, and individualization of beings, it did not thereby draw the distinction between nature and person. This distinction came later with Christian philosophy, following upon the necessity of explaining the dogma of the Trinity."

3. D. García Bacca, *op. cit.* 10.

4. X. Zubiri, "El acontecer humano; Grecia y la pervivencia del pasado filosofico," in *Naturaleza, Historia, Dios* (Madrid, 1944) 400–403.

5. Zubiri, "En torno al problema de Dios," in *Naturaleza, Historia, Dios* 432 ff.

6. Zubiri, *op. cit.* 435 ff. In a beautiful text of Richard of St. Victor (*De Trinitate* IV, 12), similar in meaning, we read: "Quod autem dicitur existere, subintelligitur non solum quod habeat esse, sed etiam aliunde, hoc est ex aliquo habeat esse. Quid est enim existere nisi ex aliquo sistere, hoc est substantialiter ex aliquo esse?" (Cf. E. G. Arboleya, "Más sobre la noción de la persona," in the *Revista de Estudio Politicos* 49 [1950], where the text alluded to is quoted and commented on.)

7. Zubiri, *op. cit.* 456, 458.

8. Zubiri, *op. cit.* 458.

9. By natural Law, all men are born free (*Inst.* I, 5, pr.) and equal (D.L. 17, 32): "Freedom is a *facultas naturalis,* and slavery is a constitutio juris gentium, qua quis dominio alieno contra natura subjicitur" (*Inst.* I, 3, 2).

10. Gayo, *Inst.* I, 52: "In potestate itaque sunt servi dominorum? quae quidem potestas juris gentium est: nam apud omnes peraeque gentes animadvertere possumus, dominis in servos vitae necisque potestatem esse."

11. Cf. R. Sohm, *Instituciones de Derecho privado romano,* special ed. (Madrid, 1936) 149 ff.

12. *La teoría egologica del Derecho y el concepto juridico de libertad* (Buenos Aires: Losada, 1944) 205 ff., 209.

13. It is a fact that, since the second half of the nineteenth century, Natural Law theory has lost much of its force in North America. But up to the present time positive Law, and the Constitution in particular, was regarded as a mere "declaration" of Natural Law based upon a deist and rationalist view of man. As Bognetti says, "The juridical system was conceived as the social recognition of the rights that the individual has from the moment of his birth, in a universe ordained by its Creator according to permanent laws" (*Il pensiero filosoficogiuridico nordamericano dell XX° secolo* [Milano: Università di Milano, 1958] 10). Cf. Leboutillier, *American Democracy and Natural Law* (1950).

14. In his unedited communication to the Congress on Comparative Law in London in 1950, "La notion juridique de la personne humaine et les

concepts relatifs aux droits de l'homme," which we had before us while preparing the present essay.

15. On this point, cf. among others J. Meinvielle, *Critica de la concepción de Maritain de la persona humana* (Buenos Aires, 1948); J. Ruiz Jiménez, *La concepción institucional del Derecho* (Madrid, 1945) 340 ff., 397 ff.; Lachance, *L'Humanisme politique de Saint Thomas* (Paris-Ottawa, 1939); L. E. Palacios, "La primacía absoluta del Bien commún," in *Arbor* 55–56 (1950); J. Ruiz Jiménez, *op. cit.* 320 ff., sets forth, with an abundant bibliography, a theory of the human person within the framework of Christian philosophy and the institutional conception of Law.

16. "En torno al problema de Dios," article cited, p. 434; cf. also "El acontecer humano," in *Naturaleza, Historia, Dios* 409, note.

17. *Sein und Zeit* (Halle, 1935), section 27, pp. 126 ff.

18. The exact equivalent of Heidegger's *Man* is "they," according to Ortega's examination of the concept.

19. Cf. *Gesellschaftslehre* (1914), especially pp. 232 ff.

20. *Grundlinien der Rechtsphilosophie,* ed. Lasson, sections 35, 36. Cf. St. Thomas Aquinas, *Summa Theologica* I–II, q. I, 3; q. III, 3.

21. To be more precise, we should speak here of "normative proposition," which is the conceptualization of the "norm" as a reality of social life; cf. L. Legaz, *Filosofía del Derecho* (Barcelona: Bosch, 1953) 210–215.

22. In his *Report* to the Congress on Comparative Law in London in 1950 (published in the *Deutsche Landesreferaten zum III. Internationalen Kongress für Rechtsvergleichung*), "Der Rechtsbegriff der menschlichen Person und die Theorien der Menschenrechte" 191, 195 ff.; he presents a summarized study of the concepts of the person and fundamental rights as proposed by Grotius, Donello, Althusius, Vultejo, Puffendorf, Thomasius, Wolff, and Heinesius. On this point, see also, besides Landeberg's classic work on the history of juridical science, some interesting paragraphs in G. Husserl, *Der Rechtsgegenstand* (Berlin, 1933) 2 ff., 70 ff.

23. On this point, cf. Legaz, "Libertad politica y libertad civil, según Joaquín Costa," in *Revista de Estudios Politicos* (1947).

24. Coing, *op. cit.* 205.

25. Cf. L. Legaz, "El individuo entre et Estado y las fuerzas sociales," in *Revista Internacional de Sociología* (October–December, 1948).

26. H. de Laboulaye, *Estudios sobre la constitución de los Estados Unidos* (a course delivered in the Collège de France in 1864), Spanish translation by J. Guichot (Sevilla, 1869) IV, 10–11.

27. *Ibid.,* prologue, p. II.

28. *Ibid.,* pp. II–III.

29. B. Constant, *Cours de Politique constitutionelle,* 3rd ed. (Brussels, 1837) 65 ff.; cf. R. Treves, *B. Croce, filosofo de la libertad* (Buenos Aires, 1944) 54–55; L. Díez del Corral, *Liberalismo doctrinario* (Madrid, 1945) 226–229, 236, 244 ff.

30. R. Treves, *op. cit.* 55; Díez del Corral, *op. cit.* 324–325, 398–400. See De Tocqueville's classic works, *De la Démocratie en Amérique* (especially vol. II, part 4, chaps. VI and VII) and *De la Revolution et de l'Ancien Régime.*

31. In a broad and formal sense. A totalitarian State is that which regards no aspect of life as indifferent. Compared with the liberal State, which is neuter, it is a "confessional" State, which means it is based upon a "faith" in whose service it is dedicated. It will affirm the primacy of the common good over private interests, and it will make use of all the means necessary to realize this idea, including entering into the fray of the economic struggle. Finally, it presupposes the presence of an "enemy," and it will make one of its reasons for existing the extermination of that "enemy." In this sense, all modern States present characteristics of totalitarianism, and the fight undertaken in democracies themselves against communism is only a proof of this, as is, in the opposite sense, the "laicism" that some democracies substitute for the indifference of their liberal predecessors. In this more concrete sense, however, as a symbol of very definite ideologies, totalitarianism is the expression of theories which deny the substantial value of man because they recognize as primary that of the State, the class, the race, etc. In the first sense, totalitarianism is not only an irresistible tendency of modern States. It can even be a good with respect to the State which is agnostic, sceptical, or abstentionist before social problems. In the second sense, the State is converted into a factor for the reinforcement of socialization, contributing itself to the socialization of spirits and to the annihilation of the sense of personal freedom, and not only is it the expression of a perfectly circumscribed political reality, but it constitutes an evil worth combating.

32. In connection with the theories that deny juridical personality, L. Legaz, *Introducción a la ciencia del Derecho* (Barcelona, 1943) 525 ff., 543 ff.; *Filosofía del Derecho* 550 ff.

33. *Storia di Europa,* 3rd ed. (Bari, 1932) 340–341, see also pp. 350 ff.; *La storia come pensiero e come azione,* 2nd ed. (Bari, 1938) 28–29; cf. R. Treves, *op. cit.* 47.

34. *Storia di Europa* 35–38; characteristic of the nineteenth century is "la lotta politica. . . . non più'di liberalismo e assolutismo, ma di liberalismo e democrazia, dalla moderata alla estrema e socialista," *op. cit.* 152; *La storia come pensiero e come azione* 256–259; *Storia di Italia* 9.

35. "Liberismo e liberalismo," in *Etica e Politica* (Bari: Laterza, 1931) 317; Treves, *op. cit.* 59 ff.

36. "Aspetti morali della vita politica," in *Etica e Politica* 285, 292 ff.; Treves, *op. cit.,* chap. III.

37. In his *Report* presented to the Congress on Comparative Law in London in 1950, *La noción jurídica de la persona humana y los conceptos relativos a los derechos del hombre.*

38. *Ibid.* 205.

1. We have elsewhere dealt in particular with the logical relation in connection with an examination of the axiom of noncontradiction as a possible universal principle of science. Here we shall speak of the logical relation only insofar as it is, in the actual work of science, complementary to the epistemological relation and to the extent that an examination of it will help for a full comprehension of this work.

2. *Determinismus und Indeterminismus in der modernen Physik* (1936), III, section 3. (English translation [Yale, 1956].)

3. Heidegger indicated certain problematical aspects in the mathematical relation of adequation which constitutes truth (*adequation intellectus ad rem*). It was, in fact, necessary to explain the concept of adequation that was traditionally employed with a badly defined meaning. But the concordance or adequation of thought with something which is heterogeneous, or the thing, can never be understood without noting that truth implies another type of concordance which is established between homogeneous or affinitive terms. In this connection, see *Metafisica de la expression,* chapter VII, and section 4 of this essay.

4. An examination of some of the modalities of this dependence, which involves the problem of historical causality, will be found in some of my other works. For the moment it is a question only of defining the structures of the third constituent relation of thought, namely, the historical relation and the primary problem of its integration with the other two.

5. See the last note. It is not the purpose of this essay to examine the dialectical articulations in the horizontal structure of the historical relation of thought. We have dealt with this more fully in an essay on historical causality. Cf. *La idea del hombre, historicismo y existencialismo, Metafisica de la expression.*

6. *Sophist* 263 a.

7. Rationalism and logicism are two of the *isms* characteristic of the first attitude. Certain forms of vitalism and historicism, like pragmatism and perspectivism—even to the point of flowing into sophism—would correspond to the second attitude. On the Spanish forms of the latter, see *Historicismo y existencialismo,* chapter IX, and *El problema de la filosofía hispanica, passim.*

8. We have to insist that the term of this transitive action is not the object but the other subject. The object is only the *means of communication,* that which makes communication possible, or the content of the communication itself. This permits (in fact, obliges) us to reject the traditional scheme of the subject-object relation even though this conflicts with established and firmly rooted notions in philosophy. In introducing this fourth constituent relation of thought, the dialogical relation, we see that the first or epistemological relation of the thinking subject with the object

thought was traditionally badly established. See Section 5 of this essay.

9. We have presented a more thorough examination of the question (which naturally would not belong in this work) in our *Metafísica de la expression*. What is said here serves only to make absolutely clear that the final object of that work is the institution of the foundation of science in general and of metaphysics itself as the first science. What we say in this essay on that theme, then, should confirm the propositions of that work if it is not clear that that work was not limited to a monographic study of expressive phenomena or of symbolic systems. The "ontology of the human" contained in that work had to be worked out only as a methodological requirement in order to come to the ontological basing of science, beginning with the primary evidences.

10. Several examples of this defective understanding were advanced among the critiques of my *Metafísica de la expression*. Hence the necessity of insisting on the point.

11. As a matter of fact, they present a problem just the same, even for the primitive man, in spite of primary evidences. The primitive also tries to explain things, or give a reason for them, even though his reason is not yet *rational*. Science eliminates these attempts at subjective explanation (in which there may be a wisdom concerning life) because it has discovered method or the faithful instrument of objective representation and of theoretical interpretation.

12. The merit of Heidegger's *Being and Time* is undeniable as an attempt at a conceptualization, in ontological terms, of the historical reality that man is: as an attempt at conceiving historicity as a constitutional character of the human being. But whatever technical opinion we form concerning this attempt, it is clear that Heidegger did not pursue the plan of work that he should have begun with that essay and that should have been completed by establishing which conditions *de principio* make science in general legitimate, in spite of science being a product of a historical being. *Being and Time* is still anthropology, even though it is already ontological anthropology. The problem of the principles of science in general is not even touched upon in that work.

13. The ontology of man is not the theme of this essay, although it is not extraneous to it nor can it be separated systematically from the theme of principles. Man is defined as the being of expression. This is a constituent character of his structure, and at the same time it is the source from which every possible phenomenological analysis of this structure proceeds. It is not expressive because it creates and employs symbolic systems of expression, but because it is itself *symbolic* in the Greek sense of the word. It is a being whose *ontological insufficiency is* compensated in action by means of the links which the *dialogical relation* establishes between it and its *ontological complement,* which is the *thou* in general. Thus the symbolic character of this being is the necessary condition of every symbolic system, the condition of the linking efficacy of any symbol. The historicity

of symbolic forms is the consequence of the historical form taken by temporality in the being that creates them. This form reveals an inner dynamic principle in the being which it has to actuate or express *in order to be what it is:* in order to complete (with the other) the original deficiency of its being. *To express in order to be* is what constitutes the human calling. See *La vocación humana,* "Expresar para ser," and *Metafísica de la expresión,* chapters V ff. The problem of science in general cannot be stated as a purely epistemological problem but only within the framework defined for the systematic analysis of the "being of truth," or the being of expression.

NOTES TO CHAPTER X
Pages 304–323

1. A growing number of soul-searching *ci-devant* linguistic philosophers might object to *any* description by claiming that linguistic philosophy is no longer "in." Since it never occurred to me that linguistic philosophy was "in," I do not feel compelled now to agree that it is "out." Whether "in" or "out," linguistic philosophy—which for the sake of historical accuracy may already be labeled "classical linguistic philosophy"—is still interesting and challenging enough to deserve critical examination. Therefore, I am not much impressed by boisterous claims that linguistic philosophers are (again) interested in realities and are even sympathetic to something that had been an anathema to them, namely, "generality." I must confess, however, that I am glad to hear that I am now allowed to do what I have been doing during all those years when I was not allowed to do it.

INDEX

379

W

Weber, Alfred, 298
Weizsacker, Von, 257, 273
Weltanschauungen, 238
Wolff, C. von, 338–9, 346
  Philosophia prima sive ontologia,
  345

Z

Zaragüeta y Bengoechea, Juan, 2
  and Manuel García Morente,
  "Fundamentos de Filosofía,"
  371 (n. 2)
Zubiri, Xavier, x, 2, 42, 94, 102, 126,
  254
  Sobre la esencia, 53

74470

B
4561
.C27

Caponigri, A.
Robert.
        Contemporary
Spanish
philosophy.

DATE DUE